D1446408

Beyond the Usual Beating

HISTORICAL STUDIES OF URBAN AMERICA

Edited by Lilia Fernández, Timothy J. Gilfoyle, Becky M. Nicolaides, and Amanda I. Seligman, James R. Grossman, Editor Emeritus

RECENT TITLES IN THE SERIES

Ann Durkin Keating, *The World of Juliette Kinzie: Chicago before the Fire*

Jeffrey S. Adler, *Murder in New Orleans: The Creation of Jim Crow Policing*

David A. Gamson, *The Importance of Being Urban: Designing the Progressive School District, 1890–1940*

Kara Schlichting, *New York Recentered: Building the Metropolis from the Shore*

Mark Wild, *Renewal: Liberal Protestants and the American City after World War II*

Meredith Oda, *The Gateway to the Pacific: Japanese Americans and the Remaking of San Francisco*

Sean Dinces, *Bulls Markets: Chicago's Basketball Business and the New Inequality*

Julia Guarneri, *Newsprint Metropolis: City Papers and the Making of Modern Americans*

Kyle B. Roberts, *Evangelical Gotham: Religion and the Making of New York City, 1783–1860*

Timothy Neary, *Crossing Parish Boundaries: Race, Sports, and Catholic Youth in Chicago, 1914–1954*

Julia Rabig, *The Fixers: Devolution, Development, and Civil Society in Newark, 1960–1990*

Amanda I. Seligman, *Chicago's Block Clubs: How Neighbors Shape the City*

Aaron Shkuda, *The Lofts of SoHo: Gentrification, Art, and Industry in New York, 1950–1980*

Mark Krasovic, *The Newark Frontier: Community Action in the Great Society*

Ansley T. Erickson, *Making the Unequal Metropolis: School Desegregation and Its Limits*

A complete list of series titles is available on the University of Chicago Press website.

BEYOND THE USUAL BEATING

The Jon Burge Police Torture Scandal and Social Movements for Police Accountability in Chicago

ANDREW S. BAER

THE UNIVERSITY OF CHICAGO PRESS | CHICAGO AND LONDON

The University of Chicago Press, Chicago 60637
The University of Chicago Press, Ltd., London

Published 2020
Printed in the United States of America

29 28 27 26 25 24 23 22 21 20   1 2 3 4 5

ISBN-13: 978-0-226-70047-2 (cloth)
ISBN-13: 978-0-226-70050-2 (e-book)
DOI: https://doi.org/10.7208/chicago/9780226700502.001.0001

Library of Congress Cataloging-in-Publication Data
Names: Baer, Andrew S., author.
Title: Beyond the usual beating : the Jon Burge police torture scandal and social movements for police accountability in Chicago / Andrew S. Baer.
Other titles: Historical studies of urban America.
Description: Chicago : University of Chicago Press, 2020. | Series: Historical studies of urban America | Includes bibliographical references and index.
Identifiers: LCCN 2019037869 | ISBN 9780226700472 (cloth) | ISBN 9780226700502 (ebook)
Subjects: LCSH: Burge, Jon. | Police brutality—Illinois—Chicago. | Torture—Illinois—Chicago.
Classification: LCC HV8148.C4 B347 2020 | DDC 363.2/32—dc23
LC record available at https://lccn.loc.gov/2019037869

♾ This paper meets the requirements of ANSI/NISO Z39.48-1992 (Permanence of Paper).

Contents

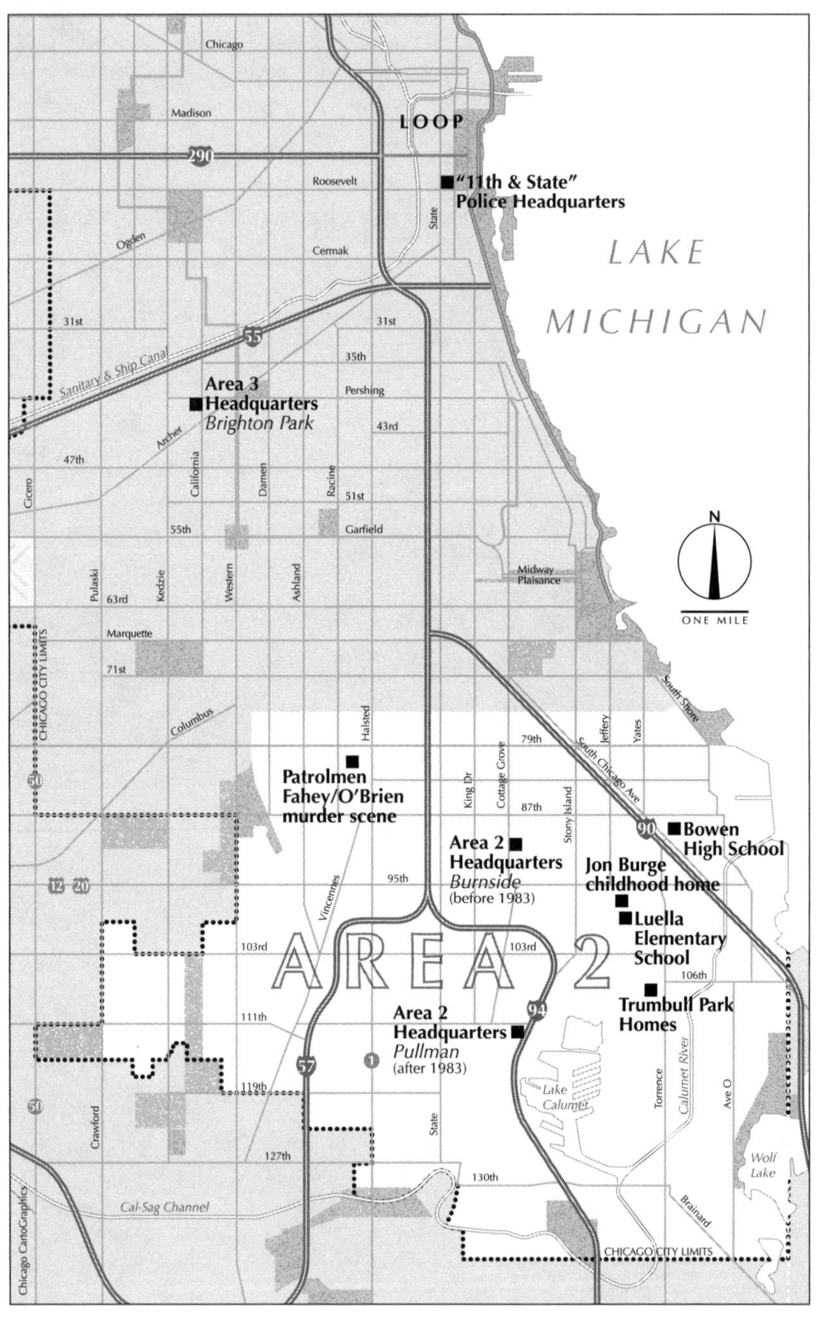

Chicago
Madison
LOOP
290
Roosevelt
"11th & State"
Police Headquarters
State
Ogden
Cermak
LAKE
MICHIGAN
31st
31st
55
35th
Sanitary & Ship Canal
Area 3
Headquarters
Brighton Park
Pershing
43rd
Archer
47th
Cicero
California
Damen
Racine
51st
55th
Garfield
Pulaski
Kedzie
Western
Ashland
Midway
Plaisance
N
ONE MILE
63rd
Marquette
CHICAGO CITY LIMITS
71st
South Shore
Columbus
Halsted
Jeffery
Yates
79th
South Chicago Ave
Patrolmen
Fahey/O'Brien
murder scene
King Dr
Cottage Grove
87th
Stony Island
90
Bowen
High School
50
Area 2
Headquarters
Burnside
(before 1983)
Jon Burge
childhood home
12
20
Vincennes
95th
Luella
Elementary
School
103rd
AREA 2
103rd
106th
Trumbull Park
Homes
111th
94
Area 2
Headquarters
Pullman
(after 1983)
57
1
119th
Lake
Calumet
Torrence
Calumet River
Ave O
50
Crawford
State
127th
Wolf
Lake
130th
Cal-Sag Channel
Brainard
CHICAGO CITY LIMITS
Chicago CartoGraphics

Introduction

On Valentine's Day, 1982, a twenty-one-year-old African American man named Jackie Wilson took a beating from white detectives at the Chicago Police Department's Area 2 headquarters on the city's Far South Side. Five days earlier, Jackie had helped his older brother, Andrew Wilson, escape after fatally shooting two white police officers. Having learned of the murders after filing out of the funeral for a third slain patrolman, Mayor Jane Byrne and her police superintendent authorized a massive manhunt for the killers that elicited sensational media coverage and allegations of brutality. Employing conventional investigative methods and illegal coercion, detectives under the command of Lieutenant Jon Burge discovered the suspects' identities, compiled evidence of their guilt, and apprehended the Wilsons at separate hideaways. Determined not only to secure confessions but also to punish alleged cop killers, detectives denied Jackie a lawyer; slapped, punched, and kicked him until he urinated; twisted his fingers; placed a gun in his mouth; and promised, "You would be wise to come clean and tell us what happened." Burge allegedly told his men: "I am getting tired of this shit. I got something that will make him talk." Pulling a black box from a bag, Burge waited while another detective attached wires to Jackie's hand. Turning a crank "like a jack in the box," Burge sent an electric jolt up Jackie's arm. Elsewhere in the building, detectives delivered electric shocks and a worse beating to the shooter, Andrew Wilson, who screamed loud enough for Jackie to hear. If the Wilson brothers expected some abuse in police custody, for Jackie, electric shock was "the last straw." Submitting, they both signed confessions. Andrew died in prison in 2007. Continuing to serve a life sentence, Jackie fought to suppress his confession and win a new trial.[1]

Over thirty-six years later, on June 14, 2018, Circuit Court judge William Hooks reversed Jackie Wilson's conviction, remanding the case back to the trial court, "where that confession may not be used."[2] Outlining what others referred to as a "mountain of evidence" supporting Wilson's torture claims, Hooks's 119-page order ended with an emotional assertion of the stakes involved. During public hearings, Hooks noted, supporters of opposing sides appeared in T-shirts reading "black lives matter" or "blue lives matter." Listing the types of people entering his courtroom—from crime victims to defendants to police officers—Hooks insisted, "All lives matter," reminding readers, "Yes, even a guilty person's life matters." Criticizing Jon Burge and his detectives for "the torture and death of nothing less than our constitution," Hooks implied the Wilson brothers' guilt but concluded: "All rights matter. The rights of the good; the bad; and the ugly all count."[3] Erin Fahey, daughter of one of the murdered officers, lamented "today's climate of police criticism" and called Hooks's pending decision "an injustice to these fallen police officers, their families, the two juries that convicted him and, ultimately, to the truth."[4] Agreeing that murder victims' families "have not been granted the small peace that might come with an end to this judicial farce," the *Chicago Sun-Times* placed "blame for this endless travesty" with a "crew of rogue officers" who tortured suspects with impunity for more than two decades.[5]

Yet Chicago's Jon Burge police torture scandal involved much more than a few bad apples. From 1972 to 1991 and beyond, dozens of detectives working alongside or under the supervision of Detective—later Commander—Jon Burge tortured or otherwise coerced confessions from over 118 African American criminal suspects at Chicago Police Department (CPD) Area 2 and Area 3 headquarters on the city's South and Southwest Sides.[6] As early as 1990, an internal investigator concluded, "The type of abuse described was not limited to the usual beating, but went into such esoteric areas as psychological techniques and planned torture."[7] Seeking to clear cases and punish wrongdoers, Burge and his crew regularly employed deception, threats, bodily discomfort, mental stress, beatings, suffocation, mock execution, and electric shock. Nearly all detectives involved were white, and virtually all their victims black.[8] Coerced confessions helped convict scores of defendants. Over a dozen wound up on death row, including innocent men who later won their release.[9] Other actors in the criminal justice system facilitated abuse as well, including patrolmen, police supervisors, prosecutors, judges, and elected officials. While stakeholders and observers bound the scandal neatly around Burge, the prevalence of similar behavior elsewhere in the department at other times and places belied the simple narrative of a few rogue cops gone bad. In response, the Burge scandal spawned

FIGURE 1 Commander Jon Burge, circa 1994. Although Burge emerged as the public face of the torture scandal, scores of other officers, police supervisors, prosecutors, and elected officials facilitated abuse at Area 2 and elsewhere during the 1970s, 1980s, and 1990s. *Chicago Sun-Times* files, Courtesy of Sun-Times Media.

or united various social movements. For over twenty-five years, a shifting coalition of torture survivors, their families, civil rights attorneys, community activists, journalists, and academics helped corroborate torture allegations, fire Jon Burge, free the wrongfully convicted, win financial settlements, empty Illinois's death row, abolish the state's death penalty, send Burge to prison, and win passage of a municipal reparations package.[10]

Through an analysis of the Burge scandal and its aftermath, *Beyond the Usual Beating* contributes to historical knowledge on race, policing, and social movements. Recent scholarship on criminal justice in the United States focuses overwhelmingly on the causes and consequences of the late twentieth-century rise of mass incarceration.[11] Borrowing a term from the social sciences, historians have outlined the origins and character of the so-called carceral state, a governing paradigm defined by law enforcement, punishment creep, and racial inequality.[12] In order to explain the "punitive turn in American life" after 1970, many publications in this burgeoning subfield adopt a top-down approach.[13] According to prevailing theses, policy makers from both major political parties responded to the gains, limitations, and excesses of 1960s-era social movements by embracing a tough-on-crime agenda in the 1970s, 1980s, and 1990s.[14] Whether by deliberate intent or unintended consequence, federal and state actors in all three branches of government erected a punitive apparatus of unprecedented scale by the turn of the new millennium. In addition to its size and reach, however, the carceral state was also defined by austerity and racial disparity.[15] Much of this story has already been told. Adopting a bottom-up perspective, this book shows how ground-level operatives perpetuated racism in the criminal justice system, uncovers grassroots resistance to the punitive turn, and challenges the paradigm of the carceral state.

Indeed, historians of post–World War II America may be assigning *too* much agency to the carceral state, a concept often applied without definition. As constituted, the carceral state thesis helps explain the rise of mass incarceration but does little to clarify the causes and character of police misconduct and state violence. After all, police brutality and racial injustice existed long before 1964, when a "major punitive turn in American policy and culture" became evident.[16] In Chicago, key developments of the Burge scandal appear disconnected from core features of the carceral state. Law-and-order rhetoric, federal funding of law enforcement, the war on drugs, mandatory minimum sentences, mass incarceration, and the militarization of police run parallel to the operation of a torture regime on Chicago's South Side but do little to explain its origin or purpose. While a larger punitive turn in American culture helped abusive officers secure impunity, police departments had never been bastions of accountability in the first place. Considering the CPD's long history of racial violence, the stubborn continuity of the third degree after the midcentury rights revolution accords the Burge scandal a haunting timelessness. If Burge's career became symptomatic of the law-and-order era, he was neither product nor producer of national trends. If social movements monitored federal and state governments, they expended most of their energy fighting local policy. National and international media events—from Rodney King to Abu Ghraib—opened windows of opportunity, but activists primarily leveraged outrage in pursuit of local goals. While the carceral state formulation helps historians understand and explain the pernicious reach of the criminal justice system, it also risks monopolizing explanatory models for historical change. If *everything* is the carceral state—and the carceral state is everything—scholars may be overlooking other historical explanations for criminal justice outcomes.

In postwar Chicago, for example, local changes in the social, economic, and demographic landscape did more to facilitate police torture than the words and actions of state and federal officials. While national efforts to crack down on crime influenced local law enforcement, patrolmen, detectives, and prosecutors usually made decisions independent of Springfield or Washington. Indeed, the Burge cases demonstrate how local—even biographical—forces helped shape the contours of repressive law enforcement. On Chicago's South and West Sides, changing neighborhood demographics—especially racial transition, rising unemployment, gang proliferation, and escalating crime rates—played a far greater role than federal legislation in convincing police departments to implement and maintain tough anticrime policies. Many of the officers involved in the torture scandal, including Burge, grew up in the very neighborhoods they later policed. Their experience—and perception—of urban decline influenced decisions to coerce confessions from black men accused of violence in formerly white neighborhoods. This is not to suggest, however, that local policemen were disconnected from federal crime policy or oblivious to national trends. Indeed, detectives had an impact on the carceral state and vice versa. Yet ordinary detective work revolved around more immediate concerns—tracking down leads, interviewing suspects, and filing reports. In a profession driven by pressure to close cases, politics and crime policy took a back seat to the clearance rate. While state and federal officials steered the nation in a more punitive direction in the post–civil rights era, local developments best explain the frequency and nature of police violence, specifically.

Exercising professional discretion within local contexts, street-level agents of law enforcement exacerbated racial disparities in the criminal justice system one case at a time. While the unintended consequences of race-neutral legislation contributed to inequality, so, too, did the deliberately racist acts of rank-and-file operatives. Indeed, police torture in Chicago was an explicitly racist practice designed to railroad black defendants into prison. According to sociologist Nicole Gonzalez Van Cleve, criminal justice institutions remained spaces where "whites were allowed to stop being nice and start acting racist," even as open expressions of racial animosity faded from public discourse after 1970.[17] Abandoning the coded speech of polite society during everyday encounters with black citizens, detectives revealed the racist motives behind their actions. For example, a white detective named Michael Kill who worked under Jon Burge admitted using the word "nigger" about "a million" times in his career.[18] Denying that race influenced police behavior, however, detectives often highlighted the moral failings—not racial background—of criminal suspects to justify abuse, as when Burge employed the phrase "human garbage" to dismiss his accusers.[19] "Coding racial divisions with a moral rather than a racial rubric," Gonzalez Van Cleve concludes, "allows professionals to ignore the ubiquity of race and racism."[20] In aggregate, the discretionary behavior of racist police officers and prosecutors helped direct the costs of the carceral state to nonwhite communities in an age of legislative and judicial colorblindness.

Despite ongoing efforts to professionalize the Chicago Police Department, shore up internal mechanisms of accountability, and improve police-community relations, administrators failed to check officers' racist application of professional discretion. Invested in a punitive model of law-and-order policing and succumbing to the growing power of police unions, reformers often favored public relations over meaningful change. Rather than eliminate corruption, professionalization drove it underground. Indeed, several illicit practices—including perjury, bribery, and excessive force—survived reform, even if employing them required tact.[21] The Burge scandal reveals the circumstances under which some officers remained willing to break the rules, violate civil liberties, and exploit vulnerable communities in order to fight crime and advance careers.

The Burge scandal also complicates standard interpretations of police militarization. According to dominant narratives, black rebellion and rising crime spurred federal funding of paramilitary equipment for local police departments after 1965. Expanded during the war on drugs and war on terror, militarization aggravated repressive policing in communities of color.[22] Crediting police militarization for contemporary state violence, however, obscures the fact that the police were always quasi-militarized and always repressive.[23] It also minimizes countervailing trends. While administrators purchased military hardware and embraced war rhetoric, they also invested in professionalization, abandoned military decorum, reinforced a "civilian orientation," relied more on non-sworn staff, prioritized community relations, hired more diverse personnel, tolerated limited civilian review, and recognized officers' right to collective bargaining.[24] Not only did the rise of police unions undermine the militarization model—soldiers, after all, cannot go on strike—it also enabled brutality by affording abusive officers greater protection.[25] Moreover, overwhelming focus on the transfer of military hardware to police departments overshadowed the concurrent transfer of military veterans, thousands of whom brought past experience in foreign war to later careers in domestic law enforcement.[26] Several officers involved in the Chicago police torture scandal, for example, served in the military before joining the CPD, including Jon Burge, whose exposure to prisoner abuse in Vietnam informed his subsequent decision to torture.[27] Finally, by affording a look at detectives instead of patrolmen, the Burge scandal suggests that demilitarizing the police would hardly check officers' capacity for racism, corruption, and abuse, none of which requires federal funding. With their phone books, plastic bags, and rigged field telephones, Burge and his men showed that repressive policing could be done on the cheap.

Exploring the role of police officers and social movements in Chicago over the span of several decades, *Beyond the Usual Beating* illuminates important urban processes. Indeed, the evolving city shaped the lives of the Burge scandal's principal figures, helping determine opportunities and constraints for white police officers and black criminal suspects alike. For example, racially disparate access to housing, education, jobs, and political patronage helped direct working-class white men and poor black men into adversarial positions in Chicago's emerging war on crime. The spatial dynamics of urban politics also helped detectives secure impunity. If crime panic spread citywide after 1965, neither crime itself nor proposed solutions proved evenly distributed. Rather, poor and black neighborhoods suffered disproportionately from both violent crime and repressive policing. More interested in mollifying white and middle-class voters than holding abusive officers accountable, public officials tolerated misconduct in support of law and order. If competitive elections, diffuse jurisdictions, and personnel turnover mitigated official misconduct elsewhere, Cook County's one-party rule, large court system, and insular law enforcement community inhibited political accountability. So did the absorption of outsiders by the political machine. While growing numbers of black police officers, prosecutors, and politicians represented a civil rights victory, their presence did not prevent police torture and its cover-up. Finally, urban conditions facilitated collective resistance. With a critical mass of activists and organizations boasting years of experience resisting oppression, the city afforded torture survivors ready-made champions and other necessary resources. Law collectives and civil rights organizations, universities and churches, prisoner reentry programs and police watchdog groups—if Chicago set the conditions for torture and impunity, it also furnished a means for indemnity.

On May 6, 2015, the Chicago City Council passed an ordinance granting reparations to survivors of police torture under Jon Burge.[28] Endorsing the $5.5 million package, Mayor Rahm Emanuel's senior legal adviser announced: "We do this not because it's required legally. We do it because we think it's the right thing to do—for the victims, their families and the city."[29] Through a spokesman, Burge wondered whether elected officials consulted murder victims' families before "giving 'Reparations' to human vermin."[30] Two weeks later, the Illinois Torture Inquiry and Relief Commission (TIRC) recommended judicial review of Jackie Wilson's torture claims.[31] Exasperated, the daughter of a man killed by the Wilson brothers again dismissed the Burge scandal as the "biggest hoax" ever committed on an American city.[32] Twice in the span of a few weeks, public officials sided with convicted murderers over the opposition of murder victims' families. Unthinkable decades earlier, the reparations bill and the TIRC ruling marked an important shift in the official response to the torture crisis. Not only had Burge and his men abused suspects with impunity for over twenty years, they also enjoyed the city's protection in the decades that followed. For example, coerced confessions won Burge's Midnight Crew commendations and promotions throughout the 1970s. Rather than punish Area 2 detectives when allegations surfaced in the 1980s, supervisors enabled them. Even as officials distanced themselves from Burge in the 1990s, they also sought to minimize culpability. As torture survivors and activists compiled victories in the 1990s, 2000s, and 2010s, officials defended Burge at great cost to the city's purse and reputation. Yet by 2015, much of the press and local government acknowledged the veracity of the torture scandal and supported redress.

To explain this change over time—from impunity to reparations—*Beyond the Usual Beating* is divided into two parts. Part 1 answers the question, How did a group of white detectives operate a torture regime with impunity for over two decades? The three chapters of this opening section focus primarily on the perspective, interests, and actions of detectives working CPD Area 2 on the city's Southeast Side during the 1970s and 1980s. Part 2 asks, How did local people win justice and relief for victims of police misconduct? Beginning with disclosure of the torture crisis in 1989, the three chapters of this closing section focus primarily on the perspective, interests, and actions of torture survivors and their allies within what I call the Chicago torture justice movement. Placing the Burge scandal in historical context, this book analyzes police violence and accountability during a period—the late twentieth century—when crime panic and the politics of law and order dominated urban policy.

Several recent books inform my inquiries and conclusions. Providing a story of "racism in action,"[33] Nicole Gonzalez Van Cleve's *Crook County* complicates the notion that structural racism "frequently functions without the active participation of any one bigoted decision maker."[34] Locating personal agency among institutional actors, she writes, "Racism is done *not* just 'out there'—in traditional measures of inequality like education, income, job prospects, and the creation of racial stigma—but also in the everyday workings 'in here'—in the interaction and social exchanges that define the experience of institutions."[35] By carrying her analysis into the interrogation room, my book complements Gonzalez Van Cleve's groundbreaking ethnography by further populating the landscape of structural racism in Cook County. Ending chronologically where my book begins, Simon Balto's *Occupied Territory* offers a comprehensive history of race and policing in the Second City between the late 1910s and early 1970s. Arguing that there was never a time "in which [African Americans] had a smoothly functioning relationship with the CPD," Balto reminds readers that racist policing, including "torture allegations," had been "routine" long before the relationship between Black Chicago and the CPD "sunk to its nadir" in the late 1960s.[36] Within this nadir, Burge and his crew flourished. Finally, People's Law Office attorney Flint Taylor's *The Torture Machine* offers an invaluable first-hand account of the Chicago torture justice movement from the perspective of a critical participant. Working on behalf of survivors for over three decades after 1987, Taylor is more closely associated with the fight for justice in the Burge scandal than anyone else—barring the survivors themselves. His detailed recollections fill important gaps in the public record. Complementing Taylor's biographical narrative, *Beyond the Usual Beating* devotes more attention to the period before the mid-1980s, places the Burge scandal in deeper historical context, and includes more sustained analysis of its broader significance.

Outlining Burge's life and career, part 1 reveals the interplay between personal bigotry and structural racism within the criminal justice system. While scholars have already explained how institutional racism exacerbated inequality after 1970, this book investigates the personal element—the intimate, everyday racism of law enforcement. According to Georgetown law professor Paul Butler, "Racial disparities have not been caused by discriminatory statutes; instead, such results have been achieved through the racialized exercise of discretion, including selective enforcement by police departments, selective prosecution, and selective sentencing by judges."[37] The Burge cases highlight more malignant types of selective misbehavior as well, including selective abuse of criminal suspects, selective coercion of statements, and selective perjury. In addition to determining when and how officers performed official duties, discretion also shaped when and how—and against whom—officers employed misconduct.

While many of Burge's methods proved extraordinary, others were representative of police action in the late twentieth-century United States. By administering more than the usual beating, Burge attracted unprecedented scrutiny to a group of actors—police detectives—who preferred to operate below the radar.[38] Allotting a rare look inside the interrogation room, multiple investigations of Area 2 not only documented unequivocal acts of torture but also uncovered the benign habits, petty racism, and minor physical confrontations endemic to criminal investigation. Discovery of officers' shortcuts, cheats, and abuses helped catalog behavior likely characteristic, rather than aberrational, of detective work in this period. It was only when Area 2 detectives crossed an invisible line that observers grew concerned. Absent electric shock, suffocation, and mock execution, regular abuse alone—the "usual beating"[39]—would not have raised alarms or triggered relief for victims.

Looking to the United Nations for reference, activists applied a broad definition of torture to the Burge scandal. Signed by the United States in 1988,[40] the UN Convention against Torture reads, in part:

> The term "torture" means any act by which severe pain or suffering, whether physical or mental, is intentionally inflicted on a person for such purposes as obtaining from him or a third person information or a confession, punishing him for an act he or a third person has committed or is suspected of having committed, or intimidating or coercing him or a third person, or for any reason based on discrimination of any kind, when such pain or suffering is inflicted by or at the instigation of or with the consent or acquiescence of a public official or other person acting in an official capacity.[41]

Under this rubric, Area 2 methods often qualified as torture, even as officers drew directly from the contemporary interrogation playbook.[42] While electric shock and mock execution brought notoriety, Burge and his men relied much more often on trickery, deception, and lies; intimidation, threats, and racist insults; slaps, kicks, and shoves; denial of food, sleep, or bathroom facilities; restricted access to family, friends, or lawyers; and the withholding of exculpatory evidence. Hardly unique to Area 2, this repertoire of dirty tricks defined detective work in the United States in the 1970s and 1980s.[43] Indeed, even Burge's signature technique—electric-shock torture—occasionally surfaced in police districts across Chicago and the nation.[44] Yet appellate courts did not need to hear of such horrors to toss confessions, reverse convictions, or invalidate sentences.[45] Threats alone, even promises of beneficial treatment, could keep a suspect's statement from a jury. While media coverage of the Burge scandal continues to highlight electric shock and wrongful conviction, most known cases involved lesser acts of abuse and targeted suspects likely guilty of the crimes under investigation. These cases, too, qualified as police torture.

Shifting focus to the Chicago torture justice movement, part 2 demonstrates the interplay between agency and contingency in the Burge scandal and its aftermath. Confounding simple cause and effect, the movement's achievements are best attributed to the convergence of perseverance and opportunity. Even when progress stalled, veteran activists kept the issue alive while opportunity structures evolved. Indeed, Burge's adversaries did not appear spontaneously, nor did they come together solely to address torture. Rather, the movement emerged from a network of individuals and groups previously active in other campaigns who broadened their coalition and added the Burge scandal to their agenda. While activists tapped old and new strategies for pressing grievances, they also benefited from the passage of time and the removal of barriers. For example, opportunity knocked when Mayor Richard M. Daley retired in 2011 after twenty-two years in office. In a political vacuum, Daley's retirement would not have had much impact on the Burge scandal. In the context of an ongoing, decades-long movement for social justice, however, the perseverance of community activists paid off. Daley's successor Rahm Emanuel hardly proved a champion for social justice, but unlike Daley, he had no direct connection to the Burge cases and seemed eager to appear progressive on issues of police violence.[46] Adapting to new circumstances, activists pressured Emanuel and negotiated a deal.[47] If Daley's absence was a necessary precondition for passage of the reparations ordinance, so was the presence of a robust and experienced social movement for police accountability.[48]

Highlighting the role of contingency, both concrete and abstract developments shaped the Burge scandal in ways activists could not anticipate. For example, external changes to the larger political culture in Chicago and the United States between the 1970s and 2010s framed opportunities and constraints. Burge and his men coerced confessions during a time of escalating crime and white backlash, when public fear and racial resentment expanded tolerance for police excess. Indeed, Burge's career timeline—from 1970 to 1991—overlaps neatly with the height of violent crime rates in post–World War II Chicago. During the 1970s, 1980s, and 1990s, many Americans tolerated—even celebrated—vigilantism in pursuit of law and order. In the midst of the Chicago torture crisis in 1982, syndicated columnist Mike Royko considered accused cop killers "lucky to be alive" after encountering Burge, suggesting that victims of police violence got what they deserved.[49] Evolving public opinion on crime and policing after 1990, however, suggests how the zeitgeist influenced outcomes. By the 2000s, plummeting crime rates, an epidemic of wrongful convictions, and a pattern of fatal police shootings eroded public tolerance for police abuse. Cultural change, of course, did not occur without human agency. Rather, the ideas, words, and actions of countless individuals helped mold a less-punitive consensus, however fragile it was. The Trump-era resurgence of law and order rhetoric notwithstanding, collective reconsideration of punitive logic in the 2000s augured well for the Chicago torture justice movement, even as its efforts to expose the Burge scandal itself helped moved the needle.

While black victimization dominates public discourse on mass incarceration, the late twentieth-century criminal justice crackdown also triggered contemporary resistance. Recovering an overlooked history of collective action against police violence from the 1970s through the early 2000s, *Beyond the Usual Beating* examines important continuities and ruptures within a larger black freedom struggle. More than simply addressing resistance after 1970, however, this book analyzes how ordinary people fighting racial injustice after the fall of Jim Crow struggled to create national movements around issues that lack the moral simplicity of desegregation and voting rights. Rising to the challenge, coalitions of small and ad hoc organizations came together to monitor, regulate, and resist law enforcement throughout the post–civil rights era. These organizations—often operating at the neighborhood or street level—have gone largely unnoticed by scholars looking at the national picture. Considering the hidden nature of police torture, the vast power disparity between perpetrators and victims, and the backdrop of punishment and impunity in which the Burge scandal unfolded, the achievements of the Chicago torture justice movement speak to the capacity for collective action among affected communities. In Chicago, survivors of police violence, their families, community activists, civil rights attorneys, journalists, academics, politicians, and various allies overcame significant obstacles to achieve lasting justice and reform, even if radical goals remain unrealized.

PART I

1

A Southeast Side Story

In the tiny neighborhood of Burnside on Chicago's Far South Side, twenty-four-year-old Jon Burge worked his first shift as a robbery detective in May 1972. Three years earlier, serving as a military policeman in Vietnam, he told friends of plans to join the Chicago Police Department (CPD), bragging that it would take him no more than five years to make detective.[1] He did it in a little over two. Entering the old brick building at 9059 S. Cottage Grove Avenue, Burge settled into a drab office space. Makeshift partitions cordoned the second story into separate offices. Desks and cabinets held files of closed and ongoing investigations. Beyond windows protected by wire-mesh grating, the real workplace spread out in all directions.[2] The Detective Division consisted of six geographic areas, each encompassing four or five districts reporting to a central area headquarters.[3] The Burnside Area—known as Area 2—was the city's largest, containing some sixty-two square miles of the Far South and Southeast Sides.[4] Long a region of bustling industry, Area 2 was in decline by the early 1970s. Deindustrialization, disinvestment, rising crime, and concentrated poverty diminished quality of life for many local residents. Others relocated. For Burge, the new assignment represented something of a homecoming. Like many of his coworkers, Burge had grown up in Area 2. His promotion offered an opportunity to serve his hometown, bring criminals to justice, and fight urban decay. Yet much had changed since Burge last lived on the Southeast Side. If the streets and parks looked familiar, it was hardly the same community.

Examining the early life of Jon Burge, this chapter demonstrates how personal bigotry and structural racism facilitated the continuity of racist police violence in Chicago after 1970. Many members of Burge's age, class, and racial cohort grew up in a lily-white world. From an early age, they watched their parents' generation fight a series of losing battles against deindustrialization, racial transition, and crime. Wanting to keep their communities lucrative, white, and safe, they spent decades fending off a series of perceived crises. Inheriting this tradition, Burge joined the CPD after most whites had abandoned much of Area 2. During his tenure, factory doors closed, murder rates skyrocketed, and life chances dimmed in Area 2 neighborhoods. For twenty years Burge participated in scores of interrogations tarnished by allegations of coercion, abuse, and torture. Most of his accusers were African American men linked to horrific crimes. From Burge's perspective, putting these suspects behind bars not only helped protect the community but also offered an opportunity to perform racial domination and punish racial subordinates. Meanwhile, the local criminal justice system incentivized coerced confessions and protected perpetrators. To explain the prevalence of torture allegations at Area 2 in the 1970s, this chapter explores the intersecting biographies of individual actors and local institutions. From a white working-class community resisting racial transition, to a school system confronting desegregation, to a losing war in a distant jungle, and back to a police department polishing an ugly image—by the time Detective Jon Burge arrived for his first shift at Burnside in 1972, he carried the weight of a young lifetime with him.

Staving Off Crisis in Postwar Chicago

Spanning several Far South Side neighborhoods, Area 2 included the furthest reaches of Chicago's Black Belt and the isolated white ethnic communities abutting Lake Michigan to the southeast. As children, Jon Burge and many of his coworkers called this place home.[5] In addition to rows of single-family houses and occasional apartments, the area contained the heart of industrial Chicago, with its sprawling rail yards and towering steel mills. If commercial bustle and civil tranquility dominated memories of the landscape, the region also bore witness to some of the city's most notorious acts of violence. University of Chicago undergraduates Nathan Leopold and Richard Loeb stashed the body of fourteen-year-old Bobby Franks near the secluded shore of Wolf Lake in 1924.[6] Police officers opened fire on union members in front of Republic Steel on Memorial Day in 1937.[7] White mobs attacked black families at Trumbull Park Homes in South Deering throughout the 1950s.[8] Richard Speck slaughtered eight student nurses in a Jefferey Manor dormitory in 1966.[9] While sensational events added local flavor, though, most residents worried more about the mundane challenges of everyday life.

Throughout America's industrial heartland, a generation born at the close of World War II spent decades fending off threats to familiar patterns of living and working. On Chicago's Southeast Side, three primary crises gripped the white working-class imagination after 1945—industrial decline, "racial succession" of neighborhoods,[10] and rising crime. Emerging from economic depression and global war, families hoped for a return to economic growth and social stability. While the postwar boom brought new opportunities, however, some challenges remained beyond residents' control. Determined to secure dreams for a better future, local whites responded to perceived threats in the 1950s, 1960s, and 1970s with a variety of methods, including organized protest and collective violence.[11] Despite the effort, Chicago's southeastern fringe proved incapable of withstanding deindustrialization and related phenomena. By the 1980s, the physical appearance, racial demographics, and economic fortunes of the area had transformed forever, at least in the eyes of those who grew up there.

In retrospect, the Southeast Side reached its economic peak in the period immediately after World War II. To local residents yearning for prosperity, the very physicality of industrial structures evoked comfort and security. Hulking factories and sprawling warehouses, however, offered only the illusion of permanence. Indeed, the Far South Side's industrial health had always been fragile. When European and American settlers began populating the Chicago periphery in the mid-nineteenth century, Lake Calumet and Lake Michigan promised to induce commercial activity among the villages southeast of downtown. Yet it took the ambitious expenditures of outside forces to truly open the South Side to modern industry. In the 1870s, Congress allocated federal funds to improve Calumet Harbor and construct a complicated series of canals and channels connecting the various natural and man-made rivers striding the local swampland. In the 1880s, many of the new railroads carrying material from the American West through Chicago wound their way across the Southeast Side, further establishing the infrastructure necessary to the later success of the steel industry. The twentieth century witnessed an explosion of industrial activity and accompanying population growth.[12]

With the outbreak of World War II, American industry entered a golden age. In the three decades after 1940, the Southeast Side of Chicago and northwest Indiana developed into what historians have called "the largest steelmaking region in the world."[13] While employment rates and wages trended relatively high throughout the 1950s and 1960s, however, ordinary people remained wary of the future.[14] The social contract established between organized labor and corporate management in the 1930s continued to deliver stability and growth, but beginning in the 1950s, rising anti-unionism and global restructuring tempered working-class optimism.[15] Citing high wages, exorbitant taxes, and foreign aid to international competitors, for example, one Chicago resident lamented as early as 1959, "The high costs of doing business in the United States is [*sic*] bankrupting American industries, is closing American plants, and is putting Americans out of jobs."[16] If most residents failed to anticipate the depth of the coming decline, few escaped economic anxiety altogether.

The postwar wave finally broke in the 1970s, a decade some observers likened to the Depression years of the 1930s.[17] Punctuating the steady decline of Chicago's meatpacking industry, the Union Stock Yards closed for good in August 1971 after more than a century of operation.[18] That same year, Amtrak's consolidation of downtown rail lines marked a crisis in the railroad industry, as shrinking passenger and freight traffic triggered plummeting demand for the manufacture of railcars and related equipment.[19] Finally, in an abrupt realization of local fears, the steel mills of the Southeast Side began laying off workers in droves. International Harvester sold Wisconsin Steel in 1977. By 1980, workers were locked out for good. Over the next three years, U.S. Steel's famous South Works plant fired nine thousand of its remaining ten thousand workers. From 1979 to 1982, the steel industry suffered more than any other sector of the ailing economy, purging over 150,000 jobs across the nation.[20] The U.S. Bureau of Labor estimated that southeast Chicago and northwest Indiana bled 187,000 steel-related jobs between 1950 and 1980.[21] Noting that "economic catastrophe" and "massive unemployment" threatened to turn a thriving "industrial center" into a placid "bird sanctuary," researchers poring over census data in the early 1980s spurned the "industrial future" of Chicago's Southeast Side.[22]

Before the decline, however, many of the economic features that bolstered industry also attracted new groups of people to the Southeast Side. Throughout the first half of the twentieth century, immigrants from across Europe and Latin America made their way to the polyglot urban capital of the Midwest in pursuit of economic opportunity.[23] Domestic migrations also fueled the city's growth. Particularly during World War II, the demands of delivering machines of war to Allied armies combined with manpower shortages, helping escalate the Great Migration of African Americans from the rural South to the urban North. New arrivals to Chicago often joined friends and family who came before, swelling the confines of the Black Belt and straining the already-tight housing supply to its breaking point. Desperate for comfortable homes, black families ventured across the informal boundaries of segregated neighborhoods throughout the 1940s and 1950s.[24]

Streets of row houses once containing only white families rapidly became all black—sometimes within the course of a few months or even weeks—through processes contemporaries called blockbusting, white flight, and racial succession.[25] If industrial vigor brought some semblance of stability to the Southeast Side, it also attracted outsiders to the doorsteps of a notoriously race-conscious group of working-class white ethnics.

Within white neighborhoods of the Southeast Side, postwar anxiety over industrial decline mixed with fears of being overrun by African American "invaders."[26] With the wartime boom came an influx of black workers eager to relocate near jobs along the lakefront. Beginning in the 1940s, residential patterns that would characterize the region for the rest of the century began to take shape. Starting in the area's northwestern corner, outgoing whites moved to the suburbs or south and east into ever-exclusive communities like East Side, a "virtual island" accessed only by drawbridge from the rest of Chicago,[27] and Hegewisch, "Chicago's most isolated neighborhood."[28] Tucked into the northwestern section of South Deering, Jon Burge's boyhood neighborhood of Jeffery Manor illustrated this trend.[29] Considered lily-white at the time of his birth in 1947, the neighborhood was "almost entirely black and Latino" by the 1980s.[30] In 1982, police officers referred to Hegewisch as the "last stand for whites" within Area 2's 4th District.[31] Decades of resistance to black migration fostered such "defensive" posturing, even if it was whites who often "flared into overt aggression" wherever people of different races met.[32]

White residents worried about deindustrialization and racial succession in part because they feared that both would lead to higher crime. Before the appearance of large numbers of African Americans, South Deering residents conflated public housing, unemployment, and government aid with crime, prostitution, and gang violence, even among poor whites.[33] When the first black families arrived in the 1950s, local whites sensationalized an alleged "recent wave of negro rapes of white girls" to rally a communal defense.[34] Insisting they were not "anti negro," a local firebrand claimed that he and his neighbors were merely defending the "American way of life" against the "savage, lustful, immoral standards of the southern negro."[35] Yet crime was hardly new to Chicago's white neighborhoods of the 1950s and 1960s. Ongoing campaigns against the high murder rate, white youth gangs, rampant vice, organized crime, drug abuse, and juvenile delinquency belied the white law-abiding ideal.[36] Racist perceptions of criminality, however, masked the ways that local institutions defined ordinary black behavior as criminal, funneled white-controlled criminal enterprises into black neighborhoods, justified white criminality, or ignored it altogether. Indeed, as historian Khalil Muhammad argues, white Americans had conflated blackness and crime for generations.[37] With crime rates low throughout the 1940s, 1950s, and early 1960s,[38] white fears owed more to racialized perceptions of threat than to real incidents of victimization. Despite the relative prosperity and peace of the postwar period the specter of unemployment, racial invasion, and crime regularly haunted Chicago's white working class.

By the 1980s, many local whites' fears appeared to have come true. The average white resident witnessed the plant close and the neighbor's house sold to a black family. In addition, the violent crime they read about in the newspaper seemed to have made its way to the neighborhood. According to a 1973 article in the *Daily Calumet*, major offenses on the Southeast Side had increased by 800 percent since 1965, when the FBI's Uniform Crime Reports placed the 4th District eighteenth out of twenty-one in terms of major offenses reported. By 1975, the 4th District's crime rate had climbed to second out of twenty-two. "Once one of the quietest districts in the city," a police officer reported in 1982, "[the 4th District] is now one of the most active." Violent crime, particularly "murder, rape and robbery," appeared to have "risen 500%, 400% and 400% respectively with no signs of letting up." Echoing conclusions drawn by local whites, the report cited the "expansion of the black ghetto in the district and the ever increasing drug problem."[39] At a time when sociologists, journalists, and politicians debated the pathology of the inner city, it was clear to many locals that the so-called urban crisis had come at last to the Southeast Side.[40] Yet white residents' fears were also self-fulfilling.[41] By choosing to relocate families, homes, businesses, and jobs, many whites also exacerbated urban decline. Far from the principal cause of their problems, the influx of African Americans even offered white property owners an occasional opportunity to recoup losses sustained by a deindustrialization process that otherwise seemed outside their control.

The Education of Jon Burge

Many of the detectives who worked at Area 2 in the 1970s and 1980s came of age during a period of social and economic insecurity, when a series of changes upended the established arrangements of local communities. In some ways, the life experiences of a young Jon Burge were typical. During early childhood, the city's longest-lasting racial housing conflict unfolded within a mile and a half of Burge's doorstep. When he was a teenager attending Bowen High School in the early 1960s, citywide struggles over the desegregation of public schools demonstrated how local policy makers bent to white resistance. After enlisting in the U.S. Army, Burge volunteered for a tour of duty in Vietnam, where he developed skills of police investigation and encountered methods of racial subjugation. By the time he was sworn in as a patrolman in the Chicago Police Department in 1970, violent crime rates on the Southeast Side and elsewhere had begun a precipitous climb. When Detective Burge first confronted black criminal suspects at Area 2 in the early 1970s, his prior experience prepared him to navigate an antagonistic relationship with black criminal suspects.

With important distinctions, Burge's background resembled that of other so-called white ethnics who populated urban America in the mid-twentieth century.[42] While not a first- or second-generation immigrant, Burge could trace his roots across the ocean and back through time to nineteenth-century Europe. Descended from a Norwegian farmer named Thomas Hansen Bjørge, Jon's father, Floyd, grew up on small farms in Wisconsin and Michigan before moving to Chicago sometime between 1930 and 1935. According to the federal census, by 1940 Floyd was married and living in a YMCA hotel. His wife, Ethel, was born in Chicago in 1916, the daughter of Lonnie and Alma Corriher, whose parents came from North Carolina and Germany, respectively. Floyd and Ethel Burge welcomed their first son, Jeffery Lon Burge, in the fall of 1942, eighteen months before Floyd joined the U.S. Navy. World War II delayed conception of their second child, but after Floyd was discharged from the service in January 1946, Ethel became pregnant again. She gave birth to Jon Graham Burge on December 20, 1947, contributing her share to America's postwar baby boom.[43]

Settling on the industrial Southeast Side, Floyd did not work in any of the local mills, yet his job at the phone company situated him firmly within the blue-collar culture of the neighborhood. Throughout the 1950s, Ethel toiled as a full-time housewife and part-time model, reaching the finals of the 1957 Mrs. America pageant, the nationally televised contest honoring married homemakers.[44] By the 1960s, Ethel had launched an eclectic career as a lecturer and advice columnist, speaking and writing to large audiences on topics familiar to the charm-school set. Doling out fashion advice and helping women to "understand the men in our lives," she reminded wives and mothers, "Men need to run things and we'd better learn to let them—with good grace and tenderness."[45] She eventually published her own book, *This Business of Dressing for Business*, in 1970.[46]

Other than Ethel's unusual glamour, the young Burge family exemplified ordinary life in 1950s Chicago. When Jon was an infant, Floyd and Ethel moved into a modern duplex at 9612 S. Luella Avenue in the new community of Merrionette Manor, Chicago's largest privately financed housing development.[47] Covering some eighty acres of South Deering's undeveloped land, the planned neighborhood epitomized postwar experiments in residential living and urban construction. Housing mogul Joseph E. Merrion welcomed the project's first homeowners in the spring of 1948, explaining his vision to reporters, "We have sought to create a model community similar to those in Chicago suburbs, and yet keep home prices within the means of the average family."[48] Even before all the buildings were completed, 205 war veterans and their families began occupying the mixed-floor, two-bedroom duplexes. Merrion arranged for the Federal Housing Authority to insure mortgages on the $9,900 homes. With a Veterans' Administration loan of $1,300 and an additional $500 down, hundreds of men joined Floyd Burge in homeownership, obtaining the crucial physical component of the American dream.[49] In accordance with local practice, all 542 of the units in Merrionette Manor were reserved for white families only.[50]

Protecting the all-white status of the subdivision, however, required vigilance. Indeed, original residents even signed clauses reading, "It is an express condition of this Declaration that the premises hereinbefore described shall not be occupied by any person who is not a member of the Caucasian race."[51] Before the ink was dry, however, a 1948 U.S. Supreme Court decision declared such restrictive covenants unenforceable.[52] Yet an intimidating spirit of communal defense lived on well into the next decade, as homeowners reacted to rumors of black purchases with organized resistance. Alert to racial conflict throughout the city, for example, the subdivision's developer protected his investment by encouraging peace through exclusion. When would-be black buyers responded to a "for sale" ad in the *Chicago Defender*, rumor had it that Joseph Merrion himself would buy the house back from the seller and place a large "Sold" sign in the yard to keep outsiders away.[53] Although many residents claimed they were "rather neutral" or even supportive of integration,[54] members of the Merrionette Manor Improvement Association pressured individuals to sell only to whites and offered to buy homes collectively rather than see them go to black buyers.[55]

Beyond powers of persuasion, however, a covert threat of violence loomed behind the communal effort to maintain racial purity in Merrionette Manor. When Jon Burge was five years old, in July 1953, a local American Friends Service Committee (AFSC) agent arranged for an African American single father named Ralph Mabry to buy the Manor home of a young white couple desperate to sell their property before departing for an extended stay overseas.[56] When word of the sale leaked, Merrion and members of the homeowners' association balked, insisting that the sudden appearance of a black family in South Deering would attract violent white protesters from nearby public housing and young toughs from "Tron Town," a colloquial name for surrounding neighborhoods of blue-collar steel workers.[57] On the evening of Friday, July 31, 1953, however, the angry crowd gathering outside 2219 East Ninety-Seventh Street—one block west of the Burge home—suggested that Merrionette Manor residents did not need to recruit outsiders to repel blacks from the neighborhood.[58] The following week, Mabry agreed to meet with the homeowners' association alone, outside the presence of his AFSC sponsors. Mabry emerged from the closed-door meeting convinced of the foolhardy nature of his decision. Instead of signing the deed, he agreed to move into a temporary apartment while the good people of Merrionette Manor found him a home in a more suitable neighborhood.[59]

Lessons from Trumbull Park

Most working-class men like Floyd Burge viewed owning a home as the culmination of a long struggle for security and status.[60] Yet in addition to bringing relief, homeownership also heightened anxiety over social, economic, and demographic change. Throughout the 1940s and 1950s, for example, massive population shifts triggered by the war taxed municipal space and resources. When African American migrants flooded Chicago's overcrowded Black Belt, city officials turned to public housing to alleviate the pressure.[61] Fearing an influx of poor tenants—particularly poor blacks—many white homeowners resisted efforts to locate public housing in their neighborhoods. On the Southeast Side, the diverging fates of neighboring communities highlighted the stakes of white resistance. In the 1940s, South Deering residents witnessed the rapid transformation of Riverdale, a small neighborhood across Lake Calumet to the southwest. In 1940, Riverdale was home to 1,509 people, only six of whom were African American. Between 1943 and 1944, however, the Chicago Housing Authority (CHA) tapped federal money to build the Altgeld Gardens public housing development. By 1950, the population of Riverdale had increased sixfold. Of the area's 9,790 people counted in that year's federal census, over 8,000 were African American, most of whom lived in Altgeld Gardens.[62] Across Lake Calumet, the people of South Deering took note.

Long before a single black family settled into the neighborhood, South Deering contained a concrete target to focus residents' abstract fears of public housing—the 460-unit, 1,700-occupant Trumbull Park Homes project located just south of the eighteen-acre park of the same name.[63] Ironically christened in honor of Senator Lyman Trumbull, who as chair of the Senate Judiciary Committee helped draft the Thirteenth Amendment banning slavery in 1864,[64] Trumbull Park Homes was one of four CHA housing developments to refuse black applicants well into the 1950s.[65] For years, CHA administrators acknowledged that state law—as well as their own policy—bound them to accept tenants based on nondiscriminatory criteria of financial need, not race.[66] Yet the project's managers bowed to local pressure, promising that "racial homogeneity would not be disturbed" in the all-white community of South Deering.[67] This agreement helped the site's wary neighbors resign themselves to the project's construction in 1936 and 1937.[68] Funded by the Public Works Administration and leased to the CHA, the $2.5 million Trumbull Park Homes welcomed its first tenants in the summer of 1938 and served to ease housing shortages during both the "long ramp up" and "longer ramp down" of World War II and beyond.[69]

Throughout the 1940s and early 1950s, the CHA diligently kept its end of the bargain, leasing low-rent apartments on a whites-only basis even as black leaders cried foul.[70] Lest downtown bureaucrats forget, occasional disturbances reminded administrators of South Deering's resolve. In 1950, local opposition effectively canceled CHA plans to purchase twenty-one acres of land for an additional three-hundred-unit expansion at Trumbull Park.[71] When a dark-complexioned Argentinean family moved into the project in 1952, angry demonstrators forced them to back out of the lease.[72] During an annual flower festival that same year, the appearance of black attendees inspired racial violence.[73] Floyd and Ethel Burge raised their young boys just a few blocks to the northwest. Throughout the 1950s, an influential group of South Deering residents celebrated a "tradition of fighting for what they think is right" and vowed to protect the community from the perceived dangers of public housing and desegregation.[74]

A clerical error finally brought explosive conditions at Trumbull Park to a head in August 1953, the very week that whites turned Ralph Mabry away from Merrionette Manor. Eager to find adequate housing and frustrated by the long CHA waiting list, twenty-two-year-old Betty Anne Howard circumvented the placement process by going directly to the Trumbull Park Homes' management office to apply for an apartment in May 1953. Although CHA policy denied black families access to Trumbull Park, the clerk mistakenly approved the application, having failed to notice that Betty Howard was African American. According to CHA director Elizabeth Wood, the fair-skinned Betty Howard "[had] not the slightest physical characteristics of a Negro" and the current address she provided was not "normally identifiable as being in a Negro area." Because Betty's husband, Donald Howard, was an army veteran and unable to get time off from his job as a mail carrier, the CHA staff waived a requisite home visit and allowed the Howards to occupy the apartment with only Betty's signature on the lease. On July 30, 1953, the Howard family—including four-year-old Cynthia and two-year-old Donald Jr.—moved into the Trumbull Park low-rises and began a nightmarish stint as pioneers on Chicago's racial frontier.[75]

Within days, local whites reacted to the "sneak attack" appearance of the Howard family with predictable violence, briefly catapulting southeast Chicago into the international spotlight as a capital of reactionary racism.[76] While a series of housing riots erupted across the city throughout the immediate postwar period, none matched Trumbull Park in terms of "duration" or "severity."[77] On August 5, 1953, fifty whites gathered outside the Howards' besieged apartment, shouting racial insults, hurling rocks, and breaking a front window. For the rest of the month and into the fall, daily crowds swelled into the hundreds, at one point reaching an estimated 1,500 persons. With the color line broken and media attention focused on the CHA's racial policies, management stood firm and allowed several more black families to move into Trumbull Park beginning in October. Through winter and into spring 1954, white demonstrators terrorized black families while police struggled to maintain order. Protestors directed verbal and physical abuse at black residents; kept them awake with explosions of fireworks and so-called aerial bombs; threw rocks and other projectiles at black passersby; stoned buses and automobiles carrying black passengers; and started fires in vacant apartments, a liquor store, and other buildings nearby.[78]

Unwilling to fall victim to what many assumed was a racial "experiment" thrust on them by "some crack-pot sociologist," local whites fought back.[79] Considering South Deering's large size, small population, and remote location, many locals perceived their community as particularly vulnerable to outside manipulation. At roughly six square miles, South Deering was the second-largest community area in the city, yet it was among the smallest by population, ranking last in population density. For comparison, the only area larger in geographic size—the 7.2-square-mile far West Side neighborhood of Austin—contained some 132,180 people in 1950, dwarfing South Deering's population of 17,476.[80] Only a square mile larger than South Deering, Austin was packed with more people than any other city in Illinois other than Chicago itself.[81] In contrast, South Deering enjoyed several miles of "vacant and undeveloped land" previously referred to as a "hunters' and fishers' paradise." As recently as 1934, South Deering residents had inhabited a mere half square mile.[82] Construction of public and private housing in the late 1930s and 1940s only marginally expanded residents' tiny footprint.[83]

When the Howard family arrived in 1953, local leaders sought to bolster the isolated community's fragile solidarity. One of Trumbull Park's earliest residents implored neighbors not to sell their property and relocate to the suburbs, writing: "Please do not forget that South Deering is a very small community as communities go. It is the smallest community in Chicago."[84] A vocal minority directed the energies of the South Deering Improvement Association toward maintaining racial purity. Residents soon launched the *South Deering Bulletin*, a weekly newsletter that grew from five hundred to three thousand subscribers in the summer of 1955, ran well into the 1960s, and boasted the masthead "White People Must Control Their Own Communities."[85] While conditions at Trumbull Park settled into "an armed truce"[86] by 1957, the general harassment of black tenants continued for the better part of a decade.[87]

White resistance to housing desegregation in 1950s South Deering took on a communal character as entire families, including women and children, participated in daily efforts to repel "unwanted tenants."[88] In his analysis of postwar housing riots in Chicago, historian Arnold Hirsch determined that 87.5 percent of those arrested during the disturbances at Trumbull Park and elsewhere in the 1940s and 1950s "lived within 1½ miles" of the events' epicenter.[89] Laid over a map of South Deering, this mile-and-a-half circle emanating from Trumbull Park would have just covered Merrionette Manor and the childhood home of Jon Burge, who turned six years old in December 1953, during the height of the violence. While police officers largely limited their arrests to young men, eyewitness accounts suggest that "the typical housing riot was a complex communal endeavor" featuring a diverse cross section of the community.[90] An observer from the *Daily Worker* noted a widespread spirit of resistance among residents of greater South Deering, claiming, "The community around the project seethes with discord."[91] There is no evidence suggesting the Burge family participated in the communal riots occurring a few blocks from their home. Yet these events, drawn out over several years of Jon Burge's childhood, served as backdrop for his early development while offering examples for adult behavior on matters of race and community.

Even if individual police officers lacked enthusiasm for integration,[92] a large contingent of patrolmen took on heightened visibility throughout the Trumbull Park disturbances. After the first crowd assaulted the Howards' apartment on August 5, 1953, police supervisors assigned a permanent

Trumbull Park detail to an abandoned unit on site, consisting of twenty-five men on twenty-four-hour watch with unpopular orders to "protect the Negro families." Within a week, supervisors learned that they needed a much larger force to contain the enormous crowds. Eventually, thousands of men from all of the department's thirty-eight districts served special duty at Trumbull Park at one time or another, with the size of the force fluctuating with conditions on site. An ordinary day in fall 1953 or winter 1954 saw anywhere from 100 to 250 officers arrive for duty. On August 11, supervisors sent an overwhelming force of 800 men to contain a crowd half that size, suggestive of officers' half-hearted commitment to the task. On October 13, a stunning force of 1,200 officers patrolled the area. With tensions stuck on high, participants fell into an uneasy routine. Administrators placed each black family under the forced watch of six to nine patrolmen, who escorted black residents to and from their homes in an uncomfortable police wagon nicknamed "Black Maria." Effecting the image of a "besieged fortress," the police erected lean-to shanties for protection from the cold and performed militarized roll calls three times a day. Officers traversed the grounds in pairs, guards stood watch in front of black apartments, and squad cars idled at trouble corners. Connecting the entire operation, a two-way communications system kept officers on high alert. Wary of media attention and desperate to avoid a full-fledged race riot, Mayor Martin Kennelly and Police Commissioner Timothy O'Connor pledged to keep South Deering under firm control.[93]

With the police operating as "a kind of occupying army" at Trumbull Park,[94] impressionable observers gleaned lessons on the mercurial nature of public service. Yet even as South Deering residents chastised the police for facilitating desegregation, their anger was not uniform. Rather, only officers who appeared to betray the white community provoked disgust. Indeed, South Deering Improvement Association leaders and the *South Deering Bulletin* regularly interspersed criticism of police action with praise for those who remembered where they came from. For example, in the summer of 1955 the *Bulletin* ridiculed a patrolman for clubbing a group of white youth during a harmless scuffle on the Fourth of July. Although the officer was white, lived in an adjacent neighborhood, played sports in South Deering, and once worked at a local factory, the paper concluded, "It's certainly odd what a policeman's uniform will do to a guy that was once known to be a swell fellow."[95] On the same page, however, the editors also thanked a "level-headed" sergeant for reversing a "sadistic" arrest of three white "boys" loitering on a street corner. The "good sergeant" not only let the "lads" go home but also gave the arresting patrolman a "swell tongue lashing."[96] As Jon Burge's childhood passed, the lessons of Trumbull Park became clear. The best police officers were those who protected the "decent, respectable, and hardworking" white people of South Deering.[97] The worst police officers were those "professional trouble-makers" who facilitated the black invasion.[98]

Race and Public Schools on the Southeast Side

Trumbull Park taught many white children of Chicago's South Side that the very presence of African Americans threatened their homes and families with some vague danger. This lesson was reinforced during ongoing struggles to resist desegregation of Chicago's public schools throughout the 1950s and 1960s. Children born during Chicago's postwar baby boom, including Jon Burge, attended school during a period of converging crises for the local Board of Education.[99] As increasing numbers of children entered the school system each year, many schools became overcrowded, triggering a succession of related problems. While construction of new facilities continued apace, frustrated officials admitted that children entered the system at "such a rapid rate" that they could not maintain optimal class sizes.[100] Creative solutions often provided only temporary relief. Administrators enrolled students part-time, operated schools on double shifts, held classes in vacant park facilities and public housing units, and considered busing pupils from crowded schools to half-empty classrooms on the city's periphery.[101] In 1958, the Board of Education predicted an annual increase of sixteen thousand students over each of the following six years, requiring an additional $5 million annually "just to keep up."[102] Financial pressure aside, the real crisis—as with so many issues in Chicago—revolved around race.

By 1963, political activists forced administrators to acknowledge the problem was not just overcrowding but also segregation.[103] Although the Board of Education spurned collecting data on the racial composition of the student population, it was common knowledge that several schools throughout the city were nearly all white or all black.[104] Between 1958 and 1964, multiple studies confirmed activists' claims that overcrowding disproportionately harmed black students even as neighboring white schools maintained empty classrooms.[105] An obvious solution called for transferring black children to white schools. Whenever officials proposed even token desegregation, however, whites rallied to the defense of the so-called neighborhood school, a euphemism employed to mask the racial nature of white resistance to student transfers.[106] Throughout the first half of the 1960s,

Superintendent Benjamin C. Willis and the eleven-member Board of Education clashed over strategies to alleviate overcrowding, mitigate segregation, and boost flagging education standards. Ultimately, school administrators succeeded only in drawing the ire of black and white parents alike, and students became pawns of political conflict.

In the 1950s and 1960s, white anxiety over the fate of public schools spread across the city, reaching even those Southeast Side neighborhoods where few black and white children attended class together. Encompassing South Deering and its adjacent community areas, Jon Burge's District 17 ranked among the top of the city's twenty-one school districts in several statistical categories.[107] With the failing districts of the Black Belt and Far South Side only a few miles away, Southeast Side parents truly felt they had something to lose. When the Board of Education included race for the first time in its official "head count" in 1963, the District 17's elementary schools were 89 percent white and its high schools 97 percent white. At Luella Elementary, where Jon Burge entered grammar school a decade earlier, there were still zero black children among a student body of 778. When Burge entered his junior year at Bowen High School that fall, over 96 percent of his 2,720 classmates were white.[108]

Despite this racial homogeneity—or perhaps because of it—local white parents joined citywide efforts to resist the transfer of black students to their schools while refusing flat out to bus their own children to distant black schools. A front-page editorial published in the *South Deering Bulletin* in October 1958 highlighted local fears of so-called mixed schools, where teachers "have not been able to cope with the integrated classes due to the huge difference in intellect, morals, customs, and intellectual heredity of the negro." Claiming that "any all-colored school is a dreg on the school system," the editorial insisted "that an integrated school is a den of riots, police-infested, and an utter lack of decent, god-fearing, studious teenagers."[109] Years before the Board of Education announced plans to reshuffle the city's student population, community leaders in South Deering steeled themselves for a fight.

In the face of local resistance, three successive transfer plans confronted Bowen High School beginning in Chicago's tumultuous 1963–1964 school year. First, the Board of Education approved a limited plan allowing top students at overcrowded schools to attend honors programs elsewhere. Buckling under pressure from white parents, Superintendent Willis unilaterally reduced the number of white schools designated to receive black transferees. Black parents from the South Side's Hirsch High School responded by winning a court order commanding Willis to comply with the original plan, triggering the divisive superintendent's public resignation. When the Board of Education refused to accept his letter and asked him to remain in office, black leaders launched a school boycott on October 22, 1963, sending over 224,000 students into the streets in protest.[110] Over several months, while the school board offered rhetorical commitment to integration, Willis's office stubbornly retained control over the permissive transfer process, ensuring that the numbers of students participating would remain small.[111]

The next major proposal, announced in November 1964, involved placing adjacent schools in "clusters" of two or three and allowing students in overcrowded facilities to transfer to another school in the group.[112] On the Southeast Side, majority-white Bowen and South Shore High Schools were placed in a cluster with majority-black Hirsch.[113] During the winter of Jon Burge's senior year, eight students from Hirsch joined the small black student population at Bowen, prompting the Harvard-educated principal to praise her allegedly progressive student body and assert that "there has been no problem at all" with the addition of the new arrivals.[114] By January, however, white resistance forced the board to cancel further transfers, ending the program short of any meaningful integration.[115]

Over the following two years, periodic resurrection of the cluster plan continued to provoke controversy on the Southeast Side. With Bowen the second-most-crowded school in Chicago—operating several mobile classrooms and two off-site branches—District 17's superintendent predicted that whites would endorse the cluster plan if administrators avoided pushing the program "to extremes" and promised to keep a close watch on the black-white ratio.[116] A spokesman for the South East Community Organization, an umbrella group of local homeowners' associations, endorsed the cluster concept in part because it allowed the parents of Hirsch High School's tiny white student population to send their children to Bowen instead of leaving for the suburbs.[117] Meanwhile, inside Bowen, a growing group of black students felt besieged by hostile white students and administrators. "We are almost two schools within a school," a white student explained in 1968.[118]

Token enrollment of black students at Bowen and other white schools elicited heated opposition, yet the process inched forward. The transportation of white students to black schools, however, never stood a chance. When the board proposed sending white freshmen to a new Bowen branch at Chicago Vocational High School—located in a rapidly transitioning community[119]—the parent-teacher association sent a letter to Superintendent Willis, reading, "Protest meetings are being held, and many families are thinking of leaving the community."[120] White resistance finally quashed the cluster plan in March 1967, when new school superintendent James Redmond suggested adding Washington High School near the Indiana state line to the Bowen-Hirsch cluster. Even before the board officially announced the plan, East Side parents presented a seven-thousand-name petition expressing disapproval.[121] Exasperated, school board members conceded that the cluster plan simply "did not work" and agreed to drop it altogether.[122]

In 1968, further elements of the so-called Redmond Plan—including designs to bus children across districts—brought the outrage of the Southeast Side to a boil. An editorial in the *Daily Calumet* called busing an "incubated plot" designed to strike at the "very bowels of the American home—its children."[123] For several days, the paper sampled "miles of letters" received from angry parents.[124] One couple refused "to pay huge taxes to bus Negroes into our community [or] send our small kids into a jungle."[125] Decrying that you "have to be black" to be heard, a Women's Auxiliary Corps private threatened to go AWOL to save her younger sisters from coming home from those "oh so safe schools beaten up, slashed, tortured, raped, and murdered."[126] On January 10, more than one thousand whites picketed downtown, singing "God Bless America" and waving "No bussing" signs.[127] Although over one thousand African Americans held their own rally in support of busing, many black parents also opposed the scheme on financial, cultural, or personal grounds.[128] In the wake of a "four-month flurry" that nearly "ripped apart the city," the board backed down. When the school year ended, administrators settled with a "small scale busing program" affecting only a few West Side districts.[129] Advocates of desegregation on the Southeast Side made do with the ineffective permissive transfer plan that had been set up years earlier.[130] Reflecting a legacy of "diverse Black educational struggles" focused on "quality education rather than desegregation,"[131] however, many African Americans instead "demanded community control" and "educational improvement" in schools where black students already attended.[132]

While the 1960s saw white community leaders achieve victories against school desegregation, the 1970s witnessed retreat. Throughout the decade, white families abandoned large parts of the South Side, relocating to the suburbs or joining a national migration to the Sunbelt. According to a former head of the Merrionette Manor Community Assembly, the first black family moved into the neighborhood in 1966 or 1967. Joining the exodus of local whites, Floyd and Ethel Burge sold their home in 1973.[133] Luella Elementary soon became predominantly black and was renamed in honor of America's first black astronaut.[134] A few blocks north, Bowen High School experienced a similar transformation. Unfortunately, the school also became a site of gang activity and episodic violence. In February 1968, for example, six members of the Egyptian Lords entered the Bowen cafeteria, upended chairs, threw bottles, and sent two students to the hospital with pellet wounds from a sawed-off shotgun.[135] In December 1974, police arrested thirty-five teenagers following a brick-throwing altercation between black and Latino students in a park across the street.[136] When a sixteen-year-old boy was stabbed and killed in a Bowen hallway in February 1982, the *Chicago Defender* wondered when the violence would end, noting that the school was "an institution with a history of racial outbursts."[137] Many white residents who remained in the area proved unable—or unwilling—to understand the complex structural forces linking race, poverty, disinvestment, and crime during the 1970s and 1980s. Looking on as Chicago public schools seemed to descend into chaos, many men of Jon Burge's age and race cohort would have experienced confirmation of a lifetime of fear and prejudice.

From the Southeast Side to Southeast Asia

The demographic changes affecting working-class neighborhoods and schools in the 1960s unfolded simultaneously with another formative experience of the postwar generation—the Vietnam War. While only a modest percentage of military-age men actually served in the armed forces during these years, a disproportionate number of working-class youth wound up in Vietnam and later transitioned to law enforcement.[138] Several detectives involved in the Chicago police torture scandal served at one time or another in the military, including Jon Burge, who was a member of the U.S. Army from June 1966 until September 1969.[139] From an early age, military service must have seemed inevitable to many of Jon Burge's generation. Indeed, the children of America's postwar working class often understood joining the military less as an option to consider and more as a "rite of passage" to endure.[140] Born in the wake of World War II and raised on the war stories of their fathers and uncles, many baby boomers expected to offer their due time in service to their country.[141]

When Jon Burge entered Bowen High School in the fall of 1961, he expected the school's acclaimed Reserve Officer Training Corps (ROTC) to prepare him for a smooth transition to the U.S. Army and the Chicago Police Department.[142] Over the following four years, Burge excelled in ROTC. Winning several commendations, he swore "to meet the high standards and ideals for which [such honors] stand."[143] Graduating in 1965, the seventeen-year-old spent a semester partying at the University of Missouri before dropping out and starting a menial job at a South Side grocery store.[144] Rather than remain vulnerable to the military draft, Burge enlisted in the Army Reserves in June 1966 with a promise that, by volunteering, he would be in a position to advance his future in law enforcement.[145] In August, civil rights activists led open-housing marches through South Deering. Confronted by a group of "good looking and intelligent" teenagers, Dr. Martin Luther King Jr. wondered, "Where did all the hate come from?"[146] While King joined the civil rights movement in the North, Burge headed south, eager to finish boot camp at Fort Campbell, Kentucky.[147]

At eighteen years old, the six-foot-two-inch, 210-pound, red-haired recruit proved a natural soldier. Following basic training, Burge finished second in a class of ninety-eight at Fort McClellan's drill corporal school in Alabama. He then spent eight weeks training for service in the Army's Military Police (MP) at Fort Gordon in Augusta, Georgia. Burge later recalled spending the remainder of his "stateside service" as a drill instructor, training MPs on their way to war. In the fall of 1967, Burge was promoted to sergeant and named Fort Gordon's "soldier of the month." The first time he volunteered to go to Vietnam, he was sent instead to the Republic of Korea, where he stood guard at a Nike-Hercules surface-to-air missile site and provided security for the MP's commanding officer. Ready to witness the war, Burge requested an intertheater transfer to Vietnam in June 1968, arriving in November as a new member of the Ninth Infantry Division's Ninth MP Company.[148]

Since February 1967, the Ninth Infantry had been stationed some forty-five miles southwest of Saigon at Dong Tam, a sprawling base built on land elevated above the "inundated and inhospitable" terrain of the Mekong Delta.[149] The placement of the Ninth Infantry in a swamp represented the army's defiant initiative to take the war into the heart of an area "infested" with Viet Cong (VC), the pejorative term Americans applied to Vietnamese communists and nationalist soldiers.[150] Dong Tam's very presence symbolized the army's commitment to bringing the battle wherever guerillas could be found, no matter how remote or unwelcome.[151] Beginning in December 1966, army engineers dredged six hundred acres of river tributary to create a small city housing over 15,000 Americans and 3,500 South Vietnamese.[152] When Jon Burge arrived, Dong Tam was still growing up from the rice paddies. Engineers and enlisted men constructed a plethora of modern facilities, replete with two-story wooden barracks, running water, an electric power plant, an Olympic-sized swimming pool, mini-golf, batting cages, and a so-called Innocent Civilian Center to house local farmers picked up on patrol.[153] Dong Tam also housed the Mobile Riverine Force, an amphibious unit that traversed local rivers and returned prisoners to a floating jail.[154] Settling into its new home, the Ninth Infantry boasted of turning delta VC from "the cockiest provincial force in Vietnam" into "a remnant of demoralized and panicky units" within the span of a few months.[155]

As the first permanent American base in the treacherous region south of the capital, Dong Tam resembled other bases designed, in part, "for the express purpose of inviting enemy attack," a strategy to raise the enemy "body count" used to measure American success.[156] Accordingly, Dong Tam was a dangerous place to live and work. Within weeks of their arrival, the Ninth Infantry fell under regular rocket and mortar fire.[157] Jon Burge would later receive the Army Commendation Medal of Valor for his actions following a January 1969 bombardment that left one MP dead and twelve wounded.[158] According to a colleague's recollection, Burge braved the falling mortars, rescued soldiers from the wreckage, and helped get the injured to jeeps for transport to medevac helicopters.[159] Similar encounters led to further honors for Sergeant Burge, who would leave Vietnam with two Medals of Valor, a Bronze Star, the Vietnamese Cross of Gallantry, and a Purple Heart.[160] Reflecting the danger, by April 1969 newspapers recognized Dong Tam as the "most frequently hit [American] target" in the delta.[161]

While occasionally dodging incoming shells, the Ninth MP Company was also a diverse unit tasked with an array of duties. The approximately two hundred MPs at Dong Tam on any given day between 1967 and 1969 guarded posts on and around base, provided security for command personnel and visiting dignitaries, regulated traffic, registered firearms, and detained enemy prisoners. They also enforced army regulations and served as general law enforcement for a base the size of a small city.[162] Because they were stationed with an infantry division in a forward area, however, the Ninth MPs were also charged with additional assignments of a distinctive nature. Philip Ash, the company's provost marshal in 1968 and 1969, described the special role of his unit. "We are not traffic cops," he explained. "Division MPs are different from post, camp or station MPs."[163] As with other military police companies sent to Vietnam, the Ninth MPs were considered a combat unit.[164] Members routinely went on patrol, either to protect the highway linking the delta breadbasket to Saigon or to gather prisoners of war from the bush. An army journalist embedded with the Ninth MPs in 1968 recalled setting off in the dark to apprehend VC responsible for nightly attacks on base.[165] Ash contrasted his troops' role at Dong Tam with military police stereotypes. While enlisted men often viewed MPs as unreasonable killjoys, the Ninth MPs fostered a different relationship with the rest of the Ninth Infantry. "The MP's are here to help the men of this division, not to make life miserable for them," Ash insisted.[166]

Jon Burge undertook a mix of assignments during his tour with the Ninth MPs, but he spent the bulk of his time as a criminal investigator, a position particularly suited for transitioning to a career as a detective.[167] According to Burge's own account of his Vietnam experience, "I performed various functions including escort of convoys, security for forward support bases, supervising security for the divisional central base camp [at Dong Tam] and I finished my tour as a Provost Marshal investigator."[168] Arriving in November 1968 and listed in an official roster as the head of a traffic section on January 31, 1969, Burge spent at least the first two or three of his nine months in country moving from one task to another.[169] Ninth MP veteran Wendell Rudacille remembered working with Burge in the Provost Marshal Investigations (PMI) office for approximately six months before their demobilization in late August 1969, suggesting that Burge held this position for as much as two-thirds of his time at Dong Tam.[170] The PMI staff investigated "less serious crimes" and worked alongside the Criminal Investigations Division (CID) on more serious cases. The MPs assigned to this office functioned much as a detective would in any municipal police department back in the United States.[171] Burge, Rudacille, and other MPs working under the provost marshal conducted investigations at Dong Tam and its surrounding firebases, building cases against American and South Vietnamese suspects alike.

Rudacille recalled two of the cases that he and Burge worked in Vietnam. The first involved staking out a postal exchange to disrupt a case of mail-order fraud. As they dissected the evidence, Burge uncovered a pattern and sent a skeptical Rudacille off to await the suspect. Eventually, the man showed, just as Burge predicted. After a high-speed chase, Rudacille arrested the American soldier and his Vietnamese accomplice in a major bust that was later credited to Burge's investigative prowess. The second case called for Burge and Rudacille to go undercover as wounded, unkempt, and "malcontent" infantrymen. Donning raggedy uniforms and driving a worn-down jeep, they joined a unit on patrol linked to a large-scale heroin ring. Although they failed to build a lead in the case, the experience helped convince Rudacille of Burge's exceptional acumen as a detective.[172] Over forty years later, following decades of experience in law enforcement, he still described Burge as "one of the finest and smartest investigators" he ever met. He remembered Burge as a "stickler for doing things the right way," the kind of detective who insisted on doing things "by the book."[173] The only fault Rudacille found in his sometime partner—other than a proclivity for chain-smoking Pall Mall cigarettes and drinking too much whiskey—was Burge's tendency to brag. As Rudacille remembered it, while Burge was a loudmouth who volunteered for the toughest assignments and boasted of his own achievements, he always "backed it up." Rudacille concluded, "The guy could produce."[174]

The aspect of Burge's Vietnam service that has received the most attention, however, concerns whether he observed or participated in the abuse of detainees.[175] The connection is obvious and reinforced by a wealth of evidence attributing atrocities to American service personnel and others throughout decades of conflict in Southeast Asia from the 1950s through the 1970s.[176] Historian Alfred McCoy traced the evolution of American interrogation techniques, including methods long categorized as torture by the United Nations, classifying a form of American torture that thrived throughout the period of engagement with enemy forces in Vietnam.[177] Developed by the Central Intelligence Agency (CIA) and government-funded psychologists in the 1950s, American torture involved the distinctive sensory deprivation and forced stress positions familiar to observers of American intelligence gathering from the Cold War through the War on Terror.[178] Typically, such methods were employed by members of an elite Military Intelligence (MI) corps or, more frequently, farmed out to foreign allies, such as the Army of the Republic of Vietnam (ARVN).[179] These intelligence and counterinsurgency methods reached a peak of excess and brutality in Operation Phoenix, the CIA-sponsored program of "systematic torture and extrajudicial executions" responsible for upward of forty thousand Vietnamese deaths.[180]

Outside the blurred lines demarcating interrogation methods sanctioned by the CIA and the U.S. Army, more gruesome techniques proliferated in Vietnam as well. While physicians and psychologists have since labeled so-called psychological interrogation techniques every bit as traumatic as physical beatings, the U.S. government overtly banned certain types of abuse while approving those that would not leave visible marks.[181] Nevertheless, political scientists documented physical torture perpetrated by democratic countries on several continents, finding that electric-shock torture "tended to spread informally and from the bottom up."[182] The first systematic use of electric shock, particularly the rigged military field telephone, appeared in Vietnam during a French crackdown on Indochina in 1931.[183] The French carried the technology to Algeria in the 1950s, and South Vietnamese officials and American advisers continued the practice after France's 1954 departure from Indochina.[184] Testimony from a 1967 citizens' tribunal organized by philosopher Bertrand Russell to look into American atrocities in Vietnam included several accounts of field-telephone torture. A military intelligence officer recalled watching his lieutenant attach the device to a suspected guerilla. "The telephones were first placed on his hands," he recalled, "and then the field telephone wires were placed on his sexual organs."[185] Sometime later, a prisoner died from heart failure following an electric-shock session.[186] Outside formal testimony, stories of the hand-cranked shocking device—sometimes referred to as the "Bell Telephone Hour," after a 1960s television show—circulated in stock tales pouring out of America's wartime experience.[187]

The nature of prisoner abuse at Dong Tam in 1968 and 1969 remains hard to extricate from rumor, myth, and speculation. While perpetrators rarely came forward, several Ninth MP veterans recalled witnessing or hearing about prisoner abuse and electric-shock torture. When journalist John Conroy described the hand-cranked shock box used by detectives in Chicago to a retired soldier who had been stationed at Dong Tam decades earlier, the man replied, "What you are talking about here, overseas in Vietnam, a lot of that went on." A second veteran told Conroy that the field-telephone technique was "not uncommon" among MI and ARVN interrogators, who would "put one [wire] around a finger and the other around the scrotum and start cranking."[188] Another Ninth MP dismissed the notion that military police deferred to MI and ARVN in all interrogations at Dong Tam and surrounding firebases, calling "bullshit" on those who denied that Ninth MPs interrogated POWs. Admitting that they often took part in interrogations, he nevertheless denied performing electric shock and simulated drowning, adding, "We were taught well on interrogation, but some of us had some class and some morals."[189] Other veterans rejected the purpose of delving into prisoner abuse altogether, preferring to bury such horrors in the past.[190]

While Jon Burge repeatedly undermined his credibility in the decades since leaving military service, his denials of having ever guarded or interrogated detainees in Vietnam hold a ring of truth. Considering the positions he held at Dong Tam, it is plausible that Burge never transported prisoners or gathered intelligence from enemy combatants. As a member of the PMI unit, Burge would have spent most of his time investigating the crimes of fellow Americans. Yet Burge's insistent claims of ignorance as to the location of the interrogation centers at Dong Tam and his refusal to concede even whispers of prisoner abuse are suspect. Both captured prisoners and unsubstantiated rumors were commonplace at any forward military base in Vietnam and would have been hard for even the most hardheaded grunt to overlook, let alone an accomplished investigator.[191] As for brutality, the capable Ninth Infantry garnered a reputation for aggression and pugnacity, important qualities for a military division engaged in guerilla war. The Ninth Division's commanding officer, Major General Julian J. Ewell, even awarded prizes to units with the highest body count.[192] The "Old Reliables"—as the division was known since World War II—were tough men, and proud of it.[193] As one veteran put it, "You didn't go in the Army to twiddle your thumbs."[194] While the highly professional Ninth MP Company did not offer formal lessons on torture, war in Southeast Asia produced atrocity wherever American GIs faced danger. Abusive interrogation methods would have been easy to pick up simply by paying attention to surroundings.

On to the Next War

Obliged to spend a full year in Vietnam, thousands of men at Dong Tam awoke one morning in summer 1969 to news of their early return home. The Ninth Infantry had been chosen as one of the first divisions to be folded up and shipped back to the States, an open fulfillment of President Richard Nixon's campaign promise to withdraw troops and hand the war back to the Vietnamese.[195] Jon Burge and the rest of the Ninth MPs left their posts for good in late August, releasing their temporary city back to the wild. By fall, South Vietnamese troops occupied a small corner of Dong Tam, and wild grass several feet tall reclaimed the rest.[196] Following an honorable discharge, Burge hung up his olive-drab uniform and prepared to don the blue dress of the CPD. While awaiting paperwork, Burge took a job at a gas station and toiled as a mechanic. Full of confidence that belied his youth, the twenty-two-year-old Military Police veteran, decorated several times over by the U.S. Army and the government of South Vietnam, easily aced the police entry exam and impressed the local bureaucrat in charge of background checks.[197] An ideal candidate, Burge was sworn in as patrolman on March 2, 1970. He spent the following six months in the Training Division before climbing behind the wheel of a Grand Crossing District patrol car.[198] Barely a year removed from his contribution to the war in Southeast Asia, Burge became a foot soldier in another conflict, this one waged across Chicago's South Side.

With violent crime on the rise, CPD administrators employed war metaphors to describe everyday police work throughout the 1970s.[199] In the five years since Jon Burge graduated high school, the annual number of total murders in Chicago had more than doubled, from 395 in 1965 to 828 in

1970.[200] Echoing national trends, local rates of so-called index crimes—murder, forcible rape, robbery, aggravated assault, burglary, larceny, and auto theft—experienced annual increases across the board.[201] Alongside rising street crime, in the three years that Burge was off fighting the Cold War racial and political tensions boiled over in his hometown. In the days following the assassination of Martin Luther King Jr. in April 1968, thousands of African Americans participated in an urban rebellion that laid waste to several city blocks west of downtown and spread to the Southeast Side as well.[202] Afterward, Mayor Richard J. Daley commanded officers to "shoot to maim" looters and "shoot to kill" arsonists in the event of future disorder.[203] Later that summer, policemen attacked protesters at Chicago's ill-fated Democratic National Convention.[204] While critics assailed the department for its public brutality, city officials praised officers for protecting the city from outside agitators.[205] Underscoring themes of warfare, snipers gunned down two veteran CPD officers from atop a Cabrini-Green public housing high-rise in July 1970.[206] Military veterans like Jon Burge joined the force at the dawn of what promised to be a violent decade.[207]

Following ten years of reform and modernization, the Chicago Police Department seemed prepared for the challenge. As recently as 1960, the CPD sat mired in a funk of political corruption, operational inefficiency, and decaying infrastructure.[208] By the end of the decade, however, Chicago boasted one of the most polished and technologically advanced police departments in the nation.[209] The metamorphosis began in the winter of 1960, when investigators busted a ring of crooked cops who were helping a burglar fence goods in the North Side's Summerdale District. Anticipating the next election, Mayor Daley turned scandal into opportunity, heading off political opponents by casting himself as an agent of reform.[210] After dumping police commissioner Timothy O'Connor as Chicago's top cop, Daley organized a blue-ribbon panel to find a replacement. The distinguished panel ultimately decided that the best choice sat at the head of their own table—Orlando W. Wilson, then serving as dean of criminology at the University of California.[211] Decades earlier, Wilson apprenticed under August Vollmer, a Progressive Era icon who helped invent the field of criminology.[212] Following service as one of Vollmer's famous "college cops," Wilson later headed police departments in a pair of medium-sized cities, helped reorganize the German police system after 1945, and established himself as an international expert on police administration.[213] Because state law dictated that Chicago police commissioners reside within city limits, the City Council created a new position—police superintendent—and offered the job to

Wilson, pending his relocation. Assured of a modicum of political independence from Mayor Daley, Wilson accepted the job in March 1960 and immediately set out to bring the CPD into the twentieth century.[214]

In light of Chicago's history of police scandal, many observers predicted that Wilson's ambitious reform agenda would fail.[215] After all, Wilson sought not only to lift performance but also to transform the very culture of a department rife in corruption. Touting police work as an honored profession, Wilson reorganized the chain of command, restructured various bureaus and operational divisions, removed uncooperative personnel, shuffled allies to new positions of authority, freed up a promotional logjam, and encouraged the hiring of African American and other nonwhite patrolmen.[216] A hardware enthusiast, Wilson delivered a fantastic array of machines and gadgets to a department that lacked a modern communications network and often forced officers to use private automobiles for investigative work. Bowing to Wilson's demands, City Council approved requisite budget increases. Taxpayers saw a quick return on their investment with the rollout of hundreds of gleaming squad cars, vans, motorcycles, and marine craft. Sporting a new white-and-blue paint scheme and rotating blue lights, the ubiquitous vehicles thrust a new aesthetic into the public consciousness. Reopening in 1963 to the tune of almost $4 million, a remodeled, state-of-the-art police headquarters housed a massive communications center where dispatchers were connected to patrolmen via two-way radio. Wilson updated buildings, furniture, and equipment; launched new tactical units; modernized training courses; expanded employee benefits; reprioritized the twenty-five-year-old crime laboratory; improved polygraph facilities; embraced scientific methods of crime detection; and hired new evidence technicians. In a few years, Wilson and his staff had refurbished much of the CPD, effectively rebranding the image of a beleaguered institution.[217]

The greatest challenge involved addressing the department's timeless reputation for physical aggression and brutality.[218] Decades earlier, when public officials launched studies of law enforcement during a 1920s crime wave, a state committee in Illinois braced for the task of surveying the Chicago Police Department, which had "for years been a storm center around which has raged conflict after conflict."[219] In 1931, President Herbert Hoover's National Commission on Law Observance and Enforcement—known popularly as the Wickersham Commission—shocked the nation with sensationalized tales of the so-called third degree, defined as "the employment of methods which inflict suffering, physical or mental, upon a person in order to obtain information about a crime."[220] Investigators working under August Vollmer found that police and prosecutors in Chicago routinely viewed interrogations as opportunities to "work" or "sweat" criminal suspects, laying into them with rubber hoses, fists, and the heavy Chicago phone book.[221] Reflecting the racial distribution of police service and abuse, Chicago's black communities remained disproportionately vulnerable to the third degree and other forms of police violence, including the use of fatal force.[222] Documenting a list of recent torture cases—including a schoolteacher beaten into falsely confessing to the Leopold and Loeb murder—the Wickersham Report concluded, "The third degree is thoroughly at home in Chicago."[223] As crime panic spread in the 1920s, so did tolerance of police misconduct.[224]

Indeed, in the midst of a popular war on crime, administrators and white residents alike seemed willing to allow a certain level of police brutality and lawlessness.[225] At the height of Prohibition, one researcher noted, "No single topic of public interest is receiving greater attention at this time than the question of crime."[226] While observers debated endless reports, many white Chicagoans viewed the beat officer, however corrupt, as the sole guardian of public safety. Lamenting citizen indifference, the Wickersham Commission concluded: "The Chicago public at the present time is much more concerned with the reduction of crime than with official lawlessness. Much crime in Chicago is committed by brutal ruffians; the public are less inclined to blame the police for beating up such men than for letting them get away scot-free."[227] Accordingly, police beatings remained commonplace. An expert witness even exclaimed, "It was an exception when a suspect was *not* subjected to personal violence."[228] Public permissiveness, however, had limits. In 1925, a "sometime police officer" and member of the Institute for Juvenile Research published a description of an electric-shock chair employed outside Chicago. According to the author: "[This] method used far surpasses in refined cruelty any case [he had heard of] and is even on a level with the ancient methods of torture. Especially is this so because of the fear entertained by nearly everyone of anything relevant to a shock." Documenting dozens of brutal examples of the third degree, the author expressed similar disgust toward only one other case, that of a sheriff who would "place a pistol against the chest of the suspect and, cocking it, tell him to [confess]."[229] Inured to the usual violence of custodial interrogation, many urban residents of the turbulent 1920s only raised alarm at extreme methods, including electric shock and mock execution.

In the 1930s, however, a series of developments helped erode public tolerance of the third degree, including the release of the Wickersham Report, appellate court decisions restricting the use of coerced confessions,[230] the repeal of Prohibition, and a general decline in violent crime rates. As violent crime rates dropped, other concerns—economic depression, the global rise of fascism—rose to the fore of national consciousness. Less worried about criminals, Americans became more critical of the third degree. Responding to demands from a nascent American Civil Liberties Union (ACLU) and other progressives, police supervisors scaled back the war footing and officially outlawed the third degree.[231] Some administrators even dismissed the method as counterproductive, finding that state lawlessness exacerbated lawlessness in the community.[232] For example, victims of abuse occasionally retaliated by kidnapping, beating, and even killing police officers.[233] By the 1940s, reformers declared the third degree largely defunct.[234] In the decades that followed, however, journalists and researchers found police administrators tight-lipped about interrogation methods, creating a public silence on the third degree easily confused with its extinction. By the late 1960s, a researcher investigating police practices focused exclusively on street-level misconduct, in part "because brutality in the precinct has become even more inaccessible to investigation."[235] While lack of empirical evidence made it difficult to determine the frequency of the third degree after 1940, the prevalence of custodial abuse at Area 2 in the 1970s suggests that violence in the interrogation room never fully disappeared.

By design, evidence of the third degree remained hidden behind closed doors. Indeed, rather than abandon the method completely, detectives learned to employ the third degree cautiously, sparingly, and only against citizens of low standing.[236] When news of physical abuse leaked to the public, it usually stemmed from an extraordinary situation, such as the murder of a police officer or other high-profile case. In 1959, however, the Illinois Division of the ACLU documented the "widespread" practice of "secret detention," whereby officers held suspects incommunicado for long stretches, sometimes days at a time, while denying them access to legal counsel, food, sleep, or basic comfort. According to the ACLU, the CPD's reliance on criminal confessions not only hampered detectives' ability to collect forensic evidence but also produced "three related evils"—police brutality, wrongful conviction, and the "deterioration of police efficiency."[237] While a few sensational cases made headlines and a small number of victims procured civil damages in court, the ongoing use of the third degree largely flew under the public radar.[238] Eclipsed by the Summerdale scandal and other corruption cases, coerced confessions remained low on O. W. Wilson's agenda during his seven years as police superintendent.

When Wilson retired in 1967, the accolades of his many admirers obscured the extent to which he failed to realize his two loftiest goals—bringing political independence and public accountability to the CPD. In both regards, he had made limited strides. When Wilson took over in 1960, the city was carved into nearly forty police districts, each corresponding loosely to the ward map of City Council.[239] For over a century, ward bosses selected district captains and other officers on the basis of political loyalty rather than professional qualifications. To lessen the influence of political patronage, Wilson cut the number of districts to twenty-one and drew a new district map detaching the department from voting precincts. Hoping to distance himself from the mayor, Wilson relocated the superintendent's office from City Hall to police headquarters. To improve accountability, he created the Internal Investigations Division to field citizen complaints.[240] While professional reforms signaled an important cultural shift, substantive change proved elusive. An honorable man by most measures, Wilson exhibited rhetorical commitment to stamping out corruption, misconduct, and brutality, as did some of the "lesser men" who succeeded him.[241] Yet meaningful and lasting improvement of the CPD required a fundamental restructuring of the premises of police power, not a doubling down on aggressive patrol. With a series of ongoing urban crises coming to a head, the CPD's bad relationship with poor and working-class people, particularly residents of color, only deteriorated in the 1960s and 1970s. Indeed, according to historian Simon Balto, "Wilson's innovations systematically turned previously informal police repression of the black community into *formal* police department policy."[242] Trouble brewed immediately following Wilson's departure, evidenced by the urban rebellion of April 1968, the police riot at the Democratic National Convention later that summer, and the police assassination of Black Panther Fred Hampton in December 1969. Jon Burge began coercing confessions soon thereafter. New mechanisms of accountability hardly operated as advertised.

The professionalization movement and its reform paradigm not only failed to prevent police torture in Chicago; it also helped perpetrators secure impunity. Above all, Superintendent Wilson was a public relations master who obsessed over the CPD's image. His greatest achievement lay in convincing a skeptical public that local police could rise above traditions of ignorance and thuggery. According to Chicago's Afro-American Patrolmen's League, however, Wilson's efforts proved little more than a "Madison Avenue type" ploy.[243] Indeed, a biographer criticized Wilson for his focus on "impressing citizens and the media with his reform efforts" at the expense of "true reform."[244] Nevertheless, when crime rates soared in the late 1960s and politicians declared a national war on crime, professionalization served to disguise the continuity of police violence and misconduct. B 1970s and 1980s, Wilson and his imitators had helped generate a con ing image of the police officer—especially the plainclothes detective—as a trained professional and skilled expert. With regard to coerced confessions, the professionalization mythos only reinforced the fiction that the Progressives had killed the third degree. In Chicago, abusive detectives who lied about police torture under oath found their credibility only bolstered by the founding fathers of police administration.

Beginning in May 1972, Jon Burge spent much of the 1970s commuting from homes on the West and Southwest Sides to Area 2 headquarters in Chicago's smallest community area of Burnside. During these years, Burnside stood in the path of the expanding Black Belt, converting from nearly all white in 1970 to almost entirely black by 1980.[245] By the end of the decade, when Burge and other detectives drove to work each day, they entered a neighborhood where nine of every ten residents were African American, seven of every ten were under the age of twenty-one, and nearly two in ten adults were unemployed.[246] Much as the U.S. military base at Dong Tam operated from the heart of enemy territory in the late 1960s, Burnside Area headquarters lay in the center of a region with one of America's highest crime rates. Around the clock, uniformed officers patrolled their beats, detectives pursued leads, and tactical units infiltrated criminal networks. To police administrators downtown, much of the South Side had become a war zone. Yet Burnside, South Chicago, Grand Crossing, Jeffery Manor, South Deering, and the rest of the community areas within Area 2 were also neighborhoods—residential communities with thousands of homes, hundreds of businesses, and dozens of parks and schools. If rising crime and political pressure influenced police brass to view the area as a tactical problem, the half million people who resided in its neighborhoods continued to see the Southeast Side as home.

For white people who left these neighborhoods in the 1960s and 1970s, returning years later could inspire nostalgia.[247] For men like Jon Burge, whose job brought him back on a regular basis, touring familiar locations in a new context could also be painful. While driving through the Southeast Side on any given day in the 1970s, Burge would have been reminded of several lost causes. Reflecting a reversal of economic fortune, plant closings transformed the physical landscape and cost workers their livelihood. Reflecting whites' failure to defend their neighborhoods, Merrionette Manor, Luella Elementary, and Bowen High School experienced rapid resegregation, going from all white to all black in a familiar, if jolting, process. Reflecting the difficulty of preventing or containing criminal behavior, crime rates soared. Even the war in Vietnam, for which many local men sacrificed, came to a disheartening end as well. With several postwar bubbles bursting, policy makers recruited local police departments to another effort that seemed likely to fail—the national war on crime. Waged primarily against African Americans, Latinos, and other poor residents of the inner city, local crime wars failed to turn the tide of the urban crisis. Facing a challenging mandate, white detectives at Area 2 turned to torture, in part, to secure an advantage against a brazen criminal element. Entangled in practical motivation, however, Burge and his men also abused black criminal suspects to assert an elusive, brutal, and racialized power over their own lives and the lives of others.

2

"They Wanted to Be Choirboys"

During the 1970s, the nation's attention focused as never before on the role of the police officer. With political protests, urban rebellion, and street crime dominating recent memory, politicians, journalists, and academics created an unprecedented volume of material probing every facet of police behavior.[1] In the entertainment world, crime fiction also experienced a renaissance. In 1970, a detective from Los Angeles named Joseph Wambaugh published the first of a series of pioneering novels challenging the tired tropes of the "police procedural."[2] Later celebrated as the "father of the modern-day cop novel,"[3] Wambaugh moved beyond showing "how the cop acts on the job" to explore "how the *job* acts on the *cop*."[4] Insisting that "police are only human," the novelist claimed to reveal "what *really* goes on in our police agencies,"[5] where exposure to the city's worst element turned good officers into disillusioned automatons, thuggish brutes, and cynical alcoholics. In the prologue to his 1975 best seller *The Choirboys*, Wambaugh, a former marine, compared the police experience to the panic and hopelessness of frontline soldiers in Vietnam. Later made into a movie starring James Woods and Louis Gossett Jr., *The Choirboys* explores a diverse squad of patrolmen who meet after hours for what they euphemistically call "choir practice," all-night binge-drinking sessions during which participants collectively drown their pain. Meant to provide comfort from their workaday lives, the last choir practice ends in tragedy—the accidental shooting of a homosexual teenager who happens upon the drunken officers in MacArthur Park.[6]

Despite Wambaugh's efforts to authenticate police culture, however, his novels further romanticized the troubled cop. Indeed, many Americans saw fictional choirboys when looking at real police. In a review of Wambaugh's first nonfiction book, *The Onion Field*, a Chicago journalist likened local officers to the author's literary characters, writing, "There are 13,000 of them in Chicago, some vicious punks, some heroes, some drunks, some compassionate, soul-searching dreamers, some conniving thieves, some intellectuals, some ignoramuses."[7] Members of the Chicago Police Department (CPD) also noted the author's ability to connote their lived experience. One officer remarked in 1976, "Rumor has it Sgt. Jon Burge . . . has been seen with Joe Wambaugh regarding a book on his exploits."[8] While Burge's colleagues joked that the young detective would make an excellent muse for a budding novelist, others worried lest fiction influence reality. When a journalist in the early 1980s wondered why police officers resorted to excessive force, CPD Superintendent Richard Brzeczek reflected: "Where does a policeman's role model come from? After *The Choirboys*, that became the image to some police officers. They wanted to be Choirboys."[9] Meant to explain a penchant for brutality, likening officers to choirboys also served to excuse or justify misbehavior.

Adopting the perspective of the police, this chapter channels Joseph Wambaugh to sketch the challenging and often horrific environment within which Area 2 detectives toiled during the violent 1970s. The pressure of police culture—combined with ambition and a racist disregard for the rights of black criminal suspects—helped inform detectives' decision to coerce confessions at Area 2. If most torture survivors from the first decade of Burge's career were suspects who detectives genuinely believed were guilty, the consolidation of torture methods in the 1970s facilitated the later abuse of suspects whose guilt was less certain or even unlikely.

The Detective Division

When Jon Burge accepted promotion to detective in May 1972, he moved along a common career track, albeit at an unusually rapid pace.[10] As in most police departments in the United States, higher-ranking officers almost always began as entry-level patrolmen before clambering upward. The CPD's rank and file qualified for promotion through seniority and performance on biannual evaluations and civil service examinations.[11] Top positions, including commander, deputy chief, chief, and deputy superintendent, were called "exempt ranks" and were held at the behest of the superintendent.[12] Supervisory personnel were thus vulnerable to turnover at police headquarters or City Hall.[13] Twenty-four years old in 1972, Detective Burge could advance his career by apprehending suspects, closing cases, and impressing superiors.[14] Early in his career, performance mattered at least as much as personal relationships or institutional politics. Considering his experience as a criminal investigator in Vietnam, Burge must have expected steady advancement through the ranks. Indeed, the department even awarded military veterans extra points on promotional exams.[15]

After stepping from a squad car for the last time, Burge reported to the Area 2 Robbery Unit, a group of over thirty investigators headquartered in an old station house at the corner of Ninety-First Street and Cottage Grove Avenue in the Far South Side community of Burnside.[16] Since reorganization of the CPD in the early 1960s, detectives were assigned to one of five sections based on criminal category—homicide, sex, and aggravated assault; robbery; burglary; auto theft; and general assignment.[17] Before 1960, most detectives had worked from bureau headquarters and drew cases citywide through a system that was both outdated and inefficient.[18] By the 1970s, however, the Detective Division consisted of six geographic areas, each with authority over cases occurring inside separate districts within its boundaries.[19] Covering much of the city's Far South Side and all of the industrial Southeast Side, Area 2 first included Districts 3 (Grand Crossing), 4 (South Chicago), 5 (Kensington), and 6 (Gresham).[20] While the districts administered patrol operations from their own station houses, detectives worked from a central area headquarters. Once nicknamed the Burnside Area, Area 2 became known as the Pullman Area in 1983, when its headquarters relocated nearby.[21] At each of the city's six area headquarters, detectives assigned to the five division sections worked cases falling under their allotted purview. During his stint with Area 2 Robbery from May 1972 to summer 1974 and again from mid-1977 until July 1980, Burge primarily investigated property crimes, although these offenses often involved violence. In addition, Burge also received special assignments that expanded his responsibilities for temporary periods.

Among the 13,000 men—and growing numbers of women—who proudly called themselves members of the Chicago Police Department in 1972, the roughly 1,300 detectives were a special class.[22] Still exclusively male, criminal investigators enjoyed prestige far surpassing their modest position a few rungs up the ladder of the department's much-maligned pay scale.[23] Their elite status—nurtured as much from within their own ranks as anywhere else—derived in part from a rare set of skills and personality traits, including a stubborn resilience and refined street smarts.[24] Outsiders admired detectives' tenacious confidence in the face of a nagging lack of job security. More than any other position on the force, investigators remained vulnerable to reassignment if they proved unable to meet the division's easily measured standards of assessment.[25] According to Superintendent O. W. Wilson, “In no branch of police service may the accomplishment of the unit and its individual members be so accurately evaluated as in the detective division.”[26] Those who proved unable to close cases found themselves out of a job or back in a squad car with the rest of the “uniform ranks.”[27] To the bosses—or “white shirts”—down on State Street,[28] detectives were only as good as the current year’s clearance rate. Even under optimal conditions—when budgets were high, staffing adequate, and caseloads manageable—pressure to perform dominated detectives’ daily lives.

In the 1970s, however, police stress rose even higher, as the number of officers failed to keep pace with soaring levels of reported crime.[29] Between 1965 and 1974, for example, the annual number of recorded homicides in Chicago more than doubled, growing 145 percent from 395 murders to 970.[30] Over the same period, the number of officers employed by the CPD grew from 10,269 to only 13,266, an increase of less than 30 percent.[31] The number of detectives inched up as well but remained consistently around 10 percent of the force.[32] Reflecting the burden of growing caseloads, homicide clearance rates dropped citywide from 91 percent in 1965 to 71 percent in 1974. Clearance rates would hover around the 70th percentile through the 1970s and 1980s, plummet in the 1990s, dip below 50 percent in the 2000s, and reach a record low of 17 percent in 2017.[33] In 1963, Superintendent Wilson anticipated that improved record keeping and growing faith in the police would trigger a slight statistical bump. Waiting for a plateau that never came, Wilson told his staff, “From now on, our figures should reflect the decrease in crimes” that he felt “certain is taking place.”[34] Instead, the nation’s second-largest police department encountered year after year of rising crime statistics, a trend mirrored in other cities. Despite an occasional drop, by the 1980s urban residents came to expect levels of reported crime that would have seemed improbable twenty years earlier.[35] Meanwhile, greater attention to crime statistics blurred distinctions between rates of reported crime and rates of actual crime, leaving observers confused as to whether an increase in the former reflected an increase in the latter.

Regardless of the reliability of the numbers, however, when Burge made detective in 1972, local law enforcement confronted a statistical crime wave that was both a quantitative burden for the police and a perceived emergency for residents. According to the FBI’s Uniform Crime Reports, known index crimes in Chicago stood at 103,343 in 1965, a slight decrease from previous years. Over the following decade, however, the numbers exploded. In 1974, Chicago reported 243,236 major offenses. Even as population dipped, reported robberies rose from 14,888 in 1965 to 26,172 in 1974; reported burglaries ballooned from 30,020 to 50,722; reported rapes increased by 60 percent; and reported aggravated assault and auto theft experienced clear increases as well.[36] For a generation or more, annual numbers of reported crime in Chicago—and in virtually every other major city in the United States—hovered around significantly higher averages than those of mid-century. By the turn of the millennium, recorded crime rates began returning to levels last seen in the early 1960s, although African American neighborhoods continued to suffer violence at disproportionate rates.[37]

Crime statistics, of course, are notoriously unreliable. Rather than reflect true increases in criminal activity, rising numbers of reported crime could mean that citizens were simply more willing or able to complain to authorities.[38] Indeed, police professionalization—an ongoing process in Chicago throughout the 1960s—often caused reported crime rates to rise, as administrators improved methods of recording, tracking, and publicizing illicit behavior.[39] Yet the actual rate of crime was likely much higher than reported, as a significant portion of crime always occurred beyond the purview of the justice system. For example, when skeptical journalists at the *Chicago Reporter* sought to counter the bias of the Uniform Crime Reports in 1977, victimization surveys suggested that "reported crime figures may *understate* the actual level of crime in Chicago, particularly in black neighborhoods."[40] Moreover, even if the observed increase did not correspond with a true expansion of crime, the larger number of offenses known to police would have nevertheless caused a real increase in the workload of individual officers.[41] For detectives, it was an academic question whether or not crime actually increased. They had more cases to solve either way. Among ordinary residents, the perception of rising crime also fueled panic regardless of its factual basis.[42] While Area 2 neighborhoods had never been crime-free, the higher visibility of street crime—particularly violent offenses that white residents historically associated with myths of black criminality—exacerbated timeless fears and raised pressure on the police department.

Perception aside, there was one criminal category—homicide—whose increase suggests the observed escalation in violent crime in the late twentieth century reflected a real expansion of violent behavior. Most serious offenses only appear in crime statistics if reported to the police. Yet many robberies, burglaries, assaults, and rapes go unreported, as do countless lesser crimes. Murders, however, are almost always reported. Accordingly, homicide rates are among the most reliable criminal statistics.[43] While police administrators can manipulate numbers, a reported doubling of annual murders—unless accompanied by growing population or declining medical care—signals a severe rise in violent crime. When the annual number of murders in Chicago doubled during a period of declining population and advancing medicine, observers lamented the arrival of a particularly violent moment in the city's history.[44] Indeed, as historian Simon Balto concludes, "criminal incidences undeniably proliferated" after 1965, when "crime *did* increase—terribly."[45] Another Chicago police historian, Peter Pihos, concurs: "It is certain that crime was increasing in these years," even if the "scale of that increase is unknowable."[46]

Within the confines of Area 2, moreover, the reported number of annual murders experienced disproportionate growth, nearly quadrupling from 59 in 1965 to 232 in 1974. Homicide detectives accustomed to opening a new investigation every sixteen days on average confronted a fresh murder on more than a weekly basis. Yet murders defied regularity, appearing at random, in groups, or following seasonal patterns in the weather. The average number of murders in Area 2 fluctuated around 152 per year throughout the 1970s, reflecting a crime rate that had become the new normal by 1980. Slight changes to geographic jurisdiction in this period did not have a meaningful impact on Area 2's share of reported crime. Heightened violence characterized the region into the 1990s, when the murder rate crept still higher.[47]

Although raw numbers provide some sense of the alarm gripping Area 2 communities during this period, they fail to capture the lived experience of local residents, criminal offenders, and crime victims. The police, too, suffered emotional strain as a result of the pain they witnessed and sometimes caused. Recalling work conditions in the Violent Crimes Unit of the early 1980s, former detective Michael McDermott recalled: "You don't believe what went on in Area 2. I mean, hundreds of murders a year. You are getting cases of rapes and robberies every day. Thousands of cases."[48] If patrolmen and plainclothes officers occasionally enjoyed the satisfaction of stopping a crime in progress or preventing one altogether, detectives almost always arrived too late. Maneuvering from one crime scene to the next—some more gruesome than others—detectives were rewarded only upon the arrest of a suspect, the closing of a case, or the conviction of yet another defendant in the city's never-ending war on crime.

In the meantime, the regular drama and intermittent horrors of Area 2 arrived in a relentless wave throughout the violent 1970s. Indeed, crime-beat reporters for the city's major newspapers regularly relied on police sources at Area 2, including Jon Burge, to gather sensational details for the front pages. A small sampling, while arbitrary, demonstrates the ubiquitous but random quality of detectives' experience with violence. Area 2 investigators responded to calls of domestic squabbles, lovers' quarrels, and hostage crises; mass homicides, serial killings, and gangland style executions; drive-by shootings, police shoot-outs, and car chases; robberies gone wrong, dice games turned ugly, and friendly arguments turned homicidal. A list of perpetrators and victims included prostitutes, drug addicts, and burglars; gang members, pimps, and the homeless; college students, military veterans, and middle-class professionals. In addition to crime, detectives also responded to accidents, overdoses, and suicides.[49] Wherever a dead body appeared, investigators followed. Mostly, however, they worked cases of routine violence—the everyday robberies, assaults, and homicides that came to define patterns of living, at least in the minds of Area 2 detectives, within their jurisdiction.[50]

If high crime rates showcased the city's capacity for human destruction, they also provided an opportunity for detectives to advance their careers. One component of police professionalization involved greater awarding and advertising of departmental commendations.[51] In press releases and a monthly newsletter, the CPD highlighted officers' frequent cunning, courage, and efficiency. Whenever an Area 2 detective closed a tough case or performed some act of skill or bravery, they could receive an official award or see their name in print. For example, in December 1971 the *Chicago Police Star* commended Area 2 Robbery detective John Yucaitis and his partners for rescuing a woman and child from an armed robber.[52] In September, 1975 the department commended Jon Burge, Michael Hoke, and others for apprehending several home invaders and armed robbers.[53] Official honors impressed supervisors and occasionally drew the attention of the superintendent. Indeed, commendations helped officers qualify for promotion, win appointment to exempt-rank positions, or otherwise enhance their power, salary, and pension. Jon Burge claimed to have received "nine or ten Department Commendations" and "approximately three Honorable Mentions" in twenty-one years of service, adding to an impressive résumé that helped propel him up the ranks.[54] Awards also bolstered Burge's credibility in front of judges and jurors during the countless criminal and civil trials in which he testified. In Chicago, ambitious detectives seized the opportunity presented by the incessant violence of the 1970s to fortify their reputations one cleared case at a time.

To close a case, however, investigators needed to convince someone from the State's Attorney's Office to approve charges. While circumstantial evidence often met the burden of proof, police manuals and training officers reminded detectives that procuring incriminatory statements remained the surest way to complete an investigation.[55] Indeed, prosecutors put great stock in confessions, as jurors found it hard to believe that anyone would admit to a crime they did not commit.[56] Consequently, as a journalist with the American Civil Liberties Union (ACLU) wrote in 1972, "The pressure on arresting or investigating officers to secure confessions [was] immense."[57] Not only did peer institutions incentivize success in the interrogation room; getting a suspect to admit a crime was often far easier than documenting guilt through other means. "For the overworked police officer," the ACLU elaborated, "the confession represents a ready-made short cut to conviction, a way of avoiding long hours of questioning witnesses, tramping the streets, and pinning down detail—work for which many officers have neither patience nor training."[58] During a time of rising crime, when wrongful convictions had yet to prick the national conscience, both the pressure to perform and detectives' natural ambition contributed to an obsessive pursuit of criminal confessions.

While the Supreme Court's 1966 ruling in *Miranda v. Arizona* affirmed constitutional protections for criminal suspects, prosecutors continued to rely on confessions in the majority of convictions.[59] Designed to force police officers to alert criminal suspects of their rights before interrogation, *Miranda* ironically contributed to wrongful convictions in certain circumstances. First, publicity surrounding the Court's decision convinced many Americans that the police were sworn to new standards of integrity. Especially as law enforcement agents condemned the decision for coddling criminals,[60] *Miranda* helped erode public skepticism about—and responsibility for—criminal confessions.[61] After *Miranda,* judges and jurors became more likely to side with detectives when defendants accused officers of malfeasance in the interrogation room.[62] Second, the ritualized reading of a suspect's rights soon evolved into a false performance of protection.[63] The legal timbre of the recitation itself—"You have a right to remain silent. If you choose not to remain silent, anything you say or write can and will be used against you in a court of law"[64]—could trick suspects into thinking the mere reading of rights provided protection. Studies of citizen comprehension revealed that "many Miranda warnings fall far short of the Court's basic requirements for clarity."[65] Early research on the ruling's implementation suggested that detectives deliberately delivered the warnings in a manner designed to confuse suspects and mitigate disruption of interrogations.[66]

A third way *Miranda* contributed to wrongful convictions involved the widespread use of printed waiver forms, which detectives would read aloud and have suspects sign.[67] In court, prosecutors presented the signed waivers as proof that suspects knew and understood their rights but waived them before giving a statement.[68] While detectives could employ a variety of dishonest or illegal means to secure signatures, the official document contained a built-in legitimacy difficult to impeach. In addition, *Miranda* barred prosecutors only from using unwarned statements at trial. It did not offer protection from coercion after detectives read the warnings and suspects waived their rights. Many Chicago police torture survivors conceded that detectives read them their rights before the abuse began.[69] In the decades since *Miranda*, however, once detectives established respect for due process by presenting signed waivers in court, it became nearly impossible for defendants to convince others they were coerced. According to legal scholar Yale Kamisar, when the Court reaffirmed *Miranda* in the year 2000, Chief Justice William Rehnquist "recognized that an effective waiver of a suspect's rights often has the effect of minimizing the scrutiny courts give police interrogations following the waiver."[70] As Nicole Gonzalez Van Cleve argues, "the performance of procedural rights" and "bureaucratic tools"—such as *Miranda* waivers—"create a façade of fairness that protects the professionals rather than the defendants."[71] Beginning in 1972, Area 2 detectives demonstrated the shortcomings of the *Miranda* prophylactic.

The Royal Family and the Decision to Torture

Allegations of prisoner abuse appeared within months of Jon Burge's arrival at Area 2. The first known case involved the coerced statements of four black teenagers linked to the assault of a young white hemophiliac whose attack made front-page news. Late in the evening of July 26, 1972, eleven-year-old Joseph O'Shea was home alone watching television when several "black youths" stormed in, gave him a beating, opened gas burners on the stove, set a small fire, and stole property before fleeing. When O'Shea's mother arrived, she found her son in a pool of blood, his cheekbone cracked, his jaw shattered, the letters "JR" written on his forehead. Outside the very hospital where his father worked security, surgeons told reporters the boy's rare blood condition made it difficult to stop the bleeding. Distraught, Mrs. O'Shea claimed they were one of only two white families on the block, the rest of the South Side community of Brainerd having "changed to practically all black about three years ago." Within hours, police officials highlighted the inscription on the boy's brow and blamed the attack on the Junior Rangers street gang. Breaking into tears, Mrs. O'Shea wondered how anyone could do this to her little boy, adding, "I'll tell you this, we're going to move out of here as soon as we can."[72] In a show of support, black residents donated blood and offered help with medical bills.[73]

The attack immediately became what detectives referred to as a "heater" or a "special," the kind of case that attracted media attention and sent added pressure down the chain of command.[74] Indeed, with unknown villains and a sympathetic victim, the story outraged much of the city and sparked fears across racial lines. In a majority-black neighborhood wracked by a string of recent home invasions, the Brainerd Community Relations Council called for greater law enforcement and organized citizen patrols to protect residents "until we get more police in the area." Dispatching protestors to the Juvenile Court, African American funeral home director and Brainerd Action Committee treasurer Howard Brookins promised to make it "hard for a judge to keep turning these punks loose."[75] Demonstrating the risks of taking a stand, someone shot a bullet through the plate-glass window of Brookins's funeral parlor.[76] Fortunately, tensions cooled when the police announced arrests in the case. Yet the *Chicago Tribune* continued to ride the story, recounting a visit to the boy's hospital room by members of the White Sox and Black Hawks professional sports teams.[77] When O'Shea returned home, he received hundreds of get-well wishes, including a personal letter from Illinois senator Charles Percy.[78]

Area 2 detectives cleared the case within weeks, satisfying the public with a quick display of investigative prowess. An editorial in the black-owned *Southeast Independent Bulletin*, however, criticized the police for their reckless attempt to placate angry residents, arguing that only because the victim was white did officers see "a need to hurriedly arrest a suspect."[79] Just three days after the attack, Detective Burge canvassed local teenagers and arrested Charles Whittenberg, a twelve-year-old black boy then on probation for burning another child in the eye with a lit match.[80] Whittenberg's family provided an alibi and Burge's colleagues in the Robbery Unit—doubting a person so young could have committed violence of that "magnitude"—reopened the case. After police arrested and procured statements from four new suspects—all black males between the ages of seventeen and nineteen—the *Independent Bulletin* commended detectives for locating the real perpetrators.[81] If the editors had known how the officers obtained the confessions, they would have been less appreciative.

On August 5, 1972, several detectives, including Burge, apprehended seventeen-year-old Rodney Mastin and eighteen-year-old Phillip "Smokey" Moore and drove them to the Burnside station. As officers led them up the stairs and down a hallway, they passed an open interrogation room where Mastin saw a black youth handcuffed to a wall. The boy appeared unconscious, his face "distorted, swollen and bleeding." Mastin thought he must have survived a car accident. Coming to a large central room, detectives told Mastin and Moore they could not leave until admitting their role in the

O'Shea beating. According to Mastin, detectives then brought the handcuffed prisoner into the open, revealing seventeen-year-old Lindsey Smith, Mastin's friend and neighbor. When officers asked the noticeably injured Smith who broke into the O'Shea home, he replied, "Rodney and Smokey did it." The detectives placed Mastin and Moore in separate rooms and Burge questioned them while others looked on. As Mastin answered, Burge allegedly circled his chair, punching the young man in the head or knocking him to the floor when he gave a wrong response. Mastin later testified to being "kicked once in the groin, slapped, backhanded, punched in the chest and face, snatched from the floor and slammed back into the chair, and hit on the head with an ashtray." He only agreed to give a statement "so the beatings would stop." Moore told a similar story. A judge later denied a motion to suppress Mastin's statement, ruling that claims of coercion were not credible in light of detectives' staid denials.[82]

While scrutiny from the O'Shea case soon passed, the rise of "one of the most vicious gangs in the city's history" brought sustained pressure to the Burnside Robbery Unit shortly after Burge arrived.[83] In early 1972, a prisoner at Illinois's Stateville Correctional Center named Roger "Cochise" Collins helped organize the Royal Family, a group of over a dozen prisoners associated with the Black P Stone Nation and other Chicago street gangs.[84] Upon release, the Royal Family coordinated a remarkable crime spree, committing more than two hundred armed robberies and at least ten murders between 1972 and 1974 alone. Briefing reporters, the Area 2 Robbery commander cited "thousands and thousands of dollar losses in stickups of dope peddlers, supermarkets, saloons, stores and residences."[85] The gang drew attention from municipal police departments, county sheriffs, the Illinois State Police, and the Illinois Bureau of Investigation, as well as the Bureau of Alcohol, Tobacco, and Firearms and the Federal Bureau of Investigation.[86] Recruiting members "by bonding them out of jail and then expecting them to go on scores with them,"[87] what really distinguished the Royal Family was its willingness "to kill or otherwise intimidate witnesses."[88] Led by a "calculating executioner," the Royal Family guarded itself against conventional methods of prosecution.[89] As an assistant state's attorney explained, "We were afraid our witnesses would be murdered."[90] Anticipating greater demand for confessions, Area 2 detectives rose to the challenge.

The CPD turned its attention to the Royal Family following the June 16, 1972, robbery of the Tally-Ho restaurant in the northern suburb of Evanston, Illinois. Just as management began closing down around 10:00 p.m., three knife-wielding men entered, forced everyone into an office, raided the safe of approximately $300, and stabbed the owner and manager to death as three tied-up witnesses cowered. In a foolish display of bravado, the culprits made no attempt to mask their faces or fingerprints, despite the fact that two of them were former Tally-Ho employees.[91] Recently paroled from Stateville following a five-and-a-half-year stint for armed robbery, twenty-four-year-old Julius Davis worked at the restaurant for one week earlier that summer. While detectives hunted Davis, fellow members of the Royal Family got to him first. On Monday morning, the Chicago Fire Department discovered his body in the trunk of a burned-out car under the elevated tracks near the Dan Ryan Expressway, seven gunshot wounds indicating the displeasure of his former associates.[92]

Less than a week earlier, Davis had narrowly escaped capture following two other daring heists in Chicago's far North Side neighborhood of Rogers Park. On June 14, 1972, Davis joined Royal Family cofounder Roger "Cochise" Collins and four other gang members in the robbery of Morseview Drugs and an adjacent tavern, netting over $900 in cash before heading toward the city's South Side.[93] Spotting the getaway car, patrolmen gave chase along a rain-soaked Lake Shore Drive, barely avoiding a spectacular three-car crash as the suspects' vehicle hurdled the median and struck oncoming traffic. "When we came over the rise we saw this car that we were chasing and it was in flames," an officer recalled, "and [another] was just flattened." The patrolmen pulled Collins—"in a shocked and dazed condition"—from the wreckage and recovered "two handguns in a brown paper bag with some money that was already burned."[94] Crawling from the twisted metal, Julius Davis escaped into Lincoln Park.[95] When witnesses identified Davis from the Tally-Ho robbery a few days later, Collins arranged Davis's execution from his jail cell, sealing a leak in the Royal Family before the Evanston double murder brought them all down. Five months later, police found the bullet-ridden bodies of two Morseview Drugs employees stuffed in the trunk of another scorched automobile.[96] Lacking eyewitness testimony, prosecutors dropped all charges in the Rogers Park holdups.[97]

Frustrated by prosecutors' unwillingness to indict, detectives decided that coercing confessions might be an efficient way to convict defendants who neutralized witnesses. In a fateful move likely inspired by Burge's service in Vietnam, officers introduced electric shock in pursuit of Anthony Holmes in early 1973. According to a probation officer's report, Holmes was born in 1945, "nurtured in an urban type environment," suffered the death of both parents by age sixteen, dropped out of high school, and supported a wife and four children through government assistance. Officials derided the family's neighborhood in the Altgeld Gardens "Public House Project" as "gang infested" and saddled with a "high delinquency crime rate."[98]

Nicknamed "Little Devil" as a child, Holmes matured into a weight lifter's body, became known as "Satan," launched a street gang named Satan's Angels, and joined the Black Gangster Disciples.[99] By 1972, Holmes's record included multiple counts of armed robbery, auto theft, and unlawful use of a firearm.[100] In Stateville prison, Holmes met Roger Collins and helped form the Royal Family.[101] When detectives brought Holmes to Area 2 in 1973, they saw only Satan, a poor, black gang member from the projects. Describing the Royal Family's encounter with Burge, Holmes explained: "I think he seen us as slum scums. I don't think he really looked at us as a real human being. He just said I think this is someone I can use."[102] Indeed, Holmes would help the Area 2 Robbery unit return key members of the Royal Family to prison.

The chain of events that brought Anthony Holmes to an Area 2 interrogation room began in a bar on December 20, 1971. Responding to a perceived insult, Holmes's twenty-year-old brother-in-law Luther Coburn fatally shot a fifty-seven-year-old patron of a Far South Side tavern called the Bus Stop Lounge.[103] At a pretrial hearing months later, the owner and bartender Joseph Murphy testified against Coburn pursuant to a murder charge. In retaliation, several Royal Family members stormed into the Bus Stop Lounge and shot Murphy eleven times as he stood behind the bar.[104] Nevertheless, Murphy's tape-recorded statement helped convict Coburn.[105] On May 29, 1973, a year after Murphy's death, Area 2 detectives arrested Anthony Holmes and locked him in a Burnside interrogation room. Six hours later, they emerged with a statement implicating Holmes, Roger Collins, and three other members of the Royal Family.[106] According to Holmes's statement, in April 1972 the gang placed a "hit" on Murphy for identifying Coburn in court. A month later, Collins called Holmes and told him, "We're fixing to make a run." Holmes then drove himself, Collins, and three others to the Bus Stop Lounge, where he waited in the car while the passengers ran inside. A few minutes later he heard multiple gunshots and saw customers pour from the entrance. When his colleagues returned to the vehicle, two of them carried guns and one told him, "It's done." On the strength of this confession, Holmes was later convicted of murder and sentenced to twenty to seventy-five years in prison.[107]

Immediately after his arrest, Holmes told several people—including a public defender—that detectives tortured him.[108] According to Holmes, detectives Burge, John Yucaitis, and others handcuffed him, beat him, and placed an empty garbage liner over his head. Desperate for air, Holmes "sucked in and bit through" the plastic, only to have detectives grab another bag. "I hollered, I screamed, I passed out," Holmes recalled, "He brought me back. I passed out again. He brought me back." Pulling a black box out of a grocery sack, Burge said, "Nigger you gonna tell me what I wanna know." Jolted by an attached wire, Holmes gritted his teeth, fell from the chair, and writhed on the floor. With "a thousand needles going through my body," Holmes watched his vision go dark and wondered if he was dying. After several hours, he finally gave in, pleading: "This is it . . . whatever you want me to say or do, I did it, whatever it is. Kill the president? Yeah, I did that, too. I don't care, I just wanted out of there."[109] By implicating other members of the gang, however, Holmes jeopardized both his freedom and his life. "You can't be no stool pigeon," he explained, "because they try to kill you." Despite the risks, Holmes cracked under the extreme pressure of an illegal interrogation, admitting, "You expect to get beat up by the police, but you don't expect to get shocked and a plastic bag put over your head."[110] While Holmes detailed his abuse in a pretrial motion to suppress his statement, the trial court conceded only that "the statement was very badly taken," not that it was illegally coerced. The judge denied Holmes's motion, and prosecutors employed the tainted confession to secure conviction.[111]

Emboldened, detectives Burge, William Wagner, and Michael Hoke employed extraordinary methods in other Royal Family cases as well. Lawrence Poree, an accomplice in the Bus Stop Lounge execution, became perhaps the only suspect to endure Burge's tactics on three or more occasions.[112] In what may be the first alleged use of electric shock under Burge, detectives tortured Poree to get him to reveal the location of Holmes in early 1973. According to Poree: "They put a bag over my head, they beat me upside the head with phone books. I mean, they really did me a job." When he refused to cooperate, "they come out with the [shock] box."[113] On another occasion that year, Poree accused Burge and Hoke of throwing him onto a table, beating him, pulling his pants down, and shocking him on the arm, armpit, and testicles. Gesturing to the apparatus, Burge told him, "This is what we got for niggers like you."[114] Two or three years later, Burge nabbed him again, "flashed his big old pistol," and said, "I'm going to get you all one at a time and blow you all away."[115] Poree would encounter Burge yet again in 1979. In the meantime, however, the Area 2 Robbery unit helped win convictions of several Royal Family members, including Cochise Collins and Satan Holmes. Garnering fanfare, detectives Burge, Wagner, and Hoke received departmental commendations reading, in part, that "skillful questioning by the officers caused Holmes to admit his guilt" and implicate "many members of the Royal Family who were also involved in the crimes."[116] Satisfied, Area 2 detectives declared the Royal Family "virtually disintegrated" by August 1974.[117]

Between 1979 and 1981, however, several members won their release and reactivated the gang. Complaining of lax parole hearings, Area 2 detectives went back to work.[118] After an armed robbery and shoot-out with the police in the summer of 1979, patrolmen found Lawrence Poree hiding in the bushes and took him to Area 2.[119] Cuffed to the wall of a familiar interrogation room, Poree knew what to expect when Burge mentioned the black box and said, "Fun time again."[120] Tracking the Royal Family to other states, Burge and his partners flew to Tennessee to retrieve suspects from Shelby County Jail. Burge told them, "Wait till we get back to the horror chamber." Joking that the officer who killed Black Panther Fred Hampton was on duty, detectives slapped James Lewis, jabbed his throat, and damaged an eardrum.[121] Officers finally incapacitated the gang's leader in 1981, when a jury convicted Roger Collins of helping murder three men found dead just blocks from police headquarters.[122] At trial, a codefendant claimed that officers placed a shotgun under his chin, asking, "How would you like it if this accidentally went off?" He also recalled Sergeant Hoke saying, "You don't deserve an attorney, you're an animal and you don't have any rights."[123] The star witness later insisted a detective threatened him with a sledgehammer, acted "like he was crazy," and persuaded him to accept a plea deal.[124] Helpful in detectives' first bout with the Royal Family in the early 1970s, coerced confessions proved even more effective during the late-decade rematch. At least seven members received life sentences. Three others, including Roger Collins, wound up on death row.[125]

Years later, Burge considered his victory over the Royal Family a résumé highlight,[126] even bragging to criminal suspects of his ability to break hardened killers with physical force.[127] Indeed, throughout the 1970s, Area 2 detectives employed ordinary methods to capture routine offenders, but they resorted to intimidation, violence, and torture to convict the toughest and most dangerous. In a case of ends justifying means, Area 2 detectives largely reserved coercive methods for what training manuals referred to as "suspects whose guilt is definite or reasonably certain."[128] Yet their judgment of guilt proved unreliable. Blinded by bigotry and tunnel vision, detectives took the law into their own hands, manufactured evidence, and violated suspects' rights, particularly in cases involving African American gang members. For example, investigating a grocery store robbery during which culprits took a police officer hostage in 1979,[129] officers allegedly struck a black suspect over the head with a flashlight, shocked him on the chest and genitals with what they called a "nigger box," and claimed, "God had diarrhea when he created you motherfuckers."[130] Even assuming that officers acted with the good intention of cleaning up the streets, their racist behavior at best distorted justice and fractured relationships with black communities. At worst, it orchestrated a human rights crisis that would take decades to repair.

Over time, Area 2 detectives grew confident that observers would not question their techniques. First, most people found torture allegations hard to believe without physical proof. In a Royal Family trial in 1981, an incredulous assistant state's attorney asked the defendant, "You are telling this jury that you admitted to triple murder because you got a beating that resulted in no bruises, no swelling, no scars, no nothing, is that correct?"[131] Second, even when evidence of abuse surfaced, detectives could expect to reap the benefit of the doubt. At the same trial, a prosecutor asked the jury rhetorically, "Do you believe Sergeant Hoke, fourteen year veteran on the Chicago Police Department or Mr. Collins," a man "convicted of ten different felonies?"[132] Third, many actors in the criminal justice system benefited directly from coerced confessions, including police supervisors, prosecutors, judges, and elected officials. When State's Attorney Richard M. Daley ran for mayor in 1983, for example, campaign fliers boasted, "The gangs have good reason not to like Daley." A list of accomplishments included "William Bracey, Roger Collins, Murray Hooper, Royal Family, death sentences for triple murder."[133] Accordingly, official mechanisms of accountability failed. The torture crisis spread. Illegal interrogation methods followed perpetrators on reassignment and appeared in cases of suspects whose guilt was "doubtful or uncertain."[134] By the 1980s, complicity in the torture regime also grew, as other actors helped enable custodial abuse at Area 2.

The Larger Scope of Abuse

Left unchecked, police misconduct evolved and expanded. The career of Deputy Superintendent Walter Murphy, one of Detective Burge's early role models, reveals how administrators carried corruption with them as they changed assignment. When Murphy was a young detective in the Area 5 Burglary Unit during the spring of 1963, a suspected thief named Raymond Kwiatowski accused him and a partner of physically abusing him inside a North Side interrogation room. According to Kwiatowski, detectives "kneed me, beat me with their fists, and finally used a sledge hammer on my left arm and legs." After the defendant revealed injuries to a bailiff, the judge ordered the detectives arrested.[135] A few weeks later, however, Kwiatowski refused to follow up on brutality allegations, opting instead to plead his Fifth Amendment right not to answer questions concerning his arrest.[136] With Kwiatowski unwilling to testify, First Assistant State's Attorney Edward J. Egan decided not to pursue the brutality complaint. Kwiatowski's self-preservation and prosecutors' reluctance to indict police officers thus stifled charges against Murphy, who returned to the job without penalty.[137] Murphy was soon promoted to sergeant and assigned to the Internal Inspections Division, created by former Superintendent O. W. Wilson to investigate accusations of police misconduct.[138]

In February 1973, the fast-rising Lieutenant Murphy was named head of the Detective Division's Robbery Section, where he administered the separate units in each of the six police areas, including Area 2.[139] For fourteen months, Murphy worked closely with Area 2 Robbery, helping shape an effective unit that cleared many a tough case and put away the Royal Family. Detective William Parker, a veteran African American detective who returned to Area 2 in late 1972 after two years away, noticed a changed culture within the Burnside station house. Regarding Murphy as the head of an "evil cabal" of five or six detectives, Parker later named Michael Hoke, James Houtsma, and Jon Burge as among Murphy's "henchmen."[140] While typing a report one day in September 1972, Parker was interrupted by a "shrill inhuman-type cry" coming from the lieutenant's office. While other detectives continued as though nothing happened, Parker got up to investigate. Rushing through the door, Parker met Jon Burge for the first time, standing over a black male handcuffed to a steam radiator, his pants around his ankles. One of two other detectives in the room snatched an object from a desk to conceal it from Parker, who slowly withdrew. Told that what he had seen "wasn't any of [his] business" and admonished not to "barge in while [other detectives] were conducting their investigation," Parker fell out of favor with supervisors and was transferred to Area 3.[141] Writing of the Cook County criminal courts, Nicole Gonzalez Van Cleve found that "attorneys inherit a culture of racism that has existed 'a priori' (before) their participation" and exists "long after they retire."[142] Likewise, Parker's recollection highlights that Burge joined—rather than inaugurated—a practice of racist policing at Area 2.

In April 1974, the superintendent promoted Lieutenant Murphy to commander of the Intelligence Division.[143] He would later take heat for coordinating the department's controversial Red Squad, a special surveillance unit accused of compiling illegal intelligence files and harassing political activists.[144] Burge must have impressed Murphy during their time together at Area 2, as he soon joined his former supervisor in the Intelligence Division.[145] After six months in Organized Crime, Burge was selected to work directly under Murphy in the division's Special Assignment Section starting in early 1975. Before long, the department promoted Burge to temporary sergeant and made him a uniform patrol supervisor in South Chicago's 4th District. Burge returned to Area 2 in the summer of 1977, resworn as career service sergeant in charge of the Robbery Unit's night shift, from midnight to 8:00 a.m.[146] It was during this period that Burge and his "midnight crew" confronted the Royal Family for the second and final time.[147]

During their absence from 1974 to 1977, the seeds of abuse cultivated at Area 2 by Murphy and Burge flourished, encompassing witness intimidation, evidence suppression, and perjury. If accusations of physical beatings and torture diminished in the interim, one high-profile case revealed the range of unethical practices prevalent in the Burnside Area in the 1970s.[148] On January 14, 1976, someone abducted an African American child model and honors student named Lisa Cabassa near her home in the South Chicago District. The next day, authorities found the nine-year-old girl—raped and murdered—in an alley a few miles away. Over the next several months, Area 2 Homicide detectives arrested multiple suspects, including seventeen-year-old Michael Evans and eighteen-year-old Paul Terry. Convicted in May 1977, Evans and Terry received sentences of two hundred to four hundred years in prison.[149]

While attorneys immediately filed an appeal, it took decades to establish prosecutors built their case on a foundation of police misconduct and perjury. Indeed, detectives sullied the Cabassa investigation from the beginning. With suspects already in custody, a sixteen-year-old Bowen High School freshman recanted testimony that first led police to make arrests. In a sixty-two-page transcript produced by Evans's attorney and sent to the *Chicago Tribune*, the teenager admitted providing a false statement to Area 2 detectives weeks earlier, explaining, "One of them said that he was going to grab me and nail me up against the wall. . . . They were hollering at me, and stuff, like I really knew something. So I went on and put a lie together just to free myself."[150] At trial, the state's case rested on the account of another tainted witness, thirty-two-year-old Judy Januszewski, who claimed she personally saw the defendants kidnap Lisa Cabassa. Januszewski later told the judge that Evans called her from jail and had friends on the outside intimidate her with threats of rape and murder.[151] Only years later would an appellate court confirm that detectives coerced Januszewski into making false statements.

When DNA evidence exonerated both men in 2004, they sued several police officers and the City of Chicago for a wrongful conviction that had robbed them of nearly thirty years. During a resultant hearing, a detective admitted to hiding results of a semen test conducted in 1976 that would have cleared Evans. While a panel of judges declined to award damages, a dissenting opinion found it deplorable that detectives "coerced and threatened their only witness to identify [Evans]; that they locked the witness's husband in a room to prevent him from telling prosecutors about the witness's eyesight and credibility problems; that they lied in saying that the witness reported threats from Michael Evans in the weeks after the murder; and that they performed genital inspections on neighborhood boys as a way to pressure them to implicate Evans (which at least one of the boys did)."[152] With Burge on reassignment, Evans avoided the physical abuse that would later cause others in similar positions to confess to crimes they did not commit. Yet Area 2 detectives still found illegal ways to clear a critical case.

In a pattern that would continue throughout the rest of Burge's career, wherever new assignments took him, torture accusations appeared. Occasionally, Burge even brought compatriots with him or recruited detectives known to possess peculiar skills in the interrogation room.[153] One case not directly involving Burge but nevertheless conforming to his style came out of Area 3 while Burge was assigned to the area's 12th District from July 1980 to October 1981.[154] On June 25, 1981, Area 3 patrolmen broke up a neighborhood squabble and arrested sixteen-year-old Mark Clements for disorderly conduct.[155] Back at the station house, officers learned that Clements was wanted for questioning in an arson that had killed four Englewood residents a week earlier. When Clements arrived at Area 3 headquarters, detectives Daniel McWeeny, James Higgins, and John McCann interrogated him for several hours, slipping into the familiar "good guy, bad guy" routine to crack the juvenile suspect—an easy target considering his social and economic background.[156] Abandoned at age three, Clements was a school dropout and a ward of the state. He was also a new father and a functional illiterate with a criminal record.[157] With McCann in the bad-cop role, detectives beat Clements in the arms, legs, back, and shoulders before bringing in an assistant state's attorney to take a statement. Clements told the prosecutor the police were beating him. The lawyer simply left the room. Detectives returned to soften Clements some more.[158] With McCann's hand painfully cupping Clements's testicles, the suspect gave in. "He *squeezed*, and *squeezed*," Clements explained, "Shoot. Hell. I woulda told him the mayor committed the crime."[159] Despite contradictory evidence, the state convicted Clements on the strength of a dithering and inconsistent confession.[160] In an eloquent, if rambling, presentence soliloquy lasting nearly two hours, Clements begged for leniency. Undeterred, Judge William Cousins condemned the teenager to life without parole.[161]

Wrongfully convicted, Clements would not win release until 2009.

Through a tireless pursuit of justice, Clements convinced prominent civil rights attorneys to pick up his case decades after conviction.[162] Investigators learned that a motorcycle gang set the 1981 fire to punish a resident for defrauding them of drug profits. Prosecutors cut a deal and released Clements after twenty-eight years.[163] Two detectives in the case later featured in other beatings and false confessions linked to Jon Burge in the 1980s and 1990s.[164] Detective Daniel McWeeny transferred to Burnside in October 1981, the very month that Burge took over as head of the area's Violent Crimes Unit, formed when the department restructured the Detective Division at the end of 1980.[165] In 1986, the department promoted Burge to commander of the Bomb and Arson Section. Two years later, he was placed in charge of Area 3 on the Southwest Side. Transferring to Brighton Park headquarters at Thirty-Ninth Street and California Avenue, Burge took McWeeny and John McCann with him. Even as the movement of personnel spread abuse across districts, misconduct also crossed institutional lines, as other law enforcement agencies cooperated with Area 2 and Area 3 detectives throughout Burge's career.

As most of these cases reveal, detectives could not sustain coercive interrogation methods without the cooperation of the Cook County State's Attorney's Office.[166] Not only did prosecutors rely on statements procured by detectives to secure plea bargains and win trials; they also were among the only people outside the police department allowed access to the interrogation room. Privy to police interviews, Chicago prosecutors had long been linked to misconduct. In the early 1930s, the Wickersham Report criticized prosecutors for enabling custodial abuse and provided examples of lawyers actively participating in physical violence.[167] In a series of decisions handed down between 1936 and 1966, however, the U.S. Supreme Court transformed police and prosecutorial procedure by tightening criteria for admissible evidence.[168] By 1970, the Cook County State's Attorney's Office had largely shed its association with the third degree and involuntary confessions, both to maintain an air of professionalism and to ensure quality cases. In the 1970s, however, rising crime rates and bulging court dockets spurred the State's Attorney's Office to create a special division to facilitate cooperation between police and prosecutors. At Area 2, members of a new Felony Review Unit faced difficult choices when confronted with the methods of Burge and his colleagues.

Felony Review emerged from the same high-pressure climate that influenced Burge's early career. As early as 1960, the State's Attorney's Office sought to educate detectives on the needs of prosecutors, writing in a CPD training pamphlet, "A policeman should do everything in his power to aid the Assistant [State's Attorney] in prosecuting any case with which he is connected."[169] In the 1970s, however, the number of criminal indictments exploded.[170] According to a veteran prosecutor, "The caseload on most of us was overwhelming."[171] More than ever, detectives and prosecutors needed to work together to produce airtight convictions. In 1972, State's Attorney Edward V. Hanrahan launched the pilot Felony Review program to help police investigators keep prosecutors' needs in mind when building cases.[172] Later that year, the National Center for Prosecution Management criticized CPD detectives for filing their own felony indictments, leading to "improperly charged" defendants and cases that were "not legally sufficient." Tasked with helping the State's Attorney spend a $50,000 grant from the federal Law Enforcement Assistance Administration, the Washington-based group recommended expanding Felony Review and making it permanent.[173] Assuming office the next year, Republican State's Attorney Bernard Carey did just that, later taking credit for the popular program launched by his Democratic predecessor.[174]

By 1975, Felony Review had become a fixture of local law enforcement. The unit employed dozens of young assistant state's attorneys (ASAs) on twenty-four-hour call, ready at a moment's notice to make their way to over two dozen station houses to advise detectives and approve charges. As former ASA Michael Ficaro explained, "It's really a screening process with a view toward the collection of additional evidence to . . . provide the best case possible."[175] Promoting Felony Review, State's Attorney Carey argued that it kept detectives from prematurely clearing cases and sending useless indictments to his office. As he told the Chicago Crime Commission: "The police are notorious for making charges. It clears their blotter."[176] Designed to sift out weak cases and make others stronger, Felony Review raised tension between ASAs and detectives. According to Ficaro, "It's often antagonistic because there's a perspective not always shared by the police upon the quantity of evidence that they have obtained, and human nature as it is when you are asking someone to do more, that person has already satisfied that they have done enough there is sometime friction."[177] Requiring evidence that could prove guilt beyond a reasonable doubt, ASAs often told detectives "it's not enough, keep on looking," sending them back to the interrogation room or into the streets for more.[178]

The implementation of Felony Review thus raised pressure on Area 2 detectives. Eager to close cases, officers' faith in a suspect's guilt occasionally rested more on gut feeling than concrete evidence. Securing confessions proved an obvious solution. According to Michael Cahill, a former ASA who tried Area 2 cases in the 1970s and 1980s, detectives viewed confessions as the "gold seal" of a good investigation.[179] While the presence of ASAs should have prevented illegal interrogations, Felony Review staff often proved unwilling or unable to intercede on behalf of future defendants. The unit typically employed young men and women fresh out of law school, anxious to bulk up résumés before heading off to private practice.[180] Indeed, ambitious attorneys often considered Felony Review a "low assignment" with bad hours and little prestige, the second rung up the ladder from traffic court.[181] According to Cahill, the average Felony Review attorney held less than three years' experience and often felt intimidated by "excellent," "well-trained," and "hard ass" detectives with greater experience compiling case files.[182] Sent to approve charges, many ASAs simply deferred to the older, more experienced, and imposing detectives working alongside Burge. Others had no qualms looking the other way or even participating in coercive methods. After all, in addition to the joint pressure of overwhelming caseloads, detectives and prosecutors relied on one another to win convictions and advance careers. Those lawyers who could not endorse the "brutish culture" of the police, however, nevertheless reconciled their complicity by locating themselves "*adjacent to*" but "not *emanating from*" the extralegal methods of unscrupulous detectives.[183]

More than simply failing to stop custodial abuse, however, the State's Attorney's Office inadvertently encouraged it. Noting a core difference between detectives and prosecutors, a 1972 study of the nascent Felony Review unit reported: "The police are motivated in charging decisions by a desire to mollify victims and to maintain a high clearance rate by arrest. They are reluctant to release an arrestee if investigation indicates a weakness in the case." Prosecutors, in contrast, were driven instead by a desire to dispose cases efficiently and maintain "high conviction rates." Accordingly, prosecutors were "more sensitive" than detectives "to the credibility and quality of evidence." The report concluded, "The police show less concern because, again, their performance is not measured by conviction rates."[184] After the launch of Felony Review, however, circumstances changed. Because prosecutors sought to avoid "embarrass[ing] their colleagues at the preliminary hearing courts or trial courts by sending them cases that are flimsy or weak," ASAs raised the bar of evidence required to approve charges. As a result, detectives confronted a higher burden of proof. Tasked with presenting slam-dunk evidence, confessions only grew in appeal. Before Felony Review, detectives pursued arrests in order to maintain clearance rates. After Felony Review, detectives pursued convictions. The need to satisfy prosecutors before clearing cases incentivized illegal interrogation methods at the very moment that Jon Burge began his detective career.

The Culture of Area 2

By the 1980s, torture was entrenched at Area 2. Buoyed by the defeat of the Royal Family and confident in the efficacy of illegal interrogations, the Area 2 Robbery Unit developed a distinct and reputedly sordid subculture. Manning the cheerless first watch, Burge's midnight crew became widely known as tough detectives who got results. In fact, though, it was the use of torture that helped elevate Area 2 clearance rates above the citywide average.[185] But if some observers admired the overnight robbery crew, others expressed suspicion and scorn. Like an untreated virus, the institutional culture at Area 2 in the 1970s infected all manner of activity. By the 1980s, sustaining the torture regime required detectives suppress exculpatory evidence, maintain a rigid code of silence, and keep black officers off related cases. Meanwhile, the prevalence of torture at Burnside Headquarters became an open secret among criminal justice practitioners and local residents alike.[186]

During an otherwise unremarkable murder trial in 1982, a rare whistleblower helped uncover a pernicious practice common to Area 2 investigations. For years, detectives concealed secret investigative files from both prosecutors and defense attorneys before criminal trials. These so-called street files represented a clear violation of the 1963 Supreme Court ruling in *Brady v. Maryland*, which required full disclosure of all material—known as exculpatory evidence—that could help substantiate innocence.[187] One day in April 1982, Area 2 Violent Crimes detective Frank Laverty read a *Chicago Tribune* account of the ongoing criminal trial of nineteen-year-old George Jones. A popular "bookworm" and son of a Chicago police officer, Jones stood trial for allegedly raping and murdering a thirteen-year-old girl and severely beating her ten-year-old brother.[188] As Detective Laverty read excerpts of trial testimony, he grew alarmed and contacted the court to prevent a wrongful conviction.

While other detectives took the primary role in the George Jones investigation, Frank Laverty assisted throughout and even went to supervisors with his own theory on how the crime unfolded. Observing the trial several months later, Laverty was convinced the state had the wrong man. Determined to prevent a miscarriage of justice, Laverty revealed to the court details from the case's street file. This separate folder—containing detectives' personal notes and memoranda—was deliberately withheld during the trial's discovery phase. The undisclosed notes, Laverty revealed, cast considerable doubt on Jones's guilt. Laverty even agreed to testify in court.[189] Shocked by the revelations, Judge William Cousins dismissed the case "with prejudice," banning the state from further prosecution.[190] A federal injunction later forced the CPD to end the practice of concealing exculpatory evidence in confidential street files.[191] Jones won $801,000 in a civil suit filed against Area 2 detectives, their supervisors, and a cooperating lab technician.[192]

When he divulged the street files fiasco, Detective Laverty also drew attention to another component of Area 2 culture—the so-called "blue wall of silence."[193] In police departments across the United States, officers regularly forged bonds of fidelity, erected barriers to outside censure, and protected one another from scrutiny.[194] While the code prevailed everywhere, the intense loyalty of the Chicago Police Department grew legendary.[195] Referencing Frank Serpico, the famous New York City police officer who exposed corruption in the early 1970s, a contemporary who fought extortion within the CPD quipped, "Chicago's police scandals have no Serpicos."[196] Sensitive to unfair judgment from a misunderstanding public, police officers held trust, discretion, and solidarity in the highest regard, at least within their own ranks.

More than just fraternal tradition, however, commitment to closing ranks was reinforced through implicit threats. Indeed, by blowing the whistle on street files—and possibly saving an innocent man from death row—Frank Laverty suffered professional retribution. For example, even before the case was dismissed, a high-ranking assistant state's attorney called Laverty, told him he was in "deep trouble," and pressured him to admit collusion with the People's Law Office.[197] Rather than punish those responsible for hiding exculpatory evidence, the department opened an Internal Investigations case against Laverty for testifying without permission.[198] Instead of honoring Laverty for doing the right thing, his fellow officers "shunned" him.[199] According to former Area 2 detective Doris Byrd, sometime after the Jones trial, Lieutenant Burge pulled his gun in front of other detectives, pointed it to Laverty's back, and said, "Bang," making it clear how supervisors felt about whistle-blowers.[200] A homicide detective with over ten years' experience, Laverty found himself assigned to a series of mundane administrative posts, ending his career by monitoring new recruits urinate into plastic cups.[201] Working days, however, allowed him to take advantage of a CPD program that paid for night classes at a local law school, leading to a better life for him. Laverty later reconciled his decision to betray the code of silence, joking that it spared him years of "taking the Fifth Amendment" alongside Burge and the rest of his former Area 2 colleagues embroiled in abuse allegations.[202]

Demonstrating the power of the blue wall, few detectives ever came for-

FIGURE 2 Gladys Lewis of Citizens Alert honors Detective Frank Laverty for his role in exposing the CPD's compilation of illegal street files, March 1985. Citizens Alert records, Special Collections and University Archives, University of Illinois at Chicago.

ward to expose custodial abuse at Area 2.[203] Not until the late 1980s did an anonymous detective write to lawyers at the People's Law Office suggesting the larger scope of the scandal.[204] In the early 1990s, African American detective William Parker, then retired, wrote civil rights attorneys to corroborate emerging details of Burge's methods.[205] No other officers came forward until a larger group of retired black detectives joined Parker in a series of sworn statements in the early 2000s.[206]

Their testimony suggests that while the CPD hired and promoted more black officers throughout the 1970s, Area 2 remained a white man's club well into the 1980s. At the old Burnside headquarters and, after 1983, the new Pullman headquarters, white detectives frequently told racist jokes and peppered their speech with racial slurs.[207] In sworn testimony, Detective Peter Dignan admitted using the word *nigger* on the job at least one hundred times, typically while reciting jokes or questioning suspects.[208] A letter sent to the People's Law Office in 1989 suggested the Violent Crimes supervisor reinforced the racist climate, claiming simply, "Burge hates black people."[209] When an acquaintance sitting at a bar with Burge in 1983 asked him why he was "ticked off," Burge allegedly explained he had been "dealing with dead fucking niggers all day."[210] The sister of Detective Robert

Dwyer overheard her brother and Burge brag about coercing confessions from "niggers" who destroyed their own neighborhoods and made police lives miserable.[211] Working alongside or under the supervision of bigoted white men, many black detectives chose to "bury [their] head in the sand" rather than jeopardize their careers confronting rumors of physical abuse.[212]

While the small number of African Americans assigned to Area 2 in the 1970s and 1980s were in a unique position to challenge the systemic use of torture against black people, a racially determined allocation of manpower limited their opportunity. Not only did fear of retaliation deter personnel of all racial backgrounds from speaking out; supervisors also deliberately kept black officers away from cases involving coercive methods.[213] During an extraordinary manhunt for two cop killers in 1982, for example, Burge sent black detectives on "wild goose chases" to hide them from Area 2 interrogation rooms.[214] In day-to-day operations, shift supervisors segregated units and assigned black detectives to weak or difficult cases. Throughout a seven-year stint at Area 2, Detective Sammy Lacey recalled working exclusively with other black partners.[215] When Doris Byrd partnered with white detective Peter Dignan, she found that "because I was black and female, he didn't want to work with me."[216] Several black detectives felt they were set up to fail. After years of high performance elsewhere, Detective Walter Young watched his efficiency rating plummet at Area 2. Describing the case management system, Young claimed white detectives received "hot cases"—promising files with known suspects—while black detectives received "blind cases"—dead-end files with few leads.[217] Competing with white detectives whose clearance rates were inflated by unfair case allocation and coerced confessions, many black detectives were soon transferred or demoted.[218]

In the rare circumstances in which black officers served in positions of authority over white detectives or were actually present during coercive interrogations, they proved unable to counter the abusive subculture of Area 2. After the 1980 reorganization of the Detective Division, two highly regarded black police veterans commanded Area 2 for most of the decade. From 1981 to 1983, however, Commander Milton Deas reportedly deferred to Jon Burge, his confident, capable, and physically imposing lieutenant.[219] According to Doris Byrd, while Deas "was in charge of the [entire] Area," he "pretty much let Burge do what he wanted."[220] Succeeding Deas as Area 2 commander and later becoming Chicago's second African American police superintendent, LeRoy Martin supervised Burge in the mid-1980s when torture allegations mushroomed.[221] A few black detectives appear to have directly participated in the torture regime. During the 1970s, African American Sergeant Alvin Palmer helped coordinate the Robbery Unit's marred investigation of the Royal Family. In the 1980s, Detective Jack Hines helped coerce confessions from several black suspects, allegedly taking a handcuffed prisoner to a remote site and threatening him with a gun in the presence of fellow black detective George Patton.[222] In 1984, a suspect accused four detectives, including African American Sergeant Rutherford Wilson, of threatening him with an electric-shock device until he confessed to bludgeoning three children to death.[223] Another suspect recalled white detectives leaving him alone with a black officer who beat a phone book on a desk to "pretend that he was torturing me," suggesting the role peer pressure played at Area 2.[224]

While greater hiring and promoting of black and Latino officers after 1970 constituted a social justice victory, nonwhite representation did not sufficiently check brutality and misconduct.[225] To be sure, many officers of color learned to mediate between their racist white peers and the black communities they served. For a variety of reasons, however, others identified more as brothers in "blue" than brothers on the block.[226] First, even as interracial conflict plagued police staff, enforcing the law engendered occupational solidarity across lines of race. Second, the power imbalance between sworn personnel and civilians corrupted officers of all backgrounds. Third, age and class difference inhibited black officers' empathy for victims of police violence. For example, Area 2 Commander Milton Deas, a black World War II veteran and son of a celebrated police pioneer, chided "responsible people" for leaving the neighborhood, bemoaned the rise of the "ghetto," and condemned black youth.[227] Writing of diversity in criminal justice institutions, Nicole Gonzalez Van Cleve concludes, "Despite the presence of people of color in leadership roles, the case of the Cook County Courts demonstrates how racism festers in culture, social processes, and institutional norms that are larger than the symbolic roles of individual actors or leaders."[228] Much could be said of the police. Echoing their white counterparts, black officers at Area 2 in the 1970s and 1980s both reflected and shaped a subculture conducive to torture. While few African Americans participated in the Burge scandal, others proved unable or unwilling to prevent it, including powerful public officials.

Chicago faced new political realities in the 1980s. A decade that began with a woman mayor—the divisive and resilient Jane Byrne—soon witnessed the rise of Harold Washington, the city's first African American mayor. "Unfortunately," writes attorney Flint Taylor, "Harold's election and the appointments of James Montgomery as the first Black corporation counsel and Fred Rice as the first Black police superintendent would have no effect on the systemic racist torture that continued under Jon Burge's command."[229] According to historian Toussaint Losier, the city's failure to check Burge and other police torturers in the mid-1980s "implicat[es] the Washington administration in a broader crisis of police accountability" that began before Harold's 1983 election and continued after his death four years later.[230] In 1989, Richard M. Daley won his first of six terms in the Mayor's Office, reclaiming the post his father held for over twenty years. Meanwhile, regardless of who captured City Hall, detectives continued to coerce confessions some fifteen miles south at Area 2. If the Burge torture regime operated in the shadows, however, it was never truly invisible.[231]

Indeed, by the early 1980s detectives on the midnight shift developed a reputation for grit and proficiency even as rumors of illicit tactics proliferated.[232] Detective Melvin Duncan, who worked at Area 2 from 1971 to 1978, understood "certain Robbery detectives used an electrical box and cattle prods on people to get confessions."[233] Detective Walter Young overheard cryptic talk of the "Vietnam Special" or the "Vietnamese Treatment." Stumbling upon a storage shelf with a strange box and an attached crank, Young recalled "stories, innuendos, [and] gossip" of Burge's notorious torture machine.[234] When Detective Sammy Lacey walked through the 5th District offices on the first floor of the old Burnside station house, patrolmen occasionally stopped him, pointed upstairs, and asked, "What are they doing to people up there on midnights?"[235] Referencing Area 2's "nasty reputation," an engineer familiar with the building conceded, "A lot of abuse went on in that station."[236] In the late 1970s, attorneys at the Cook County Criminal Courts building found accusations of torture at Area 2 "common knowledge."[237] An assistant public defender later admitted hearing "a lot of rumors and innuendos" about Burnside detectives, "particularly Red Burge."[238] Another public defender told a supervisor a client was bagged and suffocated and was told, simply, "Oh, that would be Area 2."[239] Coerced confessions, like the third degree of an earlier era, were by their very nature secretive, deniable phenomena. For every person insisting the midnight crew engaged in unethical behavior behind closed doors, another claimed to know nothing. Yet Jon Burge and his men gained a certain satisfaction and practical advantage from allowing rumors to spread.

On February 5, 1982, Area 2 detectives told Lieutenant Burge they arrested a man they believed killed a state's witness to an earlier homicide. When Burge entered the interrogation room, he asked if the suspect knew who he was. Handcuffed to a ring on the wall near an iron radiator, Melvin Jones said no. Burge threatened that before the night was through, Jones would

wish he "never set eyes on him." According to Jones, "[Burge] r
a few other guys' names[,] saying do I know Cochise [and] Sat
Jones admitted knowing who they were, Burge said "he had th
before and they both confessed and they crawled all around on
When Burge left the room, Detective Robert Flood adopted the good-cop persona, telling Jones it would be better if he just confessed. Hours later, Burge returned with the wooden box and started shouting questions. He took off Jones's boots and sweatpants and shocked him on the foot, thigh, and penis. As Jones protested, "You ain't supposed to be doing me like this," they heard a knock at the door. From a distance, Jones heard an officer tell Burge "something about a shooting at 79th [street]." Informing Jones he "had a reprieve," Burge promised Detective Flood, "When we come back it's going to be me and him." Burge gathered the shock box and left the room for good.[240]

Jones could not have known it at the time, but his interrogation had been interrupted by news that a patrolman had been shot and killed on a city bus.[241] Within four days, two more officers would be fatally shot within Area 2 as well. Once an open secret among agents of local law enforcement, Burge's distinctive methods would prove instrumental in apprehending the suspects and procuring confessions. By the end of February 1982, Burge's supervisors, the command staff of the CPD, Cook County State's Attorney Richard M. Daley, and even Mayor Jane Byrne would all know of Jon Burge and the pattern and practice of abuse at Area 2. Their silence, and even praise, would sanction the midnight crew's behavior and encourage its further slide into excess.

3

"They Believed They Were at War"

A police crisis in winter 1982 culminated in the sanctioning of torture at Area 2, leading to its expansion.[1] For nearly ten years, allegations of coerced confessions surfaced on Chicago's Far South Side. While an unknown number of torture cases likely escaped the historical record, most known allegations before 1982 involved high-profile suspects whom detectives believed responsible for sensational crimes. With abusive practices already established, Area 2 detectives responded to the murder of several law enforcement officials in early 1982 by targeting suspects and their communities with violent reprisal. On February 14, officers working under Lieutenant Jon Burge tortured twenty-nine-year-old Andrew Wilson in revenge for killing two police officers. Evidence of Wilson's treatment in custody became widely known, particularly among public officials. Rather than face punishment, however, Burge and his men received commendations. Following the indictment of Wilson, the number of known torture accusations linked to Burge grew. Indeed, Area 2 detectives appear to have become less selective in their targets, coercing confessions from suspects whose guilt seemed less than certain. During a time of widespread crime panic, the police crisis of winter 1982 opened space in which those who could have checked abuse—police supervisors, officers of the court, the state's attorney, and the mayor—instead affirmed the illegal methods employed at Area 2. Local resistance to the police terror of February 1982, however, anticipated the collective action that would bring down the torture regime and carry the fight for police accountability into the 1990s and 2000s.

The Early Life of Andrew Wilson

Andrew Wilson was born on October 6, 1952, the third son of a soap factory machinist and a waitress whose family would eventually grow to include nine children.[2] With their father commuting over fifty miles to work and their mother grinding out a living on a meager salary and tips, the Wilson children were often cared for by relatives and the family's eldest daughter, Bobbie. According to journalist John Conroy, a prison official later described the family's three-bedroom, split-level home in Chicago's Far South Side neighborhood of Morgan Park as "neat, clean, and nicely furnished," with a "small library" and an electric organ the children played by ear. Struggling with the routine challenges of working-class life, the Wilson family nevertheless enjoyed stability and a modicum of comfort.[3]

Yet Andrew proved a difficult child. Likely suffering a learning disorder or other "cognitive difficult[y]," Wilson never learned to read or write and drew labels of borderline "retarded."[4] While some observers insisted Wilson "[did] not appear to be of defective intelligence,"[5] others rejected evaluations of his intellect as biased "hearsay" or unqualified "opinions."[6] Regardless, the record suggests that from an early age Wilson experienced the growing pains of a young man resisting authority.[7] At age eleven, he started skipping school, running away from home, disappearing for days at a time, and sleeping in cars. Frustrated, his parents occasionally beat him with an electrical cord. "[We would] whup him," admitted his father, "[but] it didn't help . . . We just couldn't control him." When Wilson was thirteen, his parents enrolled him in a special school for troubled kids. Within a year he was caught stealing and sent to another institution. He lasted six weeks before running away. Busted for burglary at age fifteen, Wilson began a tour of juvenile reformatories and detention facilities. In an effort to treat "emotional disturbance and hyperactivity," doctors prescribed tranquilizers and anticonvulsive medication. While the regimen improved Wilson's mood and behavior, administrators took him off medication a few months before his release from custody.[8]

As Wilson approached adulthood, the stakes of criminal behavior grew more serious. Encouraging steady employment, Wilson's parents found him menial jobs as a busboy and member of a cleaning crew.[9] Yet he continued to supplement income with theft and burglary. Shortly after his seventeenth birthday in 1969, authorities arrested Wilson for unlawful use of a weapon and placed him on probation. Within a week, he was arrested for burglary, the first of three such arrests in as many years.[10] In the early 1970s, Wilson cut his teeth in prison at the same moment that Jon Burge began a career with the Chicago Police Department (CPD). Burge made detective in 1972.[11] Wilson moved to armed robbery a few years later.[12] On March 9, 1975, Wilson and four accomplices robbed Sambo's Restaurant in Chicago's south suburbs.[13] When a police cruiser chased the getaway car into a church parking lot, Wilson placed a sawed-off shotgun to the head of an officer and relieved him of his service revolver.[14] For this misadventure, Judge William Cousins gave Wilson an eight- to sixteen-year sentence.[15] He arrived at the state penitentiary on March 3, 1978.[16]

Over the following two-and-a-half years, Wilson adjusted to life in prison. His first stop was Joliet Correctional Center, a deteriorating complex long condemned as "unfit to incarcerate inmates."[17] When Wilson arrived, officials found him a "pathological liar" and "an aggressive, hostile, overly assertive individual with a negativistic, uncooperative and antisocial attitude."[18] Authorities transferred him hundreds of miles south to the small rural community of Chester, Illinois.[19] Downstream of St. Louis on the Mississippi River, Chester housed the maximum-security Menard Correctional Center. At Menard, Wilson further evolved into what a social worker later called "an institutionalized person," learning to master the daily routine of a state prisoner. Earning seventeen "disciplinary tickets" in three years, Wilson's "self-control" improved only through "maintaining a job" in the Menard kitchen.[20] He was later caught stealing food and penalized for "unauthorized possession of state property." Before he could return to work, he underwent "religious counseling." Enjoying chapel time, Wilson started attending Protestant services regularly.[21] Counselors noted "some improvement" in Wilson's attitude. An August 1981 report found an assignment "in the Officer's Kitchen [had] been beneficial" and applauded Wilson for amassing "90 days meritorious good time." Rewarding "steady improvement," the state paroled Wilson on October 23, 1981.[22]

Prison life, however, had not been all church service and kitchen duty. Along with most prisoners of the Illinois Department of Corrections (IDOC), Andrew Wilson found refuge from the tedium and perils of incarceration through membership in one of many gangs.[23] Extensions of street gangs on the outside, membership in the Black P Stone Nation, the Vice Lords, or the Gangster Disciples provided affinity and protection in a lonely and dangerous environment. By the time Wilson arrived at Joliet, IDOC officials had conceded gangs were a "major force in Illinois' prisons."[24] When a "gang-inspired" riot hit Joliet in April 1975, two hundred prisoners occupied a cell block and seized three hostages before guards regained control.[25] In the chaos, insurgents murdered a former gang member who broke with leadership.[26] At Menard, where Wilson bunked from 1978 to 1981, 900 of 1,400 prisoners in the mid-1970s were white, and half belonged to three white supremacist groups—the Klansmen, Vikings, and Young Nobles.[27] With IDOC confirming the prison's reputation as a "hillbilly institution," the *Chicago Tribune* labeled Menard a "Center of White Racism."[28] According to a black prisoner, "At least 70 per cent of the whites wear Nazi swastika insignia or the three K's, with open support of the administration."[29] As a Burge torture survivor later explained, it was "a little tough" to be a state prisoner in Illinois "and not be a gang member."[30] It is unknown whether Andrew Wilson, who was African American, joined a gang before or after entering prison, but once inside he must have found some measure of security among his fellow Gangster Disciples.[31]

While gang membership offered benefits on the inside, it carried obligations on the streets. When Andrew Wilson returned to Morgan Park in autumn 1981, he fell back on old social networks and resumed a life of crime. Fresh from jail, lacking formal education, and illiterate, the twenty-nine-year-old ex-con had few options. Willie Washington, a female friend of the family, gave Andrew a part-time job cleaning Willie's Beauty Salon at 1440 W. 115th Street, the site of a recent double homicide.[32] Washington gave Wilson a set of keys and let him sleep overnight. For several months, Wilson spent time with a girlfriend and their two daughters; reconnected with his younger brother, Jackie Wilson; and bonded with a former cell mate named Edgar Hope.[33] The product of a "chaotic childhood," the twenty-two-year-old Hope first affiliated with the Gangster Disciples in grammar school. His father—a reputed drunk and gambler—left the family when Hope was an infant, yet came around enough to introduce his preteen son to the gambling hall. Years before his tenth birthday, Hope would return to his mother "staggering and smelling of alcohol."[34] In 1981, Hope knew Andrew and Jackie Wilson only by their street names, "Geno" and "Bubbles."[35] The Wilsons knew Hope simply as "Ace."[36] The three shared gang affiliations and a reputation as habitual "stick-up men."[37]

Over the following four months, the Wilsons committed a series of armed robberies, often involving clever schemes or disguises.[38] On December 3, 1981, Andrew and Jackie entered the World Camera Shop at 115th Street and South Michigan Avenue. Pretending to be customers, the Wilsons pulled a gun and forced the shop owner, a clerk, and multiple patrons into a storeroom.[39] Within minutes, the brothers left with a reported $2,200 in cash—mostly from the pockets of the store's customers—and over $10,000 in camera equipment.[40] Kensington District patrolmen arrested the Wilsons less than a week later, the store's owner identified them in a lineup, and Area 2 detectives filed armed robbery charges.[41]

On parole at the time, Andrew Wilson should have been denied bail. Indeed, IDOC issued a warrant two days later.[42] Before then, however, Wilson paid a $1,000 bond and walked out of jail with no plans to return.[43] Somehow, the 5th District officers who arrested Wilson on December 7, the Area 2 detectives who interviewed him, the prosecutors who charged him, and the judge who set bail all failed to notice he was on parole. Indeed, Wilson's parole officer would not learn of her client's violation until seeing his face on the evening news months later.[44] Burge later admitted being both "unhappy with a couple of detectives" and "a little peeved at myself" for letting Wilson slip through their fingers.[45] Meanwhile, the Wilsons were due in court on December 10. Jackie arrived alone. Incredulous, the judge doubled Jackie's bail to $20,000—releasing him upon 10 percent payment—and issued a bond forfeiture warrant for Andrew.[46] Owing to a clerical error somewhere in the system, Andrew Wilson remained on the streets into the new year while he should have been locked up for violating parole.

Despite Wilson's recent run-in with the law, the twenty-nine-year-old continued to eke out a living as always—through deceit and theft. Growing more brazen, however, Wilson and crew courted violence. According to media accounts and court documents, Andrew Wilson, Edgar Hope, and possibly Jackie Wilson held up a South Side McDonald's on January 11, 1982. Accompanied by a female accomplice, Hope approached the counter and delivered a series of confusing orders to the eighteen-year-old clerk. Andrew waited outside for his cue. Reflecting the danger of the neighborhood, the restaurant employed not one, but two armed security guards—thirty-five-year-old Cook County Corrections sergeant Lloyd Wickliffe and twenty-nine-year-old Cook County Sheriff's Department investigator Alvin Thompson. Jolted from a dull routine, the guards responded to signals from the frustrated cashier and moved to confront Hope.[47]

Suddenly, Andrew Wilson stormed through the door, firing a shotgun blast into Sergeant Wickliffe, instantly killing the married father of three. Stunned, the other guard found himself shoved to the floor. Hope stood over him, smiling as he pointed the gun between Thompson's eyes. Moving to cover himself, Thompson received a bullet in the forearm instead of the forehead. Scattering, the terrified employees sought refuge in a locked basement while their attackers escaped with nothing more than the guards' firearms.[48] Within the hour, someone robbed another nearby McDonald's in similar fashion. The culprits put two more bullets into a part-time security guard and relieved the registers of $600 cash.[49] One month from the end of his criminal career, the McDonald's caper epitomized the high-risk, low-reward mentality that soon landed Wilson behind bars for the rest of his life.[50]

"It Must Have Seemed . . . an Open Season on Police"

January and February 1982 proved unusually bloody for Chicago law enforcement.[51] In addition to the shootings of Wickliffe and Thompson at the McDonald's on January 11, a veteran Youth Division officer named Edgar Clay had been injured a few days earlier during a struggle with a juvenile offender. On January 7, Clay was frisking a teenager accused of stealing property from Hyde Park Academy when the suspect attacked, knocking Clay to the ground and injuring his knee. Hospitalized with a blood clot in the leg, Clay died of a heart attack on January 25. He was fifty-one years old.[52] Eleven days later, someone shot and killed a CPD rookie on a Chicago Transit Authority (CTA) bus in Area 2, sparking a chain of events that would lead to the capture and torture of Andrew Wilson and the eventual downfall of Jon Burge.[53]

On the night of Friday, February 5, the police finally caught up with Wilson's companion Edgar Hope. At a busy transit station near the Dan Ryan Expressway, Hope boarded a westbound CTA bus around 10 p.m., already drunk on wine and high on marijuana and cocaine.[54] Climbing through a rear exit, Hope failed to notice an acquaintance of his named Charles Harris seated nearby, hiding his face behind a ball cap. When the bus reached the next stop, Harris rushed off and ran across the street to a parked police car. Harris told rookie patrolman James E. Doyle and his partner Robert M. Mantia that he spotted a man who robbed him at gunpoint last December. Advising the officers to be careful, Harris alleged that Hope had a warrant out for his arrest and was likely armed. The officers told Harris to jump in the back seat and the squad car eased from the curb.[55]

Officer Doyle edged the cruiser in front of the stopped bus at Lafayette Avenue and Seventy-Ninth Street, blocking its path. The three boarded the bus and Harris identified Hope sitting in an aisle seat wearing an ankle-length trench coat. With thick winter gloves, Doyle frisked Hope and found a plastic box containing drug paraphernalia. Satisfied, Doyle was leading the suspect to the door when Hope suddenly pulled one of two guns stashed in his waistband. Firing a stolen .38 revolver, Hope emptied the cylinder, sending one bullet into the chest of Officer Doyle and the rest careening through the crowded bus. Two of the dozens of passengers were hit, one with a critical shot to the head. Different accounts have Officer Mantia returning fire inside the bus or chasing Hope outside before shooting back. Either way, both men tossed spent revolvers within seconds. Hope then pulled a .357 Magnum taken from the McDonald's security guards weeks earlier. From behind a CTA shelter, Officer Mantia took aim with a backup weapon and dropped Hope with a final shot. Patrolman James Doyle, age thirty-four, died later that night. The police held Edgar Hope in custody at Cook County Hospital, where doctors treated him for a gunshot wound to the right torso.[56]

While Chicagoans debated the safety of public transportation, Andrew Wilson concocted a scheme to free Edgar Hope.[57] Driven by loyalty to a friend and fear of what Hope might divulge about the McDonald's robbery, Andrew and Jackie Wilson planned to don disguises, sneak into Cook County Hospital, and break Hope out, with armed force if necessary.[58] First, they needed supplies. On Tuesday morning, February 9, the Wilsons met with friends at the home of Donald White, a man they knew as "Kojak." Having outlined the plot to rescue Hope, Andrew, Jackie, and a friend named Derrick Martin left Kojak's house in a brown 1978 Chevrolet Impala they borrowed from their sister Roberta.[59] Driving along Carpenter Street, where White and Edgar Hope lived, they stopped and broke into a house mistakenly thought to belong to a police officer. Expecting to find guns, ammunition, badges, and police uniforms to wear to the hospital, they left with only a television set, clothing, liquor, and an assortment of bullets.[60] Returning to Kojak's house, they unloaded the loot and adjusted the plan, deciding instead to dress up as medical interns to enter Hope's room.[61] Back in the car, the Wilsons had just dropped off Derrick Martin when Jackie noticed a police cruiser in his rearview mirror.[62] The officer behind the wheel flashed overhead lights and motioned them to the curb.[63]

The two officers who stepped from the vehicle that afternoon had just left Officer Doyle's funeral at St. Denis Church, some four miles away, when they spotted the Wilsons' two-door Impala perform a minor traffic violation near the intersection of Eighty-First Street and Morgan Avenue.[64] Exiting the cruiser's passenger side was Patrolman William P. Fahey, a man whose life experience paralleled that of Jon Burge. Born within weeks of one another, Fahey and Burge grew up on Chicago's Southeast Side, attended rival high schools, served with the U.S. Army in Vietnam, joined the CPD in the early 1970s, and won multiple commendations. Rising higher in the ranks, Burge was married only to the job, while Fahey had a wife and three children.[65] With him that day was thirty-three-year-old Richard J. O'Brien, a physically fit, single patrolman described as a nice guy and a "tough cop."

The third son of a deceased Chicago police sergeant, Richard ignored his father's advice and mother's wishes to join the CPD, accumulating his own departmental honors over a nine-year career. Dressing for work, he proudly strapped his father's service revolver to his hip.[66] In February 1982, Fahey and O'Brien belonged to the newly created Gang Crimes South Unit, a special anticrime initiative launched by Mayor Jane Byrne. Yet they were not regular partners.[67] On Tuesday, February 9, O'Brien's sidekick and best friend called in sick to work for the first time in ten years to nurse a back sore from shoveling snow. Shift supervisors assigned Fahey to O'Brien's car instead.[68]

Not sensing danger, neither O'Brien nor Fahey bothered to radio in to dispatch before confronting the Wilson brothers.[69] While details remain contested, a basic account of what followed emerged from the memories of Andrew Wilson, Jackie Wilson, and Tyrone Sims, an eyewitness who watched the scene from the front window of a nearby home. Perhaps to keep the police from poking their heads inside the vehicle, Jackie Wilson stepped from the driver's side door and walked to meet the approaching officers. According to Andrew's later account, the "big dude"—O'Brien—questioned Jackie about someone having thrown a whiskey bottle out the window a block or so back. Jackie denied tossing anything. When he could not present a driver's license, O'Brien frisked him and moved to search the car.

Meanwhile, Andrew stepped into the street and spoke with the "little dude"—Officer Fahey—who demanded to search a jacket Andrew was holding. Knowing Fahey would find a pocketful of bullets, Andrew glanced over at O'Brien leaning into the car, scrounging the front seat, where the Wilsons had stashed a gun acquired in a home burglary. Facing yet another arrest, Andrew decided on a perilous path of action. With a sudden lunge, he reached for Fahey's belt, launching the two men into a terrifying wrestling match for the officer's loaded gun. Across the street, the eyewitness Sims watched the two men perform a deadly and silent dance on the snowy pavement. They slipped and fell to the ground. Wilson ripped the weapon from its holster, placed it against the base of Fahey's skull and fired.[70] Shoving the fatally wounded policeman's body off him, Andrew watched O'Brien remove himself from the driver's-side door and edge toward the back of the car, carrying the revolver found in the front seat. Andrew raised his arm and fired again, felling O'Brien with a shot from his partner's gun. When Jackie went to retrieve O'Brien's weapon, he noticed that the athletic patrolman was still moving. Andrew jumped onto the trunk and emptied his bullets into O'Brien from above. The brothers gathered all three handguns, scrambled into the car, and raced south down Morgan Street.[71]

News of the shooting spread quickly. The eyewitness Tyrone Sims ran to his kitchen and called the police, as did other nearby residents alerted by gunfire.[72] Andre Coulter, driving north along Morgan Avenue with Dwayne Hardin and another passenger, swerved to avoid a collision when the brown Impala tore from the scene. As they passed, Coulter noticed damage to the car's front grille, and Hardin got a good look at Andrew Wilson, smiling in the passenger seat. Coulter pulled to the curb and the three men stepped out. In front of them, the abandoned police cruiser stood silent sentry over the bodies of the two policemen bleeding out into the snow. Rushing to give first aid, there was little they could do. Dwayne Hardin climbed into the squad car, grabbed the radio transmitter, and shouted, "Help! Emergency—two police officers have been shot." Examining O'Brien's ruined body, Coulter could only comfort the dying man, placing a jacket underneath his head.[73] Hardin recalled, "He kept trying to get up, and I kept pushing him down. He knew he was dying. I went over to the other officer, and I knew he was dead." Within a few minutes, emergency vehicles began to arrive.[74]

Police Superintendent Richard Brzeczek, Mayor Jane Byrne, and members of the department's top echelon caught word of the tragedy only hours after filing out of Officer James Doyle's funeral. Brzeczek and Byrne made their way to Little Company of Mary Hospital in Evergreen Park, where police colleagues took the fallen policemen. The mayor stood vigil beside the officers' family for over three hours. Later that night, Byrne informed a crowd at a fund-raising dinner at the Conrad Hilton that it was a "sad day" for Chicago, reporting that O'Brien died shortly after arriving at the hospital while Fahey lay in a coma with severe brain trauma.[75] He passed away early the next morning.[76]

Manhunt for the Wilson Brothers

At City Hall on the afternoon of February 9, 1982, members of the Chicago City Council learned of the police shootings as they debated a controversial gun control bill.[77] The council had been drafting a limited handgun ban for weeks, a process pitting Mayor Byrne and her allies against a ragtag opposition, including independent black aldermen Clifford Kelley and Allen Streeter.[78] News of the attack on Fahey and O'Brien—coming only four days after the sensational gunfight on the Seventy-Ninth Street bus—landed in the lap of the City Council like a live hand grenade. Whether genuinely shaken by events or seizing political opportunity, the bill's supporters pounced, particularly former policeman Edward M. Burke, alderman of the Far West Side's Fourteenth Ward and chairman of the Police and Fire Committee.[79] Leading a moment of silence, the stentorian Burke let the gravity of the second and third police shootings in less than a week settle before continuing a public hearing on the gun ordinance.[80]

After City Council adjourned, the bill's opponents cried foul, accusing Burke and others of exploiting tragedy and hijacking the issue. Alderman Kelley, representing the South Side's Twentieth Ward, reminded reporters: "These men took the officers' guns. That's two more guns taken from legal gun carriers being used by criminals who can use [them] to invade the homes of innocent people who under the proposed gun ordinance would prevent them from owning a gun for protection." Voicing concern for his African American constituents, Seventeenth Ward Alderman Streeter added: "I am still opposed to this gun control ordinance even in the light of the recent shootings. If passed, it will only be enforced in the black communities and nowhere else."[81] Dismissing gun control as "people control," militant *Chicago Defender* columnist Russ Meek insisted that black Chicagoans amass firearms to fight white oppression and racial "annihilation."[82] The racial divide on gun control reflected the broader politics of Chicago in the early 1980s. As on other issues, the Fahey and O'Brien shootings split the city along familiar lines of race.

While City Council mourned and deliberated, Mayor Byrne displayed characteristic grit. For years, Byrne had trained under the best possible mentor, the late Richard J. Daley, whose death in 1976 cast her abruptly outside the Democratic machine.[83] In a stunning upset in the 1979 primary, however, Byrne toppled Daley's successor and clawed her way back to the top of the organization.[84] Once in office, Byrne pushed to head off political competition, particularly the late boss's son Richard M. Daley, by cultivating a tough reputation on matters of criminal justice. As Cook County State's Attorney from 1980 to 1989, the young Daley commanded the nation's second-largest prosecutor's office. While critics questioned Daley's qualifications, his role as Cook County's chief law enforcer afforded him law-and-order credibility that the mayor struggled to match.[85] Eager to show that she, too, was tough on crime, Byrne answered Daley by beefing up the police department.[86] If the police deaths of winter 1982 exposed Byrne to political rivals, they also presented her an opportunity to display fortitude.

Political considerations aside, Byrne took office in the middle of what many perceived as the most violent period in the city's 150-year history. In 1981 the *Chicago Reporter* labeled the 1970s Chicago's "deadliest decade," propelling the city's murder rate above both Los Angeles and New York City.[87] When Chicago's population ballooned from 109,000 to 2.2 million between 1860 and 1910,[88] the murder rate never rose above 7 per 100,000 residents. In the 1920s, the gang wars of Prohibition pushed the homicide rate to 14.6 per 100,000 before dropping to 7.9 by midcentury. In the 1960s, however, the murder rate shot upward, reaching 24 per 100,000 in 1970, 28.7 in 1980, and 32.9 in 1990.[89] No stranger to violence, by the 1980s Chicago seemed in the grip of panic. Yet if white fears of black criminality often drove policy decisions, studies revealed significant racial disparities in victimization. The growth in homicide rates disproportionately affected African Americans and Latinos.[90] With details often lost on ordinary residents, the crime wave traumatizing urban America during the last third of the twentieth century demanded a response from big-city mayors.

Indeed, elected officials' fortunes often rose and fell according to how they addressed the crime crisis. Accordingly, public relations determined much of Mayor Byrne's policy. Her most flagrant ploy came in 1981, when she and her second husband, media personality Jay McMullen, temporarily moved into a modified apartment in the notoriously violent Cabrini-Green public housing complex. Protected by a phalanx of police, Byrne failed to impress observers with recent safety improvements and briefly became the brunt of national jokes.[91] On matters of greater substance, the mayor's influence included setting an aggressive tone, pushing municipal ordinances, lobbying the state legislature, and managing the CPD. In a portentous decision, Byrne handed black voters a "slap in the face" by refusing to appoint acting superintendent Sam Nolan—the department's highest-profile black official—on a permanent basis.[92] Instead, she "kicked" Nolan "upstairs" into a largely honorary position and named Richard Brzeczek—a young, white political ally—as superintendent in January 1980.[93] Experimenting with new and reorganized units throughout her four years in office, Byrne emphasized antigang tactics, tightened security on public transportation, and moved to protect the elderly.[94] By 1981, she befriended 13th District commander Joseph McCarthy, whose reputation for harassing nonwhite youth won him the praise of supervisors and the enmity of local communities.[95] During a special meeting in his district in 1981, hundreds of residents demanded McCarthy's removal.[96] Complying, the mayor promoted McCarthy to Deputy Superintendent and placed him in charge of a powerful antigang unit reportedly orchestrated from City Hall.[97] A favorite of the mayor, McCarthy served as Byrne's personal representative on the force for the remainder of her term.[98]

When her police department came under attack in winter 1982, Byrne's ability to manage crisis and protect municipal employees was put to the test. Experiencing the deaths of the patrolmen Doyle, Fahey, and O'Brien with genuine emotion, she swore to use the Mayor's Office to assuage the pain of surviving families. Byrne knew firsthand the anguish of losing a loved one to senseless tragedy. Her first husband, U.S. Marine Corps Lieutenant William "Bill" Byrne, died in a plane crash in May 1959 when their only daughter, Kathy, was just eighteen months old. Recounting in her memoirs the moment she received word of Bill's death, Byrne broke the narrative chronology and jumped ahead to her "most hated" duty as mayor—consoling the bereaved family of "a slain police officer or a fallen firefighter." Recalling the police murders of 1982, Byrne wrote, "Sitting with the three families had drained me," as their grief was "beyond any comfort I could give." In an ominous digression, she added, "A mayor has great power." Yet the only example she gave involved sending bagpipes and a small orchestra to police funerals, her "personal way of saying thank you to the finest police department in America."[99] In addition to ceremonial trivialities, the office placed other, more concrete powers at her disposal as well.

In response to the shooting of Officers Fahey and O'Brien on February 9, 1982, Mayor Byrne and Superintendent Brzeczek authorized what would become Chicago's largest manhunt to date. Dispatching her personal representative to Area 2, Byrne placed Deputy Superintendent McCarthy in charge of the investigation. Stirred by the recent violence against police personnel, Burnside Headquarters was a hornet's nest. Hundreds of policemen swarmed about the old station house at Ninety-First and Cottage Grove.[100] McCarthy and Area 2 commander Milton Deas gave the job of directing the on-the-ground search to Violent Crimes Lieutenant Jon Burge, whose reputation for hands-on management was well known.[101] By 1982, it was an open secret that Lieutenant Burge and his midnight crew employed aggressive tactics to close cases.[102] Mayor Byrne, Superintendent Brzeczek, Deputy Superintendent McCarthy, and Commander Deas knew what they were getting when they unleashed Burge that emotional afternoon.[103]

Earlier that day, Jon Burge was detailing his car and enjoying some rare time off when an Area 2 Property Crimes detective scanned the car wash in search of the getaway vehicle. Encountering Burge, the officer briefed him on the shooting moments before supervisors messaged on an electronic beeper. Rushing to Area 2 headquarters, Burge spent most of the next five days near his desk, catching fragments of sleep in a second-floor office.[104] It had been only four days since he coordinated the investigation of Patrolman Doyle's shooting on Friday night. Members of the crime lab had transported the CTA bus to Area 2, passengers and all, to gather evidence and collect statements. Early Saturday, Burge had personally escorted Superintendent Brzeczek and other police brass through the mobile crime scene.[105] Burge must have impressed superiors with his handling of the investigation. When the deputy chief of detectives tasked him with apprehending the cop killers, Burge knew it was his "most important case," the kind of investigation that could make—or break—a career.[106]

While the police scrambled their forces, the Wilson brothers went into hiding. From the local news they learned authorities had a description of their car—a brown or burnt-orange, two-door, late-model sedan with damage to the right-front grille—that included a partial license plate.[107] The Wilsons took the vehicle to a repair shop to fix the damage and repaint the body, before ditching the Chevy in a garage. To elude capture, the brothers separated, steering clear of their home at 11409 S. May Street.[108] On Tuesday evening, Andrew called his friend Derrick Martin to brag about his exploits, urging him to watch the television news that night because he had shot two cops.[109] Wilson spent at least two of the next five nights at Willie's Beauty Salon, where he worked as a janitor. He bagged Fahey and O'Brien's pistols and the shotgun used in the McDonald's robbery and stashed them in the salon. Avoiding the search area, he rode the El train to the North Side, but wound up staying with a couple he knew on the West Side.[110] While local newspapers claimed the Wilsons went on a crime spree in their last days of freedom, the allegations were likely unfounded.[111] In the heated atmosphere following the arrest of two "professional criminals" and fundamentally "bad men," reporters fanned outrage by laying unsolved burglaries and armed robberies at the feet of the hated suspects."[112]

Considering the public mood, police efforts to locate suspects threatened to turn brutal. While Burge's detectives embraced aggressive and extralegal tactics, they also launched a more routine investigation. First, they interviewed the witnesses Sims, Coulter, and Hardin to get a description of the suspects.[113] They also determined the owner of a pair of eyeglasses left at the scene, linking them to Andrew Wilson through an optician who crafted lenses for state prisoners.[114] After matching bullets recovered from the slain officers with computerized serial numbers and handgun records, they identified Fahey's gun as the murder weapon.[115] In what CPD officials referred to as "the largest and best-organized search in the department's history," all twenty-four district commanders hunted the suspects' vehicle inside an exhaustive "grid-like" pattern.[116] On Wednesday, a top police administrator insisted that they employ a hypnotist to cull the full license-plate number from the memory of Tyrone Sims. Ignoring the State's Attorney's Office, who feared a defense attorney would claim the hypnotist planted testimony inside Sims's brain,[117] the hypnotist extracted a nonsensical set of letters and numbers incongruent with any Illinois license plate.[118] To jump-start civic responsibility, Mayor Byrne announced a $50,000 reward for news leading to arrest. The Fraternal Order of Police added another $10,000 to locate the men who killed two of their own.[119]

Alongside conventional efforts, however, the CPD also unleashed a five-day "reign of terror" on black Chicago.[120] With a mandate to leave no stone unturned, McCarthy, Burge, and other coordinators of the manhunt dispersed hundreds of angry police officers across the South Side. While Burge sent the small number of black detectives to the North Side or otherwise had them guarding witnesses away from the action, white detectives went to work.[121] Officers apprehended, manhandled, detained, interrogated, and generally harassed any African American male matching even the vaguest description of the suspects.[122] They stormed into homes without warrants, ransacked apartments, bombarded residents with threats and racial slurs, and held innocent citizens at gunpoint.[123] On the second floor of Area 2 headquarters, detectives held suspects for hours without access to lawyers, food, or a restroom. A few men accused detectives of physical and mental abuse.[124] For example, Donald "Kojak" White claimed that detectives beat him during an interrogation at police headquarters. According to White, when he refused knowledge of the crime, Detective Fred Hill told him, "I am tired of this fucking shit," draped a black garbage bag over White's head, and allowed others to beat him. Nearly losing consciousness, White recalled someone placing a gun in his mouth before he agreed to provide a statement dictated by his tormentors.[125] A female witness to abuse recalled a woman officer telling her, "We just buried our brothers," referencing the cop killings to justify excess.[126]

Eventually, Burge and his men got results. According to the *Chicago Sun-Times*, a "black elected official" arranged a secret meeting with Mayor Byrne and an anonymous tipster at a vacant City Hall on Friday evening. The informant told of two brothers bragging about killing cops and robbing a camera store.[127] In an unexplained coincidence, Sims falsely identified the Wilson brothers' friend Kojak as the shooter in a photo lineup the same day. Through Kojak's interrogation, detectives learned the names of Andrew and Jackie Wilson, present at his home before and after the shooting. Kojak led officers to Willie's Beauty Salon, where a morning search on Saturday, February 13, yielded the murder weapons.[128] After nightfall, Burge plotted a raid on a West Side apartment where it was believed the primary suspect lay hiding. Burge summoned detectives to a planning session sometime after midnight. They were closing in. Around 4:30 a.m. on Sunday, February 14, a mixed unit assembled at a park near a quiet garden-level apartment. Officers donned weapons and bulletproof vests from a CPD "war wagon" and received a final briefing before making their way to 5301 W. Jackson Boulevard.[129] Attorney Flint Taylor later likened the "show of force" to the infamous 1969 raid leading to the police killings of Black Panthers Fred Hampton and Mark Clark.[130] Under the cover of darkness, several unmarked police cars rolled up to the three-story brick condo, awakening Wilson with the sound of squeaking tires and crunching snow.[131] It was almost five o'clock in the morning—dawn of what would prove a pivotal day in the Chicago police torture scandal.[132]

February 14, 1982

As the policemen stepped from their cars, Wilson sat up from a couch and peered out a window. Adding to the tense atmosphere, Deputy Superintendent McCarthy had allowed several members of the Gang Crimes Unit to ride along based on their personal relationships with Fahey and O'Brien.[133] Alerted by the sudden clamor of officers working their way into the building, the apartment's inhabitants emerged from their bedroom. One of them turned on a light and scurried to open the door before the police clawed their way through. From the couch, Wilson watched a throng of cops wrestle the metal burglar bars blocking an open door. With weapons drawn, the police commanded Wilson to stand and place his hands on the wall. Frustrated by the security gate, officers sent for bolt cutters, prompting the female resident to hand over keys. "She was so scared," Wilson recalled, "she like handed them . . . just dropped them or something and ran back into the room."[134] In another account, Burge told of picking the lock with a "single-digit rake and tension bar" before entering.[135]

The officers surged in, led by Burge and McCarthy. The deputy superintendent and an Area 2 sergeant seized Wilson by both arms, dragged him around a corner, and threw his hands against a wall. As they rummaged Wilson's pockets, Burge—described by Wilson as "clean cut, heavy set"—asked if he had a weapon. Jerking his restrained left arm, Wilson gestured to a gym bag nearby, prompting McCarthy and the other officer to slam him to the floor. Thinking Wilson moved for a weapon, Burge recalled growing "con-

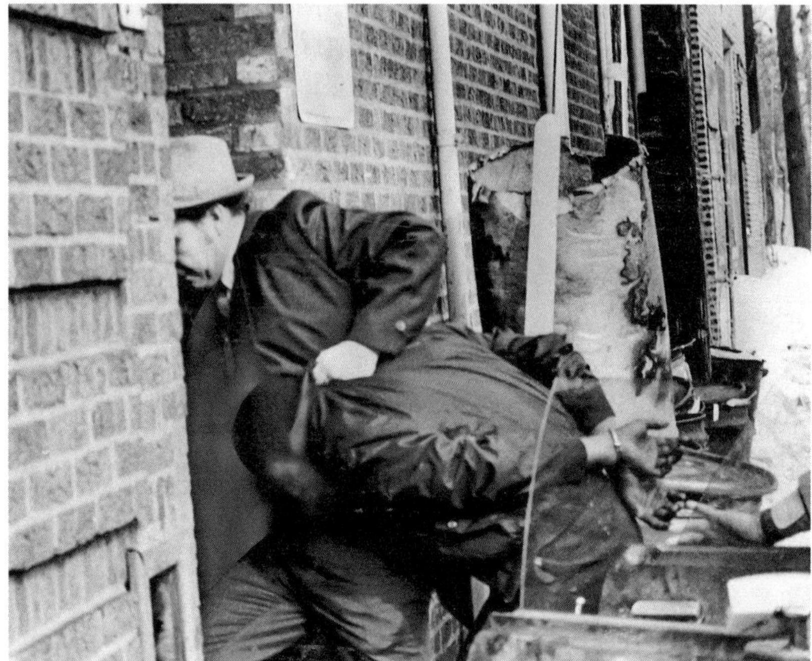

FIGURE 3 An unknown detective escorts Jackie Wilson through a backdoor of Area 2 headquarters, early morning, February 14, 1982, where he joined his brother Andrew Wilson in police custody. Frank Hanes/1982/Chicago Tribune/TNS.

cerned for my safety." Accordingly, he "knelt on the back of [Wilson's] neck, [and] placed all of my weight on him to pin him in that position."[136] Securing the gun, detectives handcuffed Wilson, lifted him up, tossed a jacket around him, put boots on his feet, and escorted him to an unmarked car. Burge later described the arrest as "anticlimactic," prompting one of Wilson's lawyers to speculate, "No doubt because Andrew did not offer them the opportunity to kill him."[137] Ordering Detective John Yucaitis to drive Wilson to Area 2, Burge warned: "Don't let anybody get to him. Don't let nobody talk to him. Treat him right." Wilson claimed Burge added, "We will get him at the station."[138] Sandwiched between two burly detectives in the back seat, the diminutive Wilson and four officers sat in silence for the twenty-minute ride to Burnside.[139]

According to an African American detective who worked at Area 2 during Burge's tenure, it was common for officers to perform a "shell game" with criminal suspects, bringing them through a back door so front-desk personnel would not have to lie when denying knowledge of prisoners' whereabouts.[140] As the sun began to rise over Lake Michigan, detectives brought

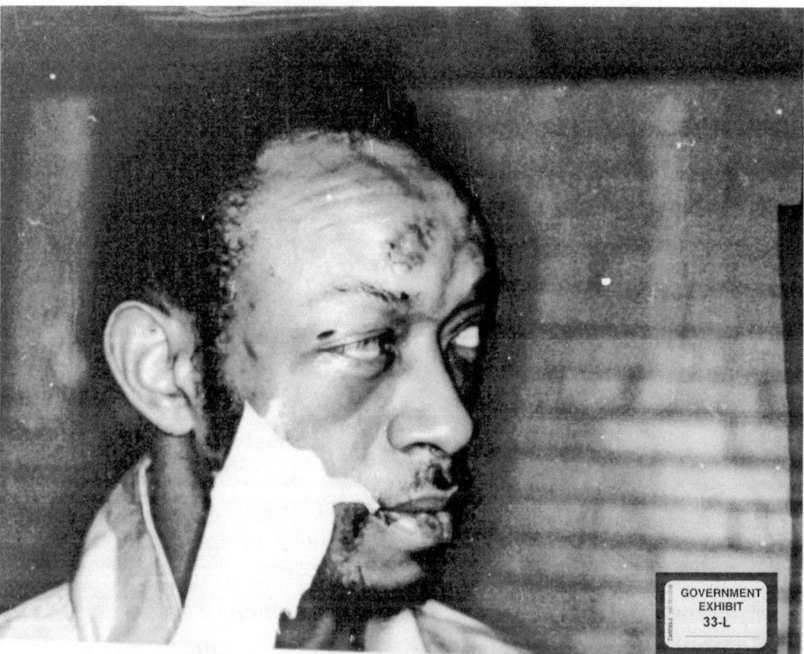

FIGURE 4 Public defender Dale Coventry captured photographic evidence of Andrew Wilson's injuries within days of his arrest on February 14, 1982. Marks of a beating appear on Wilson's face and head. U.S. Attorney's Office Trial Exhibit.

Wilson through the back, up a flight of stairs, and into a room on the second floor. Other officers—all white men in plainclothes—joined them. Someone removed Wilson's watch, threw it to the ground, and "stomped it," contributing to his confounded timeline of the day's events.[141]

With the door closed and Wilson still in handcuffs, the officers delivered a vicious beating. According to Wilson, they were "hitting me, kicking me, slapping me. Basically just beating on me." A punch knocked him to the floor, followed by a kick to the eye. From his knees, Wilson managed to fight back—"I bit one of them"—before someone removed a garbage liner from a trash can and forced it over Wilson's head, pulling it tight around his face from behind. Unable to breath, Wilson bit through the plastic to get air into his constricting lungs—"I was panicking." With the bag punctured, an officer hurled Wilson against a wall, breaking the window behind a metal screen and showering the floor with broken glass. They shoved him to his knees and beat him some more. An officer dragged a lit cigarette across his arm. The assault ended only when Lieutenant Burge entered and scolded them for causing visible damage. According to Wilson, Burge told them "he wouldn't have messed my face up" and locked him in an interrogation room alone to catch his breath.[142]

Wilson's account acquired minor inconsistencies over the course of multiple legal proceedings from 1982 to 1992—particularly relating to time, sequence, and detail—but the core narrative remained consistent. Following the initial beating, detectives sat Wilson in a chair against the wall of a small interrogation room and handcuffed his right wrist to a metal ring next to a hissing steam radiator. Burge and other detectives came and went throughout the morning and afternoon. At some point, according to Wilson, "[Burge] told me about I'm going to make a statement; that his reputation was at stake." A short time later, Detective Yucaitis and another officer came in carrying a brown-paper grocery sack, which Yucaitis placed at Wilson's feet. The detective reached down, rustled inside, and pulled out a hefty "black box," described by Wilson as having a "crank on the outside and two wires." Leaning forward, Yucaitis attached one wire to Wilson's left ear and another to his left nostril using metal alligator clamps extending from the wires. The cold, pinching grip of the wires portended worse to come.[143]

Apprehensive, Wilson first felt nothing. Yet when Yucaitis turned the crank, Wilson recalled, "It shocked me." The first jolt "didn't last long," however, because Wilson "kneed" Yucaitis "in between his legs" as he crouched in front of him, causing him to stop. With a jarring punch to Wilson's face, Yucaitis returned to his task. "Hollering" loudly, Wilson recalled "[the electric shock] wasn't that long because I was making too much noise to where [someone] knocked on the door and he stopped and it was over then." The door opened, Yucaitis set the bulky machine on the floor, and both officers stepped outside. Yucaitis returned, stuffed the black box into the brown bag, and left.[144]

Thinking Wilson had enough, Detective Patrick O'Hara took him to another dingy room where another white man in a suit, Assistant State's Attorney Lawrence Hyman, prepared to take a statement. When they sat Wilson across from Hyman, however, the battered captive looked up, muttering, "You want me to make a statement after they been torturing me?" Hyman asked, "What?" Wilson just stared back at him. Disgusted, Hyman allegedly barked at O'Hara, "Get the jagoff out of here." The detective agreed—Wilson was not ready to cooperate. O'Hara returned Wilson to the interrogation room, chained him back to the wall using two pairs of handcuffs, and left him alone to stew. Burge and Detective Fred Hill soon entered. Burge told Wilson it was "fun time" and pulled the shock box from the paper bag with purpose.[145]

After they had Wilson kick off his old boots, Burge placed a third pair of handcuffs around Wilson's ankles, clamped the electric wires to his captive's ears, and "started cranking." According to Wilson: "I grinded my teeth. Every time right off the bat when he was cranking I just rubbed it off, I rubbed it off." Restrained and nearly helpless, Wilson violently shook his head from side to side, desperate to rip the clamps from his ears with his shoulders "to stop it from hurting." Every time Wilson tore the clamps loose, Burge replaced them. Throughout the ordeal, the room remained eerily quiet. With his jaw clenched and teeth grinding, Wilson was unable to speak or shout. Meanwhile, Burge "wasn't saying nothin' . . . he was just cranking it." Finally, one of the wires slipped off and landed in Wilson's hand, nearly knocking him from the chair in pain. Wilson threw the clamp to the floor and Burge, frustrated, stopped cranking.[146]

Burge and Hill then unlocked one of Wilson's handcuffs from the ring and stretched his left arm across the steam radiator. Against the force of two solid men estimated at weighing over two hundred pounds each, Wilson resisted. "It took them—I'd say a minute," he believed, "but it took them a while to get me over this." They attached his left handcuff to a protrusion on the other side of the ribbed radiator, exposing Wilson to a nearly open-armed hug of a series of scalding metal pipes. The radiator resting under his chin, his chest nearly pressing against it, Wilson could not remember the steam burns, so focused was he on the terror of electric shock. Sitting calmly in the chair, Burge attached the clamps to Wilson's pinky fingers, where he could not rub them loose. His prisoner helpless, Burge "just kept cranking." Wilson started "hollering for help." Finally, he "spit some blood out" on the floor and Burge quieted the machine.[147]

When the cranking stopped, Burge reached into the bag and "got the other one out."[148] Wilson described the second device as "something like a hair dryer, round and black and had wires sticking out of it with a plug."[149] Wilson managed to stand up, still stretched across the radiator, his back to the room. "He run it between my legs," Wilson recalled. "He wasn't touching my privates. He just went between my legs and he would bring it up and he'd go back down. You can feel it . . . He's so close. It was a lot of current was coming out of that thing because I could feel it tingling. And he did that about . . . three or four times . . . [O]n the last pass he jabbed me with it. When he jabbed me with it, the force of it slammed me into the window . . . and knocked me back down to the floor." On his knees in pain, Wilson coughed a mess from his lungs. Burge glared, "You spitting blood on my floor?" Wilson insisted "No," and Burge removed him from the radiator, unlocked one pair of handcuffs, and sat him back down. Detective Hill, who had been kicking Wilson into the radiator throughout the shocks, wiped

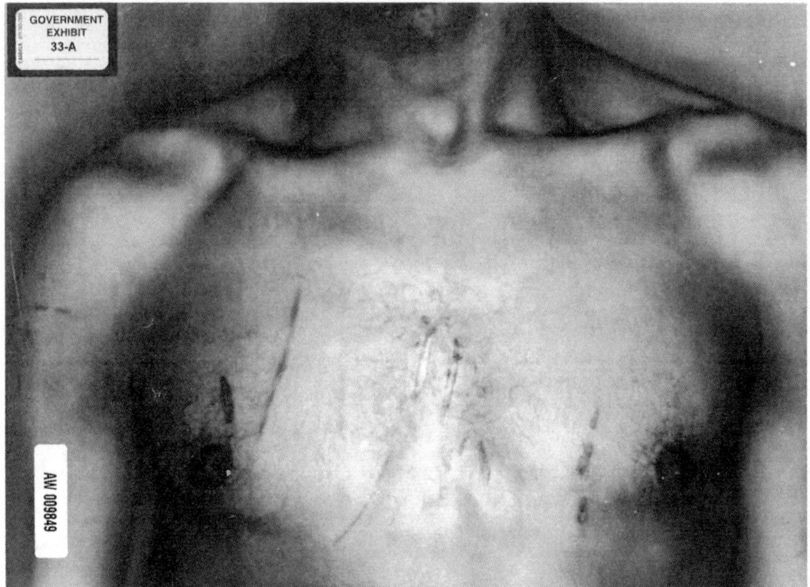

FIGURE 5 Burn marks on Andrew Wilson's chest support allegations that detectives forced his body against the hot pipes of a steam radiator at Area 2 on February 14, 1982. U.S. Attorney's Office Trial Exhibit.

blood from Wilson's face and cleaned the floor. Burge gathered his tools, leaving Wilson alone with his thoughts and pain.[150]

The worst was over, but Wilson's ordeal continued throughout the day. Around 3:00 p.m. detectives brought him to Area 1 headquarters, where Sims and another witness picked both Wilson brothers out of a lineup.[151] Jackie Wilson, too, had suffered a round of torture under Burge earlier that morning.[152] Andrew later claimed Burge threatened him again as they prepped the lineup, "playing with his gun in my mouth" and promising to end the abuse if he confessed. Finally, Wilson gave in, agreeing to "make a statement to keep from getting shocked anymore."[153] After the lineup, two detectives drove him back to Area 2, where ASA Hyman recorded the official statement. From 6:05 to 6:26 p.m., Wilson dabbed at a sore over his right eye while recounting his role in the shooting of Patrolmen Fahey and O'Brien. The requisite parties signed the documents and detectives arranged Wilson's transport to overnight lockup.[154] Before Wilson left Area 2 for good, however, Burge stuck his head in the room one last time, gloating, "They gonna fry your black ass."[155]

Around 10:00 p.m., two wagonmen—William Mulvaney and Mario Ferro—arrived to escort Wilson to a waiting police vehicle.[156] Mulvaney,

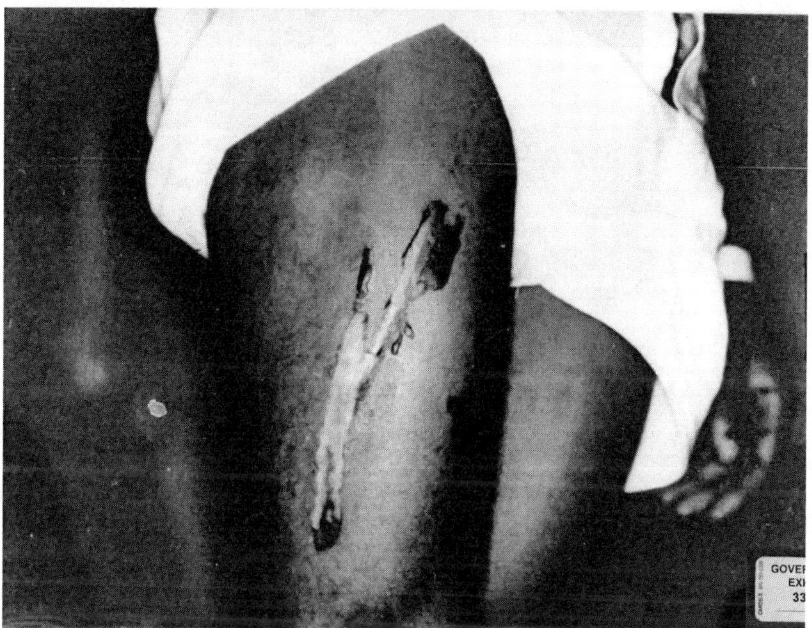

FIGURE 6 A burn on Andrew Wilson's thigh, allegedly caused by detectives' forcing him onto a steam radiator, February 14, 1982. U.S. Attorney's Office Trial Exhibit.

a purported friend of one of the slain officers, released his anger on Wilson as they walked. He squeezed Wilson's groin, tried to trip him down a flight of stairs, and threw him into a ceramic tile wall, tearing open an old forehead scar that started bleeding down his face.[157] According to Wilson, Detective Hill suggested they put Wilson in a cell with other prisoners "so it look like they beat me up."[158] Down at police headquarters, Mulvaney pistol-whipped Wilson on the back of the head as they rode an elevator. Seeing the damage, an unknown lockup keeper refused to accept the prisoner in such condition. Mulvaney and Ferro agreed to take Wilson to Mercy Hospital, where a doctor examined him despite the officers' refusal to holster their weapons on the ward floor. Before the medical staff finished, however, Wilson reported that the officers convinced him, "If I knew what was good for me I'd refuse treatment." They returned to the lockup. After more than sixteen hours of interrogation, physical abuse, and torture, Wilson fell asleep alone in a cell in plain sight of a guard.[159] He would spend the next twenty-five years—the rest of his life—behind bars.

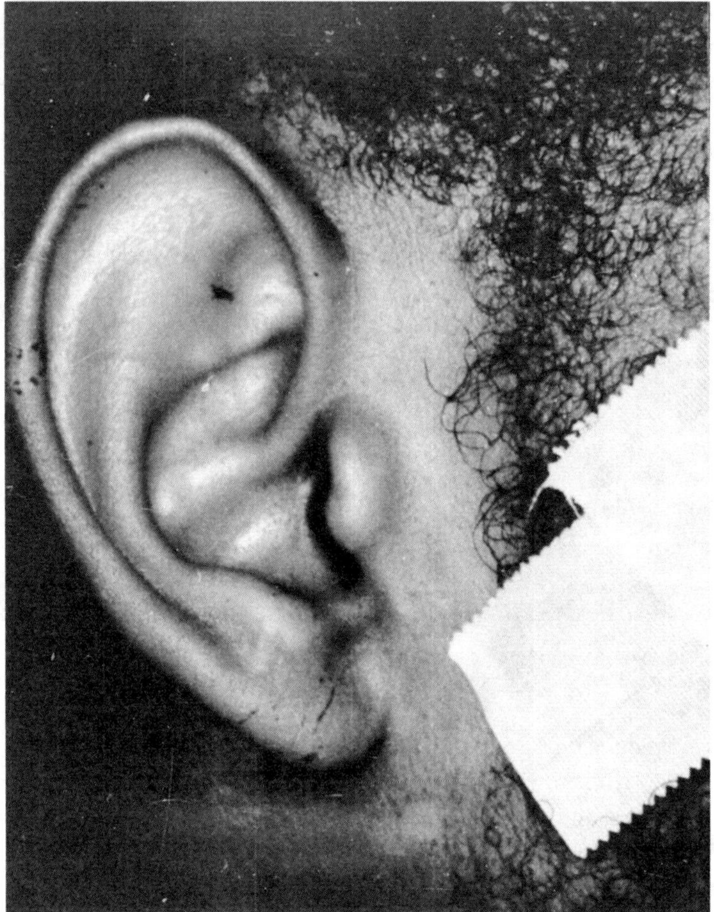

FIGURE 7 Next to a bandage on Andrew Wilson's face, spark burns and abrasions in the shape of alligator clips on his ear support Wilson's claims of electric-shock torture at Area 2 on February 14, 1982. U.S. Attorney's Office Trial Exhibit.

Living in a War Zone

As Wilson's treatment demonstrates, there was another side to winter 1982 beyond police victimization. Historian Adam Green reflected on "two very different stories presented" by the city's daily newspapers following the cop killings of February 9.[160] The *Chicago Tribune* and the *Chicago Sun-Times* largely lamented the killing of three dedicated patrolmen in less than a week, celebrated the "magnificent police work" leading to the suspects' capture, and criticized a system allowing such violence to flourish.[161] The black press went further, however, highlighting the police misconduct endemic before and after the officers' tragic deaths. The staff of the *Chicago Defender*, for example, refused to ignore the outrageous police abuse accompanying the manhunt for the Wilson brothers.

Well into March, nearly every issue of the *Chicago Defender* blamed police tactics for turning black communities into a "war zone."[162] Indeed, the extreme harassment of the manhunt only exacerbated fear and resentment already prevalent in targeted neighborhoods.[163] For nearly a week, law enforcement agents stormed into homes unannounced, violated due process, removed black men at gunpoint, and dragged them to Area 2 for abusive interrogation.[164] A participating officer likened the events to the Nazi Kristallnacht of 1938.[165] On the night of the police shooting, for example, upward of thirty officers rushed into the home of Francis Pinex, trained guns on her children, destroyed property, and arrested her eighteen-year-old son, Alphonso. Demonstrating the salience of race, she emphasized, "only 5 . . . officers were black."[166] Early the next morning, approximately seven officers broke into another home, threw sheets off a sleeping couple, and forced the family against a wall. An officer put a gun to a twelve-year-old girl's head and threatened her father with a shotgun. Refusing to provide identification or a warrant, officers removed eighteen-year-old Anthony Smith on suspicion. "We live in a war zone. The black community is under occupation," the Reverend Jesse Jackson told reporters.[167]

In referencing war, however, Jackson cited more than the manhunt. Rather, he alerted city leaders and apathetic whites to the everyday violence of the nation's racially motivated crime wars. According to Jackson, while war metaphors evoked combatants squaring off across a shared battlefield, Chicago resembled more an occupation. "Both groups got guns; both groups know how to shoot guns," Jackson conceded, yet "it is a known fact, that the police can, will, and do brutalize black people."[168] Chicago's black residents did not need reminding. "When white people kill blacks, no one cares," argued a letter sent to the black-owned *Chicago Metro News*, "but let a white policeman be killed, regardless of how rotten or dirty he might be, and it's a city-wide catastrophe." Another letter insisted: "There's just no way we can even tally up how many innocent blacks have been killed by white policemen. But the number of white policemen killed by blacks is so minute, that the count isn't even worth talking about. Things just don't balance out. Some folks just must think it's time for revenge." Others agreed: "I think all this crime against police is a reflection on police brutality. Black people are tired of being abused."[169] Indeed, many South Siders interpreted recent antipolice violence through the old adage of chickens coming home to roost.

As downtown newspapers posted the names of officers killed in the line of duty, black residents countered with a longer list of black men killed by the police. Condemning the recent manhunt, Russ Meek of the *Chicago Defender* criticized "the Mayor of Chicago and her police" and urged African Americans to arm themselves against "police brutality and police killings of blacks."[170] Meek cataloged recent victims of excessive force, identifying only names to an audience familiar with details. Meek's record included the Soto brothers, sixteen-year-old John and nineteen-year-old Michael, fatally shot by the police in two separate incidents in October 1969.[171] He referenced the infamous police assassination of Black Panthers Fred Hampton and Mark Clark later that year.[172] Also on Meek's list were Wallace Davis and Richard Ramey. Owner of a popular rib restaurant, Davis had called the police after subduing a pair of would-be robbers on March 8, 1976. Arriving officers mistook Davis for a suspect and shot him in the back.[173] Losing his gall bladder, part of his spleen, and 107 pounds as a result of the shooting, Davis sued the city for $15 million and joined movements for police accountability.[174] In July 1980, Richard Ramey died after three officers beat him during an arrest for smoking on a mass-transit platform. Considered one of Cook County's "most controversial police brutality cases," Ramey's death resulted in a rare criminal conviction of police officers. In December 1981, a judge found two of Ramey's attackers guilty of involuntary manslaughter, contributing to the divisive context of the Wilson case and its aftermath.[175]

Even as the black press meditated on recent police violence, conflict between officers and residents continued to make headlines. On Sunday night, February 21, an African American Muslim named Patrick Crigler held what he called a "one-man protest" against police brutality.[176] According to the *Chicago Defender*, Crigler dressed himself in a full-length white "African robe" and engaged in a "wild" shoot-out with the police from inside his home, firing nine shots from an M-14 rifle and destroying the engine of a police cruiser. Officers fired back, sending Crigler's wife and six children running for cover. After an hour-long standoff, police arrested Crigler before anyone was injured. A friend told reporters Crigler was "fed up with police harassment during the recent manhunt for two fugitives."[177] A few days later, police responded to a domestic violence call in West Englewood. A twenty-year-old white woman had gotten into a fight with her forty-five-year-old African American boyfriend, Fred Kemp, over who was to look after their two-year-old son. When the police arrived, they shot and killed Kemp—already paralyzed below the waist—in front of his girlfriend and infant child.[178]

While Andrew Wilson's experience fit patterns of violence between black residents and local police, the sensational details garnered special attention. On February 17, the *Chicago Sun-Times* published a front-page sketch of Wilson covered with bruises and bandages.[179] Wilson's public defender told reporters that officers beat his client in custody, adding, "He's not the only one in the black community who got worked over."[180] In an emotional op-ed, columnist Roger Simon chided the police manhunt: "I wonder what would have happened if two black cops had been killed by two white men. What would have happened if squads of shotgun toting black cops had kicked down doors in [white neighborhoods]? What would have happened if whites walking down Lake Shore Drive were suddenly thrown up against walls and roughly searched? Actually, I don't have to wonder. It would never happen." Yet Simon understood that political pressure dictated police action. "No Chicago Police superintendent is ever going to get in trouble because a few blacks get roughed up," Simon explained. "But he will get in trouble if he doesn't catch cop killers."[181] Not everyone shared Simon's misgivings. "Those people crying about police brutality are lucky to still be breathing," retorted an anonymous reader. "You bleeding hearts always cry about the niggers, but you never cry about the dead cops."[182] Lauding police "restraint," columnist Mike Royko reminded readers "there was a time when suspected cop-killers had little chance of being taken alive."[183] Parsing the "mixed emotions" aroused by the case, African American journalist Nate Clay doubted that many observers would raise "any serious questions about the beating of Andrew Wilson." After all, those who did were "roundly attacked." According to Clay, "Knowing that most whites would back them, the cops felt no particular reason to restrain their anger." Unable to hold perpetrators accountable, Clay expected police misconduct to continue.[184]

In the midst of a rare public reckoning, however, some locals fought to win justice for brutality victims. Led by black residents who were affected by the raids, civic groups and neighborhood associations held meetings and filed complaints with the department's Office of Professional Standards (OPS).[185] In a testament to its reputation for whitewashing investigations, however, the OPS reported only eighteen complaints. Citing a then-recent audit discovering a backlog of one thousand cases—including over one hundred missing—the *Chicago Defender* dismissed the OPS as a "sloppy, badly managed organization."[186] In contrast, Operation PUSH, the Afro-American Patrolmen's League, and the Cook County Bar Association had received over 230 complaints by February 18 alone.[187] On February 20, police Superintendent Brzeczek met with Jesse Jackson and fourteen local ministers.[188]

FIGURE 8 Illustrator John Downs sketched the Wilson brothers during a court appearance shortly after their arrest, placing Andrew Wilson's injuries on the front page of the *Chicago Sun-Times* on February 17, 1982. John Downs, Courtesy of Sun-Times Media.

In March, the ad hoc Community Commission on Law Enforcement held public hearings at which residents confronted law enforcement personnel.[189] The police watchdog group Citizens Alert formed the Coalition to End Police Abuse and Misconduct and arranged meetings with Superintendent Brzeczek and Mayor Byrne. Disappointed with results, coalition spokespersons skewered Brzeczek for his "total disinterest and disregard" for what he called "frivolous and garbage" complaints.[190] Leaving Byrne's office months later, Citizens Alert reported: "It is obvious that the Mayor is not concerned. . . . She defended the abusive tactics [and] equated good policing with instilling fear of police in innocent people to retain control." Announcing that she would "make no changes in response to the Coalition's critical recommendations," Byrne dug in until the crisis passed.[191]

Few observers expressed surprise when accountability mechanisms failed in the winter of 1982. Despite documented evidence of brutality, the OPS chose not to discipline CPD personnel, the State's Attorney and the U.S. Attorney decided not to charge officers, and interest in police watchdog efforts waned. In a measured understatement before a federal judge some three decades later, historian Adam Green assessed the response to the police terror of 1982: "One would have to conclude that those efforts failed."[192] Yet by meting out more than the acceptable level of abuse, Burge and his men crossed an invisible line. If Area 2 detectives could fend off allegations of electric shock and mock execution in pursuit of a cop killer, they could not avoid scrutiny forever. The police accountability movement, however, faced challenges of its own, including a complicit and secretive municipal government, a vengeful or apathetic public, and—in Andrew Wilson—an unsympathetic victim. While public officials sanctioned police torture that winter, survivors of police violence received their own affirmation, yet again, that the rights and safety of black people held little value in times of crisis.

For a variety of reasons, Andrew Wilson emerged as the poster child of the Burge torture scandal. Wilson's murder of two police officers was the highest-profile crime Burge ever investigated. Area 2 detectives got sloppy with Wilson and left physical marks. Wilson's record included clear photographs of injuries taken within days of the abuse.[193] Wilson was also among the first Burge survivors to sue the city. It was during the course of Wilson's civil trials that lawyers and activists learned of further victims.[194] The Wilson case inspired the first comprehensive piece of investigative journalism on the Burge scandal in 1990.[195] The CPD fired Burge on the strength of Wilson's testimony in 1993.[196] A federal jury relied in part on Wilson's posthumous testimony to convict Burge of perjury and obstruction of justice in 2010.[197]

The Wilson case also demonstrates how public officials came to sanction illegal interrogations at Area 2. During and immediately after the manhunt for the Wilson brothers, supervisors and administrators learned of the methods employed to secure confessions. Within a week of the abuse, Superintendent Richard Brzeczek received a letter from Dr. John Raba informing him of injuries discovered during an examination of Wilson at Cook County

FIGURE 9 Mayor Jane Byrne and CPD Superintendent Richard Brzeczek attend the funeral of Patrolman Richard J. O'Brien, St. Denis Catholic Church, Chicago, February 12, 1982. Dismissing allegations of police abuse during the manhunt for O'Brien and Fahey's killers, syndicated columnist Mike Royko argued, "The Wilsons . . . are not only alive, but appear to be healthy and sound of limb. That shows some restraint by the police, considering the frame of mind they must have been in after three cop funerals in a week." Mike Royko, "Celling the Idea of More Jail Cells: Some Arresting Ideas," *Chicago Sun-Times*, February 17, 1982. Jerry Tomaselli/1982/Chicago Tribune/TNS.

Jail. Lest the superintendent fail to appreciate the gravity of the allegations, Raba included, "[Wilson] also stated that electrical shocks had been administered to his gums, lips, and genitals."[198] Brzeczek claimed he confronted two deputy superintendents, the chief of detectives, and Area 2 commander Milton Deas with the allegations but received only "a lot of blank faces."[199] On February 25, Brzeczek sent a copy of Raba's letter to State's Attorney Richard M. Daley, assuring the county's chief prosecutor he would not investigate the allegations if Daley's office thought it might "jeopardize the prosecution's case" against Wilson.[200] In 2006, special prosecutors investigating Burge told Daley, "It is our understanding that this letter was received by your office." Asked if he became aware of the letter at the time, then mayor Daley admitted, "Yes, I did."[201] In 1982, Brzeczek initiated an OPS investigation that went nowhere.[202] Daley ignored the allegations and allowed prosecutors to admit tainted confessions in the Wilson brothers' subsequent criminal trials.[203]

Despite her denials, Mayor Jane Byrne likely learned of the torture of Andrew Wilson as well.[204] Years later, Superintendent Brzeczek insisted he called the mayor in February 1982 to let her know Wilson was in custody, but he could not be certain he disclosed Dr. Raba's allegations.[205] However, Byrne's reputed representative on the force, Deputy Superintendent Joseph McCarthy, was allegedly present at a meeting of command personnel in which Brzeczek waved the Raba letter, asking, "How could this happen?"[206] McCarthy—who oversaw the search for the Wilson brothers but denied any such meeting—earned a reputation for aggressive tactics long before Byrne promoted him.[207] Moreover, there is no evidence the mayor disapproved of how her department conducted the manhunt. Byrne received regular progress reports from McCarthy and actually visited Area 2 more than once during the search. Marking the only time in a twenty-year career that Burge recalled receiving a visit from a Chicago mayor during an investigation, Byrne personally encouraged detectives' efforts to locate the culprits.[208] In a series of anonymous letters written under a CPD letterhead, Andrew Wilson's lawyers from the People's Law Office later received insider information that blew the torture cases wide open. In one note, a secret police source insisted, "Mayor Byrne and State's Attorney Daley were aware of the actions of the detectives" and "ordered that the numerous complaints filed against the police as a result of this crime not be investigated."[209] At the very least, it is unlikely the mayor remained ignorant of Wilson's abuse during her term. Allegations appeared both in the press and in Wilson's pretrial testimony prior to Byrne's leaving office in 1983.[210]

The tragic killing of local law enforcement personnel in the winter of 1982 created the crisis necessary to officially sanction the Area 2 torture regime, then entering its second decade. Whereas public officials could plausibly deny knowledge of Burge's methods in the 1970s, few could claim ignorance after 1982. Balancing the desire to bring cop killers to justice on the one hand and preserving civil liberties on the other, officials chose the easier route and embraced extralegal tactics. Retired Area 2 detective Doris Byrd claimed it was an "open secret" in February 1982 that officials ordered Lieutenant Burge to do "whatever he had to do to clear [the Wilson] case." According to Byrd, the mandate came straight from the top—"The mayor of Chicago . . . Jane Byrne."[211] Rather than face punishment for abusing suspects, Burge was rewarded first with the opportunity to make a name for himself during the manhunt. Second, he was given a public commendation for his role in closing the case.[212] Finally, he was later promoted to commander of Area 3, where abuse continued into the early 1990s.[213]

Before 1982, Area 2 detectives operated a torture regime in secret, even as rumors circulated in surrounding neighborhoods and criminal courtrooms. Weighing the consequences, Burge and his men might have wondered what trouble they would get in if evidence of abuse surfaced. In February 1982, however, supervisors learned of widespread misconduct—including coerced confessions and electric-shock torture—and looked the other way.

PART II

4

"Before Our Communities Become Virtual Armed Camps"

In December 1969, an African American man from the South Side of Chicago named Leonard Richardson filed a complaint with the Chicago Police Department (CPD). A month earlier, two white officers had stopped Richardson on the way to the hospital for driving a car with a cracked windshield and broken taillight. According to Richardson, officers berated, frisked, and bullied him while his pregnant wife went into labor in the passenger seat. In a letter to police superintendent James B. Conlisk, Richardson acknowledged the need for vigilance, particularly "with times being as difficult as they are, with tensions at an all-time high, and with general havoc a part of our daily life." But, he added, police misconduct must not go unchecked. "As the father of eight, as a husband trying to provide for a family, as a leader in my church, community and social and civic groups, I too echo the cry of 'law and order,'" Richardson pleaded, "but I also feel that the words in themselves mean nothing unless tempered with the word 'justice.'"[1] With this letter, Richardson epitomized the spirit of local campaigns to improve policing in Chicago's African American, Latino, and poor white neighborhoods in the 1970s. Desperate for security in a violent decade, ordinary black residents and community leaders demanded a better war on crime, one that protected law-abiding citizens, respected the constitutional rights of criminal suspects, and catered to the needs of local people.

Shifting perspective from Area 2 detectives, this chapter explores how ordinary Chicagoans reacted to competing threats to public safety after 1965.[2] While the city's poorest neighborhoods confronted a vaguely defined urban crisis, the most sustained solution—greater law enforcement—often made things worse. Underscoring the agency of local people, however, widespread community activism for police accountability paralleled the criminal justice crackdown. Indeed, grassroots organizations addressed a series of overlapping emergencies in the 1970s and 1980s, particularly rampant street crime and police misconduct. Insisting that black communities were both "over-policed and under-protected,"[3] a diverse network of activists fought to transform criminal justice in Cook County. Few did more than Citizens Alert, Chicago's only permanent organization engaged in the daily fight against police abuse. Meanwhile, the police torture crisis at Area 2 evolved after February 1982, as detectives under the command of Lieutenant Jon Burge grew less selective in targeting suspects, leading to several wrongful convictions. By 1989, Burge had been promoted to commander and placed in charge of Area 3 on the Southwest Side, where new torture allegations surfaced, including a rare Burge-related case involving a Latino victim.[4] When litigation brought by a torture survivor introduced public details of abuse that summer, Chicago's established network of veteran activists organized an immediate response.[5]

The Urban Crisis and the Criminal Justice Crackdown

The urban crisis, as a political idea, was a 1960s invention. Sometime during the Kennedy administration, an influential coterie of pundits and policy makers awoke to a new realization that something was seriously wrong with the nation's cities. Helping burst the bubble of postwar optimism, Michael Harrington's *The Other America*, published in 1962, helped expose an obvious paradox.[6] Despite unprecedented prosperity, pockets of poverty and hopelessness continued to blight large portions of the American metropolis.[7] Confident in the efficacy of progressive government, experts set out to adapt urban reform traditions to the style and scale of the dawning space age. Of course, the struggling mass of people living and working in American cities long understood the challenges of urban life. Kennedy-era technocrats merely arrived late, if eager, to an ongoing discussion. With an optimism born of privilege and a habit of success, liberal elites turned their expertise to solving the problems of the modern city. Within a few years, a repackaged articulation of an old problem—what contemporaries referred to as the urban crisis—emerged as a bipartisan topic of conversation across the United States.

In the 1960s and 1970s, however, the urban crisis meant different things to different people and those meanings changed over time. Following Harrington's lead, early theorists questioned the collective morality of ignoring poverty in a nation of wealth. Yet recurring urban rebellion each summer after 1964 tempered idealistic policy makers with practical emergency. By the late 1960s, the urban crisis became synonymous with "lawlessness."[8] While political conservatives railed against civil disobedience, crime, and disorder, liberals presumed that social reform would preempt civil unrest before it began.[9] By the mid-1970s, presidents Richard Nixon and Gerald Ford cited a string of quiet summers and plateauing crime rates to declare victory over the urban crisis or deny its existence altogether.[10] Objecting, liberals insisted the problem was always about more than just "riots and robberies."[11] Economists, meanwhile, focused on "cash flows and unbalanced budgets."[12] Some observers denied the crisis completely. In 1966, former assistant secretary of labor Daniel Patrick Moynihan attributed new grievances to "higher standards."[13] Similarly, conservative political scientist Edward C. Banfield blamed a spate of "spurious" outrage on "rising standards and expectations."[14] Sociologists Francis Fox Piven and Richard Cloward suggested that administrators could easily solve municipal problems if they would just stop pandering to the racist fears of constituents.[15] Others saw crises over every horizon. By the late 1970s, suburban boosters hosted stops along the "Urban Crisis Tour," an academic lecture series on containing inner-city pathologies.[16]

With important exceptions, policy makers' take on the urban crisis favored a white, middle-class perspective.[17] Implicit in many contemporary analyses, fixing the American city meant enticing white homeowners and businesses not to leave. In a 1966 interview, for example, Moynihan refused to admit that policy makers' main goal was to "hold the white middle class in the city." Moments later, however, he added, "Let us say that measures could be taken to make the city attractive to people of different income levels and different circumstances."[18] In 1970, Banfield conceded, "The fact is that until very recently most of the talk about the urban crisis has had to do with the comfort, convenience, and business advantage of the well-off white majority and not with the more serious problems of the poor, the Negro, and others who stand outside the charmed circle."[19] While the needs of black communities demanded attention, white, middle-class interests took precedent. Accordingly, policy makers prioritized crime and law enforcement above competing concerns.

Long before Michael Harrington and others alerted whites to the urban crisis,[20] however, black journalists, academics, and politicians catalogued a breadth of related hardships.[21] A partial list includes concentrated poverty, unemployment, low wages, racial segregation, inadequate housing, overcrowding, inferior schools, crumbling infrastructure, spotty municipal services, credit shortages, substandard health care, political corruption, pollution, isolation, white violence, substance abuse, domestic violence, gang proliferation, crime, and police brutality.[22] While decades of reform produced limited results, fully resolving these issues required fundamental transformation of American institutions. Ideologically opposed, lacking political capital, or simply unimaginative, most policymakers resisted radical change. Instead, politicians and administrators rallied around a rare set of issues enjoying bipartisan support—crime control.[23]

Indeed, crime panic dominated public discourse in the late 1960s and 1970s. In Chicago, Renault Robinson of the Afro-American Patrolmen's League conceded in 1972, "Everybody agrees on both sides that there is a horrible crime problem in this city; moreover, no one has found a solution."[24] If white conservatives led cries for law and order, however, black communities also demanded state action.[25] After all, not only did Chicago experience a dramatic rise in violent crime rates after 1965; the increase in murders was "demographically concentrated" among young black males.[26] According to the Illinois Criminal Justice Information Authority, between 1965 and 1981 African Americans comprised approximately one-third of Chicago's population but 70 percent of its murder victims.[27] While the white murder rate barely moved and never rose above 8 per 100,000, the black murder rate grew to "a whopping" 56 per 100,000 in 1970, easing slightly to 49 per 100,000 in 1980.[28] Describing murder as a modern "black plague," the *Chicago Reporter* revealed in 1981 that while "predominantly white, middle-income areas of the city remain virtually unscathed by violent crime," over 40 percent of Chicago murders occurred within only seven of the city's twenty-four police districts. These "veritable battlegrounds" included areas of the city that were predominantly black and poor.[29]

Grasping for solutions, local politicians settled on gun control. By the late 1970s, academics reported increased gun ownership among street gangs and greater use of firearms during robberies and assaults.[30] In 1977, the University of Chicago's Center for Studies in Criminal Justice reported, "It is clear from this data that much of the increase in homicides in Chicago from 1965 to 1974 can be accounted for by the addition of many more homicides with guns."[31] The data supported local speculation. Eager to curb the "free wielding use of cheap and easily accessible handguns," in 1975 Chicago Urban League director James W. Compton called for immediate legislation before "black on black crime reached epidemic proportions."[32] According to the *Chicago Reporter*, at least four hundred thousand handguns circulated in the 1970s, roughly one for every eight residents.[33] Reducing stockpiles, however, never seemed viable. While the City Council passed a stringent handgun ban in 1982, the ordinance proved difficult to enforce and later fell to constitutional challenge.[34] Frustrated with local efforts to alleviate the urban crisis through crime control, Chicagoans also looked to the federal government.

In the 1970s, however, federal policy makers grew less inclined to answer the urban crisis with broad reform or social welfare. Reviewing a decade of collective hand-wringing over the plight of the American city, National Urban League executive director Vernon Jordan Jr. denounced the inaction of President Jimmy Carter in fall 1977. "The so-called urban crisis," Jordan lectured, "[had] become almost a cliché, stripped of meaning by repetition and misunderstanding." Rejecting the empty rhetoric of the Washington beltway, Jordan reminded listeners that "the urban crisis has a human face to it," often with a dark complexion. Castigating policy makers for scapegoating the poor, he accused politicians of facilitating blight to justify urban renewal and gentrification. "If our cities are dying," Jordan insisted, "it is not through natural death or even self-inflicted suicide; it is through local policies aimed at killing inner-city neighborhoods that they may be reborn for the benefit of the well-off." Weary of endless discussion, he demanded action on behalf of black and poor residents. "Cities have to be saved, not for those who abandoned them and then changed their minds, but for those who live in them today," Jordan concluded.[35]

While the urban crisis involved a complex range of problems, the political climate favored narrow solutions. Obsessed with crime, local politicians answered with attitude and repression. Washington responded with money. By the late 1960s, years of protests, assassinations, and disorder begot near "hysteria" nationwide, prompting police departments to demand more training, personnel, and hardware.[36] The Johnson administration placed a tentative toe in the water with the Law Enforcement Assistance Act of 1965, a preliminary foray into the federal financing of local law enforcement.[37] Three years later, Congress passed the Omnibus Crime Control and Safe Streets Act of 1968, expanding the Law Enforcement Assistance Administration (LEAA) into a giant clearinghouse for the disbursement of federal funds. According to historian Elizabeth Hinton, by the time the LEAA folded in 1981, the agency "had funded roughly 80,000 crime control projects and awarded 155,270 grants amounting to nearly $10 billion in taxpayer dollars," with nearly 75 percent of funds going to local police departments.[38] By the mid-1970s, *Chicago* magazine reported that federal revenue sharing programs, including the LEAA, indirectly footed the bill for a sizable portion of Chicago police salaries.[39] As police departments procured an array of paramilitary equipment, including automatic weapons, bulletproof vests, armored assault vehicles, and helicopters, critics decried the overwhelmingly repressive nature of the program. "The police are being armed to the teeth," warned *The Nation* in 1970.[40]

Carried out with unusual bipartisan fervor, the criminal justice crackdown of the late 1960s proved the most sustained response to the postwar urban crisis. While African Americans demanded relief from the crime wave that disproportionately ravaged Chicago's South and West Sides after 1965, government action often devolved into an indiscriminate assault on black communities. Indeed, as the 1960s gave way to the 1970s, the war on poverty withered and the war on crime thrived.[41] Where urban policy makers had once advocated remedy, reform, and rejuvenation, they instead embraced police, prosecutors, and prisons.[42] Anticipating that a crime war would bring atrocities, however, black residents, community leaders, and their white allies made simultaneous demands for police accountability.

The Chicago Campaign for a Better War on Crime

Even as authorities launched a criminal justice crackdown in Chicago after 1965, a loosely connected network of individuals and organizations sustained collective resistance to both rising street crime and endemic police misconduct. Marking a new peak in an old tradition of struggle, temporary organizations representing various interests worked independently and together to make communities safe throughout the 1970s, 1980s, and beyond. This fluid social movement included established civil rights organizations, black nationalists, street gangs, public housing tenants, women's groups, gay rights activists, lakefront liberals, religious congregations, government officials, academics, journalists, civil rights attorneys, bar associations, black police officers, crime victims, survivors of police abuse, and their families. By the 1980s, police accountability movements were a fixture of Chicago politics. When news broke of the Jon Burge police torture scandal in 1989, veteran activists mobilized to stop torture, free the wrongfully convicted, and punish perpetrators.[43] While mass incarceration and racial inequality defined the criminal justice system throughout the last third of the twentieth century, community activists cultivated resistance and compiled an impressive list of accomplishments.

At least four broad phenomena contributed to the persistence of social movements for public safety and police accountability after 1965. First, ongoing traditions of racist policing conditioned local people to concentrate on improving law enforcement. Indeed, black Chicagoans had always fought to improve policing in their communities, even if, as Simon Balto argues, "their criticisms largely fell on deaf ears."[44] Second, the Watts rebellion in California in August 1965 focused national public attention on the explosive implications of police brutality as never before. Triggered by a routine confrontation between white patrolmen and black residents, Watts and other civil disorders highlighted the stakes of improving police-community relations nationwide.[45] Third, rising crime in Chicago intensified local anxiety, increased pressure on community leaders, and magnified the role of the police, particularly in black neighborhoods, where much of the crime increase occurred.[46] Finally, an emerging war on crime generated outrage at police excess, punctuated by national assaults on the Black Panther Party and other radicals between 1967 and 1972. Coordinated by the Federal Bureau of Investigation (FBI) and local police, efforts to neutralize the radical Left affirmed activists' fears of a rising "police state" and helped recruit ordinary people to the movement for police accountability.[47]

As national news focused attention on race and policing, however, social movements continued to prioritize local efforts. For example, a decade-long fight against a controversial stop-and-frisk policy in Chicago demonstrated the pull of immediate concerns. In 1965, an African American judge freed on a technicality two Latino men accused of slashing a white off-duty police officer with a broken bottle.[48] Within weeks, the Illinois General Assembly drafted a bill allowing officers to "stop and frisk" anyone suspected of committing a felony.[49] While Democrats stalled passage and Governor Otto Kerner issued a veto in August 1965, persistent Republicans touted a "total war on crime" and introduced similar legislation in January 1967.[50] Capping a "burst in anti-crime actions," legislators passed the bill in July 1968.[51] Unpopular on Chicago's South Side, stop-and-frisk inspired black police officers to announce formation of the Afro-American Patrolmen's League and publicly condemn the policy.[52] In 1969, the Chicago Urban League and the Kenwood-Oakland Community Organization accused the CPD of abusing stop-and-frisk to harass street gangs.[53] Undeterred, officers told the Mayor's Office in 1972 that stop-and-frisk "helped them to apprehend criminals and to confiscate guns."[54] When civil rights groups recruited State Representative Harold Washington to repeal the bill, the Fraternal Order of Police rallied a successful defense.[55] Citing the 1968 ruling in *Terry v. Ohio*, the U.S. Supreme Court further buoyed stop-and-frisk in June 1973, impeding legal challenges in Illinois.[56] Despite defeat, the campaign invigorated local resistance to the criminal justice crackdown and trained activists' attention on local policy.[57]

For decades, self-professed "responsible" black organizations, including the National Association for the Advancement of Colored People (NAACP) d the Chicago Urban League (CUL), provided an organizational base for confronting law enforcement.[58] Yet many observers criticized the civil rights establishment for its moderate agenda, middle-class aspirations, and relationship to white elites.[59] By the late 1960s, the Black Panther Party (BPP) modeled an alternative vision. Founded in Oakland, California, in 1966, the BPP disseminated a radical critique of state power and influenced struggles for police accountability across the United States. Characterizing the police as an army of occupation, the BPP crafted its Ten-Point Program, focused heavily on criminal justice. Point 7 called for the "immediate end to police brutality and murder of black people." Point 8 demanded "freedom for all black men held in federal, state, county, and city prisons and jails." Point 9 insisted "all black people when brought to trial . . . be tried in court by a jury of their peer group or people from their black communities."[60] According to cofounder Huey P. Newton, the Panthers "emphasized" police brutality because it was "a major issue in every black community."[61] Unlike the NAACP and the CUL, the BPP grounded its critique of law enforcement in Marxist, anti-imperialist rhetoric and explicitly identified with alleged criminals.[62] As punishment for impugning local police, practicing armed self-defense, and modeling Black Power in action, dozens of Black Panthers suffered harassment, imprisonment, serious injury, and death.[63]

In Chicago, activists Bobby Rush and Bob Brown recruited a charismatic young organizer named Fred Hampton to help secure an Illinois Chapter of the Black Panther Party in spring 1968.[64] Raised in the suburbs, Hampton was a gifted orator and a "fearless" presence among West Side militants.[65] Under Hampton's leadership, the Chicago chapter grew in numbers and influence throughout its first year, riding a wave of "national notoriety" that helped draw recruits to the Panthers wherever they appeared.[66] Dedicated to serving the people, the Panthers offered a number of survival programs, including free health clinics, free busing to state prisons, and free breakfast for children.[67] In 1969, the Chicago Panthers organized a local Rainbow Coalition of working-class radicals from a variety of backgrounds.[68] Historically divided by racial hostility, African Americans, Latinos, and poor whites united around shared experience with police brutality.[69] Under Hampton's direction, the Panthers' collaboration with groups like the Black P Stone Nation, the Young Lords Organization, Students for a Democratic Society, the Young Patriots, and Rising Up Angry represented an apex of interracial organizing around issues of race, class, and community control of police.[70]

Preferring to focus on community service, however, the Chicago Panthers exhausted resources responding to police harassment.[71] According to local activists, police orchestrated over thirty raids on BPP offices nationwide between 1967 and 1969, "with equipment smashed, food and medicine destroyed, money taken," 20 Panthers killed, and 247 arrested—all of this likely undercounted.[72] In Chicago, police action against the Panthers throughout 1969 included harassment, entrapment, mass arrests, multiple raids of BPP headquarters, destruction of property, and armed assault. In retaliation for police shootings that left several Panthers dead or wounded, party member Spurgeon Jake Winters ambushed a group of patrolmen on November 13, 1969, injuring nine and killing two before succumbing himself to police gunfire.[73] On December 4, 1969, fourteen officers working under State's Attorney Edward V. Hanrahan raided a West Side apartment on the pretense of executing a search warrant. Unleashing a fifteen-minute barrage of bullets, officers killed twenty-one-year-old Fred Hampton and twenty-two-year-old Mark Clark and seriously injured four others.[74] While officials characterized the incident as a shoot-out with dangerous revolutionaries, formal inquiries accused officers of deliberate assassination.[75]

Meant to quell a rising insurgency, the assassination of Fred Hampton instead energized movements for police accountability.[76] While the Black Panthers enjoyed wide popularity among working-class blacks and radical whites, not everyone warmed to their provocative posturing. In moderate circles, the Panthers represented a regrettable militant turn in the black freedom struggle, a threat to the politics of respectability, and a glamorization of hoodlumism.[77] To conservatives, however, the Panthers represented something worse—an existential threat to the established order. By ruthlessly repressing the Panthers—and disrupting their popular survival programs—authorities united progressive people who, while not in full agreement with the BPP, recoiled at naked brutality. "Whatever the Panthers believe in," argued the director of the Chicago Urban League, "they shouldn't be shot down like dogs in the street."[78] Jesse Jackson agreed, concluding, "If it happened to Fred, it could happen to us."[79] Averse to armed revolution, liberals and moderates appreciated the need for police vigilance but balked at the CPD's racist excess.[80] After 1969, residents of high-crime communities learned to demand greater policing and greater accountability in the same breath.

In the new decade, even mainstream civil rights organizations asserted that law and order without accountability imperiled justice. In 1970, for example, the CUL launched Action for Survival, joining over forty community groups in a "war on all crime in black Chicago."[81] Denouncing black criminals, the CUL also highlighted the role of local whites. According to Action for Survival, white criminals cornered the market in illegal drugs and firearms, white police officers brutalized black residents on a "daily" basis, all-white juries condemned black defendants, and a white "Criminal Syndicate hover[ed] over black Chicago like a huge vulture waiting to pick our bones dry."[82] Seeking protection, however, activists hesitated to call on police. Indeed, Action for Survival described black Chicago as "overwhelmed by crime on the one hand and official repression on the other." Pursuing relief from both, speakers insisted: "Protection for ourselves and our youth must be provided on *our* terms. We cannot permit the authorities to engage in a genocidal campaign against young black men and women under the guise of protecting the community."[83] Volunteers led "Survival Workshops" in local neighborhoods, educated residents on the criminal justice system, informed suspects of their constitutional rights, and referred defendants to affiliated attorneys.[84]

Yet tension between protecting civil liberties and fighting crime continued to surface, particularly in efforts to police street gangs. Uniting young men and women of similar ethnic background for decades, neighborhood clubs and organizations served a variety of complex and conflicting purposes. In the early twentieth century, for example, street gangs offered white, working-class youth entrée to the rough-and-tumble world of Chicago crime, business, and politics. Well into the 1950s, white street gangs helped forge racial identity, nourish social networks, and bolster white privilege.[85] In the 1960s, African Americans and Latinos began organizing on a larger scale, combining street- and neighborhood-level groups into so-called nations or super gangs that spanned multiple community areas and cultivated citywide—even regional or national—allegiance.[86] While gangs of all races participated in much antisocial behavior, including violent crime and extortion, they also provided "pro-social" benefits to underserviced communities.[87] In the late 1960s, black and Latino gangs developed a political consciousness, joined civil rights and Black Power movements, and ran their own community programs.[88] A regular presence in everyday life, street gangs played an ambiguous role in Chicago neighborhoods, eliciting contradictory feelings of anger, affection, fear, and respect.[89]

As crime rates soared after 1965, however, residents of high-crime communities demanded action.[90] Convinced the costs of gang activity outweighed the benefits, some Chicagoans risked the repressive hand of law enforcement as the lesser of two evils. The CPD created the Gang Intelligence Unit in 1967.[91] Two years later, State's Attorney Hanrahan launched a Special Prosecutions Unit to coordinate an all-out "War on Gangs."[92] Predicting that most citizens would turn a blind eye, officers often employed extralegal tactics to rid the city of an apparent public menace. Looking back, organizer Ruth Wells acknowledged that black communities struggled to reconcile calls for police accountability with the need for get-tough policing. "When, in the past, liberal and radical groups dealt only with the 'brutality' aspect of police work without giving sufficient weight to the brutality and oppressive nature of street gang violence," she explained, "we helped to divide the community within itself."[93] Too often, local residents asked themselves, "Who's worse—the police or the gangs?"[94] According to Wells, when offered a choice between "offing the pigs" and embracing Hanrahan's "war on street gangs," most people "went to Hanrahan," at least until the Hampton raid exposed the danger.[95] Facing a crime crisis, local people wanted law and order but worried about the cost.

Indeed, public support for the war on gangs went only so far.[96] When a police supervisor admitted in 1969 that his unit occupied itself with "keeping things stirred up" between rival gangs, black residents petitioned for the Gang Intelligence Unit's dissolution. Acknowledging the need for rigorous law enforcement, petitioners insisted gang members had rights too. "Stirring things up," they argued, involved a breadth of malevolent behavior, from "lying, to perpetuating violent confrontations in between youth organizations, to the extreme of assassinating a key figure in one of these organizations, to lengthen[ing] gang wars."[97] Residents' need for security, while palpable, did not blind them to injustice. When off-duty police officer James Lamb fatally shot Manuel Ramos of the Young Lords Organization on May 4, 1969, hundreds of activists and sympathizers rallied, marched, and protested in solidarity.[98] By the mid-1970s, Ruth Wells noted a new sophistication among "grass roots groups and councils in the inner city." Whereas urban residents responded to police violence with rebellion in the 1960s, Wells reported, "Some of the explosive violence-begetting frustration of the past is giving way to meaningful efforts for change" in the 1970s. Optimistic, Wells concluded that "communities are coming together" to better address both street crime and police misconduct.[99]

Throughout the 1970s and 1980s, local groups operated a web of programs to improve Chicago's war on crime, often articulating parallel demands for police protection and police accountability. For example, the black-led Coalition of Concerned Women in the War on Crime sought police reform and justice for crime victims, announcing, "While we fully recognize the twin problems of police corruption and police brutality, we firmly believe that there must be a partnership between law enforcement officials and the people they serve."[100] Gay rights activists also escalated efforts to protect their communities from street crime and police harassment.[101] With the president of Mattachine Midwest referring to State's Attorney Hanrahan as "an enemy of the people," gay liberation groups resisted police harassment with "unprecedented brazenness" after 1970.[102] Meanwhile, the Latin American Citizens League, the Native American Committee, the Japanese American Citizens League, and other civil rights groups joined coalitions to demand better protection from the police.[103] Poor whites from the North Side's "Hillbilly Ghetto" joined the Panthers' Rainbow Coalition, explaining, "Most people don't understand we are kicked around as bad as Negroes and Puerto Ricans by police."[104] Religious groups and nonprofit organizations operated anticrime and accountability programs as well. In 1980, a Catholic-run prisoner reentry program begged to keep federal funding, writing, "We cannot throw up our hands and give up on crime."[105] While the CPD hoarded weaponry and equipment, ordinary people proposed an alternative crime war.

Caught in the spotlight, police officers across the country redoubled efforts to win union recognition. While fraternal organizations, social clubs, and trade unions emerged decades earlier, the 1960s witnessed the rise of "blue power" on a "revolutionary scale."[106] To the alarm of critics, police associations lobbied legislatures, fought civilian review, and initiated "strikes, work stoppages and slow downs."[107] The "police militancy" of the late 1960s laid the groundwork for official recognition of public unions in the 1970s and 1980s, helping offset improvements to accountability for the rest of the century and beyond.[108] While police unions defended errant officers, Chicago's Afro-American Patrolmen's League (AAPL) fought to improve labor conditions for black patrolmen and combat misconduct. Formed to address everyday police abuse as well as sensational events like Mayor Daley's "shoot-to-kill" order of April 1968, the AAPL vowed to bring "Black Power" through policing to Chicago.[109] In the words of historian Peter Pihos, the AAPL looked to "use racial solidarity to make police agents in helping black people."[110] The AAPL fielded brutality complaints, supported civilian review, and filed a federal antidiscrimination suit against the city. With federal revenue sharing partially fronting the bill for CPD salaries, the AAPL won a court ruling freezing payment in 1975. Rather than hire and promote more black officers, Daley borrowed $55 million from local banks to keep the department afloat.[111] Wanting "in on the war on crime," the AAPL helped charter a National Black Police Association boasting fifteen thousand members in twenty-two states by 1976. According to AAPL leader Renault Robinson, "It's ridiculous for a government to have a war on crime and not include the people in [its] midst."[112] Representing a broad constituency of black policemen and black civilians alike, the AAPL embodied local efforts to bring law, order, and justice to Chicago.

Facing competing interests, elected officials struggled to balance crime control with police accountability. The Chicago City Council, for example, often divided over fighting crime and reforming police. While machine loyalists dominated the chamber, a few independent aldermen—black and white—tried to soften the edge of law and order.[113] In majority-black wards, however, most aldermen toed the party line and supported the mayor and his police. According to council member Leon Despres, Ralph H. Metcalfe and other black aldermen operated as "the machine's invaluable mouthpiece in corralling and controlling the vote" in black wards throughout the 1960s.[114] After his election to U.S. Congress in 1970, however, Metcalfe rallied around the one issue uniting black residents "across the class spectrum"—police brutality.[115] When two black, middle-class constituents suffered police abuse in back-to-back incidents in spring 1972, Metcalfe broke ranks and held a series of high-profile hearings on the CPD's history of brutality.[116] Insisting that "it's never too late to be black," Metcalfe surprised critics by organizing Concerned Citizens for Police Reform (CCPR) and thrusting a list of demands on City Hall.[117] Under pressure from the CCPR and other community groups, in 1974 the CPD launched the Office of Professional Standards, a complaint review section staffed by civilian investigators working under the police superintendent.[118] Other politicians, particularly black elected officials independent of the Daley machine, sought to embed accountability mechanisms within anticrime measures as well. In 1970, for example, the "Black State Legislators of Illinois" held a three-day conference titled "Freedom from Fear, Crime in the Community" to promote improvements to the war on crime.[119]

While many individuals and organizations drew attention to crime and policing after 1965, most focused on a particular constituency—residents of local neighborhoods, members of certain ethnic groups, gays and lesbians, troubled youth, ex-offenders, black police officers, or other groups. A few organizations catered to all victims of police abuse but not exclusively. The Black Panther Party, the American Civil Liberties Union, the Afro-American Patrolmen's League, the Alliance to End Repression, and others regularly addressed police misconduct but also devoted resources to competing issues. Other permanent, ad hoc, or umbrella organizations addressed law enforcement as well, typically publicizing a specific case, providing an institutional base for a charismatic personality, or consolidating a temporary coalition. Examples include Congressman Metcalfe's CCPR, journalist Russ Meek's Search for Truth, Jesse Jackson's Operation PUSH, the Committee to End Murder of Black People, the United Front for Black Community Organizations, the Organization for People's Rights for Blacks, the Coalition to Combat Police Misconduct, and countless others.[120] After

1967, however, a small group of committed activists calling themselves Citizens Alert operated Chicago's "only permanent, broad-based coalition [dealing] with on-going, day-to-day problems that citizens face with the police."[121] In the decades-long struggle to win justice for survivors of police torture under Jon Burge, no group—with the exception of the People's Law Office—worked longer or helped accomplish more than Citizens Alert.

Citizens Alert

In April 1967, five white male professionals from Chicago and nearby suburbs officially certified Citizens Alert as a nonprofit organization in the state of Illinois.[122] Over the previous year, the group's founders—two "civic-minded" businessmen, an attorney, a Methodist minister, and a local director of the American Civil Liberties Union (ACLU)—worked to improve relationships between police and local residents, often showing up at lockups to check the status of criminal suspects.[123] "Very often the police would treat them more carefully after that because we had shown an interest," explained cofounder Jack Korshak, "You know, we were lawyers from the suburbs, and they were mostly poor black people."[124] The group's statement of purpose read, "To bring about better understanding between the police department and the overall community to the end that mutual respect shall characterize their relationship and each fulfill in greater harmony its obligation and responsibilities to the other."[125] For several years, Citizens Alert operated almost unnoticed, its few volunteers wakening to the realization that meaningful reform of the justice system demanded greater commitment. Following the assassination of Fred Hampton and Mark Clark in December 1969, Citizens Alert experienced turnover in leadership, as a multiracial cohort of volunteers fought to expose the true nature of the Hanrahan raid.[126]

In early 1970, Citizens Alert merged with a fledgling coalition called Alliance to End Repression (AER). Within weeks of Hampton's death, Richard Criley of the Chicago Committee to Defend the Bill of Rights met with colleagues from the ACLU, the Independent Voters of Illinois, and the United Methodist Church to answer a recent "wave of oppressive action by police and other government agencies."[127] By April 1970, activists had launched the AER, an "action-oriented alliance" of over thirty-five organizations determined to "counter growing trends toward a police state on local, state and national levels."[128] While the war on the Panthers jolted white liberals into action, the Black Coalition for United Community Action and other representatives of Chicago's African American poor reminded board members that "institutionalized repression had been around a long time for them—especially in the denial of criminal justice."[129] In addition to demanding that a grand jury investigate the Hanrahan raid, the AER organized a series of permanent task forces on related issues, including legislation, bail policy, prison reform, jury selection, gay rights, media relations, and police accountability.[130]

Mobilizing "concerned citizen power," the AER united "storefront community groups" in black and Latino neighborhoods with "human relations units in the suburbs." According to activist Mary Powers, "The name of the organization conjures an image of young militants, but among the Alliance to End Repression's activists are middle-aged, well-groomed, and soft-spoken adults sharing responsibilities with bearded, denim-clad students." Reverend John Hill added, "We have a kind of collective, non-charismatic style" among "basically white, middle-class and non-abrasive" members who "don't grab the microphone" or "work in the streets." Rather, AER members "go directly to the decision makers," "move from protest to program," and "stay on the case." Above all, the AER emphasized "presence and persistence." Organizer Betty Plank explained: "We are like the widow in Jesus' parable. We keep coming to the 'judges' and whether they believe in the rights for which we push or not, they give, little by little, to get rid of us. They know we won't go away."[131] Seeking to make the "struggle against repression not just a movement but an institution," activists gained experience and expanded networks throughout the 1970s, winning a series of victories along the way.[132] Their greatest win came in 1982, when a federal judge terminated the CPD's controversial Red Squad, an intelligence unit known for illegally spying on civilians, community organizations, and opponents of the political machine.[133] By then, however, the AER had all but ceased to exist, a victim of waning funds and dwindling volunteers.[134]

Its nonprofit status secured in 1967, Citizens Alert operated as the AER's police task force through much of the 1970s. Considering themselves crusaders in the local crime war, volunteers insisted that law and order threatened vulnerable communities. "To reassure the middle-class citizen that his rights will not suffer," explained a 1975 position paper, "a double standard of justice is projected, which exempts officialdom—including policemen—from the rule of law, and accords the white collar criminal mercy and compassion, while dealing 'without pity' with the 'criminal classes'—the poor, the alienated, the black and Latino."[135] Catering to survivors of police abuse, Citizens Alert hosted a series of "accountability sessions" with local residents and public officials and crashed monthly meetings of the Chicago Police Board, an appointed body responsible for reviewing regulations, adopting budgets, and approving discipline.[136] In 1973, Citizens Alert won a federal LEAA grant to pay the salary of coordinator Ruth Wells, its first full-time staffer.[137] In 1974, the organization proved "a catalyst for the establishment" of the CPD's Office of Professional Standards, launched to review citizen complaints.[138] In 1976, Citizens Alert persuaded Cook County to replace its "archaic, often ineffective" coroner with a professional medical examiner.[139] Nearly folding when grant money ran out, Citizens Alert attributed its "difficulty in securing funds" to its "critical stance taken toward the police."[140] Yet the organization survived financial woes and the demise of the AER, pursuing a range of activities throughout the 1970s, from fighting racist police in downstate Cairo, Illinois to demanding psychological testing of CPD recruits and fielding brutality complaints.[141]

Despite its small membership and inability to afford paid staff, Citizens Alert survived on the extraordinary commitment of a close-knit community of activists. Looking back on the organization's first quarter century, a reporter wrote in 1992, "Over the years, membership has shifted gradually from the original core of North Shore liberals to a mix of whites, blacks, Hispanics, Native Americans, Asian-Americans and gays and lesbians."[142] Yet its board of directors had been multiracial as far back as 1970. Staggered turnover aside, its nucleus of volunteers remained consistent for years on end. Between 1970 and 2010, nine board presidents—white and black—kept Citizens Alert running, including attorney Fred Glick of the American Jewish Congress, Milton Cohen of the Jewish Council on Urban Affairs, businessman Tom Peters, Reverend Willie Baker, Mary Powers of the Winnetka Human Relations Committee, Juanita Van Dorn of the First Unitarian Church of Chicago, Gladys Lewis of the Supreme Life Insurance Company, and community activists Mary L. Johnson and Gerald Frazier. Lewis, an African American graduate of Wilberforce University who moved to Chicago in 1960, led the board for all but five years between 1984 and 2014.[143] According to Johnson, who joined after her son suffered abuse under Jon Burge in 1982, "Citizens Alert provides victims and their families a shoulder to lean on, a voice to publicize complaints and grievances and a platform for the broader non-victim population of greater Chicago to learn about the urgent continuing problem of police abuse."[144] For over forty years, the multiracial volunteers of Citizens Alert forged enduring bonds through the tedium of community organizing, confrontation with state authorities, the rush of victory, and the heartache of defeat.

While many volunteers deserve credit for the work of Citizens Alert, the longest-tenured and most visible was Mary D. Powers. Born in 1922, Powers grew up in East Lansing and Flint, Michigan. Her father, a manager

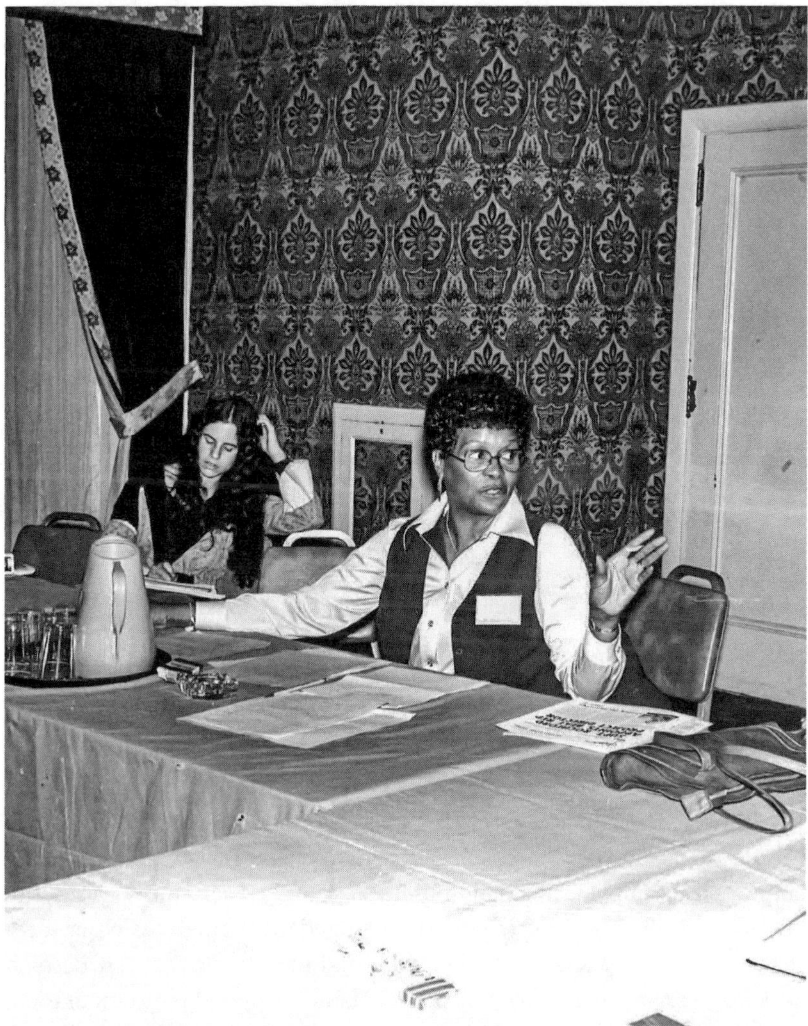

FIGURE 10 Citizens Alert executive director Ruth Wells, October 1976. According to Wells, "Police brutality sabotages the war on crime by alienating the community from the police." Wells to *Chicago Sun-Times*, July 26, 1974, Citizens Alert records, folder 32-544, Special Collections and University Archives, University of Illinois at Chicago.

at Oldsmobile, moved Mary and her mother, a schoolteacher, to Wisconsin during World War II. After the war, Mary wed William Powers, a sales manager in the publishing industry, with whom she raised three children in Chicago's North Shore.[145] Graduating with a sociology degree from the University of Wisconsin–Madison and doing postgraduate work at Michigan State University and Loyola University Chicago, Powers worked as a

FIGURE 11 Citizens Alert board members attend the Citizens Alert Eighth Annual Police Conference, Mt. Carmel A.M.E. Church, Chicago, November 10, 1979. From left to right: Howard Saffold, Milton Cohen, Boris Brail, Dorothy Tollifson, Juanita Van Dorn, Reverend Marty Gool, Lieutenant Arthur T. Lindsay, Mary Powers, Charles Washington. Citizens Alert records, Special Collections and University Archives, University of Illinois at Chicago.

social worker for the Red Cross and as a personnel counselor for Western Electric and Time.[146] In the late 1940s, Powers counseled gay and lesbian employees fearful of losing their jobs because of their sexuality. In 1965, she hosted Martin Luther King Jr. when he stumped for fair housing in the north suburbs. A few years later, she helped found the Illinois Gay and Lesbian Task Force. When the police killed Fred Hampton and Mark Clark in 1969, she joined hundreds of local people in tours of the ravaged apartment.[147] Shocked at the stark brutality, Powers, then president of the Winnetka Human Relations Committee, joined the Alliance to End Repression.[148] She soon emerged—in the words of attorney Flint Taylor—as a "suburban warrior for police accountability."[149] From 1970 until 2014, when Citizens Alert finally folded, Powers, Gladys Lewis, and countless other volunteers anchored Chicago's multiracial anti–police abuse movement.[150]

By the 1980s, many community activists, public officials, and neighborhood residents recognized Citizens Alert as an effective lobby for justice. For example, after persuading the State's Attorney's Office to indict a security guard who shot and killed a handcuffed purse snatcher in 1980, the Citizens Alert Cabrini-Green Committee forced the CPD to remove a makeshift police station from a ground-floor apartment in the public housing high-rise.[151] Not only did tenants resent the constant police presence; they also reported hearing officers beat detainees, often by placing buckets over their heads and banging them with clubs.[152] "These Citizens Alert ladies live in a different environment and social level," explained a grateful Cabrini resident, "they are articulate and have influence so they can get others to look at what is going on here."[153] Giving voice to the voiceless, Citizens Alert helped family members of victims of police violence to lobby lawmakers for redress in 1984.[154] Following a series of accidents involving CPD squad cars, Citizen Alert convinced the department to alter its "hot pursuit" policy in 1985.[155] Whenever a death or suicide occurred in police custody, Citizens Alert questioned official accounts and demanded independent investigations.[156] As the years passed, Mary Powers and other volunteers turned Citizens Alert into a clearinghouse of citizen complaints and information on police accountability.[157] Meanwhile, one of the most egregious human rights scandals in CPD history was unfolding behind closed doors at Area 2.

The Evolving Torture Regime

After February 1982, Lieutenant Jon Burge and the detectives under his command grew comfortable that supervisors approved their illicit interrogations under certain circumstances. With coerced confessions all but guaranteeing the conviction of cop killers Andrew Wilson and Jackie Wilson, the torture regime at Area 2 basked in the praise of its investigative prowess. For the remainder of the decade, a small circle of detectives continued to utilize physical and psychological abuse to close important cases at the South Side's Area 2 and—after Burge's 1986 promotion and transfer to Brighton Park in 1988—the Southwest Side's Area 3. During this period, the number of known allegations escalated and targets expanded to include suspects whose guilt was less certain or even unlikely. If the first decade of the torture regime from 1972 to 1982 involved high-profile or extraordinarily violent criminals who detectives genuinely believed committed the crimes under investigation, then detectives had become less selective during the 1980s. More than 75 of the People's Law Office's 118 documented Burge torture survivors appeared after February 1982.[158] Over a dozen wound up on death row. At least seven of these were later exonerated or otherwise released.[159] Month after month, year after year, Burge and his men routinely coerced confessions from a variety of suspects, including suspected murderers whose guilt was easily established, men with criminal records who detectives believed were at least guilty of something, and likely innocent men who simply fit a certain profile.

Following the electric-shock torture of Andrew Wilson on Valentine's Day 1982, the next accusation against Burge surfaced in June when a "high-ranking El Rukn gang leader" named Michael Johnson told anyone who would listen that Area 2 detectives abused him.[160] According to activist Mary L. Johnson, Michael's mother, the CPD targeted her son for harassment as early as 1970, when officers beat the sixteen-year-old and his friends in a local park. Conceding Michael was never a "saint," Mary filed a brutality complaint. In retaliation, officers arrested him for petty offenses seventeen times in six months. When he was seventeen, Michael went to prison on a shooting charge, emerging two years later with a drug habit. Poised for a "a life of crime," he bumbled a scheme to rob a drug house and wound up in an interrogation room with Jon Burge.[161] Johnson alleged Burge beat him, applied electric shocks to his genitals, placed a gun to his head, and referred to his attorney Cassandra Watson as a "nigger bitch."[162] Watson, an assistant public defender and former Black Panther, also represented another man, Melvin Jones, whom Burge allegedly tortured four months earlier.[163] After his release, Johnson complained to the CPD's Office of Professional Standards and reported his abuse to the FBI.[164] He later went to prison on unrelated kidnapping and murder charges. In 1987, a court convicted Johnson of arranging the murder of a prison guard, a charge his mother maintained was a frame-up.[165] Special prosecutors investigating the Burge scandal later found Johnson's torture allegations among the most credible.[166]

Lists of torture survivors include repeat offenders suspected of cruel acts of violence, suggesting that detectives used physical abuse not only to aid investigation but also to punish those they saw as a worst class of criminal. While Area 2 detectives encountered horrific crime scenes on a regular basis, some cases struck a chord. For example, in the predawn hours of September 9, 1982, a thirty-three-year-old white woman named Karen Byron awoke in an alley—bruised, burned, and bloody—and stumbled toward the lights of a gas station at Seventy-Sixth Street and Jeffrey Boulevard. An "admitted alcoholic," Byron had spent the previous day drinking with friends before heading alone to find a party.[167] As Byron approached a liquor store, twenty-four-year-old Rodney Benson and friends pulled up in a red automobile. Benson recognized Byron as "K.B.," a "neighborhood party girl" who "went around trading sex for alcohol."[168] Benson refused to buy K.B. a drink. She jumped in his car and they began arguing. A police sergeant drove by and asked if Byron needed help. According to Benson, K.B. was already "falling down, sloppy drunk" at this point, but they convinced the officer she was in good hands.[169]

Over the next few hours at least five men assaulted, raped, and tortured K.B. in an attic above the home of twenty-eight-year-old Stanley Wrice, an acquaintance of Rodney Benson who lived nearby. When police officers found her at the gas station the next morning, K.B. was in severe pain, her body covered in bruises, abrasions, and second- and third-degree burns. It appeared as though someone had pressed heated cooking utensils and a hot clothes iron to her "face, neck, chest, breasts, thighs, back, and buttocks."[170] Within hours, Detective Peter Dignan and Sergeant John Byrne apprehended several suspects—including Rodney Benson, Stanley Wrice, Michael Fowler, and Lee Holmes—and brought them back to Area 2 for questioning.[171] K.B. later underwent skin-graft surgery. She suffered permanent scarring and lost part of a nipple.[172]

After several rounds of interviews, detectives emerged with statements incriminating Benson, Fowler, and Holmes in lesser charges and pinning the worst on Stanley Wrice. All four suspects accused detectives Dignan and Byrne of abuse.[173] Wrice recalled Dignan announcing that they were "fixing to do some police brutality" before officers beat him with a long flashlight and a rubber hose in an abandoned jail cell on the first floor. Sitting on the second story of the Burnside station house, Wrice's sister overheard sounds of a beating and men "hollering from the basement." An officer allegedly told her "they would not hurt [Wrice] too badly." To avoid further abuse, Wrice gave a statement to an assistant state's attorney with information fed him by detectives. A paramedic noted superficial injuries the next day. Wrice later discovered blood in his urine and sought medical treatment in Cook County Jail.[174]

Years later, Rodney Benson described two "big white guys" working under Burge escorting him to a dark cell on the first floor of the Burnside station in September 1982. "Well," he began, "down the stairs I got there, and they told me I was fixing to learn a lesson. I come in the room, looked up. They had this noose hanging there. I'm thinking, oh, shit, here we go. They sit me down on a little stool, cuffed my hands up underneath them, and just started to do their little thing." Wielding rubber hose and flashlight, the burly detectives beat him all over his body. One assured him, "All tough mother fuckers holler sooner or later." Benson continued: "[He] hauled off and hit me in the chest with the damn thing. I just kind of looked at him, and then he took the mother fucker and jammed it into my nuts and that's when I said, fuck this, I started hollering." As the beating continued for what seemed an eternity—"Time sort of lost itself with me then"—Benson abandoned his will to resist. Throughout the ordeal, a third man hovered in the shadows, "standing in my peripheral, [where] I can't see." Before finishing, "They made sure I looked up at the noose and told me that those—what's that old story again? We'll hang your ass; tell everybody that you hung yourself, but we hang niggers here all the time." When he finally agreed to implicate Wrice, the detectives told him, "You did good. Tell the same thing to the state's attorney." Returning to the second floor, Benson learned his companions had suffered a similar fate. "All I could hear was the same thing that I was going through," he recalled, "swack, swack, ouch, ouch, ouch, ouch."[175] Benson, Fowler, and Holmes pleaded guilty to aggravated battery.[176] A jury found Wrice guilty of rape, deviate sexual assault, armed violence, and unlawful restraint. A judge sentenced him to one hundred years in prison.[177]

Thirty years later, a court allowed Wrice to file a postconviction petition, reiterating that "use of a defendant's physically coerced confession as substantive evidence of his guilt is never harmless error."[178] A judge overturned Wrice's conviction, finding that Byrne and Dignan "committed perjury when they testified in 1983 that they did not beat [Wrice] to secure his inculpatory statement."[179] With one witness dead and another recanting, the state chose not to retry Wrice. Yet a judge denied a certificate of innocence, finding evidence sufficient to prove Wrice guilty of assaulting Karen Byron even without the coerced confession.[180]

While Wrice provided details of police torture during his 1983 trial, not all suspects in the case raised an immediate outcry. Decades later, lawyers investigating the Burge scandal asked Rodney Benson why he did not complain about abuse. "I just tell you the truth," Benson answered. "I wasn't saying nothing to nobody in that police station about nothing that happened to me in that police station until I got out of that police station, if I got out of there." Justifying himself to white attorneys all those years later, Benson grew frustrated with their inability to grasp obvious realities. "I'm a black kid in the City of Chicago with some white cops and a white state's attorney in [1982]—huh uh," he explained. "It doesn't work." Understanding why Benson would not mention abuse to other detectives, the lawyers wondered why he did not at least tell the ASA who took his statement. Benson shook his head: "Assistant state's attorney that came in laughing and joking with the same police officers that hit me? No good." The interviewers reminded him that lawyers were "sworn to uphold the law"—certainly, they could be trusted. "That's true," Benson replied, "[But] by the same token, aren't those same police officers sworn to hold the law like that? They did it anyway." Asked why he did not file a complaint with the Office of Professional Standards (OPS), Benson answered: "One, I probably didn't even know what

OPS was. . . . Not to mention there might have been some retaliation." For weeks after he left the station, friends and relatives repeatedly told Benson not to fight the CPD because he simply "can't win." The lawyers still did not understand. "I was a black kid and it wasn't going to work," Benson insisted.[181]

Elaborating, Benson explained that he came from a world where police could not be trusted. Asked if he ever heard details of custodial abuse, Benson nearly laughed: "I'm sorry. This is Chicago, right? Yes, I had." Pressed, Benson gave a list—"pistol whooped, rubber hose, flashlights, dunked in the [lake], hit with bricks, telephone books, padded baseball bats, golf clubs. I've heard all the stories." They wondered if neighbors shared stories of abuse. "All my life," he affirmed. "You hear suicide in prison. It's not suicide in prison." Lest they dismiss his musings as the paranoid mythology of a criminal underclass, Benson clarified, "Those weren't [just] gang members saying that." Rather, "Those were ordinary people, like my stepfather and his friends." He continued, "Most gang members would never admit [to being abused by the police]. At least not back then. Not the ones I knew. Everybody was tougher than tough." Simply put, tales of police brutality permeated the neighborhood's every social circle for as long as he could remember. To Benson, police violence was inevitable, even among the innocent. "Somebody's going to take a whooping, somebody's guilty," he promised.[182]

Indeed, Area 2 detectives often acted as though locating and punishing the guilty was less important than making sure someone—anyone who fit the right profile—answered for a crime. Accordingly, several men, mostly young black gang members, paid a steep price. On October 28, 1983, detectives arrested a nineteen-year-old Gangster Disciple named Gregory Banks for shooting two men during an armed robbery of codeine and cough syrup.[183] A lengthy interrogation with African American detectives Doris Byrd and Sammy Lacey soon went nowhere. When the shift changed, however, Lieutenant Burge gave the case to incoming members of the midnight crew. According to Byrd, a visit with Burge's "A-Team" suddenly made Banks "very cooperative."[184] At a pretrial hearing on a motion to suppress his confession several months later, Banks testified that Sergeant John Byrne "pulled out a nickel-plated .45 and put it in my mouth," hit him in the chest with a flashlight, and knocked him to the ground, where Detective Charles Grunhard kicked him repeatedly. Detective Peter Dignan then tugged a plastic bag over Banks's head. "I couldn't breathe," Banks recalled. "I was handcuffed, so there was nothing I could do." Detectives left the room, came back, and suffocated Banks until he confessed.[185] Lieutenant Burge allegedly "peeked in" the door throughout.[186]

With Banks's coerced confession, detectives secured probable cause to arrest an accomplice, nineteen-year-old David Bates on October 29, 1983. In what Bates later claimed was his "first experience with white people,"[187] Sergeant Byrne and detectives Robert Dwyer and Charles Grunhard allegedly interrogated him "on and off" for two days, beating, bagging, and suffocating him "until he hollered or pretended to lose consciousness." When he resisted, detectives told him: "That's okay, we'll take care of you on the graveyard shift. We're gonna take you outside in the forest or somewhere over there where we can do what we want to. You'll say something then."[188] Eventually, he confessed. "They beat the hell out of me," Bates recalled, "They were enjoying beating Black men."[189] A few weeks later, Dr. John Raba, hospital director at Cook County Jail, wrote a letter to the OPS demanding detectives account for corroborating injuries discovered during an examination of both defendants.[190]

While Banks and Bates may have been responsible for the deaths of two men, false confessions allowed the state to convict on more serious charges than evidence warranted. At trial, Banks testified to shooting one victim in the leg as a warning and killing the other with a ricocheted shot fired on accident during a scuffle for the gun. The coerced confession, however, had Banks deliberately shooting to kill. Deflecting abuse allegations, Detective Peter Dignan testified that he "punched [Banks] a couple times" during a failed escape attempt.[191] Banks spent over five years in prison before an appellate court overturned the conviction in December 1989, finding "his confession was procured through police brutality and racial intimidation."[192] In a warning to Cook County jurists, the court added, "Trial judges must bear in mind that while we no longer see cases involving the use of the rack and thumbscrew to obtain confessions, we are seeing cases, like the present case, involving punching, kicking and placing a plastic bag over a suspect's head to obtain confessions."[193] Barred from submitting the tainted confession, prosecutors declined to retry Gregory Banks, who received a $92,000 settlement from the city in 1993. Appellate courts twice remanded Bates's conviction. He settled with the city for $66,000.[194]

Within days of abusing Banks and Bates, Area 2 detectives coerced a confession from thirty-three-year-old El Rukn gang leader Darrell Cannon in an unrelated murder. On October 26, 1983, patrolmen found the body of a suspected drug dealer dumped in a prairie behind the Altgeld Gardens public housing project. Detectives identified the victim as Darren Ross. Ross's family introduced investigators to a witness who saw two brothers—Tyrone and Andrew "A.D." McChristian—confront Ross about stealing from the El Rukns mere hours before his death. Bloodstains found inside a car registered to one of A.D.'s aliases matched Ross's blood type. Detectives found Tyrone McChristian at a billiard hall and took him to Area 2 for questioning. In a statement that he claimed was both false and coerced, Tyrone told detectives Cannon gave A.D. a .38-caliber revolver, which A.D. then used to shoot Ross in the head in the back seat of the car while Cannon drove.[195] Unable to locate A.D., detectives stormed Cannon's home on the morning of November 2, 1983, waving guns and threatening to kill Cannon and his fiancée as they roused from sleep.[196] A former bodyguard of Black P Stone Nation leader Jeff Fort, Cannon was on parole after serving only twelve years of a hundred- to two-hundred-year sentence for fatally shooting an elderly man during a toy store robbery in 1970.[197] Detectives demanded Cannon tell them where to find McChristian and sign a statement corroborating their account of the murder. While Cannon admitted to being present when McChristian shot Ross, he denied any advance knowledge of the crime and insisted he did not give A.D. the weapon.[198]

Determined to get a convicted murderer off the streets, Sergeant John Byrne and detectives Daniel McWeeny, Raymond Madigan, Peter Dignan, Michael Bosco, Ray Binkowski, and Charles Grunhard allegedly coerced an inculpatory statement from Cannon using psychological and physical torture. According to Cannon, Detective Dignan struck him across the knee with a flashlight on the ride to Area 2 headquarters, demanding, "Nigger, where's A.D.?" Revealing they had "scientific ways" of getting people to talk, detectives told Cannon he was in store for the "hardest day of his life." Once in the interrogation room, Cannon refused to cooperate as officers coached him through a statement corroborating Tyrone McChristian. Insisting, "Nigger, you going to tell us where A.D.'s at," Detective Bosco opened a brown sack and showed Cannon an electric-shock device resembling a cattle prod. When Cannon continued to resist, detectives dragged him outside and placed him in an unmarked police car.[199]

Detectives drove Cannon to a remote location on Chicago's industrial Southeast Side and maneuvered through a narrow viaduct near 126th Street and Torrence Avenue.[200] A trailing car blocked the entrance. Detectives removed Cannon, bombarded him with questions, threats, and racial slurs, and lifted him off his feet by a pair of handcuffs.[201] With a misty rain falling, Dignan removed a shotgun from the trunk, turned his back, said, "Now listen, nigger," and mimicked the sound of loading a shell. Turning back around, Dignan forced the barrel into Cannon's mouth. Another detective told him, "Pull the trigger, blow that nigger's head off." The gun clicked, but nothing happened. Dignan repeated the mock execution twice more. Experiencing the fear of death, Cannon recalled, "It seemed like, when I heard the trigger click, that the back of my brains was being blown out. That's what my mind was telling me, and as a result from that I could feel my hair stand up on my head." Next, detectives stretched Cannon across the back seat of the car and pulled his pants and underwear down to his ankles. Sergeant Byrne pressed the electric-shock device against Cannon's penis and testicles multiple times, telling him he was a "strong nigger" and threatening to turn the device to a higher setting.[202] Finally, Cannon surrendered. They drove back to Area 2 and signed a sworn statement implicating Cannon in Ross's murder.[203]

The procedural history of Cannon's case demonstrates how detectives caught torture survivors in a complicated web. Relying on a coerced confession, prosecutors convicted Cannon of murder in the courtroom of Thomas J. Maloney in April 1984.[204] Maloney later went to prison for taking bribes to fix murder trials.[205] Although Cannon did not pull the trigger, jurors convicted him through Illinois's accountability statute, allowing a person to be legally accountable for the conduct of another—ironic considering a jury later acquitted "A.D." McChristian.[206] Receiving a life sentence, Cannon appealed. The appellate court reversed on the state's use of peremptory challenges to strike African Americans from the jury but rejected the torture claim.[207] In a second trial, Judge John J. Mannion chose not to hold a hearing on the merits of the confession, but then recused himself for having previously worked as a detective at Area 2.[208] A second judge, however, also denied a motion for a suppression hearing. In 1994, Cannon was again convicted and given a life sentence. Three years later, an appellate court remanded the case for a third trial, ruling that emerging details of the Burge scandal warranted a fair hearing of torture allegations.[209] In 2001, Cannon pleaded guilty to lesser charges in exchange for an early release. The Illinois Prisoner Review Board, however, refused to let Cannon go, insisting that his arrest for Ross's murder in 1983 violated his parole from the 1970 toy-store murder. Allowing Cannon off the hook for the plea bargain, the state dropped all charges in 2004. Yet the parole board continued to stonewall, keeping Cannon behind bars until 2007.[210]

Meanwhile, in 1986 Cannon sued the city for violating his civil rights. Counseled to take a paltry settlement, Cannon accepted $3,000, of which he received only $1,247.[211] As other Burge torture survivors settled for millions of dollars, Cannon filed a new suit in 2004, arguing that ineffective assistance of counsel, new evidence of a pattern and practice of torture at Area 2, and a history of cover-up voided his earlier settlement. While the court originally sided with Cannon when the city tried to have the suit disqualified, a judge reversed the ruling in 2011, granting the city summary judgment and preventing Cannon from pursuing further damages.[212] In 2015, however, Cannon applied for reparations payments. Promising to buy a motorcycle and cruise around City Hall, Cannon cashed a check for nearly $100,000, which he claimed was not enough to compensate for what detectives put him through thirty-three years earlier.[213]

Throughout the 1980s, detectives working under the supervision of Jon Burge regularly performed some combination of abuse experienced by Andrew Wilson, Michael Johnson, Stanley Wrice, Rodney Benson, Gregory Banks, David Bates, and Darrell Cannon. Indeed, journalist John Conroy once quipped, "Gathered together, the Area Two cases make for repetitive reading."[214] The majority of detectives' targets boasted gang affiliations and criminal records. Most were somehow connected to, if not directly responsible for, the crime under investigation. Not all torture survivors from the 1980s, however, fit the profile. For example, detectives helped send Madison Hobley to death row following an apartment fire that killed seven people, including Hobley's wife and infant son, in January 1987. While the soft-spoken Hobley had no serious convictions, no history of gang affiliation, and little incentive to commit arson, detectives employed physical abuse to coerce a confession. When Hobley held firm, detectives swore under oath that he gave an oral confession they could not corroborate.[215] In the 1990s, Hobley helped organize the Death Row 10, a group of prisoners sentenced to death on the basis of confessions secured by detectives connected to Burge.[216] Some of these prisoners almost certainly committed awful crimes.[217] Others, like Hobley, offered persuasive claims of innocence. None deserved the brutal treatment they received at the hands of the police.

Despite the complaints flowing from Area 2 and Area 3 throughout the 1980s, those in positions of power within the Cook County criminal justice system failed to expose and end police torture until they were forced to act by torture survivors, lawyers, and activists in the 1990s. Burge's supervisors, the command staff of the CPD, the Felony Review Unit of the State's Attorney's Office, the prosecutors who tried cases in court, State's Attorney Richard M. Daley, several mayors, including the mayors Washington and Daley, and multiple circuit court judges either failed to notice the pattern of abuse or chose to ignore it. Indeed, detectives selected their victims well. Most of the men abused at Area 2 and Area 3 were persons the law-abiding, middle-class-aspiring world simply did not care much about. During a time of heightened fear, with crime and drug wars raging at all levels, with street gangs, drugs, guns, and violence dominating headlines, public officials and ordinary people often ignored the atrocities of Chicago's crime war. Buttressed by tacit approval in pursuit of cop killers in 1982, police torture might have continued indefinitely.

Not everyone, however, buried their head in the sand while Burge and his men ran amok. By the 1980s, a healthy network of veteran activists organized around local criminal justice issues, helping keep residents safe from violent criminals and lawless police alike. Struggling to survive an era of crime panic and mass incarceration, the police accountability movement persisted through frequent disappointment, defeat, and setback, poised to take advantage of changes to the political opportunity structure. Citizens Alert first heard rumors of torture under Jon Burge in February 1982, when a public defender representing Andrew Wilson came asking about electric shock in police custody.[218] It would take years, however, for community activists to fully appreciate the extent of the torture crisis.

5

Third-World Torture—Chicago Style

News of the Burge scandal finally broke during two civil trials in summer 1989.[1] For the next three decades, a complex network of individuals and organizations fought to end torture, secure relief for survivors, and hold perpetrators accountable. The twenty-year practice of abuse at the Chicago Police Department's (CPD) Area 2 and Area 3 headquarters between 1972 and 1991 and the ongoing cover-up involved scores of detectives, police administrators, municipal officials, prosecutors, and judges. While few detectives received formal punishment and only one faced criminal charges, grassroots activists achieved a great deal between 1989 and 2019.[2] Defying simple generalization, the Chicago torture justice movement revolved around the leadership and interests of African Americans directly affected by the torture crisis but also united other people across lines of race, class, gender, and age.[3] Participants included torture survivors, state prisoners, and their families; veteran activists, volunteers, and civil rights attorneys; journalists, academics, and politicians. Fluid and evolving, the movement persevered by cultivating personal bonds, adapting to changed conditions, and recruiting new allies. Its mixed record reveals the challenges of sustaining social movements for police accountability at a time when most victims of state violence failed to inspire widespread sympathy. Spanning from 1989 to 1993, the movement's first successful campaign focused on getting Jon Burge fired.

The People's Law Office and *Wilson v. City of Chicago*, 1986–1989

With roots in several ongoing struggles against repression, the Chicago torture justice movement began in state prison in 1986, when torture survivor

Andrew Wilson filed a civil lawsuit against Jon Burge and the City of Chicago for violating his civil rights years earlier. Whether executing routine investigative work, exorcising personal demons, or simply exacting revenge on an unrepentant cop killer, Area 2 detectives went too far when they tortured Wilson on Valentine's Day 1982. In their zeal, Burge and his men left too many marks on Wilson's five-foot-eight, 135-pound frame—a mosaic of bruises, burns, and abrasions that demanded explanation.[4] Questioning Wilson about his injuries later that night, the emergency room staff at Mercy Hospital began a collective thread pulling that would, eventually, unravel a decorated career and expose naked brutality within the nation's second-largest police department.[5] The loose knitting together of lies, fear, and apathy covering the torture regime, however, took years to come undone.

Immediately after his encounter with Area 2 detectives in February 1982, Andrew Wilson understood the stakes of suppressing his coerced confession. Facing capital charges for murdering two police officers, Wilson needed to convince a criminal court judge to keep his damning statements from the ears of a Cook County jury. Andrew's younger brother and codefendant, twenty-one-year-old Jackie Wilson, faced dire consequences of his own. He, too, sought to quash a coerced statement linking him to the crime. On the advice of counsel, the Wilson brothers filed motions to suppress their statements and offered detailed accounts of torture during pretrial hearings in fall 1982. Under oath, several Area 2 detectives and Felony Review attorneys answered with steady denials. The judge denied the motions and prosecutors presented incriminating statements to the jury. Almost a year to the day after the deaths of officers William Fahey and Richard O'Brien, an all-white jury convicted both Wilson brothers on February 4, 1983, sending Andrew to death row and condemning Jackie to a life sentence.[6] On appeal, however, the Illinois Supreme Court ruled that the state's inability to account for Andrew's injuries in custody should have barred use of the confession.[7] Following a second trial, a jury convicted again, this time without hearing the coerced statement. Sparing him the death penalty by one vote, the second jury sentenced Andrew to life in prison without parole.[8]

Even as the lengthy appeal process unfolded, Andrew Wilson initiated a civil suit against the officers who tortured him and the public officials who facilitated it. Dictating the complaint from inside Illinois's Pontiac Correctional Center in 1986, Wilson claimed he was "beaten, burned, shocked by electrical devices, and received many injuries . . . to my body and mind." Seeking to have his "conviction reversed and illegally obtained evidence excluded," Wilson demanded "ten million dollars so they don't ever do that kind of thing again."[9] Despite the corroborating evidence in the case, few attorneys proved willing to represent such an "unpopular" client.[10] Not only was Wilson well known for committing a horrific crime; many local people—including attorneys and potential jurors—denied, even justified, Wilson's abuse. Still on death row and growing desperate, in 1987 Wilson reached out to activist attorneys at the People's Law Office (PLO) in Chicago. Looking back, attorney Flint Taylor recalled Wilson's determination to win his release and make officers pay for excessive force. While criminal suspects expected a beating in police custody, electric shock and sexual humiliation went too far. According to Taylor, "the attack on [torture survivors'] genitals" was "symbolic going all the way back to slavery."[11] While Wilson could not let that go, the PLO hesitated. "Here's an uneducated, black cop-killer," Taylor explained. "Got the death penalty originally. Filed his own suit. No lawyer would represent him or when they did get appointed, they quickly jumped ship. And we take it over. What expectation of money do we have? Zero. All we knew is, you shouldn't torture people."[12] With "some trepidation," the PLO took the case.[13]

Opened as a law collective representing radical activists in the late 1960s, the People's Law Office proved an ideal champion for Andrew Wilson. In April 1968, attorneys Dennis Cunningham and Jeffrey Haas met while wandering through police headquarters looking for potential clients arrested during the urban rebellion following Martin Luther King Jr.'s assassination. Cunningham grew up in Winnetka, graduated from the University of Chicago and Loyola University School of Law, bartended at the Second City comedy club, and represented activists arrested during protests.[14] Haas grew up outside Atlanta, graduated from the University of Michigan, joined the U.S. Army Reserves, earned a law degree from the University of Chicago, and later became part of the Legal Assistance Foundation.[15] Several months later, Cunningham and another movement lawyer, Ted Stein, assisted the Chicago Legal Defense Committee represent protestors arrested at the Democratic National Convention. Wondering how to handle three hundred misdemeanor cases, Cunningham and Stein discussed forming a law collective.[16] Stein brought in lawyers Donald Stang and Francis "Skip" Andrew, also at Legal Assistance. According to Haas, Stang "came from a liberal, Jewish, upper-middle-class family in New York" and had recently graduated from Harvard Law School. Andrew, son of an Iowa minister, previously served with the Peace Corps in the Dominican Republic. He had a degree from Northwestern University Law School and, according to Haas, "looked older and more conservative than the rest of us."[17] Blurring the lines between attorney and activist, Cunningham, Haas, Stein, Stang, and Andrew debated joining the movement full-time.

Meanwhile, law enforcement harassment of local radicals drew lawyers deeper into the struggle. In late 1968, a filmmaker working with Haas's wife introduced Dennis Cunningham to Black Panther leader Fred Hampton. Two months later, in February 1969, Hampton recruited Cunningham to represent him on bogus charges stemming from a protest in Maywood, Illinois. In his first criminal trial, Cunningham won an acquittal.[18] In May, however, a jury convicted Hampton of robbing an ice-cream truck. Skip Andrew and Don Stang attended the trial and agreed to represent Hampton on appeal.[19] Barred from taking criminal cases, Legal Assistance attorneys felt growing pressure from the Panthers, the Young Lords, the Young Patriots, the Concerned Citizens of Lincoln Park, the Latin American Defense Organization, and Students for a Democratic Society and its splinter group, Weatherman.[20] That same month, Haas, Ted Stein, and other lawyers marched in support of Manuel Ramos, a Young Lords leader killed by an off-duty policeman.[21] Led by Jose "Cha Cha" Jimenez, the Young Lords had transitioned from a street gang to a community organization, joined a multiracial Poor People's Coalition, and resisted urban renewal and police brutality.[22] In May 1969, the Young Lords occupied Lincoln Park's McCormick Theological Seminary. Their list of demands included money for the fledgling PLO "to represent people in the community."[23] Successive police raids of the Black Panthers kept movement lawyers busy throughout the summer, with "multiple appearances in the branch courts almost every day."[24] To coordinate the work, lawyers officially opened the People's Law Office inside a converted Lincoln Park sausage shop on August 1, 1969.[25]

The original firm included lawyers Dennis Cunningham, Jeff Haas, Skip Andrew, and Don Stang. Ted Stein and Burt Steck operated the Chicago Legal Defense Committee and the Chicago Area Military Law Project in an adjacent room. Mariha Kuechmann, Norrie Davis, and Eugene Feldman soon rounded out the staff. Law students also joined, including Seva Dubuar, Ray McClain, and G. Flint Taylor.[26] Born in Farmington, Maine, in 1946, Taylor grew up in suburban Massachusetts. A ten-sport athlete in high school, Taylor majored in history at Brown University before pursuing law at Northwestern in 1968. Influenced by an older sister, Taylor embraced the counterculture and supported the civil rights and antiwar movements.[27] According to Haas, "[Taylor's] hippy exterior, including long, reddish-blond hair, disguised a tireless work ethic."[28] At Northwestern, Taylor met Dubuar, a student activist he described as "much more advanced politically." In spring 1969, Dubuar recruited Taylor "into going and working with civil rights lawyers who were representing . . . all of the radical and revolutionary organizations who were getting busted." At a crossroads, Taylor made the "life-altering decision" to turn down a summer job with Senator Ted Kennedy in order to collect affidavits in support of Fred Hampton in Chicago. "That summer," Taylor explained, "not only did I work on legal cases, I also met a lot of Black Panthers and their families." The Hampton family, in particular, "had an extremely profound impact on me because—as a white kid from a white suburb—I really hadn't much contact with African American people." While the media depicted the Panthers as a "violent, racist people," he reflected, "in fact they were quite the opposite." In the fall, Taylor brought Fred Hampton to Northwestern to lecture elites on the merits of revolution.[29] Awakened to struggle, Taylor helped run the PLO for the next five decades.

Conceived as a true collective, the People's Law Office evolved in the 1970s and 1980s. Determined to "raise their voices, and their fists, in court to show their solidarity with their clients," members of a nascent people's law movement inspired by the likes of William Kunstler and Charles Garry first launched experimental collectives in Los Angeles and New York.[30] In Chicago, Jeff Haas explained his reluctance to forgo steady paychecks for collective insecurity, admitting, "The hardest thing was casting my lot outside the mainstream."[31] In the early years, all PLO members—lawyers and nonlawyers alike—split salaries equally or according to need. Clients paid what they could afford. The office made decisions through equally weighted votes. Members even maintained a collective home. Operating inside the "belly of the beast" of capitalist America, the PLO embraced "radical"—even "revolutionary"—ideas, attacked "bourgeois society, imperialism, and patriarchy," and drew harassment from authorities, including the CPD's notorious Red Squad.[32] Anticipating raids, attorneys outfitted the office with a concrete barricade and steel gate, stashed firearms in a safe, and took target practice.[33] Ambitious and idealistic, PLO attorneys resisted the norms of a traditional law firm.

To survive, however, the office adopted more conventional arrangements in the 1970s. Indeed, as practical realities destroyed similar organizations, the PLO evolved, emerging by 1973 as the nation's "oldest existing legal collective."[34] While members remained committed to uniform compensation and prioritized paying nonlawyers when money was tight, attorneys typically made higher salaries.[35] While staff embraced democratic decision making, only "full-time PLOers got the vote."[36] Communal living endured, but most members eventually adopted traditional homes. If PLO attorneys often worked cases pro bono or on reduced fees, they also insisted on payment. As one member explained arrangements in the 1970s: "We are no longer bleeding hearts. If we have to get up at nine in the morning and contribute, we feel that our clients should contribute something too."[37] Burdened by expenses, PLO staff were not afraid to "lean on people" to collect, even while charging "generally only one-third or one-fourth" the going rate.[38] Meanwhile, they barely scraped by. "Every few years," admitted Taylor, "the office [went] through a cycle where we [didn't] really know how much longer financially we [could] persevere." Occasionally, lawyers found themselves "hustling $100 bond slips" just to "make enough money to pay that $100 a week to everybody."[39] In two profiles published decades apart, the *Chicago Reader* applauded Haas and Taylor for passing up "prestigious LaSalle Street offices" to chase "things other than money or success."[40] While colleagues found lucrative careers in corporate law firms, PLO attorneys found greater reward advancing social justice.

In its first two decades, the People's Law Office racked up an impressive record. In addition to providing legal aid to indigent clients, the PLO spent its early years representing various activists, radicals, and political prisoners, particularly the Black Panthers and the Weather Underground. After police officers killed Fred Hampton and Mark Clark in December 1969, the PLO represented survivors in protracted litigation stretching into the 1980s. In 1971, the PLO opened a branch in downstate Carbondale to serve local Panthers and associated activists. Following the 1971 Attica prison uprising, PLO attorneys relocated to Buffalo, New York, to aid survivors' legal defense. Indeed, the PLO fought for prisoners' rights across Illinois and beyond throughout the 1970s and 1980s. Alongside the National Lawyers Guild, the PLO worked its strategy of "litigate and demonstrate" in support of Puerto Rican independence, Palestinian liberation, the anti-apartheid movement, anti-nuclear proliferation, women's rights, peace in Latin America, employment discrimination, aid to the homeless, and other progressive or radical causes. In 1983, PLO attorneys won a $1.85 million settlement in the Fred Hampton case. In 1985, they won $350,000 for members of the Communist Workers Party who survived a fatal 1979 shooting at the hands of Nazis and Klansmen in Greensboro, North Carolina. In 1987, the PLO won $1.5 million in the case of George Jones, who sued the city following a 1982 murder trial that exposed illegal street files at Area 2. By the late 1980s, the office's history of representing "a large number of people who had been beaten, wrongfully arrested or otherwise abused at the hands of police, prison guards and other government agents" attracted unpopular plaintiffs seeking justice against powerful state actors.[41]

In addition to their ideological fit and experience, PLO lawyers were also affordable. While the Chicago elite secured the best counsel money could buy, indigent criminal defendants and prison litigants made do with the public defender's office, nonprofit law clinics, pro bono assistance, and civil rights firms. Relying on minimal fees and occasional awards for survival, the PLO remained a source of cheap representation for clients with nowhere else to turn. Following passage of the Civil Rights Attorney's Fees Award Act of 1976, the PLO could litigate more cases without charge, hoping to reap compensation by settling out of court or winning outright. Promoted as a mechanism for enforcing civil rights statutes, the act allowed judges to award fees to prevailing parties, offering financial incentive to private attorneys who might otherwise avoid costly civil litigation.[42] According to Taylor, "Periodically [the PLO won] a big recovery and that kind of cover[ed] our work," at least until the next "dry spell." In the meantime, he elaborated, "we [paid] whatever staff we had with whatever little money we had and just hope[d] that we [won] another case."[43] Agreeing to litigate Andrew Wilson's civil suit in 1987, the PLO worked for nearly a decade without payment.[44]

Amended by the People's Law Office, Wilson's complaint rested on 42 U.S.C. 1983, a Reconstruction-era statute known popularly as "Section 1983." A component of the Civil Rights Act of 1871, Section 1983 allowed citizens to sue individuals for violating their civil rights under state authority. While the statute lay "dormant" for nearly a century following the collapse of Reconstruction in the 1870s, plaintiffs rediscovered Section 1983 during the Second Reconstruction of the 1960s.[45] Citing the Fourth and Fourteenth Amendments to the U.S. Constitution, the PLO accused the City of Chicago, former CPD Superintendent Richard Brzeczek, Jon Burge, and several other officers of violating Wilson's right to due process and equal protection of the law. Demanding $10 million in compensatory and punitive damages, the PLO claimed officers "unlawfully" held Wilson, "torture[d] him as punishment for the alleged murder of the two police officers," and "force[d] him to make an inculpatory statement." Broadening the scope of the complaint, the PLO accused detectives of pursuing a "de facto policy, practice and/or custom of the city of Chicago, its police department, and defendant Brzeczek" of "isolating," "physically abusing," and "exacting unconstitutional revenge and punishment" against defendants, especially those accused of injuring or killing "a fellow officer." Insisting detectives upheld these policies "in practically every felony arrest that occurred in Chicago in 1982," the complaint carried implications far beyond the Wilson case.[46]

To answer the charges, the city hired former First Assistant State's Attorney William J. Kunkle, an esteemed prosecutor lionized for putting away serial killer John Wayne Gacy in 1980.[47] While Kunkle left the State's Attorney's Office for private practice in 1985, he led the prosecution of both Wilson brothers in 1983 and returned for Andrew's second conviction in 1988.[48] For Kunkle, Wilson's 1989 civil trials would be the third and fourth round of a five-round, ten-year bout. This time he stood in the defendants' corner, representing the City of Chicago and Jon Burge—a decorated Vietnam veteran and high-ranking police commander—against a career criminal and convicted cop-killer. Sitting ringside, journalist John Conroy described the case as "the underclass . . . having a go at the establishment."[49] Echoing earlier proceedings, Kunkle countered Wilson's allegations with the rehearsed denials of sworn detectives and prosecutors. Shown photographs of the plaintiff taken in February 1982, a medical expert dismissed burn marks on Wilson's body as "friction abrasions" incurred, perhaps, during the struggle with Patrolman Fahey days earlier.[50] In his closing argument, Kunkle laid bare the simple task before the jury. "You are being asked to believe [Wilson] over the policemen," he explained. "It is up to you to decide who is telling the truth."[51] While an appellate court already concluded officers abused Wilson, the jury waffled. "We're sure something happened to him," one juror reported afterward, "but maybe he inflicted it himself."[52] On March 30, 1989, the jury acquitted two of the officers but divided over the culpability of Jon Burge. Declaring a mistrial, Judge Brian Barnett Duff of the district court scheduled another trial for later that year.

Even as they litigated the first trial, Jeff Haas, Flint Taylor, and John Stainthorp of the People's Law Office uncovered additional torture allegations going back to the early 1970s. When the day's mail arrived at the PLO's downtown office on the morning of February 3, 1989, Taylor pulled a one-page letter from an envelope with no return address. In clipped prose, an anonymous author with intimate knowledge of Area 2 purported inside information on the Wilson case, hinted at additional torture victims, and implicated powerful public figures. Begging for secrecy, the author revealed that in February 1982 "several witnesses" associated with Wilson "had been severely beaten" at CPD headquarters in front of high-ranking officials, including Superintendent Brzeczek and top members of the state's attorney's office. "Mayor [Jane] Byrne and States Attorney [Richard M.] Daley were aware of the actions of the detectives," the letter explained, yet both "ordered that the numerous complaints filed against the police as a result of this crime not be investigated." While the officers involved had a history of abusing suspects with various "torture machines," the author continued, the main device had been "destroyed by throwing it off Lt. Burge's boat." The letter insisted that many Area 2 detectives believed "torture was not necessary" and remained "disgusted." Signing off, the author instructed Taylor to place a cryptic ad in a neighborhood newspaper if he wanted more information.[53] With jury selection only weeks away, PLO attorneys had little time to question the letter's validity or chase its tantalizing leads.

Like a paperback plot device, three more letters arrived over the next four months, teasing PLO attorneys with puzzling clues. One thing seemed clear—they had stumbled upon a much larger story. Following instructions, Taylor placed a short ad in the classifieds section of the *Southtown Economist* on February 7, 1989, reading, "Further information sought on Wilson case, Call."[54] As weeks went by, the civil trial moved forward without word from the mysterious whistle-blower. Then on March 7, another letter appeared with the same typewritten text, this time in an envelope marked with a seal: "City of Chicago, Department of Police." Signed only "T.Y.," the letter announced, "I believe that I have learned something that will blow the lid off of your case." Demanding secrecy, the author complained, "Your ad in the newspaper was a little to [*sic*] obvious." Providing a list of detectives present at Area 2 in the early 1980s, the short message separated twenty officers, including two women, into two categories—"Burge's Asskickers" and "Weak Links." Sergeant John Byrne, Burge's "main man," topped the list of ass kickers. Another, Detective Fred Hill, allegedly earned a "[ch]oice job" at the criminal courts building as a result of his involvement. The "weak links" included at least two black detectives as well as Frank Laverty, whose role in exposing dirty tricks within the unit led to his ostracism and transfer.[55] Hungry for more information, the attorneys accommodated the confidentiality concerns of the anonymous T.Y.—whom Taylor referred to as "Deep Badge" in a wry allusion to the famous Watergate informant Deep Throat.[56] Taylor and his colleagues embedded a coded message into another ad in the *Southtown Economist* a week later.[57]

Two final letters from Deep Badge offered more information and set the PLO on a path to fresh discovery. Postmarked March 15, a third letter placed T.Y. further out on a limb, prompting the author to plea, "I do not wish to be shunned like Officer Laverty has been since he co-operated with you." Despite the risks of coming forward, several former Area 2 detectives "[did] not approve of the beatings and torture" and wanted to see Burge punished. Adamant of Wilson's guilt, however, they also wanted assurances that monetary damages would go to "the families of the [slain] police officers" and not to Wilson or his dependents. To secure these ends, T.Y. directed the PLO to Melvin Jones, a criminal suspect tortured by Burge just days before Wilson in February 1982. Sitting in Cook County Jail awaiting trial on unrelated murder charges, Jones would corroborate Wilson's story. "You will also find," T.Y. added, "that the State's Attorney knew that [Jones] was complaining and that is why [earlier] charges were dropped. That decision was made in the top levels [of the Criminal Courts Building] at 26th and California."[58] Busy with Wilson's ongoing trial, PLO attorneys scrambled to locate and interview Melvin Jones.

The last anonymous letter arrived on June 19, several months after the first hung jury. With a second trial set to begin within days, Deep Badge narrowed attention to the torture regime's ringleader. "The common cord is Burge," the letter insisted. "He was always present, the machines and the plastic bags were his and he is the person who encouraged their use."[59] In an earlier letter, T.Y. told Taylor: "Burge hates black people and is an ego maniac. He would do anything to further himself."[60] The author elaborated: "You will find that the people with him were either weak and easily led or sadists. He probably did this because it was easier than spending the time and the effort talking people into confessing." Lazy or not, Burge was proud of his work. According to T.Y., "Burge thinks this is his most important case and he brags about it. You could check in the taverns at 103rd and 92 and Western and you will find that Burge youse [*sic*] to brag about everyone he beat." Collectively, the four letters painted a clear picture. Burge began torturing suspects "right after becoming a detective" in 1972.[61] Corroborating evidence could be found in brutality complaints or in the record of pretrial motions to suppress statements going back to the 1970s. Implicating other officers in additional cases, Deep Badge tried to clear the names of detectives who, the author persisted, "had nothing at all to do with Burge and his crew."[62] Prodding Taylor to fish for further victims, T.Y. warned of bogus allegations. From these letters, the PLO formulated a growing list of reliable claims, eventually over one hundred names, that would help construct a skeletal narrative of the Burge scandal. Taken together, they hoped, the list would provide legitimacy to individuals who otherwise appeared incredible in isolation.

Armed with explosive new information, the PLO attempted to transform the nature of the second civil trial, spanning eight weeks, from late June through August 1989. First, Wilson's attorneys sought to have Judge Brian Barnett Duff recused from the proceedings, claiming he displayed a clear "bias or prejudice" in favor of the defendant police officers and an outright hostility to Wilson and his attorneys.[63] Indeed, Flint Taylor depicted Duff's behavior as bordering on the pathological. Not only did Duff routinely side with the defense; he also fought openly with PLO attorneys, threatened them with contempt on multiple occasions, and referred to Wilson off the record as the "scum of the Earth."[64] Unfortunately for Wilson, a higher court denied the motion, forcing the PLO back into Duff's courtroom for another go. Facing a new jury, the plaintiffs planned to build a foundation of other cases in order to establish the pattern of abuse at Area 2. Convinced they were "sitting on an iceberg of torture evidence," PLO attorneys no longer relied simply on Wilson's word against detectives'.[65] When the time came, however, Judge Duff refused to allow jurors to hear testimony from any of these old cases, finding the evidence irrelevant to Wilson's claim.[66]

As for defense strategy, William Kunkle dropped the expert testimony dismissing the burns on Wilson's chest and thigh as friction abrasions, a revealing change from the first trial.[67] Instead, Kunkle brought in a former cellmate of Wilson's to explain how the injuries, by then conceded to be burns, may have occurred. According to the jailhouse informant, a notorious con man from England with a record of making deals with prosecutors, Wilson once admitted he caused the injuries himself, leaning into a hot radiator at the police lockup to corroborate the torture claims and suppress his confession.[68] Judge Duff also permitted Kunkle to bombard the jury with numbing details from Andrew Wilson's life of crime, describing at length the murders of Officers Fahey and O'Brien. Objecting, Wilson's attorneys argued that such detail was irrelevant to the question of police torture. From their perspective, and that of the law, it did not matter what Wilson stood accused of in 1982. He was not on trial. The only relevant question was whether detectives abused Wilson or not. By allowing Kunkle to fuel the jury's personal fear and hatred of Wilson, Judge Duff played right into the strategy of the defense.[69]

In an unusual outcome in a federal civil rights trial, the judge requested a "special verdict" at the close of proceedings.[70] Rule 49 of the Federal Rules of Civil Procedure authorized a federal judge to order a jury bring a special verdict regarding specific facts of a case rather than a general verdict of guilt or innocence.[71] In this particular case, while the jury found Wilson's constitutional rights had been violated, jurors also found none of the accused officers personally responsible. In addition, while the CPD did, in fact, have a "de facto policy authorizing its police officers physically to abuse persons suspected of having killed or injured a police officer," the jury concluded that the policy "had not been a direct and proximate cause of the physical abuse visited on Wilson."[72] Applying these findings of fact, Judge Duff acquitted all defendants. Although a federal jury confirmed Burge supervised the torture of a criminal suspect, the verdict also cleared Burge, allowing him to remain in charge of detectives at Area 3. While the jury legitimized

Wilson's claims, he received no judicial relief and zero monetary damages. As expected, the PLO appealed and the case dragged on for years.[73]

"We Cannot Have Guardians That Have to Be Guarded," 1989–1993

While two federal juries refused to hold detectives responsible for documented abuse, publicity garnered by the proceedings dragged the torture regime out of the shadows once and for all.[74] Published accounts of Area 2 torture began appearing at the start of the first trial in February 1989.[75] The earliest article expressing unequivocal disgust and linking prisoner abuse to State's Attorney Richard M. Daley appeared in *Crain's Chicago Business* on February 20, just days before Daley's first victory in a mayoral primary. Witnessing opening arguments, journalist Rob Warden argued that Chicago was home to serious police violence. "Not your garden-variety police brutality," Warden insisted, "[but] real torture in the Third World sense."[76] In a longer treatment published in March, the *Chicago Lawyer* offered play-by-play of the first civil trial, implicated Burge by name, and presented evidence kept from the jury. Alongside color photographs of Wilson's injuries, the author concluded, "Authorities empowered to investigate such charges—the state's attorney of Cook County, the U.S. attorney for the Northern District of Illinois, and the Chicago Police Department's internal investigative unit—have known about the evidence for years, but have done nothing."[77] As Judge Duff considered allowing testimony from other torture victims, an April 1989 article claimed he also informed the U.S. Attorney of the allegations. If proven, Duff explained, he would demand a federal investigation of Burge. If not, he added, "An inquiry should also be made into whether a conspiracy was engaged in by the other side [the PLO] to suborn perjury and/or interfere with the process of this court."[78] The city's major daily newspapers offered cursory coverage of the trials as well, albeit without the editorial outrage appropriate for such serious revelations.[79]

When they first learned of the Burge scandal, the small but influential network of community organizers, volunteers, and progressives active in the decades-long fight for police accountability in Chicago reacted with shock and anger. Conditioned to channel outrage into action, activists went to work. For years, the League of Women Voters of Illinois and other civic groups sent court watchers to monitor legal proceedings and publicize issues that had an impact on the community.[80] Continuing this tradition, the police watchdog group Citizens Alert regularly dispatched volunteers to

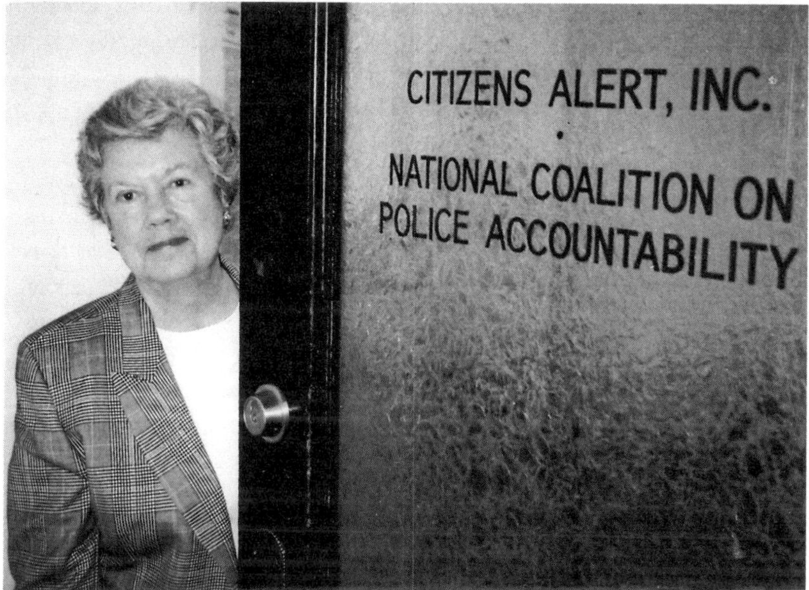

FIGURE 12 Mary Powers, pictured here in the early 1990s, fought for police accountability in Chicago for more than forty years as a member of Citizens Alert. Jennifer McClory, Courtesy of Sun-Times Media.

audit trials related to police misconduct. When lawyers at the People's Law Office disseminated torture allegations following Wilson's first civil trial in spring 1989, Mary Powers and other members of Citizens Alert decided to make themselves fixtures in the gallery of the summer retrial.[81] Since at least the early 1980s, the PLO and Citizens Alert forged a friendly working relationship, with activists referring clients to the law collective for legal consultation.[82] As the number of known torture survivors grew, Flint Taylor handed the list over to journalists and community activists. When the second trial began in June 1989, protestors circulated fliers outside the courthouse demanding a "fair trial" and an official investigation. Publicly criticizing Judge Duff for "[continuing] the cover-up," activists invited supporters to "express your outrage at the blatant disregard for the law and human rights of people [merely] *accused* of committing crimes."[83] The fight against Burge had been joined.

Indeed, within weeks of Wilson's testimony an evolving coalition of individuals and organizations initiated collective action to confront the emerging scandal. Once in motion, the Chicago torture justice movement survived for the next thirty years and more, strategically shifting direction, altering priorities, or changing emphasis as conditions dictated. Rallying disparate actors around a vague mandate for simple justice, the movement employed a range of strategies and tactics. Torture survivors and their families shared their stories, imparted emotional gravity to the struggle, and directly participated as activists and leaders. Civic and religious groups held meetings, spread awareness, and rallied support. Ordinary citizens and volunteers attended rallies, petitioned public officials, and initiated accountability mechanisms. Lawyers litigated cases, elucidated complex legal matters, and navigated establishment circles. When circumstances required more immediate pressure, militants and radicals led public protests and disrupted normal procedures. Representing a softer approach, journalists and academics researched, published, and broadcast information and arguments to a wider audience. While diverse methods occasionally worked at cross-purposes, allies recognized shared goals and negotiated disputes. Never formally constituted or institutionalized, the shifting parts of the Chicago torture justice movement nevertheless operated with consistency, unity, and resilience. In response to wide exposure of the torture crisis in 1989, for example, the movement began with a coordinated campaign to get Jon Burge fired.

Looking for leverage, veteran activists immediately tapped a number of long-established relationships. On July 26, even as the second civil trial dragged on, Mary Powers sent a letter directly to David Fogel, chief administrator of the CPD's Office of Professional Standards (OPS), demanding Burge's suspension pending investigation. Powers had nurtured a cordial relationship with Fogel since his appointment in 1984, praising his efforts to reform the department's much-maligned and ineffective internal investigations unit.[84] While the OPS closed Wilson's complaint four years earlier with a finding of "not sustained," Powers appealed to Fogel's pride and independence, writing, "The previous attempt occurred prior to your appointment and typified the shortcomings behind the call for the abolishment of [OPS]."[85] Lest new cases uncovered by Deep Badge and the PLO slip through the cracks, Powers formally registered new OPS complaints on behalf of Wilson, Melvin Jones, and Donald White, the man who gave the Wilson brothers up to detectives after a torture session in February 1982.[86] Responding with unusual speed, Fogel met with Powers and representatives of several other organizations the next day, agreeing to "reopen the investigation into Andrew Wilson's allegations of police torture once the current court case is ended and to open investigations into [the] two other cases."[87] While Fogel's pledge fell short of the urgent action demanded by Citizens Alert, local activists considered it a good start.

Turning to other time-honored connections, Citizens Alert spent August resuscitating the coalition of community organizations, churches, and individuals that came together in the wake of the manhunt for the Wilson brothers seven years earlier. In a newsletter sent to old friends and allies on August 1, Powers wrote: "Your participation was important when we confronted Mayor Byrne on this issue in 1982. [Now] it is really vital to our efforts to confront an even more serious situation."[88] Later named the Coalition to End Police Torture and Brutality, the umbrella group united over thirty-five community organizations in a concerted effort to force the CPD to act.[89] Members included Citizens Alert, the People's Law Office, the Chicago Committee to Defend the Bill of Rights, the Illinois Coalition Against the Death Penalty, the Japanese American Citizens League, the Jewish Council on Urban Affairs, the National Alliance against Racist and Political Repression, the National Council of Black Lawyers, the National Lawyers Guild, Operation PUSH, and dozens more.[90]

Having won the verbal support of OPS Director Fogel, the coalition moved to its next target—the Chicago Police Board. Appointed to locate and hire a new police superintendent in the wake of a serious police scandal in 1960, the members of the Chicago Police Board were later tasked with narrowly defined bureaucratic responsibilities that included approving disciplinary action against individual officers.[91] Sometime in 1970, Citizens Alert volunteers stumbled on the obscure Illinois Open Meetings Act and decided to crash the board's monthly closed-door meetings. Through a pious determination to attend each and every session, by the late 1980s the Chicago Police Board had become something of a public forum for the airing of citizen complaints.[92] Responding to the torture crisis, the coalition ambushed the "normally sedate" meeting on August 17, 1989, leading a brief protest outside police headquarters before ushering upward of seventy activists into the auditorium.[93] After taking care of routine business, the board yielded the floor to the public. Representing the coalition, Mary Powers outlined the nascent narrative of the torture scandal and repeated demands sent to the OPS—Burge's suspension followed by a "broad investigation." She further requested that the board hold public hearings so torture survivors and their families could have their voices heard. Before passing the microphone, Powers added that if their demands were ignored, "the Coalition will hold hearings on its own." Another community leader suggested the board convene meetings somewhere other than police headquarters, where officials could "assess what is actually happening" in the neighborhoods and experience the visceral anger of local people firsthand.[94]

As one agitator gave way to the next, beleaguered board members deflected, repeatedly citing their lack of power to initiate investigations or punish officers directly. Near the end of the meeting, police Superintendent LeRoy Martin announced he already sent for a transcript of the Wilson civil trial. He promised to look it over and make a personal decision regarding disciplinary action. Accusing police supervisors of ignoring evidence of prisoner abuse at Area 2 for years, People's Law Office attorney Jeff Haas rejected the trial transcripts as too narrow, reminding Martin, "The Department could have much [more] information concerning allegations of torture if it chose to secure that information."[95] Shuffling out of the auditorium, activists knew they would need to sustain pressure on the police board, the superintendent, and other officials before meaningful action would be taken.

At the next meeting in September 1989, Powers again took the floor to ask about the Burge investigation. A noticeably irritated Superintendent Martin told the crowd he would "act when he finds evidence of wrongdoing, not when a citizens group feels he should act."[96] Pressed for results at another meeting two months later, Martin wondered why activists did not "follow up on the murder of Police Officer Elijah Harris, whose funeral was held last Tuesday, in the same way [they were] pursuing the Burge case."[97] Honoring activists' request, the board held its December meeting at the Center for Inner City Studies on the city's South Side. Unveiling a new monthly ritual, board members began with a standing ovation for recent recipients of departmental commendations, publicizing the meritorious service of brave officers to a crowd demanding accountability for police torture. Absent for the touching display, Superintendent Martin sent a deputy in his stead.[98] The department's intransigence did not surprise an audience that had long considered the Chicago Police Board—with the superintendent lording over its proceedings—a weak mechanism for accountability.

Recent developments had made the Chicago Police Board even less likely to accommodate the movement's demands. Since voters had elected Harold Washington Chicago's first black mayor in 1983, the police accountability movement nurtured a cautious optimism. In November 1987, however, Washington replaced the competent, affable Fred Rice—the CPD's first African American superintendent—with LeRoy Martin, a black career officer with a reputation as a "tough cop."[99] To prove his mettle, Martin famously boasted, "When you talk about gangs, I've got the toughest gang in town: the Chicago Police Department."[100] Martin even served as commander of Area 2 for nine months in 1982 and 1983, when Violent Crimes detectives tortured confessions from Darrell Cannon and other criminal suspects.[101] Less than a month after Martin's promotion, Mayor Washington died, opening a vacancy in City Hall later filled by Richard M. Daley, scion of Chicago's first family and head prosecutor during the height of the torture regime. Sitting beside Martin at monthly meetings throughout 1989, the board consisted of nine men and women—white, black, and Latino—appointed by the mayors Byrne and Washington, including Nancy Jefferson, an African American civil rights activist and former Citizens Alert board member.[102] Jefferson was among the last holdouts from what Mary Powers referred to as a "Camelot-like era" of open communication between police watchdogs and the late Washington administration.[103] Eight weeks later, Mayor Daley replaced two-thirds of the board, leaving Jefferson "the only real 'community' person" still serving.[104] With just one ally remaining, activists held little faith in the Chicago Police Board, especially considering Superintendent Martin and Mayor Daley's direct link to the Burge scandal.

The campaign to fire Burge dragged on for several more years. Accustomed to the long game, the Coalition to End Police Torture and Brutality drew from a repertoire of protest activities developed over decades of related struggle. Volunteers affixed thousands of signatures to a petition, bombarded politicians and police administrators with letters and phone calls, and persuaded progressive city council members to sponsor a resolution calling for Burge's firing.[105] They held regular meetings across the city, issued press releases, and organized rallies at Area 3 and police headquarters.[106] Activists mounted an art exhibit dramatizing police abuse and sponsored a documentary film on the Burge scandal.[107] Hedging their bets, coalition leaders went over the heads of Chicago officials, inviting independent investigations by the U.S. Attorney's Office, the FBI, and Amnesty International.[108] Citizens Alert sent a grant application to the American Friends Service Committee and raised thousands of dollars through local fund-raising.[109] In April 1991, a rally outside Mayor Daley's home exposed a rift within the coalition, as Citizens Alert criticized the "more radical" Task Force to Confront Police Violence and opted not to attend.[110] Having nurtured professional relationships with local law enforcement officials for more than two decades, Mary Powers and other so-called lakefront liberals chafed at the task force's "past modus operandi, agitation and militantism [*sic*]."[111] Subsumed for the greater good, however, ideological differences did not derail the movement's momentum.

In the early years of the Chicago torture justice movement, activists often referred to Burge's methods as "third-world torture tactics."[112] In a speech designed to sway skeptical members of the City Council, for example, a Citizens Alert spokesperson asserted, "Electroshock, beatings, intimidation by suffocation by placing plastic bags over the heads of suspects are all charges we are accustomed to hearing from Central America and other third world countries. Chicago is joining their ranks!"[113] Andrew Wilson's lawyers beseeched jurors in 1989: "This isn't Chile. This isn't El Salvador. This is the United States of America."[114] Evoking international scandal well into the 1990s, activists contrasted routine police abuse with egregious acts of torture. Aware that many Chicagoans tolerated—even celebrated—a limited degree of police violence, activists framed Burge as having gone too far. Confronting widespread apathy, activists knew tales of routine deception, manipulation, and psychological stress alone would not raise concern over coerced confessions. Prior to the War on Terror, so-called first-world torture—the stress positions and sensory deprivation developed by the Central Intelligence Agency in the 1950s—had yet to become a focal point of national criticism.[115] To drum up support, the movement relied on the most sensational details of the Burge scandal, hence the proliferation of third-world analogies. By the mid-1990s, however, activists dropped the by-then-politically-incorrect term and adopted a more sensitive, if still controversial, phrase—police torture.

For two years after the summer of 1989, community activists and city officials maneuvered in stalemate. As corroborating evidence piled up, however, official denials became less defensible. In the absence of official hearings, Citizens Alert made good on its promise to hold its own "People's Tribunal" on police torture, offering a forum for citizens to air general grievances against a range of police behavior.[116] In August 1989, patrol officers deliberately stranded two black teenagers in the hostile community of Canaryville, a white, working-class enclave a few blocks from Mayor Daley's home in Bridgeport. In a matter of minutes, a gang of white teenagers beat one of the boys to within an inch of his life.[117] With black communities seething, City Council commenced public hearings on police brutality in September and October, providing occasion for more torture allegations to surface.[118] In a parallel development, an appellate court overturned the conviction of torture survivor Gregory Banks on December 28, ruling that "his confession was procured through police brutality and racial intimidation."[119] Bundled with other rulings, including those of Andrew Wilson's criminal and civil trials, judicial authority provided the strongest evidence condemning Burge and his men.

Other sources added substance to the allegations as well. At the end of January 1990, journalist John Conroy published the first of several long-form articles on the Burge scandal in the independent *Chicago Reader*. The previous year, Conroy sat brainstorming a book on torture when a friend told him about Andrew Wilson's civil suit.[120] Attending court alongside Mary Powers, Conroy fully appreciated the severity of the allegations. After months of research, and a rare interview with Burge himself, Conroy sent his story to press. Titled "House of Screams," Conroy's exposé made little splash at the time but would go on to become the standard published account of the Wilson case and the Burge scandal.[121] Armed with hundreds of photocopies, Citizens Alert made sure each member of the Chicago Police Board got one.[122] Unable to dodge controversy forever, City Council finally allowed torture survivors, their family members, and allies to address the public in an open hearing at the end of 1990.[123] In an obvious attempt to blunt its impact, Alderman Edward Burke scheduled the hearing for Christmas Eve.[124] Undeterred, dozens of supporters "packed" the chambers to witness testimony on Area 2 torture going back more than a decade.[125] A few weeks later, Amnesty International concluded its own cursory investigation, releasing a small report in January 1991. With its global reach and reputation, the human rights organization drew wider publicity to the scandal, prodded federal authorities, and further legitimized the campaign to fire Burge.[126]

As pressure mounted, public officials delayed. Although OPS's Director Fogel reopened complaint files on Andrew Wilson, he could not guarantee the superintendent would honor the findings or release them to the public. In a confidential memo sent to Mayor Washington in 1987, Fogel had criticized the "politically corrupt heritage" of his own agency and lambasted its "irremediably incompetent investigators."[127] Condemning his predecessors for "institutionaliz[ing] lying, subterfuge, and injustice," Fogel concluded that the OPS regularly "immunized police from internal discipline" rather than bring wayward officers to heel.[128] Yet in one of his last acts before stepping down, Fogel assigned two civilian investigators to examine the case on March 27, 1990. For the following six months, Francine Sanders investigated torture allegations related specifically to Wilson, and Michael Goldston assessed "systematic abuse at Area 2 during that period" and the "culpability" of command personnel.[129] Upon completion, new OPS chief administrator, Gayle Shines—a Daley appointee—handed the Goldston and Sanders report to Superintendent Martin, adding, "Both investigators have done a masterful job of marshaling the facts in this intensive and extensive project and their conclusions are compelling."[130] Apparently, Martin disagreed. Finding the report "incomplete" and in need of further analysis, he waited three months before returning it to Shines for "additional information and work on the project."[131] Twelve weeks later, Shines reported that Goldston and Sanders stood by their conclusions and urged Martin to act. In May 1991, Martin alerted Commander Burge and two detectives, Patrick O'Hara and John Yucaitis, of possible disciplinary action, giving lawyers from the

Fraternal Order of Police until July to prepare a written defense.[132] Hoping the crisis would blow over, the CPD delayed accountability for over two years after news of the Burge scandal broke.

Local activists, however, would not let the torture issue go away. Indeed, national news forced police brutality on the public conscience in dramatic fashion in 1991. On March 3, a group of police officers physically beat African American motorist Rodney King following a high-speed chase through a residential neighborhood in Los Angeles, California. Grabbing a handheld video camera, a concerned citizen filmed the beating from his apartment and delivered the tape to local news.[133] As the footage spread, Citizens Alert seized the opportunity to unite affiliated organizations into a National Coalition on Police Accountability.[134] According to Mary Powers, not only did the video make Rodney King an unlikely American icon; it also "brought police brutality into the living rooms of the nation" as never before.[135] Attempting to shape consensus during a rare moment of shared outrage, the National Interreligious Task Force on Criminal Justice concluded: "As an isolated incident, the Rodney King case is a historic and verifiable fact that police violence is alive and well in America. When put in the context of what is a national epidemic of police abuse, the King case is only another example of the racist and repressive tactics that have become normative procedure and a matter of course in police departments across the country."[136] As King's beating came to define police brutality in the public imagination, the Burge cases failed to fit the paradigm. Andrew Wilson's ordeal did not look like Rodney King's. Nevertheless, rising awareness of police brutality provided activists leverage in their efforts to legitimize torture allegations in Chicago.

While national news provided larger context, local developments finally gave activists the crisis they needed to draw public officials against Burge. On October 1, 1991, twenty-nine-year-old Carolyn Wiggins asked Operation PUSH to help get her teenage son out of police custody. Wishing to file a complaint against Area 3 detectives, Wiggins eschewed OPS and pursued a referral to Citizens Alert. A few days earlier, Marcus Wiggins, age thirteen, was hanging out on a street corner around 8:00 p.m. when shots rang out, killing another young man in what police later reported was a gang-related shooting. Marcus and his friends ran from the scene but were picked up by detectives and taken to Area 3 for questioning. Along the way, officers threatened Wiggins and struck him with a flashlight. During the interrogation, the detectives John Paladino, Anthony Maslanka, James O'Brien, and Kenneth Boudreau allegedly punched and intimidated Wiggins before shocking him with a black box attached to his hands with electrical wires.

Although Wiggins was a minor who suffered a history of violent crime and exhibited an acute learning disability, officers refused him access to his mother or an attorney.[137] When Carolyn Wiggins recounted her son's story to Citizens Alert days later, she had only spoken to him briefly on the telephone. Mary Powers told her about the pattern of torture connected to Area 3 Commander Burge and asked permission to tell Wiggins's story to the *Chicago Reader*, the PLO, and Amnesty International.[138] As if activists needed any reminding, the Wiggins case highlighted the urgency of their efforts. While public officials deflected, Jon Burge continued to work each day at Area 3, personally supervising investigations and overseeing interrogations.

Even as the Coalition to End Police Torture and Brutality continued its protests, Superintendent Martin sought to discredit and suppress the Goldston and Sanders report. Requesting an external review by the Police Foundation, a private agency chaired by conservative political scientist James Q. Wilson, Martin was pleased when the appraisal found "the data base limited, full of missing data, and in need of much more thorough analysis." Far from a slam dunk, the review argued, the data "hardly amounts to [even] a 'preponderance of evidence.'"[139] Unfortunately for Martin, highlighting the obvious flaws in the OPS investigation did little to calm community anger or reduce pressure on City Hall. On October 10, torture survivor Gregory Banks filed a civil suit against Burge, four other detectives, Superintendent Martin, and the City of Chicago.[140] Three weeks later, the City Council approved a $5,000 settlement in the civil suit of Alphonso Pinex, tortured in two separate encounters with Area 2 detectives in 1982 and 1985.[141] While settlements prevented the publicity of trial and allowed Mayor Daley and others to escape depositions, they also garnered headlines and lent credibility to further allegations. As evidence against Burge multiplied, LeRoy Martin caved. On November 9, 1991, the superintendent officially filed administrative charges against Burge, O'Hara, and Yucaitis, suspending them without pay while they awaited hearings before the Chicago Police Board. Charged with violating administrative rules, they would be terminated if found guilty.[142]

Pleased with Martin's bold—if belated—action, the Coalition to End Police Torture and Brutality filed an amicus brief with the Chicago Police Board and awaited the outcome.[143] Considering the board's history of reducing superintendents' recommended punishments, few activists were optimistic.[144] Meanwhile, officers' supporters geared up for a fight. Michael Fahey, brother of one of the patrolmen Andrew Wilson killed ten years earlier, secured thousands of names on a petition supporting the suspended officers.[145] Rallying behind Burge, O'Hara, and Yucaitis—affectionately referred to by their initials as the "BOY" officers—the Fraternal Order of Police (FOP) paid for the return services of private attorney William Kunkle and raised money to support the accused and their families.[146] Fearful that a guilty ruling would only encourage "the People's Law Office and other defense attorneys [to] continue their conspiracy with their convicted criminal clients, and initiate factually baseless lawsuits," FOP attorneys unsuccessfully sought a restraining order to block the hearings altogether.[147] On February 25, 1992, the FOP held a twenty-dollar-a-plate banquet for the BOY Committee fund.[148] Held in a reception hall at Teamster's union headquarters, the event was disrupted by the Task Force to Confront Police Violence, a "radical off-shoot of the coalition,"[149] whose members urged counterdemonstrators to "Shout, Dance & Demonstrate Against Their Torture Party."[150] In a show of petty retaliation, FOP members fought to block check-off donations to the United Way after hearing false rumors the charity once contributed to the People's Law Office.[151] While the sideshow unfolded, the main event got under way in the sixth-floor auditorium at police headquarters.[152]

Three days before opening arguments, the CPD lost a major public relations battle when Flint Taylor, litigating another torture case, won partial release of the Goldston and Sanders report.[153] According to Citizens Alert, whenever activists met with Superintendent Martin to discuss the OPS investigation, "he went through an elaborate charade of shuffling through papers on his desk," issued empty promises, and stalled for time.[154] Tired of delay, activists collected names on a petition while PLO attorneys filed motions in federal court.[155] Ignoring objections from the FOP, Judge Milton I. Shadur lifted a protective order on the report—minus the superintendent's signature—on February 7, 1992.[156] In sixty-six pages, Sanders outlined the Wilson case and sustained charges against the BOY officers.[157] Goldston provided a partial database with the names of fifty men alleging abuse at Area 2 as far back as 1973. The real bombshell came in Goldston's brief summary. "The preponderance of evidence is that abuse did occur and that it was systematic," the department's civilian investigator concluded, adding: "The type of abuse described was not limited to the usual beating, but went into such esoteric areas as psychological techniques and planned torture." In condemning high-ranking personnel, Goldston wrote, "particular command members were aware of the systematic abuse and perpetrated it either by actively participating in same or failing to take any action to bring it to an end."[158] Quoted at length, the report garnered the Burge scandal its first national headlines.[159] Calling the report "too broad," Mayor Daley dismissed it as inconclusive. Denying implications of his own culpability, Superintendent Martin told reporters: "It's a lie, an outright lie. Whoever said that doesn't know what they're talking about."[160] Ridiculing Martin's denials, Citizens Alert announced, "If he was not aware of it, he should have been!"[161] The Chicago Police Board added the reports to the record and scheduled the first day of the hearing for February 10, 1992.

Lasting six weeks, the hearings must have elicited feelings of déjà vu for attorney William Kunkle and anyone else familiar with the Wilson case. After two criminal trials and two civil trials, the Chicago Police Board hearings saw lawyers rehash a lot of old evidence. Despite its formal trappings and judicial procedure, however, the board was not a civil or criminal court. Sessions unfolded within a vacuous police auditorium or, on special occasions, in a large room provided by Kunkle's law firm in a premier Loop skyscraper.[162] Lacking a jury to sway with dramatic appeals, attorneys spoke for the benefit of a court reporter, whose meticulous record of proceedings later went before the nine-member board, none of whom sat in attendance. Because Burge, O'Hara, and Yucaitis were accused of breaking departmental rules, not the law, attorneys referred to them as "respondent officers," not "defendants." In lieu of a judge, an administrative officer sat awkwardly on the bench, often relaxing legal procedure and allowing testimony restricted elsewhere.[163] While participants performed professionally and respected the gravity of the charges, both supporters and critics of the CPD cynically wondered whether the outcome was predetermined one way or the other. Accusing Superintendent Martin of scapegoating the officers to protect himself and Daley, the FOP bristled at the "trumped up" and "manufactured" charges.[164] Wary of a whitewash, the Chicago torture justice movement worried that the hearings would acquit the officers and return them to the force.

Cognizant of public perception, the city hired former assistant U.S. attorney Daniel E. Reidy to present the department's case against the officers. In the 1970s, federal prosecutors chose a twenty-seven-year-old Reidy to spearhead Operation Greylord, an unprecedented, massive prosecution of local law enforcement officials considered "one of the most complex and far-reaching government corruption investigations in U.S. history."[165] Reidy's $500,000 fee alone should have silenced skeptics about the sincerity of the city's effort to fire Burge.[166] Picking up where Wilson's public defenders and the People's Law Office left off, Reidy and his team built a strong case. In between appearances by multiple law enforcement and medical experts, they elicited testimony from several torture survivors, including Melvin Jones and Wilson himself, escorted in chains from Pontiac Correctional Center some one hundred miles southwest of Chicago.[167] Kunkle and the defense team countered with expert testimony of their own, as well as the staid narration of events from several former Area 2 detectives, including a polite and cooperative Commander Burge, who denied abusing anyone and dismissed his accusers as unreliable.

Answering questions in a lighthearted yet professional manner, Burge appeared confident and comfortable, occasionally displaying a witty sarcasm his adversaries dismissed as arrogance.[168] Admitting he "dealt with some pretty non-credible bad ex-convict pieces of garbage over the years," Burge conceded his distaste for Andrew Wilson, a man who "never worked in his entire life" and "preyed on the citizenry around him." Proud of removing such men from society, Burge explained, "The average law abiding citizen on the street had much less of a chance remaining alive with those people out there." Discussing Wilson's arrest, Burge recalled "a great deal of venom let out by a lot of police officers that day" and admitted he "probably said several unkind words to him at the scene." Refusing to elaborate, he pleaded, "I would be rather embarrassed in front of all the females in the audience to recite it." Insisting he told detectives to "treat [Wilson] with kid gloves," Burge explained how abuse allegations "stood a very good chance of jeopardizing the admissibility of any statement . . . and therefore jeopardizing the prosecution." He knew of superficial injuries Wilson incurred during transfer to lockup but found it "humorous" how attorneys inflated minor altercations. "I saw an artist's sketch of Mr. Wilson with the turbine bandage and big patch on his eye," he recalled, "and my personal opinion was they were really playing it up grand." In twenty years on the job, he had seen "a lot of fights between police officers and suspects, but I wouldn't consider any of it mistreatment." Burge also admitted operating electric field telephones in Vietnam and developing a "rudimentary familiarity with a car's electrical system" in a short stint as a mechanic.[169]

Struggling to account for physical evidence, the defense offered several explanations for the marks on Wilson's body, recycling contradictory testimony from earlier proceedings.[170] For example, Kunkle submitted multiple decorative roach clips used by prison inmates to smoke marijuana cigarettes, suggestive, he claimed, of how Wilson faked the alligator-clip marks on his ears and nostril.[171] Had it been a criminal trial, with the state needing to prove guilt beyond a reasonable doubt, suggesting the reasonable possibility that someone other than the accused officers abused Wilson may have been enough. Yet the burden of proof in the administrative hearing was much lower. The city's attorneys needed only suggest by a preponderance of evidence that Burge and his men likely abused Wilson. With no jury and a lower standard of proof, Kunkle faced tough odds of convincing the board of Burge's innocence.

Attorneys presented closing arguments in late March 1992. Devoting some effort to dismissing the evidence against his clients, William Kunkle's main strategy hinged not on denying torture but on justifying it. "What we're losing sight of here," he told the board, "is what these guys do all year, every year at a place like Area 2 headquarters. What we're losing sight of is how many homicides there are in this city and in this area every year and how many armed robberies and how many rapes and how many gang killings and how many drug deal killings and how many witness killings and doubles and triples."[172] Balancing contradictory arguments—Wilson was not tortured, but if he was, he deserved it—Kunkle's appeal to the ambiguity of justice had worked well with federal jurors three years earlier.

Rejecting Kunkle's emotional, fear-driven justification, Reidy reminded board members of their duty. It fell to them to uphold the highest principles of the U.S. Constitution. Acknowledging widespread disgust with the accusers, Reidy emphasized the board's decision would not "make Andrew Wilson rich," an outcome "too much for anybody to stomach and [that] may explain some of those civil verdicts as well as anything." Soft-pedaling his criticism of police behavior, Reidy laid bare the implications of official collusion in brutality. "They did something they thought was to a guilty person," Reidy explained. "They did something to someone they viewed as a piece of human garbage, and they did it to him to secure a conviction that the man richly deserved. But we simply cannot have it. The costs of misconduct like this are not acceptable. We cannot have guardians that have to be guarded."[173] With proceedings closed, the hearing officer sent the final transcript—at over 3,800 pages the "most voluminous" in the board's thirty-year history—to the board members for review and decision.[174]

Those expecting swift punishment—or, alternately, an immediate acquittal—grew frustrated when progress turned to delay. Again, national events influenced local decisions. Just as board members settled into the lengthy transcript, on April 29, 1992, a jury in Simi Valley, California, acquitted officers accused of beating Rodney King. Later that day, Los Angeles erupted in the nation's most destructive urban rebellion since the New York City draft riots of the Civil War.[175] In Chicago, public officials noted the tense nature of police-community relations and wondered aloud whether the Chicago Bulls' pending repeat as champions of the National Basketball Association might trigger a similar riot.[176] While the Chicago Police Board considered the Burge case, Citizens Alert sought to channel community anger over the King verdict. "This should be a wake-up call to the general public," wrote Mary Powers, "a call to action—not to take to the streets—but to become involved in holding police accountable for their behavior."[177] Less interested in quelling rage, the Task Force to Confront Police Torture marched outside CPD headquarters in July to demand the board announce Burge's termination. Broaching the specter of the LA riots, activists distributed leaflets reading, "No Simi Valley in Chicago!" and "Could the Rodney King verdict happen here?"[178] Rumored to be reconsidering an earlier decision to exonerate Burge, the board responded with silence.[179]

While most observers awaited the fate of Burge and his men, others acted to ensure their protection. On April 7, 1992, State Senator Walter Dudycz—a former member of the Chicago Police—introduced Senate Bill 1789 to legislative committee in the General Assembly in Springfield.[180] Creating a three-year statute of limitations on allegations of excessive force, the bill was designed, in part, to save Burge and others from criminal assault charges.[181] Receiving little fanfare, the bill passed in June with a 55–0 vote in the Senate and a 98–7 vote in the House.[182] Awaiting the signature of Governor Jim Edgar, SB1789 came to the attention of Citizens Alert in July when a volunteer cut an article out of a local newspaper and brought it to a meeting of the Coalition to End Police Torture and Brutality.[183] Fearing it was too late, Mary Powers wrote Edgar begging for an eleventh-hour veto. Other letters implored coalition supporters, CPD Superintendent Matt Rodriguez, and the Chicago Police Board to urge the governor to quash the bill. In August, activists held a series of press conferences and protests at the Chicago Police Board, downtown Chicago's State of Illinois building, City Hall, and police headquarters. With editorial support from the *Chicago Sun-Times*, the campaign garnered vocal backing from several local institutions.[184] Weeks after meeting the governor's representatives, Citizens Alert celebrated a mixed victory when Edgar issued a veto on September 3, 1992.[185] Passed later that year, compromise legislation raised the statute of limitations from three to five years. Not retroactive, however, the bill did not protect officers, like Burge, accused of abuse before 1993.

The Chicago Police Board finally issued its ruling on February 11, 1993, nearly a year after the hearings closed. In a fifty-nine-page report, the board found the officers guilty of several violations, concluding only that Burge "mistreated" Wilson and that O'Hara and Yucaitis did nothing to stop or report it. The board suspended O'Hara and Yucaitis for fifteen months and fired Burge outright.[186] Bitter in defeat, the FOP sent an application to the South Side Irish Parade Committee proposing a float for the upcoming St. Patrick's Day festival. Titled "Travesties of Justice," the proposed design showcased Burge, O'Hara, Yucaitis, and the officers responsible for facilitating the 1989 attack on the two black teenagers in Canaryville. Led by the African-American Police League, renamed to reflect the role of women officers, protestors convinced the committee to reject the FOP's application.[187] Considering the officers' ongoing suspension as time served, the board allowed O'Hara and Yucaitis to return to duty. Leaving Chicago in disgrace, Jon Burge relocated to a "modest ranch home" in Apollo Beach, Florida, where he later worked as a freelance security guard and collected a healthy pension.[188] Eager to cite the board's ruling in other cases, the People's Law Office claimed victory. Hoping the decision would influence the outcome of his criminal and civil cases, Andrew Wilson pressed ahead with appeals. Citizens Alert relished a rare victory and basked in the praise of Chicago Police Board president Albert Maule, who told reporters that activists deserved credit for keeping the torture issue alive, "for better or for worse."[189] Outranking some "99 percent" of the force, Burge became the "highest ranking police official to be dismissed in over twenty years"—a great victory for the police watchdog community.[190] The fight for justice in the Burge scandal, however, had only just begun.

While public officials pointed to Burge's firing as proof the system worked, other observers drew more complex conclusions from the nearly four-year battle. Police accountability mechanisms may have improved since the 1960s, but the overall record remained discouraging. For example, not only did the Chicago torture justice movement compel the Chicago Police Board to respond to community pressure; it also forced the Office of Professional Standards to corroborate charges of violent misconduct. Yet considering the scope and gravity of the Burge scandal, the results hardly seemed proportional. In response to scores of torture allegations involving dozens of detectives and prosecutors, the CPD suspended only two officers and fired another. Moreover, even this minimal response required unusual effort from community activists. Meanwhile, prosecutors did not file criminal charges against perpetrators of torture. Courts did not proactively review cases of state prisoners convicted on the strength of coerced confessions. Officials made no apology, started no thorough investigation, granted no restitution. Nor did they reevaluate procedures, reorganize agencies, or establish new safeguards. If Mayor Richard M. Daley, the state's attorney, and the police superintendent thought justice could be bought so cheap, they were mistaken.

6

The Chicago Torture Justice Movement

For over twenty-five years following the firing of Jon Burge in 1993, the Chicago torture justice movement fought against great odds to realize a moral resolution of the torture crisis. Outraged by the scope of the scandal and its cover-up, a network of dedicated individuals and organizations struggled to illustrate the depth of injustice to an apathetic public. Yet convincing local people to set aside fears of crime, to honor due process, and to support the torture victims proved a constant challenge. Indeed, Burge and his men targeted suspects whose deviance and criminality—as well as race and class—yielded credibility and sympathy to the police. The largest obstacle to justice in the torture cases, however, remained the intransigence of local officials. Inside Cook County's incestuous criminal justice system, too many people working in the State's Attorney's Office, the Leighton Criminal Court Building, and City Hall in the 1990s and 2000s shared damning connections to the allegations at Area 2 and chose to protect themselves and their colleagues rather than correct injustice. Nevertheless, a steady stream of victories won by the torture justice movement—indeed, its very existence and endurance over time—signifies an overlooked history of resistance during an age of repressive policing and mass incarceration. While activists pressured local officials to provide relief for survivors, they also benefited from changes in the larger political opportunity structure, demonstrating the interplay between agency and contingency in the determination of social movement outcomes.

The Death Row 10 and the Anti-Death Penalty Movement

For much of the 1990s, the torture justice movement struggled to corroborate accusations and counter denials. If sporadic reference to police torture at Area 2 surfaced in Criminal Court transcripts throughout the 1980s, few persons outside the Public Defender's Office ever connected the dots.[1] Following Burge's firing in 1993, however, the kaleidoscope of cases on the appellate docket began twisting into a clear pattern. For example, Gregory Banks left prison when an appellate court tossed his coerced confession in 1989.[2] His codefendant David Bates won reversal on appeal in 1994.[3] Both men sued and received financial settlements in the tens of thousands of dollars.[4] In 1995, city attorneys flipped strategy in the ongoing civil suit brought by Andrew Wilson, finally stipulating that Burge had, in fact, tortured the plaintiff in 1982. But, they argued, the city was not responsible for civil damages because Burge acted "outside the scope of his employment."[5] The court disagreed.[6] After a decade of litigation, Wilson settled for $1,100,000 in July 1996. The People's Law Office received $900,016; the family of slain patrolman William Fahey received $100,000; and Andrew Wilson received nothing, having lost his claim to damages in a wrongful death suit brought by the Faheys years earlier.[7] These and other cases legitimized the torture allegations. In 1999, a federal judge declared, "It is now common knowledge that in the early to mid-1980s Chicago Police Commander Jon Burge and many officers working under him regularly engaged in the physical abuse and torture of prisoners to extract confessions."[8] By the early 2000s, the courts had long affirmed much of the social movement's basic narrative of the Burge scandal.[9]

While several interested parties cared deeply about righting the wrong of coerced confessions, corroborating the torture allegations became a matter of life and death for a key subset of survivors. More than a dozen men who encountered Jon Burge or his colleagues wound up on death row, where, facing extreme deprivation, they launched a campaign to win their release and abolish the death penalty in Illinois. Despite material and emotional barriers to forming any union with fellow prisoners, torture survivors found clever ways to communicate with one another and forge a collective identity.[10] In sporadic conversation with other prisoners—often shouted from one cell to another[11]—Chicago native Aaron Patterson discovered other men, like Stanley Howard, with near-identical claims of torture at the hands of detectives. In the summer of 1998, Patterson, Howard, and eight other prisoners formed the Death Row 10 (DR10) to collaborate for new hearings on the validity of their coerced confessions.[12] By 2003, the DR10 had grown to include thirteen men: Frank Bounds, Madison Hobley, Stanley Howard, Grayland Johnson, Leonard Kidd, Derrick King, Ronald Kitchen, Jerry Mahaffey, Reginald Mahaffey, Andrew Maxwell, Leroy Orange, Aaron Patterson, and Victor Safforld (also known as Cortez Brown).[13] They would enjoy their greatest success in partnership with the Campaign to End the Death Penalty (CEDP), a radical offshoot of the International Socialist Organization,[14] in the late 1990s and early 2000s.[15]

Already the "best-known" member of the DR10 at the time of its formation,[16] Aaron Patterson approached the fight with unapologetic anger.[17] Considering the weakness of the state's case against him, the credibility of his torture allegations, and his strong—if difficult—personality, Patterson emerged as an effective leader of an unconventional organization. In earlier efforts to organize outside pressure for his release, he and his mother, Jo Anne Patterson, had launched the Aaron Patterson Defense Committee in 1995.[18] Following their lead, all DR10 members argued that they deserved judicial relief because they were both tortured and innocent. Most of their cases, however, did not neatly fit the frame of innocence, making it a challenge for activists to rally mass support on the outside. Adding to the difficulty, details of their alleged crimes competed with details of alleged torture, obscuring personal information on the prisoners' character and life stories. Accordingly, activists, journalists, and academics struggled to depict the DR10 without reducing their lives to two critical moments—their involvement in violent crime and subsequent experience of torture.

In an effort to humanize the anti-death penalty movement and sway public opinion in their favor, the Death Row 10 worked to disseminate personal biographies beyond the prison walls. Aaron Patterson was born in 1964. The son of a Chicago police lieutenant, he grew up in a middle-class family, graduated from the prestigious De La Salle Institute, and briefly joined the National Guard. By his early twenties, Patterson also had compiled a lengthy criminal record and earned a reputation as a gang enforcer.[19] Learning of his arrest for assaulting a fellow gang member, detectives grabbed Patterson from a patrol precinct on April 30, 1986, and took him to Area 2 headquarters for questioning in a recent double homicide. According to detectives, Patterson first denied involvement but, after failing a polygraph, gave a statement to a court reporter outlining how he and a codefendant fatally stabbed an elderly couple during an armed robbery. On the advice of his grandmother and a lawyer, however, Patterson refused to sign the statement. Regardless, several detectives and an assistant state's attorney swore at trial that Patterson freely volunteered the confession. Despite a dearth of physical evidence, Patterson was convicted and sentenced to death.[20]

Challenging detectives' account of his interrogation, however, Patterson accused officers of threatening and beating him, twice suffocating him with a plastic typewriter cover, and forcing him to sign a false confession. In the midst of a twenty-five-hour ordeal, Patterson recalled Burge telling him not to tell anyone about the abuse, as it would be "your word against our word," and "who are they going to believe, you or us?"[21] Left alone for long stretches, Patterson used a discarded paper clip to etch a crude message on a metal bench and doorjamb, reading, "Aaron 4/30—I lie about murders—police threaten me with violence—slapped and suffocated me with plastic—No lawyer or DAD—No phone."[22] Attorneys submitted photographs of the etchings as proof of immediate outcry, but the judge denied Patterson's motion to suppress and allowed prosecutors to introduce the confession. Affirming Patterson's conviction on appeal, the Illinois Supreme Court ruled the torture allegations unfounded.[23] Nevertheless, Patterson's version of events gained credibility as lawyers working on other cases uncovered evidence of an historical pattern of torture at Area 2 and Area 3.[24]

Over the course of the 1990s, Aaron Patterson's exceptional determination and militancy attracted the attention of the anti–death penalty movement. With help from his mother, Aaron worked tirelessly to spread awareness of his case among influential persons on the outside, writing letters, making phone calls, and nurturing grassroots support for his release.[25] Before long, the Aaron Patterson Defense Committee began drawing supporters to local events. A flier promoting a rally at Area 2 headquarters on June 1, 1996, showed Patterson in prison clothes and handcuffs, standing before a bookcase, holding an opened law book, urging supporters to "speak out and demonstrate against police torture."[26] Harnessing Patterson's unique persona and persuasive claim to innocence, the anti–death penalty movement appealed to local residents uneasy with the state's growing list of wrongful convictions.

Fellow prisoner Stanley Howard also proved instrumental in organizing the DR10.[27] On November 1, 1984, Area 2 detectives arrested Howard on suspicion of breaking into a home in Blue Island, Illinois, tying up a male resident, sexually assaulting a woman, and robbing both of $800. During the course of several lineups held the next day, witnesses implicated Howard in additional crimes, including multiple sexual assaults and the robbery of two off-duty police officers. Recognizing a pattern in Howard's alleged offenses, detectives questioned him about a similar crime from six months earlier. Howard later accused detectives of beating him and suffocating him with a plastic bag until he confessed to fatally shooting a forty-two-year-old man on May 20, 1984.[28] Another suspect present at Area 2 that day claimed Howard told him officers were "trying to clear their books on him."[29] At trial, Judge John J. Mannion denied Howard's motion to suppress and allowed the jury to hear the allegedly coerced confession. A jury found Howard guilty and sentenced him to death.[30] Lawyers and journalists later uncovered compelling holes in the state's case.[31] Yet Howard was also convicted of two other violent crimes and sentenced to an additional seventy-eight years in prison.[32] With an "extensive history of violent criminal activity,"[33] Howard struggled to appear credible and sympathetic, even if claims of torture and wrongful conviction rang true. Nevertheless, Howard spent his time on death row awaiting progress in his appeals, learning the trade of a jailhouse lawyer, and helping rally support for the DR10 through written contributions to anti–death penalty publications.[34]

Shortly after helping found the DR10 in April 1998, Howard wrote the Campaign to End the Death Penalty looking to form a partnership.[35] The request included ideas for direct action, including a letter-writing campaign targeting Illinois Attorney General Jim Ryan and Chicago Mayor Richard M. Daley. Howard included a flier—produced in prison with cut-and-pasted headlines from the *New Abolitionist* and *Socialist Worker*—promoting the first DR10 demonstration rally.[36] Conceived by prisoners and orchestrated by CEDP, the event brought more than seventy protestors together in a public march around a Chicago police precinct in September 1998.[37] Despite their confinement, the prisoners signaled their partnership with the CEDP would not be one-sided. According to a 1999 summary of the fledgling alliance, the DR10 "risked retribution to organize themselves inside Illinois' prison system" while "the campaign on the outside . . . developed from community meetings to rallies, marches and civil disobedience acts."[38] Howard made the stakes of the movement explicit, writing: "Me, I'll work for justice in here. You, you work for justice out there. If not, these people are actually gonna kill us. It's gonna be a party, or it's gonna be a funeral. It's just that simple."[39] Within a year of forming, the DR10 began to attract support and enjoy victory in the courtroom.

The first significant achievement of the DR10 and the CEDP came in the appeal of Aaron Patterson's criminal conviction. In what the Illinois Supreme Court described as a "circumstantial evidence case," activists and attorneys focused attention on the dubious confession.[40] While Patterson's 1989 criminal trial occurred the same year as Andrew Wilson's civil trials, several years passed before the emerging torture scandal corroborated Patterson's allegations. Meanwhile, the state's only witness recanted her testimony, claiming she only implicated Patterson out of fear of the police.[41] As evidence against Burge mounted, not only did Patterson's original alibi gain credibility; missing fingerprint, palm-print, and shoe-print evidence became more suspicious.[42] Even the state's highest court conceded, "No physical evidence was presented linking defendant to the murders."[43] Further, Patterson's interrogation-room etchings, immediate complaint to a judge, and consistent story bolstered claims of custodial abuse.[44] Indeed, Patterson's early outcry belied critics who dismissed him for joining the torture bandwagon only after Wilson's civil suit. When Patterson refused to drop the torture allegations in exchange for his release in 2001, supporters marveled at his dedication. "Aaron is literally putting his life on the line so the truth of police torture can be exposed," explained a leading anti–death penalty activist.[45]

Through steadfast effort and clever articulation, Aaron Patterson and other condemned prisoners helped bring national attention to the DR10.[46] In 1998, over sixty opponents of the death penalty from across the nation, including political activist and former model Bianca Jagger, added their names to a petition filed on Patterson's behalf by the University of Chicago's MacArthur Justice Center.[47] In May 1999, *Newsweek* featured Patterson in an article profiling Northwestern journalism professor David Protess, whose undergraduate students worked to free the wrongfully convicted.[48] In November, the *Chicago Tribune* published a series of articles placing the DR10 within a broader context of miscarriages of justice in Illinois.[49] On December 2, the *Chicago Reader* published a cover article on Patterson written by journalist John Conroy, the latest in a years-long exposé on the Burge scandal and its cover-up.[50] Later that week, CBS broadcast Patterson's story on a primetime episode of *60 Minutes II*.[51] Other DR10 members captured the spotlight drawn by Patterson as well, culminating in a special live broadcast of the *Oprah Winfrey Show* in 2003 that featured Patterson and two of his fellow prison mates.[52]

While Aaron Patterson and Stanley Howard worked to publicize the DR10, Madison Hobley garnered the most sympathy. Prior to January 1987, Hobley had never been in serious trouble with the law. A few months earlier, however, the married twenty-six-year-old made a costly mistake, turning a chance encounter with an attractive young woman into a sordid affair. Within weeks, Hobley secured an apartment for his new girlfriend and considered leaving his wife, Anita, and infant son, Philip. Coming to his senses, Hobley reversed course just before Thanksgiving, ended the affair, recommitted to Anita, and moved his family into the apartment instead.[53] Weeks later, around 2:00 a.m. on January 6, 1987, he woke to a blaring smoke alarm and walked to an interior hallway of the twenty-two-unit, three-story brick building to investigate. Creeping dozens of feet from his open doorway, Hobley turned to find smoke and fire blocking his return. He cried for Anita to grab Philip and go to their third-floor window while he escaped through a rear exit. Barefoot in the snow, wearing only shorts and a T-shirt, Hobley stood below while smoke—and eventually flames—poured through a small space below their cracked bathroom window. As fire gutted the building, Hobley moved desperately through the chaos, begging others to save his family, receiving pants, shoes, and a coat from strangers, and helping catch a child dropped from above.[54] While firemen rescued over thirty people, at least nine residents suffered injuries, including broken bones and cuts caused by daring leaps from smoke-filled windows.[55] Wading through the predawn wreckage, firefighters discovered the charred bodies of seven victims, including Anita and Philip.[56]

The tragedy that killed his family also brought Madison Hobley into the professional orbit of Jon Burge, whose recent double promotion to commander found him briefly in charge of the Bomb and Arson Unit at police headquarters.[57] Poring over evidence from what journalists described as a "well-kept" building in a "middle-class South Side neighborhood," investigators soon ruled arson the cause of the fire.[58] To solve the case, Burge's new unit worked alongside his old crew at Area 2 Violent Crimes, then under the command of Lieutenant Philip Cline.[59] Within hours of the fire, detectives Robert Dwyer and James Lotito brought Hobley in for questioning. According to the suspect's later testimony, detectives allegedly punched and kicked him, suffocated him with a plastic typewriter cover, called him "nigger," kept him from a lawyer, and demanded inculpatory statements. During a polygraph examination at police headquarters, Sergeant Patrick Garrity allegedly kicked Hobley when he refused to cooperate. Despite the abuse, Hobley never broke, maintaining his innocence hour after hour. Suggesting his ex-girlfriend may have set the fire, Hobley refused to sign a statement and told reporters flanking a televised perp walk, "I didn't do it, they got the wrong person."[60] Ignoring his protests, the State's Attorney's Office announced it would seek the death penalty.

During the two-week trial in July 1990, three detectives testified that Hobley orally confessed to setting the fire to free himself from an unwanted marriage. No written documentation of the statement existed, they claimed, because Detective Robert Dwyer spilled liquid on his notes and threw them away weeks before writing his report.[61] To corroborate the undocumented confession, prosecutors introduced testimony from Andre Council, who claimed he saw Hobley purchase gasoline the night of the fire. They also introduced a gas can allegedly found under the sink of a second-floor apartment of the gutted building. During cross-examination, defense attorneys sought to reveal Andre Council's alleged link to two other arsons set within weeks of the fatal blaze only a few blocks away. The judge sustained the state's objection and told jurors to disregard the line of questioning.[62] Years later, Hobley learned that Commander Burge took the extraordinary step of quashing another investigation of Council for criminal property destruction in order to protect the credibility of his key witness. Defense attorneys also attacked incongruent testimony regarding discovery of the gas can, suggesting that Area 2 detective John Paladino clumsily planted it hours after the arson.[63] Following lengthy deliberations dominated by a foreman who happened to be a suburban police officer, the jury convicted Hobley and sentenced him to death on August 4, 1990.[64]

For the next twelve and a half years, Madison Hobley braved the brutal realities of death row, struggling to secure his freedom with the help of private attorneys, fellow inmates, and community activists. While state-appointed lawyers from the cash-strapped appellate defender's office filed the requisite appeals, the case soon attracted attention from a private law firm with deeper pockets. Convinced of Hobley's innocence, attorneys Kurt Feuer and Jon Stromsta agreed to take the case pro bono. As postconviction dismissals and denials mounted, a mutual friend connected Hobley with Andrea Lyon, founder and director of the Illinois Capital Resource Center.[65] Known locally as the "Angel of Death Row," Lyon cut her teeth in the late 1970s and early 1980s as a member of the Cook County Public Defender's Homicide Task Force.[66] In 1979, she became the first woman in the United States to serve as lead counsel in a capital defense. By the time she joined Hobley's team in 1994, she had represented dozens of men and women in capital trials. Not one of her death-eligible clients ever received a death sentence.[67] Lyon's investigators soon uncovered evidence that not only supported Hobley's innocence but also bolstered torture allegations and highlighted police and prosecutorial misconduct.[68] In 1998, their work helped convince a federal judge to reverse Hobley's conviction and remand the case back to the circuit court for a new evidentiary hearing.[69] Enduring myriad delays, Hobley joined the Death Row 10 and helped draw support to its cause, only to face disappointment. On July 8, 2002, Judge Dennis Porter dismissed Hobley's claims and denied further relief.[70]

While the DR10 publicized the peril of wrongful conviction, not all members made credible claims of innocence or actively participated in the campaign. Together, however, each case helped corroborate the pattern and practice of the Burge torture regime. Indeed, as a veritable "mountain of evidence" against Area 2 and Area 3 detectives accumulated, all torture survivors enjoyed greater credibility.[71] Yet evidence of torture did not always counter evidence of guilt. It was one thing to persuade observers that suspects were coerced into confessing to horrible crimes; it was quite another to prove they did not commit the crimes in the first place. The DR10 and their supporters often obscured this distinction. Fully committed to condemning torture against the innocent and guilty alike, activists nevertheless chose to frame the DR10 campaign around wrongful conviction. As a series of high-profile exonerations captured the nation's attention as never before, activists strategically embraced innocence in order to undermine support for capital punishment. Accordingly, the few DR10 cases involving almost certain guilt presented a conceptual conundrum.[72]

Indeed, detectives deliberately coerced confessions from men they believed would not elicit wide support, typically suspects with extensive criminal records, gang affiliations, and some direct connection to the crime for which they were later convicted. Lacking the articulate voice of Aaron Patterson or sympathetic narrative of Madison Hobley, most struggled to connect with the largely white, middle-class audience targeted by activists' media campaign. For example, in 1984 Leroy Orange and his half brother Leonard Kidd were allegedly bagged, beaten, and tortured by electric shock to the head, genitals, and anus until they both confessed to stabbing four persons, including a ten-year-old boy, before setting the crime scene on fire.[73] A jury convicted Orange the following year. Kidd pleaded guilty. They both received the death penalty.[74] While Orange fought to prove his innocence, activists struggled to counter adverse elements of the case. First, both Orange and Kidd insisted they were present at the scene of the crime and imbibed cocaine and alcohol but left before the murders occurred.[75] Second, in a failed attempt to save his half brother from the death penalty, Kidd took the stand at Orange's trial and testified that he, Kidd, committed the murders on his own.[76] Prosecutors seized Kidd's rambling, half-crazed testimony to sidestep allegations of police coercion and confirm the original confessions.[77] Third, Kidd later received a second death sentence for setting an earlier apartment fire that killed ten children between the ages of seven months and seventeen years.[78] With activists focused on wrongful conviction, some cases fit the frame better than others.

Few of the DR10 cases proved more resistant to claims of innocence than that of brothers Jerry Mahaffey and Reginald Mahaffey, whose story activists distorted or kept in the background. On August 28, 1983, Jerry, twenty-seven, and Reginald, twenty-four, drove a borrowed van to the North Side neighborhood of West Rogers Park to burglarize the Off the Rax clothing store.[79] Spotting an idling police vehicle, however, they parked at a nearby hospital, shut off the engine, and sat waiting in the dark until a dead battery left them stranded.[80] Experienced burglars, the brothers improvised. Searching for a car to steal, they noticed an open window in the bathroom of a first-floor apartment. Peering inside, they saw windows stripped of curtains and a collection of boxes near the front door. Unbeknownst to the Mahaffey brothers, the sleeping residents were on the eve of relocating to a new home in the northwest suburb of Skokie. Assuming the place to be vacant, the Mahaffeys tore the mesh screen from the bathroom window and climbed in, leaving a shower rod and a bottle of shampoo littering the bushes. Thirsty, they drank Kool-Aid from the refrigerator, pilfered $11 from a wallet on the kitchen table, grabbed a knife from a cutlery set, and entered a dark bedroom.[81]

Eleven-year-old Ricky Pueschel awoke to a stranger suffocating him with a pillow. To keep him quiet, Reginald put Ricky in a headlock while Jerry stabbed the boy six times in the back. Reginald grabbed a nearby baseball bat and knocked Ricky cold with two blows to the head. Moving on, the intruders found an adult couple asleep in their bed. Dean Pueschel—six-foot-three and 230 pounds—had no time to react before the Mahaffey's rained blows upon him with his stepson's Little League bats. Next, they took turns sexually assaulting Dean's wife, Jo Ellen Pueschel, in the kitchen and across the armrest of a living-room couch. When they heard Dean groaning from the master bedroom, Jerry returned and stabbed him nearly twenty-five times.[82] The brothers then forced Jo Ellen to disable the alarm on a red 1982 Chevrolet Camaro before loading the vehicle with stolen guns, jewelry, a television, VCR, videotapes, and an Atari video-game console. Returning to the kitchen, the Mahaffeys debated what to do with Jo Ellen. Ricky staggered into the room as Jerry decided they had to "kill this bitch, too." Clutching her son and begging for their lives, Jo Ellen agreed to lie down on the floor next to Ricky. With his head on his forearms, the terrified child watched as Reginald Mahaffey repeatedly clubbed his mother in the back of the head with a handgun. Reginald later recalled walking outside to the sound of "solid hits" as his brother "finish[ed] the lady and her son off with the bats." Around 4:00 a.m., the Mahaffeys drove off in the family sports car. Ricky, critically wounded, later wandered into the street, where his grandfather—Jo Ellen's father—found him covered in blood the next morning. Ricky survived. His mother and adoptive father did not.[83]

The random and brutal nature of the attack on the Pueschel family shocked the city, turning the investigation into a classic heater case with all the attendant pressure and scrutiny.[84] Echoing the fear and anxiety of local residents, the *Chicago Tribune* reflected: "No place is safe. . . . It can happen anywhere."[85] A neighbor of Jo Ellen Pueschel's father expressed the primal emotions felt by many when he told reporters, "It's not fair the good people die and the rats are still out there."[86] The press highlighted the courage of eleven-year-old Ricky, who told a priest visiting the hospital: "I'm okay. Mommy and Daddy are with God in heaven."[87] In the months that followed, Ricky received hundreds of presents, letters, and cards, some containing cash or checks signed by ordinary Chicagoans shaken by the tragedy.[88] Soon after doctors cleared Ricky to leave the hospital, Chicago Bears running back Walter Payton escorted him on a tour of the team locker room and gave the recovering boy a signed ball from a winning touchdown drive.[89] Nearly a decade later, the press still referred to the case as "one of the most shocking crimes of the 1980s."[90] In the days immediately following the attack, public attention focused on the investigation as local detectives hit the streets.[91]

Relying on an informant with intimate knowledge of the crime and employing illegal interrogations to secure confessions, detectives did not require crack investigative skills to clear the case. On the night of the Pueschels' funeral, September 1, 1983, Cedrick Mahaffey received a phone call from his brothers Reginald and Jerry asking for help moving pilfered merchandise. Shuffling jewelry and electronics from one apartment to another, Jerry coldly explained to Cedrick that "they had to kill a couple of white people to get the stuff." Laughing in disbelief, Cedrick turned to Reginald, who confirmed the revelation. "All the way home I was scared," Cedrick admitted. "My hands were trembling. I had it in my mind, should I tell or should I keep my mouth shut?"[92] Sitting across from Area 2 Sergeant John "Jack" Byrne some hours later, Cedrick gave up his brothers' addresses and detailed a list of stolen items detectives would find if they executed a search warrant.[93] Cedrick had his own troubles with the law and considered himself a loyal family man. Yet he could not stop thinking about the Pueschel family or shake the moral lessons of his mother. "She raised us saying that you just don't go around hurting people for nothing," he explained, "and that is what bothered me about what my brothers did. They didn't have to kill those people and beat that little boy. There was no cause."[94] Area 2 detectives rushed to Reginald's and Jerry's apartments, arrested them separately, and secured court-reported confessions from both.[95]

During a pretrial hearing on a motion to suppress their confessions held on February 9, 1984, the Mahaffeys challenged detectives' account of their interrogation. Months earlier, on September 2, 1983, Sergeant Byrne—Burge's reputed "right-hand man"[96]—led an early-morning raid of a West Side apartment. The legal tenant claimed that officers "pointed their weapons at him and forced their way into the apartment" before "forc[ing] him to sign a form consenting to the search."[97] Believing their suspect armed and dangerous, detectives proceeded with caution into a bedroom where Reginald Mahaffey lay sleeping on the ground, surrounded by property stolen from the Pueschels' home, including two firearms. Officers woke him up, led him to the kitchen, and began a rough interrogation. According to Reginald, one officer forced him to the ground with a punt to the groin while another kicked him about the head and ribs. Leading him up the stairs of the basement-level apartment, officers allegedly tripped him and later smacked his forehead as he rode in an unmarked car. Arriving at Area 2, Reginald sat handcuffed to an interrogation-room wall while an officer "repeatedly hit" him in front of others. The same "curly brown-haired" detective—whom the judge identified as Detective John Yucaitis—struck Reginald's abdomen, back, and shoulders with a flashlight. Officers placed a plastic bag over Reginald's head, cracked his skull against the wall, and told him he would die if he did not confess. Afraid for his life, Reginald agreed to provide an inculpatory statement to Felony Review supervisor Irving Miller. In the presence of Yucaitis and a court reporter, Miller read the statement back to Mahaffey, who could not read, instructing the suspect to affix his initials to corrections made on each page. With the confession signed, detectives called a paramedic to attend to Reginald, who vomited and complained of rib pain and a headache.[98]

Joining Reginald at the motion to suppress hearing, Jerry Mahaffey and his wife, Carol Mahaffey, also accused detectives of misconduct during the arrest and interrogation. According to the married couple, officers arrived at their apartment at 5:40 a.m. on September 2, 1983, pounded on the door, and forced their way inside "with their pistols drawn." In sight of Carol and the couple's two young daughters, detectives physically assaulted Jerry while bombarding him with questions. Jerry accused officers of punching him in the face, throwing him into a wall, putting a gun to his face, kicking him in the groin until he curled into a ball, booting him twice in the ribs, and suffocating him with a plastic bag. A neighbor recalled waking to sounds of a scuffle, hearing Jerry scream, and a voice yelling, "Get up!" With blood dripping from Jerry's nose to his pajamas, officers forced him to change clothes before driving him to Area 2. In the squad car and again at the station house they threatened to kill him if he did not confess. Around 1:00 p.m., Jerry finally provided a statement to Irving Miller and another assistant state's attorney. Having left school after the eighth grade, Jerry struggled with reading comprehension. He signed the confession and initialed each page, he claimed, without reading a word.[99]

To counter defendants' accusations, the state called ASA Miller and at least seven Area 2 detectives to deny abuse under oath. Prosecutors presented Polaroid photographs depicting both Mahaffey brothers seated on the morning of September 2, 1983, with no discernible signs of injury or distress. Two medical technicians who examined the Mahaffeys at Cook County Jail on September 3 corroborated the lack of physical injury. At the close of the hearing, Circuit Court Judge Thomas A. Hett denied both motions, explaining that his decision "boiled down to a question of credibility."[100] "There is no substantial evidence," he clarified, "to support the claims of brutality and there is overwhelming evidence to refute them."[101] Weighing conflicting accounts, Hett concluded, "Detective Yucaitis' testimony is far more credible than the self-serving statements of the defendant in this regard."[102] Ironically, the *Chicago Tribune* published an article that very morning with the headline, "Cop 'Black Box' Torture Charged," revealing similar accusations in the case of Leonard Kidd and Leroy Orange unfolding down the hall. Buried in a back section above a large advertisement for Toys "R" Us, perhaps the article failed to attract the judge's attention.[103] Having lost the suppression motion, defendants faced a daunting record of incriminating evidence. In addition to their own damning statements, they had to answer the eyewitness testimony of Ricky Pueschel; the hearsay testimony of Cedrick Mahaffey; a large collection of personal items belonging to the Pueschel family found in defendants' possession, including several pieces of jewelry with Ricky and Jo Ellen's names engraved on them;[104] as well as multiple murder weapons, including two blood-soaked baseball bats found at the Pueschels' home. Prosecutors also presented a .357 Magnum coated with blood "consistent with Jo Ellen's blood type" found next to Reginald on the morning of his arrest.[105] With the trial looming, defendants' outlook appeared grim.

The Mahaffey brothers, however, had one last adventure left in them. Several weeks after Judge Hett denied their motion to suppress, Reginald and Jerry joined four other prisoners—the reputed "baddest of the bad"—in a daring escape from Cook County Jail on March 23, 1984.[106] Weeks earlier, the mastermind of the breakout paid a paramedic $75 to sneak two handguns into the sprawling complex at Twenty-Sixth Street and California Avenue. Armed, the six men overpowered several correctional officers, stole their uniforms, and made their way through concrete corridors to the grounds outside.[107] Along the way, they took several guards hostage and threatened or manhandled others. One later described the prisoners' desperation. "I know both the Mahaffey boys," he told reporters. "I met them when they were students and I was a teacher's aide at the Lawndale Academy. But that didn't matter during the escape. Reginald was like a crazed animal. He kept waving the gun, growling and biting his lips."[108] Following an armed standoff, guards recaptured three of the would-be fugitives, including Reginald.[109] The remaining three fled into the surrounding neighborhood. All were recaptured within a week. On an anonymous tip, police ambushed Jerry as he got out of a cab at a public housing high-rise forty-eight hours after the jailbreak.[110] By then, his younger brother lay in a coma at Cook County Hospital.

On the night of the escape, Reginald fell through a closed window of a second-story interrogation room in the Marquette District station house. An assistant state's attorney and several detectives claimed he jumped.[111] His attorneys insisted he was thrown.[112] Still wearing a stolen correctional officer's uniform, hands cuffed behind his back, Reginald landed on his head and lay crumpled on the sidewalk when a *Chicago Tribune* photographer snapped his picture.[113] One of Reginald's sisters claimed she saw on a local news broadcast officers helping her brother walk under his own power into the back of an ambulance following the fall.[114] By the time he arrived at St. Anthony Hospital, however, he was unconscious and severely injured. Emergency-room records reveal fractures of the skull, pelvis, left clavicle, and ribs.[115] The next day, Reginald's father and sister, and his mother, Myrtis Mahaffey, made separate visits to the CPD's Office of Professional Standards to file a complaint. Fresh from the hospital, Myrtis described her son as "bloated," with "swollen" eyes and injuries to the liver, spleen, and brain. The family insisted Reginald could not have sustained his injuries from the fall alone. Rather, his flight out the window was a horrifying reprieve from a beating that began in the police station and continued in the ambulance.[116] Another escapee, the convicted cop killer Ray Greer, witnessed Mahaffey's fall and claimed officers told him, "You better say he jumped or we'll push you out, too."[117] Investigators later ruled the Mahaffeys' complaint "not-sustained." Reginald awoke from the coma six weeks later, but those who knew him assert he never fully recovered.[118]

The Mahaffey brothers were tried together, found guilty, and sentenced to death in February 1985.[119] Reversing Reginald's conviction four years later, the Illinois Supreme Court ruled the state should have severed the cases and tried them separately. Since prosecutors used Jerry's confession to convict Reginald, the judge should have allowed Reginald's lawyers to cross-examine his brother, who asserted his right to not take the stand.[120] In the second trial, however, Reginald waived his right to counsel and represented himself. Predictably, his unhinged performance helped dig his own grave. Not only did Reginald fail to offer any evidence in support of his defense, he also volunteered details of his criminal past and admitted his presence at the crime scene, conceding, "I was there alright. . . . I'm not going to deny it."[121] As a public defender waited useless in the wings, he further alienated the jury with an insensitive cross-examination of the state's key witness, the then eighteen-year-old Ricky Pueschel.[122] In the sentencing hearing following his conviction, Reginald offered no evidence in mitigation. Six years earlier, Reginald insisted at the close of his first trial that jurors "don't have no control over whether I live or not. It's up to God. It ain't up to nobody if Reginald Mahaffey lives."[123] Given another opportunity to plea for his life, according to appellate court documents, Reginald again fell "under a religious delusion that he could not be found guilty and sentenced to death," believing instead that "he had been found free of sin by God because he had survived a life-threatening fall from a second-story window in 1984" and had thus been acquitted by a higher power.[124] Failing to sway the jury, Mahaffey received another sentence of death.[125]

As the Chicago torture justice movement built momentum in the 1990s, the Mahaffey brothers' attorneys seized on budding evidence of Area 2 torture to craft new appeals around old claims of coercion.[126] Indeed, by the end of the decade, their singular voice had joined a growing chorus. With the formation of the Death Row 10, activists began leveraging the Burge scandal to abolish capital punishment in Illinois. The Mahaffey brothers, however, resisted frames of actual innocence. While tainted confessions helped send them to death row, the state could likely prove guilt beyond a reasonable doubt without them. Dissenting in Reginald's 1989 reversal, an Illinois Supreme Court justice wrote, "In view of the substantial evidence of Reginald Mahaffey's guilt, I do not believe that it can be said that he was prejudiced by the State's use at the joint trial of his brother's confession."[127] Affirming Reginald's second conviction in 2000, the same court argued, "In light of the overwhelming evidence establishing defendant's guilt, confidence in the outcome of defendant's trial is not undermined, even assuming the claimed error." That error—police torture—was thus ruled harmless in light of the "totality of the evidence" marshaled by the state. Indeed, Reginald was wearing one of Dean Pueschel's rings at the time of his arrest.[128] Jerry had a video recording of the Pueschels' wedding stashed in his bedroom.[129]

Eager to win new trials for Burge survivors, the Death Row 10 and its allies in the Campaign to End the Death Penalty struggled to maintain a consistent narrative in cases like the Mahaffey brothers'. While activists presented well-rehearsed arguments against the death penalty under all scenarios, standard attacks on the immorality, inefficiency, and inequality of capital punishment often yielded to simple frames of innocence, even when doing so required obscuring facts of the case. For example, in a 2002 profile designed to evoke sympathy for the DR10, an activist opened, "On September 2, 1983, Reginald Mahaffey's nightmare began."[130] Not only did starting the narrative with Mahaffey's interrogation erase the nightmare of the Pueschel family altogether, it also implied Reginald's innocence, as did other partial or misleading details. First, the author suggested that Reginald was thrown from a station-house window during his interrogation instead of following his escape from jail six months later. Second, the author failed to distinguish the all-white jury that decided Mahaffey's reversed conviction from the later jury that convicted him a second time.[131] Third, the author highlighted Ricky Pueschel's inability to identify the Mahaffeys in a police lineup but did not mention the severe injuries impairing Ricky's judgment at the time or his later courtroom testimony, where he identified them with great certainty. In the context of an ongoing "innocence revolution," activists might be excused for employing wrongful conviction to undermine capital punishment in all cases, even those involving likely guilt.[132] Accordingly, the Mahaffeys played a negligible role in the campaign to free the rest of the Death Row 10.

Regardless of guilt or innocence, all thirteen members of the DR10 highlighted problems of capital punishment in action, offering activists compelling narratives to employ in support of otherwise abstract arguments. Indeed, their efforts put living faces on a range of related issues, including false confessions, ineffective assistance of counsel, mental fitness, bribery, perjury, and torture. Emphasizing the movement's urgency, DR10 member Frank Bounds died of cancer in 1998, just months after the Illinois Supreme Court remanded his case back to trial.[133] Meanwhile, the DR10 helped bridge the gap between Chicago's burgeoning antitorture movement and the established anti–death penalty movement. By the late 1990s, local activists engaged both issues simultaneously. In a 2002 pamphlet demanding criminal indictments for perpetrators of police torture, the diverse coalition spoke in a unified voice: "As in the days of the lynching era in this country, Jon Burge and the rest of his lynch mob are in a position to get the vigilante justice they have sought because the authorities look the other way. The difference, though, is that we, the law-abiding citizens of this community can stop them." Reminding supporters that Jim Crow–era violence entailed "sudden events under cover of night by an anonymous mob," the document described the Burge scandal as "slowly unfolding before our eyes for many years." Inspired by the DR10 and other Burge survivors, however, the Chicago torture justice movement expressed renewed optimism, concluding, "We know who the vigilantes are, we know what they are doing, and we have time to act."[134]

"The Illinois Capital Punishment System Is Broken"

In the five years following the formation of the Death Row 10 in 1998, the terms of the capital punishment debate in America rapidly evolved.[135] Whereas the 1990s witnessed an explosion in the number of executions in the United States, the 2000s saw a period of decline.[136] Illinois proved pivotal in this about-face. Between 1963 and 2019, Illinois executed twelve men, all in the 1990s. Ten of these executions occurred in a concentrated spurt between 1994 and 1998.[137] Yet in January 2000, Governor George Ryan placed a moratorium on all executions.[138] Three years later, he emptied death row with unprecedented blanket commutations.[139] Swept up in a national innocence movement fueled by the DNA revolution and a stream of exonerations, Illinois entered the vanguard of America's reexamination of capital punishment.[140] The Burge scandal played an important role in propelling this transformation.

Constrained by incarceration, the Death Row 10 benefited from the support of veteran activists with over two decades' experience fighting capital punishment in Illinois. In 1972, the U.S. Supreme Court ruling in *Furman v. Georgia* effectively invalidated all state capital-punishment statutes and halted executions nationwide.[141] Four years later, in *Gregg v. Georgia*, the Court approved new model statutes to reconcile executions with the Eighth Amendment's ban on cruel and unusual punishment.[142] Guided by *Gregg*, Illinois legislators met in Springfield to draft new death penalty statutes in 1977. Outside the capital, activists rallied in opposition. Led by coordinator Mary Alice Rankin, members of the new Illinois Coalition against the Death Penalty (ICADP) worked to block reinstatement and, when that failed, to force repeal.[143] A former high school teacher from suburban Oak Park, Rankin was white, middle-aged, and a widowed mother of five. In a previous life, she considered herself a conservative Republican. In 1975, however, Rankin joined the Alliance to End Repression and began lobbying for gay rights, prison reform, and police accountability.[144] After *Gregg*, the American Civil Liberties Union tapped her to coordinate collective action against the death penalty in Illinois.[145] Rankin ran the ICADP until her death in 1990, when the fight took on greater urgency.[146]

Indeed, by the 1990s the ICADP had become inured to defeat. Looking back on the tally of wins and losses from the year 2000, an attorney at the Illinois Office of the State Appellate Defender remarked: "In 1977, our state's death penalty statute contained six factors that qualified a defendant for the death penalty. That list has since expanded to twenty, averaging a new factor every eighteen months."[147] With few allies in Springfield, the ICADP accomplished little more than a slowing of the death machine. When Illinois executed its first prisoner in twenty-eight years in 1990, observers anticipated a dramatic increase in the frequency of state-imposed death.[148]

As the turn of the century neared, the number of executions in Illinois and across the nation escalated to levels not seen since the early Cold War. "More Americans were executed in 1999," an activist reflected, "than any year since 1952. In the past decade, the execution rate has risen 800 percent."[149] Rising homicide rates after 1965, combined with declining faith in rehabilitation and a collective embrace of harsher sentencing, triggered a hike in death sentences after the court-imposed moratorium ended in 1976. Yet lengthy appeals produced a predictable lag in executions as condemned prisoners pursued postconviction relief. When their options ran out, the logjam broke free. Although Illinois had not executed anyone since 1962, a sense of crisis gripped the anti–death penalty movement. "We need your help!" the ICADP wrote to supporters in 1995, "Illinois' death penalty, long dormant as condemned prisoners pursued appeals, is now in full force."[150] Emotionally invested in saving lives, activists suffered on all twelve occasions when Illinois executed a state prisoner between 1990 and 1999.

Alongside the taxing parade of executions, however, appeared a quieter march of exonerations. In 1987, the state released Darby Tillis and Perry Cobb, the first persons freed from Illinois's death row after the reinstatement of capital punishment in 1977.[151] Subsequent exonerations occurred within a short span: Joseph Burrows in September 1994;[152] codefendants Rolando Cruz and Alejandro Hernandez in 1995;[153] Verneal Jimerson, Dennis Williams, Gary Gauger, and Carl Lawson in 1996;[154] and Anthony Porter and Steven Smith in February 1999.[155] The horse race of executions and exonerations—twelve killed, thirteen freed as of 2001—captivated observers.[156] Eager to shape the narrative, the ICADP asserted, "These men did not get off on 'technicalities.'" Rather, "Their convictions were damaged by flawed police investigations, questionable conduct by prosecutors, inadequate legal representation, a statute lacking appropriate safeguards, and a narrow, restrictive system of judicial review."[157] Activists highlighted the Burge scandal and the fate of survivors still behind bars. "A documented system of police torture in a Chicago police precinct resulted in the commander's termination," pleaded the ICADP, "yet 10 victims of his torture remain on death row because of forced confessions."[158] Reflecting the regularity of exoneration, state officials drafted a form letter, reading, "We regret the impersonal nature of this communication, but given the recent increase in the number of special cases like yours, we're sure you'll appreciate our swift and certain attention to this matter." The document concluded, "Your incarceration will no longer be required by the State of Illinois, due to (check one): ___ new DNA analysis; ___ a confession by someone not previously suspected; ___ new evidence brought to light by Northwestern University journalism professor David Protess and his students."[159] Activists cataloged this Kafkaesque token to highlight the pathology of a broken system.

The debate over the death penalty in Illinois reached a crossroads in 1999. In January, the *Chicago Tribune* published a five-part series accusing local state's attorneys of facilitating an epidemic of wrongful convictions. Titled "Trial and Error: How Prosecutors Sacrifice Justice to Win," the weeklong feature highlighted several high-profile scandals, including the railroading of the so-called Ford Heights Four.[160] Following a notorious rape and double murder in suburban Cook County in 1978, prosecutors sent four innocent men to prison, including two—Verneal Jimerson and Dennis Williams—who sat on death row until 1996.[161] Within weeks of the *Tribune* exposé, trial began in the case of the DuPage Seven, four sheriff's deputies and three assistant state's attorneys accused of falsifying evidence and conspiring to wrongfully convict suspects—including death-row exonerees Cruz and Hernandez—in the kidnapping, rape, and murder of a ten-year-old girl in 1983.[162] Ironically, the special prosecutor orchestrating such "extraordinary" indictments was none other than William Kunkle, who prosecuted Andrew Wilson and defended Jon Burge years earlier. "In a free society," Kunkle told reporters, "there must always be a line between vigorous prosecution and official misconduct."[163] As always, Kunkle's willingness to police this line came at a cost—roughly $1.1 million in legal fees.[164] While a jury acquitted the defendants in June, the trial represented a rare effort to hold law enforcement agents criminally responsible for wrongful convictions.[165] A barrage of headlines in similar cases hammered away at the public's toleration for error in capital cases.

The greatest blow came in early February, when the state released condemned prisoner Anthony Porter some forty-eight hours before his scheduled execution. Jurors sent Porter to death row for fatally shooting two teenagers in Chicago's Washington Park in August 1982.[166] While attorneys lost a series of appeals, Professor Protess and his students went to work.[167] With less than a week to go, Protess delivered two timely depositions on February 1, 1999. The first came from an eyewitness to the 1982 murders who recanted his testimony and accused officers of coercing his statement during a fifteen-hour interrogation.[168] The second came from a state prisoner who swore that his uncle, a Milwaukee man named Alstory Simon, confessed to the crime years prior. Within days, Protess presented videotape of Simon accepting full responsibility.[169] Porter walked free while Simon went to prison.[170] Yet controversy surrounded the exoneration from the beginning.[171] Accusing a private investigator of coercing his statement with tricks and promises, Simon later recanted. The state set him free in 2014, triggering wide criticism of Protess and his methods.[172] Nevertheless, Anthony Porter's eleventh-hour escape in 1999 marked a turning point, as ambivalent residents pondered the possibility of executing an innocent man.[173] Highlighting the stakes involved, Illinois exonerated one prisoner and executed another within six weeks of Porter's release.[174]

Responding to public pressure, state and local officials moved to present the appearance of action. In March 1999, the state's top judicial body created the Special Supreme Court Committee on Capital Cases to investigate the death penalty and recommend ways for courts to prevent wrongful conviction.[175] In April, the Illinois Attorney General called a special meeting of lawyers involved in death penalty cases, bringing together some twenty-five state's attorneys and three defense attorneys to draw up "special review procedures" for prosecutors. The ICADP likened the effort to putting the "foxes" in charge of "the hen house."[176] In Chicago, City Council held a series of public hearings on the Burge scandal at which Mary Powers of Citizens Alert demanded the videotaping of police interrogations; the removal of the OPS from the Superintendent's Office or the creation of an independent civilian review board; greater scrutiny of the Fraternal Order of Police contract; changes to the department's hot pursuit policy; an end to racial discrimination within the patrol division; and the reopening of several investigations of police torture, including those of Melvin Jones and members of the Death Row 10.[177] Accustomed to being ignored, Powers instead enjoyed a rapt audience. Collective frustration over capital punishment opened space for activists to press grievances in the Burge scandal.

With ultimate responsibility for passing or repealing capital-punishment statutes, the Illinois General Assembly became the epicenter of debate. Long before the innocence crisis of the late 1990s, a small number of state legislators championed abolition with little hope of success. From 1979 to 1988, State Representative Carol Moseley Braun sponsored several bills to halt executions and reexamine their efficacy.[178] Others picked up where she left off, particularly those from predominantly black districts where a disproportionate number of condemned prisoners and their families called home. After his election in 1997, State Senator Barack Obama routinely sided with abolitionists in efforts to reform capital punishment.[179] Following Porter's exoneration in 1999, legislators Emil Jones, Coy Pugh, and others sponsored reform bills, created the Capital Litigation Trust Fund to support capital defense, and convened the Legislative Task Force on the Death Penalty.[180] The task force urged Illinois's governor and the Illinois Supreme Court to impose a moratorium on executions while it held public hearings across the state. Throughout fall 1999, activists bombarded the governor with letters, phone calls, and e-mail.[181] In November, the *Chicago Tribune* published another scathing series: "The Failure of the Death Penalty in Illinois."[182] Succumbing at last, Governor George Ryan announced a moratorium in January 2000 and appointed the Governor's Commission on Capital Punishment to settle the issue once and for all.[183]

With the moratorium in effect, activists visualized a set of circumstances that might force the state to end capital punishment altogether, but they needed to act before the rare window of opportunity closed. Experiencing 1999 as a "watershed year" for the "struggle against the death penalty," the ICADP organized community meetings, speaker forums, and protest rallies.[184] Having spent decades swimming against the tide of public opinion, abolitionists appreciated the sea change wrought by a wave of national exonerations. "This sequence of events suddenly moved abolition from bleeding heart liberal fringe to respectability," wrote an ICADP fund-raiser. "All of a sudden, people were open to the idea that the death penalty could go seriously wrong."[185] Capitalizing on the favorable climate, the ICADP dispatched supporters to hearings of the governor's commission in Chicago and Springfield.[186] Foregrounding "Commander Burge, forced confessions, and 10 men on death row," activists explicitly linked the moratorium to the police torture scandal.[187] As the commission's work stretched into a second year, activists fought to keep the issue alive. For example, in April 2001 the Illinois Death Penalty Moratorium Project and the Campaign to End the Death Penalty brought exonerees and family members of prisoners on death row to college campuses to recruit support.[188] Other events dovetailed with politicians' efforts to pass an abolition bill in the General Assembly.[189]

By spring 2002, rumors circulated that Governor Ryan was considering unilateral action to prevent further miscarriage of justice. Speaking before a death penalty conference at the University of Oregon in March, Ryan not only promised to review the case of every condemned prisoner in Illinois but also teased the notion of blanket commutations.[190] Releasing its report a few weeks later, the Governor's Commission on Capital Punishment recommended eighty-five changes to the capital justice apparatus.[191] Echoing activists' arguments, all fourteen commissioners agreed that "no system, given human nature and frailties, could ever be devised or constructed that would work perfectly and guarantee absolutely that no innocent person is ever again sentenced to death."[192] A "narrow majority" recommended complete abolition.[193] Acting on the commission's recommendations, Ryan's staff prepared a bill and located a legislative sponsor.[194] Anticipating a long political fight, however, activists moved to sidestep the assembly and nudge Ryan toward executive action. In a bold move, attorneys from the Office of the State Appellate Defender filed separate petitions for executive clemency on behalf of more than 140 persons on death row, including several who preferred to await appeals or welcome execution.[195] Answering their gambit, the state insisted on public hearings for each case.[196] When the Illinois Attorney General lost a suit to stop proceedings, the stage was set for a dramatic showdown.[197]

In October 2002, the Illinois Prisoner Review Board conducted nine days of hearings across two weeks, pitting convicted murderers against murder victims' families, civil rights attorneys against prosecutors, and anti-death penalty activists against proponents.[198] As expert witnesses flew in from across the country, over three hundred lawyers prepared briefs.[199] Conference rooms in Chicago and Springfield filled with survivors of violent crime, many wearing yellow ribbons in support of lost loved ones. Outnumbered, friends and family of condemned prisoners sat among a hostile crowd.[200] Meanwhile, participants vied for the hearts and minds of appointed board members, whose recommendations could force or stay the governor's hand. While prosecutors relitigated some of Illinois's most notorious crimes, petitioners put the state's capital punishment system on trial.[201] Yet the ceremonial review of each case backfired on abolitionists. Preparing dozens of briefs in opposition, the Cook County State's Attorney's Office regaled the audience with gory details of more than 250 murders committed by 142 petitioners.[202] The sheer number of cases benefited the state. While board members typically reviewed around three hundred cases per year, they heard nearly half that number in two weeks.[203] The bloody repetition of countless murders, rapes, and manslaughters diminished whatever impact petitioners hoped to score with less sensational accounts of police perjury, witness intimidation, and coerced confessions.[204]

Dissatisfied with a mere recitation of facts, state officials hyped the audience with hyperbolic descriptions of the petitioners and their alleged crimes. For example, prosecutors referred to Death Row 10 member Stanley Howard as a "heartless predator" always "on the prowl," poised to commit "evil deeds" and spread "death and human misery." Denying claims of abuse, the state reminded observers, "[Howard] is a remorseless killer and a sadistic sexual predator [whose] efforts to masquerade as a victim himself are the lowest form of insult to the judicial system and serve only to re-victimize the people whose lives he has already destroyed enough." The brief concluded, "Petitioner's is a life not worth sparing."[205] Seeming annoyed at having to answer petitioners' claims at all, prosecutors wrote in another DR10 case: "Leonard Kidd has been convicted of killing more people [fourteen] in the State of Illinois than any other person currently on death row. Further, he has the dubious distinction of having killed more children [eleven] than anyone else in the history of the State of Illinois." In a flourish of exaggeration, the brief credited Kidd with "a commitment to death and destruction that is virtually unparalleled in modern history."[206] Describing Reginald Mahaffey as "the 'poster child' for the death penalty," prosecutors opined that his victims' family "deserve[d] to see him executed" and "can only hope and pray that he will then burn in hell."[207] Begging, "Please, please, let it finally be over," thirty-year-old Ricky Pueschel—then a police sergeant in Schaumburg, Illinois—asked the board to deny mercy to his parents' killers.[208] Through exhaustive replay of the most terrifying acts of violence in living memory, the hearings left many observers convinced capital punishment was not only necessary but also in need of shoring up.[209]

Facing an onslaught of unfavorable press, anti-death penalty activists struggled to redirect the narrative.[210] While none of the 142 petitioners appeared, dozens of lawyers presented briefs on their behalf. Yet condemned prisoners could do little to counter the weight of their alleged crimes with the injustice of capital punishment. Efforts to portray the system as arbitrary, expensive, and inhumane simply could not compete with the state's "theater of pain."[211] Refusing to yield, however, activists rallied support outside the hearings.[212] With Chicago hosting the annual conference of the National Coalition to Abolish the Death Penalty in late October, some four hundred sympathizers attended meetings, packed rallies, and distributed fliers.[213] Demanding the state "Stop Legal Lynching!," a characteristic handbill highlighted the plight of "wrongfully convicted police torture victims, the Death Row 10."[214] According to much of the press, however, it was too late—prosecutors had won the public relations battle.[215] Indeed, with intimate tales of gore and grief leading the nightly news, sober reflection on due process faded, reinforcing activists' impulse to foreground actual innocence.

Accordingly, the anti-death penalty movement considered Burge torture survivors among the hearings' true headliners. Unable to corroborate the pattern and practice of Area 2 torture in their original criminal trials, petitioners marshaled a breadth of evidence supporting claims of coerced confessions. Indeed, by 2002 the People's Law Office had spent years disseminating material unearthed during the discovery phase of civil litigation. "We've always thought that an important function of fighting [a] case," explained Flint Taylor, "[is] when we get the information . . . it should get to the public in one form or another."[216] Sometimes, attorneys "walked on the edge" of judges' protective orders.[217] For example, Taylor and his colleagues risked running afoul of a federal court in 1997 by circulating sealed documents in the case of torture survivor Marcus Wiggins. Ruling in their favor, however, Judge Ruben Castillo noted, "The public has a right to know whether allegations of police torture are appropriately investigated and resolved by the City of Chicago."[218] Preferring to ask forgiveness rather than permission, activist attorneys "aggressively" sought evidence of official misconduct and "not only [left] it in our files, but [got] it to people like Mary Powers and Mariel [Nanasi]" of the Task Force to Confront Police Violence. "When it's not under protective order and it's important to the community," Taylor concluded, "we put it out there. That's part of why we're the People's Law Office."[219] As the clemency hearings came to a close, widespread evidence of custodial abuse bolstered petitioners' claims of wrongful conviction.

With Governor Ryan set to leave office within months and facing serious allegations of political corruption in unrelated matters, critics speculated he might clear death row to distract the public and save a tarnished legacy.[220] Defense attorney Andrea Lyon even suggested that prosecutors threatened to indict Ryan on old charges of fraud and conspiracy if he moved forward with commutations.[221] Demanding that he respect the judicial process and deny clemency, supporters of capital punishment delivered a petition signed by over three hundred people, including Dean Pueschel's sister and a sibling of James Doyle, the patrolman murdered on a CTA bus in February 1982.[222] In December, Ryan met with murder victims' families.[223] Some found him cold and detached. Others believed he listened to their pleas and would leave sentences intact.[224] Not to be outdone, the anti–death penalty movement applied pressure as well. On December 15, scores of exonerees from across the nation shared their stories at a conference hosted by the Center on Wrongful Convictions at Northwestern University Law School.[225] The next day, Gary Gauger and other exonerees launched a "Dead Men Walking" march from Stateville prison to downtown Chicago carrying a letter addressed to the governor.[226] In an early January meeting between Ryan and the families of forty-five prisoners on death row, Robin Hobley pleaded for her brother's life, saying, "It's time for Madison to come home."[227] As the state held its breath, observers rued the pain the decision would bring to one side or the other.[228]

In two speeches delivered the final weekend of his term, Governor Ryan finally ended the suspense. Speaking at DePaul University on Friday, January 10, 2003, Ryan lamented the "manifest injustice" of wrongful convictions, highlighted the horrors of the Burge scandal, and pardoned four members of the Death Row 10. Wielding the awesome powers of his office, Ryan concluded, "Today I shall be a friend to Madison Hobley, Stanley Howard, Aaron Patterson, and Leroy Orange."[229] In a speech at Northwestern the following day, Ryan commuted the sentences of all 163 persons facing capital punishment in Illinois, effectively emptying death row in a dramatic change of heart.[230] As minority leader in the state legislature, Ryan had voted with fellow Republicans to reinstate the death penalty in 1977. "I had to think about it very hard," the Kankakee, Illinois, pharmacist and machine politician reflected at the time, "and I was upset about it the whole day. But I feel I did the right thing."[231] Over twenty-five years later, Ryan credited lawyers, professors, journalists, state prisoners, and their families for changing his mind. "I started with this issue concerned about innocence," he explained, "but once I pondered what had become of our justice system, I came to care above all about fairness." Referring to capital punishment as "one of the greatest civil rights struggles of our time," Ryan answered the pleas of Nelson Mandela and Desmond Tutu with quotes from Mahatma Gandhi and Abraham Lincoln. Paraphrasing former justice of the Supreme Court Harry Blackmun, Ryan concluded, "Because the Illinois death penalty system is arbitrary and capricious—and therefore immoral—I no longer shall tinker with the machinery of death."[232] A total of forty-eight capital sentences had been reduced nationwide since 1977.[233] Ryan quadrupled that in a single day.

Among predictable reactions, murder victims' families felt betrayed.[234] Opening one of countless red, white, and blue envelopes sent to explain the governor's decision, a surviving family member choked back tears, asserting, "This man is stepping on the graves of my sister and her children."[235] Local prosecutors balked. Insisting that the commutations would be remembered as "among the most irresponsible decisions ever taken by a state's chief executive," Cook County State's Attorney Richard Devine said: "In one stroke, he tossed aside the work of police, prosecutors, trial court judges, juries and appellate judges. The system is now indeed broken, and the governor walks away."[236] Of the pardoned members of the Death Row 10, Patterson, Hobley, and Orange walked free.[237] Owing time on another conviction, Stanley Howard joined the mass exodus to general population.[238] The ICADP rejoiced, holding a "victory party" at the home of Anthony Porter the day after the commutations. With hugs all around, Madison Hobley told supporters,

"I just can't thank you all enough."[239] State and federal legislators vowed to reexamine capital punishment nationwide.[240] Ordinary people celebrated Governor Ryan across the globe.[241] Nominated for a Nobel Peace Prize, he received federal indictments instead.[242] In April 2006, a jury convicted Ryan on eighteen felony counts for funneling state business to personal associates in exchange for cash and gifts.[243] While he served a six-and-a-half-year sentence, his wife, Lura Lynn Ryan, died of cancer. Widowed, stripped of his pension, and pushing eighty years old, Ryan returned home to Kankakee in January 2013.[244]

"At Last a Modicum of Justice"

Even as the struggle against the death penalty monopolized resources, the Chicago torture justice movement continued efforts to hold Burge and his men criminally responsible.[245] Once the immediate threat of executions passed, it was time to send a message that local people would not stand for human rights abuse in Chicago. Yet activists would go on to toil for over twenty years to punish perpetrators with little success. While the campaign to fire Burge paid off in 1993, simultaneous demands on the Office of Professional Standards (OPS), the Chicago Police Board, the State's Attorney's Office, and the U.S. Attorney to investigate other officers went nowhere. By the early 2000s, it became clear that local agencies could not be trusted to police their own. The appointment of a special prosecutor, however, also brought disappointment. Frustrated at home, activists took their grievances abroad, lobbying for relief before the Organization of American States, the International Olympic Committee, and the United Nations. In 2008, federal authorities finally yielded to sustained pressure by arresting Jon Burge on charges of perjury and obstruction of justice.[246] Demanding more proportional accountability, activists nevertheless acknowledged a rare achievement. Exhibiting remarkable perseverance, the Chicago torture justice movement endured years of official intransigence and public indifference while the political opportunity structure evolved. Indeed, activists' own efforts to frame police torture within a larger context of racial inequality helped change local narratives and alter expectations.

Throughout the 1990s, many activists still believed they could force police administrators to discipline officers responsible for torture. After all, by combining ordinary methods of redress with extraordinary community pressure, actors in the social movement had pressured the department to fire Burge and reopen prior complaints. Indeed, during the fallout from

Burge's police board hearings, director of the OPS Gayle Shines instructed her staff to reexamine nine old cases. Yet when investigators found six complainants credible, Shines refused to recommend disciplinary action, changed four rulings to "not sustained," and buried the reports in a filing cabinet.[247] After her retirement in 1998, an incoming director located the files and sent them to CPD's Superintendent Terry Hilliard. After cursory review, Hilliard's lead counsel concluded: "Bringing charges against any of the remaining accused at this time would deprive those officers of an opportunity to present a full defense. More importantly, the lengthy delay between the date of the initial complaint and the present day makes it virtually impossible to conduct any kind of meaningful inquiry into the matters in issue." Preventing further action, Hilliard's office instructed the OPS "to classify all of the allegations in the above-referenced complaint register files as 'not sustained.'"[248] When the memo leaked, Hilliard claimed prior ignorance of the files and regretted that so much time had passed. Suspecting a cover-up, activists labeled Hilliard's explanation "highly suspicious" and abandoned efforts to win relief through the OPS.[249]

Pursuing new strategy, on April 5, 2001, activists petitioned the chief judge of the Cook County Criminal Court to appoint a special prosecutor to investigate the Burge scandal. Alongside Mary Powers of Citizens Alert, lead petitioners included activist Mary L. Johnson, mother of torture survivor Michael Johnson, and Larry Kennon, former president of the Cook County Bar Association.[250] Outlining the parameters of the Burge cases, the petition accused Cook County State's Attorney Richard Devine of a conflict of interest. Not only did Devine serve as first assistant to State's Attorney Richard M. Daley at the height of Burge's career, he also worked for a private law firm that represented Burge in the early 1990s.[251] During a public rally in June, approximately one hundred supporters launched a formal Campaign to Prosecute Police Torture.[252] In November, Chief Judge Paul Biebel held public hearings where torture survivors, their family members, activists, and attorneys testified to torture's wide impact.[253] In what Mary Powers considered the first time a Cook County judge "ever aggressively pursued evidence of torture in the 50 cases in which it was raised by defendants in a courtroom,"[254] Biebel agreed to appoint a special prosecutor in April 2002.[255]

When activists learned that the special prosecutor and his assistant would be both "white" and "politically connected," however, optimism gave way to "consternation and skepticism."[256] While the Special Prosecutors Committee pressured the judge to appoint an African American cocounsel, the top job fell to former appellate justice Edward J. Egan, a longtime ally of the Cook County Democratic Organization. Serving as first assistant state's attorney from 1961 to 1964, Egan later sat on the circuit court from 1964 to 1972.[257] Four years later, Mayor Richard J. Daley slated him to challenge Republican Bernard Carey in the Democrat's unsuccessful bid to reclaim the State's Attorney's Office in 1976.[258] Astute observers wondered whether Egan and assistant Robert D. Boyle possessed the independence required of an impartial investigation.[259] Decades earlier, Egan had quashed efforts to prosecute Detective Walter Murphy for abusing criminal suspects in 1963.[260] Murphy later served as Burge's first supervisor at Area 2 in the early 1970s.[261] As an appellate court judge, Egan once denied an appeal in Andrew Wilson's criminal case.[262] Activists later learned that Egan's family tree included multiple CPD veterans past and present, including a nephew who helped arrest torture survivor Gregory Banks in 1982.[263] Ignoring public criticism, the Office of the Special Prosecutor set up shop in the Leighton Criminal Court Building and began gathering evidence and interviewing witnesses.[264] Four years and $7 million later, several police officers and a former prosecutor tried to block publication of the final report.[265] Tired of protecting the "ruthless" Jon Burge, the Black Caucus of the Chicago City Council demanded transparency, as did dozens of protestors.[266] Finally, Judge Biebel ordered the report released in July 2006.[267]

To the "disappointment and dismay" of community activists, the 292-page Special Prosecutor's Report corroborated only a handful of allegations, claimed the statute of limitations had run on potential charges, and recommended zero indictments.[268] Dismissing the process as a "whitewash," the Chicago torture justice movement organized a team of lawyers to draft a response.[269] Led by the People's Law Office, the ad hoc committee released a fifty-page report in April 2007 "rectifying, supplementing and refuting much of the incomplete and distorted context of the original document."[270] Boasting the endorsement of hundreds of leading activists, attorneys, scholars, civil rights organizations, and community groups, the so-called Shadow Report blasted the special prosecutor for challenging torture survivors' credibility, favoring the statements of police and city officials, and refusing to label the abuse "torture."[271] Residents voiced their dissatisfaction in public hearings held by the Cook County Board and the Chicago City Council.[272] Yet despite its shortcomings, Egan's report corroborated several abuse claims and further legitimized the movement's narrative.[273] By refusing indictments, however, Egan appeared to sink the possibility of ever holding perpetrators criminally responsible.[274]

Stonewalled on all sides, activists continued to look beyond Chicago for relief. Back in July 1999, a delegation of lawyers led by U.S. Congressman

Bobby Rush met with U.S. Attorney General Janet Reno in Washington, DC, to demand federal oversight of the CPD.[275] Considering the Daley family's close relationship with President Bill Clinton, participants tempered their expectations. Reno entertained for forty-five minutes before showing them the door.[276] Unable to recruit allies in Washington, activists looked further afield. Following the terrorist attacks of September 11, 2001, policy makers' decision to launch the global War on Terror attracted worldwide attention to American law enforcement and military personnel.[277] As the Egan investigation unfolded locally, photographs of U.S. soldiers abusing prisoners at Abu Ghraib prison in Iraq triggered international outrage in April 2004.[278] Exposing a breadth of questionable and illegal interrogation methods employed by U.S. operatives in Iraq, Afghanistan, and Guantanamo Bay, Cuba, the scandal thrust torture to the fore of international debate.[279] Similarities with Chicago did not go unnoticed. Finding details of Area 2 torture "reminiscent of the news reports of 2004 concerning the notorious Abu Ghraib facility," federal Judge Diane Wood drew direct parallels between foreign and domestic atrocity.[280]

With American torture drawing unprecedented attention, activists seized the opportunity to attract an international audience. "Here we are in 2005," explained Chicago attorney and civil rights activist Standish Willis, "over 20 years of evidence of torture, and absolutely nothing has been done to prosecute. We are moving to a different level."[281] In August 2005, a coalition of lawyers and activists sent a letter to the Inter-American Commission on Human Rights (IACHR) requesting an investigation of the Burge scandal.[282] In October, representatives of the People's Law Office, the National Conference of Black Lawyers, and Chicago-area law clinics witnessed torture survivor David Bates testify before an IACHR hearing in the nation's capital.[283] While the United States never signed the organization's American Convention on Human Rights, its three-member committee heard activists' pleas and issued recommendations. Unable to bring formal charges before the Inter-American Court of Human Rights, the commission explained, "We believe [the report] carries moral weight and political weight, but it does not carry the force of a court decision."[284] Encouraged by the reception and publicity, representatives of the Midwest Coalition for Human Rights, Positive Anti-Crime Thrust, and the African-American Police League invited the IACHR to Chicago for further investigation.[285]

Activists next turned to the United Nations. In May 2006, Joey Mogul of the People's Law Office led a delegation to Geneva, Switzerland, to charge the United States with violating the UN's Convention against Torture (UNCAT).[286] Inspired by the presentation, UNCAT commissioners devoted a section of their 2006 report to "allegations of impunity . . . in respect of acts of torture or cruel, inhuman or degrading treatment or punishment" in the United States, particularly the "limited investigation and lack of prosecution in respect of the allegations of torture perpetrated in areas 2 and 3 of the Chicago Police Department." Validating activists' long journey, commissioners urged the U.S. government to "promptly, thoroughly and impartially" investigate the Burge scandal.[287] In 2007, the UN special rapporteur on torture referenced "at least" twenty-four men "serving prison terms on the basis of confessions which may have been obtained by torture or ill-treatment." In 2008, torture survivors David Bates, Darrell Cannon, and Anthony Holmes testified before the special rapporteur on racism in Chicago.[288] According to Mogul, UN support "provided us emotional motivation" and reminded local authorities "the whole world is watching—you're not gonna just keep this in Chicago."[289] Pleased with results, Standish Willis founded Black People against Police Torture and pressured the International Olympic Committee to reject Chicago's bid to host the 2016 Olympic games.[290] Once an open secret on Chicago's South Side, the Burge scandal was now circulating across the globe.

Meanwhile, a small group of detectives, including several who previously worked under Burge, continued coercing confessions from black criminal suspects at Area 3 and elsewhere.[291] Belying the notion that Burge was simply a bad apple who had gone rogue, police torture in Chicago endured after 1991. Indeed, in some ways the torture crisis worsened after Burge's firing, even if allegations of electric shock faded. For over twenty years, Burge demonstrated a craven disregard for basic civil liberties. Yet he also operated the torture regime under a lawless code of professional misconduct that typically reserved torture for suspects likely guilty of heinous crimes. When Burge left, however, so did his limited restraint. Free of supervision, detectives Kenneth Boudreau, James O'Brien, Michael Kill, John Halloran, James Pienta, and others compiled a long record of brutality complaints from a particularly vulnerable group of criminal suspects—black juveniles with mental handicaps, emotional disabilities, and little or no direct connection to the crime under investigation.[292] By singling out Burge and ceremoniously firing him, public officials obscured the scope of the torture crisis and inhibited further scrutiny of the department, even as coerced confessions continued to make headlines.[293]

Even those who understood the depth of the Burge scandal found it difficult to win relief within Cook County's incestuous criminal justice system. Throughout the United States, detectives, prosecutors, and judges belonged to the same "courtroom work group," an extended network of professionals relying on one another to accomplish respective tasks.[294] Over the course of long careers, individuals at all levels of law enforcement forged professional and personal relationships of extended duration. Interpersonal bonds, however valuable, could complicate the delicate system of checks and balances necessary to prevent misconduct.[295] In the Circuit Court of Cook County, once the "largest unified court system in the nation," conflicting loyalties often inhibited norms of political accountability.[296] Simply put, too many persons with power to repair Burge's damage held some damning connection to the larger scandal.

Looking to get their cases reassigned in 2001, attorneys representing twelve torture survivors revealed that at least fifty of the sixty-one judges in the Criminal Division's felony courts previously worked in other local law enforcement agencies. Their number included forty-one former Cook County assistant state's attorneys, four former assistant corporation counsels, two former assistant attorneys general, and five former Chicago police officers. Moreover, "at least eighteen had material involvement in the torture cases, either by obtaining the allegedly coerced statements, by approving charges based on them in Felony Review, by using the confessions . . . as trial prosecutors, and/or by participating in Burge's defense as lawyers or witnesses."[297] For example, Judge John J. Mannion—who refused to suppress Stanley Howard's confession in 1987—previously served as both an Area 2 homicide detective and an assistant state's attorney.[298] In 2004, Judge Nicholas Ford dismissed a postconviction petition filed by Keith Walker, who claimed Area 3 detectives tortured him by electric shock thirteen years earlier. In an obvious conflict of interest, it was Judge Ford who, as an assistant state's attorney, recorded and signed Walker's allegedly coerced statement in 1991. According to John Conroy of the *Chicago Reader*, "The prosecutors who sent police torture victims to prison are now the judges who keep them there."[299] Indeed, a private attorney speaking to researcher Nicole Gonzalez Van Cleve described the "insular culture" of the Cook County criminal courts as a "good-ol'-boys club where judges are not only accountable to their former peers but have a desire to be in the prosecutors' inner circle."[300] Eager to punish perpetrators, activists needed to go beyond what critics referred to as "Crook" County.[301]

Yet efforts to recruit federal prosecutors often went nowhere.[302] Indeed, Citizens Alert lamented the indifference of the U.S. Attorney's Office as early as 1990, conceding, "All of our efforts to obtain an investigation of Burge's conduct through the usual sources have been fruitless."[303] Shifting political fortunes, however, offered hope. Acting on the recommendation of U.S. Senator Peter Fitzgerald, an ultraconservative "maverick" Republican whose single term fell between those of Carol Moseley Braun and Barack Obama, President George W. Bush appointed New York prosecutor Patrick Fitzgerald (no relation) to serve as U.S. Attorney for the Northern District of Illinois in 2001.[304] A graduate of Harvard Law School, Patrick Fitzgerald won renown for prosecuting those responsible for bombing the World Trade Center in 1993 and U.S. embassies in East Africa in 1998.[305] Representing the establishment against those who challenged its authority, Fitzgerald seemed an unlikely champion of state prisoners and their radical allies. Yet by helping convict former governor George Ryan in 2006 and Washington insider I. "Scooter" Libby in 2007, Fitzgerald also earned a reputation for fighting corruption.[306] With a New York Republican at the helm of the Northern District of Illinois, activists sensed an opportunity. "Remember this was under Bush's Administration," explained PLO attorney Joey Mogul, "and when Bush was going to the UN Committee against Torture, their arguments were essentially, 'Yes, we made some missteps in the War on Terror . . . and at Abu Ghraib and Guantanamo, but look at us domestically, we are the beacon of human rights.'"[307] Responding in part to pressure from the Chicago torture justice movement, Fitzgerald's office finally impaneled a grand jury in 2008 to investigate charges against Burge.[308]

With all its flaws, however, the 2007 Egan report concluded correctly that "the statute of limitations had run on all offenses" of physical abuse and torture committed by detectives in the 1970s, 1980s, and 1990s.[309] Yet the People's Law Office helped outline other areas where Burge and his men remained vulnerable to prosecution.[310] Scouring the record, federal prosecutors focused on a civil suit filed by Madison Hobley. After Governor Ryan's 2003 pardons, Hobley sued Burge, the City of Chicago, and other public officials for violating his civil rights pursuant to a wrongful conviction.[311] During pretrial proceedings in November 2003, Burge and other detectives signed sworn interrogatories denying any knowledge of—or participation in—acts of torture. Fitzgerald seized on these sworn denials to charge Burge with lying under oath and obstructing justice.[312] If this seemed a roundabout way to convict a torturer, Fitzgerald likened the indictments to those brought by Eliot Ness in the 1930s. "If Al Capone went down for taxes," Fitzgerald explained, "it's better than him going down for nothing."[313] On October 21, 2008, federal agents arrested sixty-year-old Jon Burge at his home in Apollo Beach, Florida, nearly seventeen years after he worked his final shift with the Chicago Police Department.[314]

Delayed while Burge received treatment for prostate cancer, *United States v. Burge* went to trial on May 26, 2010.[315] For four weeks, prosecutors rehashed a handful of cases familiar to observers of the decades-old scandal. Torture survivors Anthony Holmes, Melvin Jones, Gregory Banks, and Shadeed Mu'Min each took the stand.[316] While Andrew Wilson died in prison in 2007, the judge allowed lawyers to read his prior testimony into the record.[317] For two days in June, Burge testified to a packed gallery. In a polite, professional cadence, Burge played the humble public servant and denied all torture allegations. Portraying him as a professional liar, prosecutors jumped on his admission that he "lied to defendants all the time." Sensing a trap, Burge deflected, "You're making a big issue out of something that was routine and accepted practice and legal, sir." Revealing Burge once owned a boat named *Vigilante*, prosecutors inquired "whether you were proud of your reputation for taking the law into your own hands." Sharp as ever, Burge answered, "That's like a [']when did you stop beating your wife['] question." Nonplussed, he added, "I'm proud of my reputation, but not for taking the law into my own hands, counselor." When prosecutors suggested it took extraordinary effort to catch "sophisticated criminals," Burge quipped, "I never met a sophisticated criminal."[318] On redirect, defense attorneys challenged the relevancy of Burge's boat and established detectives' right to deceive criminal suspects. Stepping from the stand, Burge left his fate to the jury.

In closing arguments, Assistant U.S. Attorney David Weisman told jurors, "It is your time to say that Jon Burge is not above the law." Suggesting criminal suspects "expect to get smacked around a little by the police," Weisman's colleague April Perry insisted, "what [Burge] did was different. What he did was torture." In response, defense attorney Richard Beuke countered, "Those detectives who worked murder after murder, rape after rape, armed robbery after armed robbery back in the [1970s and 1980s], they were honorable true heroes." Indeed, he argued, Burge and his men "were the only people that the South Side of the city had" to protect them from the "Anthony Holmeses," "Shadeed Mu'Minses," and "Gregory Bankses of the world." Meanwhile, he mused, "somewhere in the darkest, dingiest corner of hell, Andrew Wilson has to be sitting and laughing hysterically as to how he has managed to manipulate this system." According to Beuke, the government's witnesses had turned nice neighborhoods into "crime infested, drug infested, gun infested cesspool[s]." Linking past and present, he added, "evil still lurks on those streets. There [are] monsters all over the South Side." Referring to Burge, Beuke concluded that crime victims "would be better off if this gentleman was still there. He has nothing to come into this court and apologize for." In rebuttal, Perry placed her witnesses' flaws in context. "We did not pick these victims," she reminded.

"[Burge] picked them because he thought they were bad people, who would never be believed."[319] By 2010, however, decades of collective struggle had tipped the scales decisively in their favor.

On June 28, 2010, jurors found Jon Burge guilty on all counts.[320] While federal guidelines recommended a sentence of only two years in prison, prosecutors calculated Burge could face up to thirty years or more, a veritable life sentence for a man of advanced age and poor health.[321] Prior to sentencing, Judge Joan Lefkow requested victim-impact statements and letters from Burge supporters. During an emotional public hearing, torture survivor Anthony Holmes explained how his experience proved "hard on me and my family." His wife divorced him. He had trouble maintaining relationships with his eleven children. Several family members died while he was in prison. He suffered post-traumatic stress. "[Burge] tried to kill me," Holmes recalled. "It leaves a gnawing, hurting feeling. I can't shake it."[322] After careful deliberation, on January 21, 2011, Judge Lefkow sentenced Burge to four and a half years, double the suggested time for perjury and obstruction of justice, noting, "These offenses were committed in order to conceal the commission of other offenses."[323] Blaming police supervisors and prosecutors for enabling Burge's behavior, however, Lefkow refused to frame the scandal solely around the defendant's character. "There are those who believe you are deeply racist," she expounded, "and there are those who believe you could not possibly have tortured suspects. I doubt that my opinion or what happens here will change anyone's views. You are the person you are, neither all good, nor all evil, just like the rest of us."[324] Outside the courthouse, torture survivors and their attorneys, families, and supporters celebrated a hard-fought victory. While many participants of the Chicago torture justice movement considered Burge's sentence too lenient, most appreciated the accomplishment. Having realized some semblance of justice, activists maintained efforts to hold others accountable and repair affected communities.

The fate of torture survivors still behind bars took precedent. While Governor Ryan's 2003 commutations alleviated the danger of executions, dozens of men continued to languish in prison despite the clearing out of death row. Many voiced compelling claims of innocence. Others insisted that false confessions exacerbated the charges and punishments they faced. Activists and attorneys did not turn their backs on these men. Shortly after his release, Aaron Patterson called for shifting resources from the Death Row 10 to the "Burge 66," a contemporary estimate of the number of prisoners impacted.[325] Meanwhile, Burge's indictment, trial, and conviction legitimized activists' narrative and helped survivors win their freedom. For example, the state vacated the conviction of DR10 member Ronald Kitchen in July 2009, freeing codefendant Marvin Reeves as well.[326] A year later, DR10 member Victor Safforld pleaded guilty to one murder in exchange for the state's dropping charges in a second and setting him free.[327] In March 2011, prosecutors finally honored the logic of Patterson's 2003 exoneration by freeing his codefendant Eric Caine.[328] Indeed, the plight of DR10 codefendants Reeves and Caine underscored the challenges facing wrongfully convicted prisoners who were not sentenced to death. Escaping capital charges, they did not enjoy the automatic appeals, litigation funds, or media attention that often accompanied a death sentence. In another noncapital case, a judge overturned Stanley Wrice's conviction in December 2013, freeing the fifty-nine-year-old torture survivor some thirty years after his coerced confession.[329] While justice delayed remained justice denied, activists welcomed every belated act of judicial relief.

Victory against Burge in federal court also bolstered the fight against capital punishment. Ten days before Judge Lefkow sentenced Burge in January 2011, the Illinois State Senate in Springfield passed legislation abolishing the death penalty in Illinois.[330] Democratic governor Pat Quinn spent the next six weeks weighing arguments before signing SB3539 on March 9, 2011.[331] Announcing his decision, Quinn cited twenty exonerations in Illinois since 1987, the most of any state.[332] Echoing Governor Ryan, Quinn also commuted the sentences of all fifteen persons sent to death row since the 2003 commutations.[333] In the *Chicago Tribune*, journalist Eric Zorn honored those responsible for the victory, including Rob Warden of the *Chicago Lawyer*; John Conroy of the *Chicago Reader*; Professor David Protess and his students at Northwestern; the Center on Wrongful Convictions; defense attorney Andrea Lyon; PLO attorneys Joey Mogul and Flint Taylor; Aaron Patterson, Mark Clements, and other former prisoners-turned-activists; the late Mary Alice Rankin and the ICADP; former Governor Ryan and his Commission on Capital Punishment; and current and former state legislators, including Carol Moseley Braun and the sponsors of the bill, Kwame Raoul and Karen Yarbrough.[334] Zorn might also have thanked Jon Burge, who reported to the Butner Federal Correctional Complex in North Carolina to begin his sentence one week after Quinn signed the abolition bill.[335] For twenty-five years, Burge offered the movement a galvanizing symbol of how capital punishment could go horribly wrong.

Epilogue

The Chicago torture justice movement did not end with the conviction of Jon Burge and the abolition of the death penalty in Illinois in 2011. Flush with victory, activists renewed efforts to win judicial relief for torture victims still in prison, memorialize the torture scandal, and secure reparations for survivors. Indeed, myriad streams of related action continued apace throughout the campaign to prosecute Burge. In 2005, attorney Standish Willis launched Black People against Police Torture and drafted legislation to provide a range of services to Burge survivors.[1] Shorn of a comprehensive reparations package, the bill led to the creation of the Illinois Torture Inquiry and Relief Commission (TIRC) in 2009.[2] Sponsored by State Senator Kwame Raoul, the TIRC bill tasked the commission with fielding applications for judicial review from state prisoners convicted on the strength of allegedly coerced confessions linked to Burge.[3] Five years later, however, Judge Paul Biebel concluded that "there is no confidence that the [TIRC] will ever have the funding and resources to achieve its intended purpose and give finality to this painful issue."[4] Accordingly, in March 2014 Biebel appointed a "special master" to "locate the individuals with a 'valid claim' of a Burge-related coerced confession who are still languishing in Illinois penitentiaries."[5] Both the TIRC commission and the special master documented scores of abuse allegations, including many unrelated to the Burge scandal, and offered hope to prisoners looking to win their release.

Meanwhile, lawyers and activists founded the Chicago Torture Justice Memorial project (CTJM) in 2011. CTJM sponsored art exhibits, poetry readings, dance and music performances, and other creative means of publicizing police abuse and commemorating the movement. At a retreat in May 2013, CTJM participants decided to adapt Willis's reparations bill for introduction in the Chicago City Council. Aldermen Howard Brookins and Joe

Moreno, who once worked with the Campaign to End the Death Penalty, cosponsored the bill in October 2013. The ordinance attracted little attention and soon disappeared in committee. Determined to raise awareness of the reparations push, CTJM sponsored a series of public actions throughout the fall and winter, including an ongoing art exhibit and rally outside City Hall involving dozens of volunteers from Amnesty International.[6] If the ordinance seemed unlikely to ever see the light of day, activists at least hoped to spark a citywide conversation.[7]

With the reparations bill stalled, national events in the late summer of 2014 opened a window of opportunity for local activists to frame the ordinance in new context. On August 9, a white police officer killed African American teenager Michael Brown in Ferguson, Missouri. The latest in a string of high-profile police killings, Brown's death made Ferguson an epicenter of protests for police accountability.[8] Rallying around the slogan "Black Lives Matter," activists in Chicago escalated ongoing efforts to hold abusive officers accountable and challenge the policies of Mayor Rahm Emanuel and State's Attorney Anita Alvarez. Old and new organizations, including Amnesty International, Black Youth Project 100, CTJM, Project Nia, We Charge Genocide, and others invigorated campaigns to win justice on several related issues. Inspired by Ferguson, CTJM launched a concentrated campaign to win reparations for Burge survivors with an October 2014 Twitter "power hour" designed to force the hashtag "#RahmRepNow" to the top of the social media platform's trending list. For six months, participants in the #RahmRepNow campaign relied on social media to coordinate and publicize a series of public protests. Activists circulated T-shirts, fliers, and reading material; participated in train takeovers, teach-ins, and sing-ins; packed City Council meetings and subcommittee hearings; stood outside the mayor's home with signs spelling "Reparations Now" in electric light; organized rallies and marches; and employed social media to recruit supporters, pressure public officials, and document their actions in real time.[9]

Even as the #RahmRepNow campaign unfolded, external events intervened to align the interests of the mayor and the movement. On October 20, 2014, police dashcam video recorded white Chicago police officer Jason Van Dyke shooting seventeen-year-old Laquan McDonald sixteen times as other officers looked on. While footage of the black teenager's killing would not surface for over a year, Mayor Emanuel knew what it revealed and urged City Council to offer a financial settlement to the McDonald family.[10] In February, an independent journalist suggested a cover-up.[11] Two weeks later, voters forced an embarrassing runoff election in Emanuel's bid for a second term. Desperate to avoid negative press and eager to appear progressive on issues of police accountability, the mayor suppressed the McDonald video and began negotiations with CTJM representatives.[12] Unbeknownst to protestors, the city agreed to virtually all of the CTJM's demands, balking only at the $20 million price tag. Determined to win at least $100,000 each for approximately sixty eligible torture survivors, CTJM insisted on a $5.5 million package.[13] Before an ecstatic crowd of torture survivors, activists, and supporters, the mayor's chief attorney announced the deal during a Finance Committee hearing on April 14, 2015.[14]

Originally written by People's Law Office attorney Joey Mogul and titled "Reparations for Burge Torture Victims," the bill represented a landmark achievement for the local police accountability movement.[15] The ordinance acknowledged the verity of the torture scandal and highlighted its systemic nature. In addition to financial payouts, some fifty-seven claimants would also receive privileged access to psychological counseling, health care, and vocational training as well as tuition-free enrolment in City Colleges for themselves, their children, and grandchildren. The ordinance required the city offer an official apology, erect a public memorial, create a permanent community center for victims of police violence, and develop a public-school curriculum to teach the Burge scandal to eighth- and tenth-grade students.[16] Some torture survivors and their allies criticized the bill for narrowing eligibility to only those men tortured under Burge or his men between 1972 and 1991. Others objected that the bill forced claimants to waive their right to sue the city for civil damages or otherwise fell short of guaranteeing survivors' income or employment. Following celebrations, activists turned to the implementation fight to ensure meaningful delivery of services in a timely fashion.[17]

As the reparations campaign demonstrated, the goals and tactics of the Chicago torture justice movement changed over the course of its quarter century of existence, with immediate crises often determining the allocation of resources at any given moment. In 1989, when the coalition first came together and Burge remained in charge of detectives at Area 3, activists concentrated on ending torture, locating victims, and removing perpetrators from the department. With Burge fired after 1993, efforts shifted toward winning the release of the wrongfully convicted, suing the city for civil damages, and preventing executions. The clearing of death row in 2003 ended an immediate threat and allowed activists to concentrate on getting criminal indictments for perpetrators. Burge's 2010 conviction led to renewed efforts to win judicial relief for torture victims still behind bars.[18] The appointment of a state commission and special master to adjudicate prisoners' allegations opened space to secure reparations. Even as the movement's priorities shifted, however, objectives overlapped.

Indeed, to accomplish its goals, the movement developed an informal division of labor. Lawyers filed briefs and litigated cases. Activists organized events and led marches. Torture survivors and their families made public appearances. Journalists investigated stories and interviewed officials. Yet traditional roles often blurred, as attorneys spoke at rallies, prisoners researched legal procedure, and activists launched alternative media. Throughout the process, activists demonstrated the necessity of working both inside and outside established channels of accountability. On the occasion of Burge's conviction in 2010, Citizens Alert paused to acknowledge the perseverance of a multitude of participants, writing:

> Whether you were able to monitor civil trials, to pressure the Chicago Police Board to fire Jon Burge (as they did in 1993), to petition the courts for appointment of a Special Prosecutor, to write letters urging legislation to require videotaping of interrogations, to promote establishment of the state-wide 'Torture Commission,' whose appointments will be announced later in the month, to promote international pressure on the U.S. to insist on Chicago prosecution of torture charges, or to attend demonstrations to keep the issue alive in public awareness, your role was significant and your efforts important to this overall victory in the courts.[19]

While activists celebrated, however, they never lost sight of challenges ahead.

By the 2010s, decades of sustained action had illuminated the nature of the movement's principal obstacles. First, there was the difficulty of defining a constituency, representing its interests, and broadening support. The direct beneficiaries of the movement consisted of men convicted of serious felonies, including several still behind bars, as well as their families, friends, and communities. Activists struggled to rally mass support for victims who otherwise failed to elicit sympathy or compassion. Many of the men who claimed they were tortured were likely guilty of awful crimes, including arson, rape, and murder. Indeed, Area 2 detectives deliberately targeted suspects who fit a certain profile—young, poor, and black—with lengthy criminal records, known gang affiliations, histories of violence and drug abuse, as well as some connection to the crimes under investigation.[20] Officials easily denied, even justified, abusing such men. Second, the hidden nature of police violence—particularly torture perpetrated during custodial interrogation—made it nearly impossible to corroborate accusations and counter denials. Third, the movement's diversity, while celebrated, contributed to internal conflict and inhibited unity of purpose. Finally, there existed a great power disparity between the movement and the institutions it targeted. Whereas the Chicago Police Department, the City of Chicago, and Cook County wielded great influence and wealth, the movement struggled to assert credibility or raise funds. Its qualified success testifies to activists' ability and perseverance.

Yet the Chicago torture justice movement also experienced regular disappointment and defeat. For example, even after the CPD fired Burge in 1993, other detectives continued coercing confessions throughout the 1990s and 2000s. While elected officials placed a moratorium on executions in 1999 and abolished the death penalty in 2011, Illinois remained a national capital of wrongful convictions. While judges ruled in favor of torture survivors in multiple proceedings, they also denied petitions and rejected appeals in countless more. For every prisoner released, another one or more remained behind bars. Each time a survivor accepted a financial settlement, perpetrators and collaborators escaped depositions. Indeed, former mayor Richard M. Daley dodged testifying under oath time and time again.[21] Every survivor who cashed a reparations check signed away his chance to sue for larger damages. While a handful of perpetrators faced disciplinary action for their role in the torture scandal, only Burge faced criminal charges. If activists helped close the chapter on the Burge regime, racist police violence continued to plague the city.[22] As late as 2019, dozens of torture survivors remained behind bars without ever having aired their allegations before an impartial judge. Others who served their time or won their freedom endured the consequences and stigma of a criminal conviction. Many suffered post-traumatic stress.[23]

For over twenty years after 1970, personal bigotry and structural racism converged to shape outcomes for countless individuals affected by the Burge scandal. At Area 2 headquarters, white police officers predisposed to racial animosity thrived in a system rewarding certain kinds of misconduct. As caseloads expanded and pressure mounted in the 1970s and 1980s, local law enforcement agencies deprioritized civil liberties, encouraged shortcuts, and incentivized coerced confessions. Lacking robust accountability, perpetrators largely avoided detection. From this milieu emerged the Area 2 torture regime. In Burge, the CPD found a skilled and ambitious investigator, raised on traditions of white resistance, trained as a soldier, and seasoned in Vietnam. In the CPD, Burge found an institution with a history of racial violence, a practice of masking misconduct, and a need to streamline convictions. Together, Burge and the CPD fomented abuse and exacerbated the challenges facing black Chicago, including deindustrialization, concentrated poverty, rising crime, and police brutality. Removing Burge, however important, failed to address the structural inequality driving racial disparities in housing, education, employment, income, health care, and criminal justice. Yet the failure of accountability mechanisms mobilized social movement actors, whose efforts to win justice for Burge survivors continued beyond 2019.

Meanwhile, Burge finished his sentence and returned to central Florida on a taxpayer-supported pension.[24] Continuing to plead the Fifth Amendment in ongoing litigation, he broke silence only following passage of the reparations bill in May 2015. In a statement released through a local supporter, Burge found it "hard to believe that the City's political leadership could even contemplate giving 'Reparations' to human vermin" like Darrell Cannon, Madison Hobley, Anthony Holmes, and members of the Royal Family. Attacking a "Northwestern cabal" of "academics and students" for their "unethical" efforts to "free guilty, vicious criminals," Burge also condemned "human vultures" like "G. Flint Taylor and his ilk" for pushing a "radical political agenda" while "getting rich . . . filing specious lawsuits." In his last public comments, Burge defended himself and other "dedicated Chicago Police Detectives who fought, as best we could, the worst, most violent predators on the South Side." Predicting he would be "vindicated" while his accusers "[paid] the piper," Burge appeared broken and bitter.[25] Disturbed that the disgraced commander seemed unwilling to seek redemption, Taylor rejected claims he had some "personal vendetta" against him. "I don't hate the guy," Taylor admitted in May 2018, adding: "Maybe that's easy for me because he didn't torture me. But, he's a dying old man now and there's more important things to deal with." Yet Taylor could not deny all satisfaction, concluding: "I've got my health, he doesn't, and I'm still fighting and he's not. So, I guess you could say we won that one."[26] Jon Burge died on September 19, 2018, at age seventy.

Less than three weeks later, a jury convicted Jason Van Dyke of second-degree murder in the shooting death of Laquan McDonald. Many of the same activists who fought for justice in the Burge cases took credit for the victory.[27] Exposing the CPD's shameful history of racism, violence, and cover-up, both scandals demonstrated the barriers to meaningful accountability and the efficacy of social movement activism. Rather than isolated events separated by decades, however, Burge's shock box and Van Dyke's sixteen shots represent a tradition of extraordinary events exposing ordinary misconduct. Indeed, in 2018 attorney Joey Mogul rejected the standard narrative of the Burge scandal, insisting, "The problem with this story is that it's just all about Burge." Citing endless reports of similar abuse, Mogul concluded: "Let's not pretend that this is some isolated racist who did all this damage. This is about a community, a culture that, to be honest, exists to this day."[28] Drawing lessons from the Chicago torture justice movement, the fight against racist police violence continues.

Acknowledgments

I could not have finished this book without the help of scores of people, all of whom made the final product better. I begin by thanking Martha Biondi, an ideal mentor who directed me to the topic and sustained me when my confidence lagged. Martha continues to inspire with her scholarship and commitment to social justice. When in doubt, I often ask myself, What would Martha do? Then I try to do that. I thank Michael Sherry for the conversation, support, and good humor. His approach to historical inquiry, writing, and teaching is simply unparalleled. I thank Henry Binford for his creative suggestions, tough queries, and expertise on urban history. I thank Kevin Boyle for his exceptional collegiality and suggestions for improving narrative style and organization. Other faculty at Northwestern University deserve credit as well, including Michael Allen, Anthony Chen, Kate Masur, Melissa Macauley, and Dylan Penningroth, for their advice on writing, teaching, and applying for external funding. Thanks to the Northwestern History Department staff—Paula Blaskovits, Annerys Cano, Susan Delrahim, Susan Hall, Liz Murray, and Eric West—for all their hard work and encouragement. Thanks to my editor at the University of Chicago Press, Tim Mennel, for believing in the project and helping tighten my arguments. Thanks to Katherine Faydash for the meticulous copyediting. Thanks to Lilia Fernández for her insightful review and critique. Thanks to the anonymous reviewers for their time and suggestions.

A fellowship from the American Bar Foundation (ABF), the Law and Society Association, and the National Science Foundation carried me through critical steps of completion and introduced me to important new ideas. I'd particularly like to thank Bernadette Atuahene, Traci Burch, Amanda Ehrhardt, Terence Halliday, Joshua Kaiser, Richard Leo, Ajay Mehrotra, Bob

Nelson, Laura Beth Nielson, Christopher Schmidt, Jill Wienberg, and Vicky Woeste for their hospitality and guidance at the ABF. I am also grateful for the friendship and advice of former ABF fellows Amanda Hughett and Matthew Shaw, whose contributions extend well beyond scholarship.

Participation in countless research and writing workshops exposed me to a breadth of talented historians whose work informed my own. From the Newberry Library Urban History Dissertation Group I thank Devin Hunter, Kyle Mays, Christopher Ramsey, Chloe Taft, and many others. I thank Robin Bartram, Anya Degenshein, Mary Patillo, and the rest of the Northwestern Sociology Department's Urban and Communities Workshop for putting up with a historian's sixty-page chapter submission. Michael Sherry's American history writing workshops were essential. I thank many friends in attendance, particularly Laila Ballout, Ashley Johnson Bavery, Kyle Burke, Myisha Eatmon, Bonnie Ernst, Michael Falcone, Alex Gourse, Mariah Hepworth, Alistair Hobson, Zachary Jacobson, Valeria Jimenez, Donald Johnson, Matthew June, Matthew Kahn, Amanda Kleintop, Sam Kling, Rebecca Marchiel, Jesse Nasta, Wen-Qing Ngoei, Adam Plaiss, Aram Sarkisian, Ian Saxine, Leigh Soares, Andrew Warne, and many more. Thanks to Jon Briggs and Jamie Holeman for the support and advice. Thanks to all of the Chicago historians and police historians who have sat with me on panels or in attendance at various conferences, including Christopher Agee, Richard Anderson, Simon Balto, Max Felker-Kantor, Erik Gellman, John Hagedorn, Jeff Helgeson, Brandon Jett, Julilly Kohler-Hausmann, Nora Krinitsky, Toussaint Losier, Gordon Mantler, Sam Mitrani, Melanie Newport, and Peter Pihos.

I thank my colleagues at the University of Alabama at Birmingham (UAB) for their collegiality and support, including Jordan Bauer, Jill Hamilton Clements (and Jason Clements), Colin Davis, Harriet Amos Doss, Michele Forman, DeReef Jamison, Andrew Keitt, Pam King, George Liber, André Millard, Stephen Miller, Kathryn Morgan, Pam Murray, Brian Steele, John Van Sant, Jeff Walker, Walter Ward, Jonathan Wiesen, Will Womack, and Natasha Zaretsky. Thanks also to Melanie Daily, Alisa Dick, and Jerrie McCurry. Funding through UAB's Faculty Development Grant Program helped push the manuscript over the finish line. I also thank my students for their insight and inspiration and for being a sounding board for many half-baked ideas.

Various archivists, activists, attorneys, and community members provided suggestions and assistance as well. I thank the wonderful staff of the Special Collections Library at the University of Illinois at Chicago, particularly Dan Harper, Valerie Harris, and Gretchen Neidhart. I thank Peter Alter and the archivists and staff at the Chicago History Museum, the Special Collections Library at the University of Chicago, the Municipal Reference Library at the Harold Washington Library Center, and the Vivian G. Harsh Research Collection at the Chicago Public Library. I thank Max Caproni and the Chicago Police Board for providing research material and the U.S. Attorney's Office for the Northern District of Illinois for providing exhibits from the 2010 Jon Burge criminal trial. I thank Chicago Police Department officer Jack Enter for candidly explaining the failure of my repeated Freedom of Information Act requests. I thank James Sorrels for the many exciting conversations and for sharing research materials and off-the-record film interviews. Thank you to John Conroy for providing the foundation for all scholarship on the Jon Burge scandal. Thanks to the People's Law Office, particularly G. Flint Taylor and Joey Mogul, for speaking with me and sharing an incredible amount of documentary evidence. Thanks to Charles Hoffman and Rob Warden for useful email exchanges. Thanks to Andrea Lyon for her candor and encouragement. Thanks to the many activists who spoke to me at protest rallies or agreed to sit with me in person or on the telephone, including Darryl Cannon, Mark Clements, Alice Kim, Gladys Lewis, Marlene Martin, Noreen McNulty, Mary Powers, and Jane Ramsey. Thanks to the veterans of the Ninth Military Police who spoke with me despite reservations about the nature of my project, including Michael Cahill, Steve Gustat, John Patterson, and Wendell Rudacille. Thanks to Elliot Dellman and Charlie Ochs for their insight into Burge's childhood neighborhood and the Ninth MPs, respectively.

Finally, I thank my mentors, friends, and family. Len Lempel at Daytona Beach Community College convinced me I belonged on a college campus. The late Alan Petigny at the University of Florida convinced me I could be a historian. Kyle Burke, Matt June, and Brian O'Camb sustained me through the difficult early stages of an academic career. Jesse Russell, Nick Knapp, and Matt Deruntz offered shelter outside academia. Ben Burbank, Mike Kemick, Josh Knight, and Jason Molohon remain with me to this day, even across distances of time and space. Of course, no one has done more to help than Mariah Hepworth, beside me every step of the way, through each self-righteous high and self-pitying low. Her unique empathy and penchant for the big idea make me a better historian. Thanks to my grandmother, Eileen Baer, for igniting my interest in history. Thanks to my mom, Cindy Baer, for helping me understand the lived meaning of justice, sacrifice, and empathy. Thanks to my dad, Jeffrey Baer, for teaching me responsibility and affection.

Thanks to Terry Baer for the peace of mind. Thanks to my sisters, Jackie Baer and Jenni Baer, for the lifelong comfort, security, and companionship. And thanks to my nephew, Benjamin Henry Baer, for giving it all purpose. And finally, thanks to the fine people at Panera Bread, for all the free Wi-Fi and Dr. Pepper.

Abbreviations

AAPL: African American Police League Records, Chicago History Museum

AER: Alliance to End Repression Records, Chicago History Museum

AFSC: American Friends Service Committee Papers, University of Illinois at Chicago Special Collections Library

CAOF: Citizens Alert Office Files, unprocessed material located in the Citizens Alert offices shortly before their closing, now housed at the University of Illinois at Chicago Special Collections Library.

CAR: Citizens Alert Records, University of Illinois at Chicago Special Collections Library

CCCA: Cook County Clerk of the Circuit Court Archives.

CCUA: Chicago Council on Urban Affairs Records, University of Illinois at Chicago Special Collections Library

CHAIII: Cyrus Hall Adams, III Papers, Chicago History Museum

CHC: Committee for Handgun Control Records, University of Illinois at Chicago Special Collections Library

CHM: Chicago History Museum

CPB: Chicago Police Board Archive

CUL: Chicago Urban League Records, University of Illinois at Chicago Special Collections Library

HWLC: Municipal Reference Library, Harold Washington Library Center

ICADP: IL Coalition to Abolish the Death Penalty Records, University of Illinois at Chicago Special Collections Library

LMD: Leon M. Despres Papers, Chicago History Museum

LOC: Len O'Connor Papers, Chicago History Museum

LWVIL: League of Women Voters of Illinois Collection, University of Illinois at Chicago Special Collections Library

MAB: Michael A. Bilandic Papers, University of Illinois at Chicago Special Collections Library

OWWP: Orlando Winfield Wilson Papers, University of California Berkeley.

PLOTF: People's Law Office Torture Files. The People's Law Office put these documents on a disc and gave them to the author. They were then downloaded or printed and held in the author's possession. The People's Law Office also gave this material (and much more) to the Pozen Family Center for Human Rights at the University of Chicago for use in its torture archive. Briefly opened to researchers in 2016, the archive is closed as of summer 2019.

RJD: Richard J. Daley Collection, University of Illinois at Chicago Special Collections Library

RSR: Red Squad selected records, Chicago History Museum

TIRC: Illinois Torture Inquiry and Relief Commission decisions, https://www2.illinois.gov/sites/tirc/Pages/TIRCDecision.aspx.

TMB: Timuel M. Black Papers, Vivian G. Harsh Collection, Chicago Public Library

Notes

Introduction

1. "Memorandum Opinion and Order," *People v. Wilson*, 82 C 001211-02, 88 CR 07771-01, June 14, 2018, 8–17, 81–88.

2. "Memorandum Opinion and Order," *People v. Wilson*, 82 C 001211-02, 88 CR 07771-01, June 14, 2018, 119.

3. "Memorandum Opinion and Order," *People v. Wilson*, 82 C 001211-02, 88 CR 07771-01, June 14, 2018, 110, 116–119.

4. Erin Fahey, "Alleged Torture of Jackie Wilson Doesn't Diminish His Guilt in Cops' Murders," *Chicago Sun-Times*, June 13, 2018.

5. "Lessons of the Jackie Wilson Murder Trial Saga," *Chicago Sun-Times*, June 18, 2018.

6. Journalist John Conroy and attorney G. Flint Taylor crafted the standard narrative of the Jon Burge police torture scandal. See John Conroy, "House of Screams," *Chicago Reader*, January 20, 1999; Taylor, *Torture Machine*. The number 118 comes from "118 Documented Burge Area 2 and 3 Torture Victims 1972–1991," People's Law Office, http://peopleslawoffice.com/wp-content/uploads/2014/01/1.6.14.-Documented-TortureSurvivorsunderBurge.pdf.

7. Michael Goldston and Francine Sanders, *Office of Professional Standards Special Project* (Chicago Police Department, 1990), 6, People's Law Office, https://peopleslawoffice.com/wp-content/uploads/2012/02/Goldston-Report-with-11.2.90-Coversheet.pdf.

8. Flint Taylor, "Racism, Torture and Impunity in Chicago," *The Nation*, February 20, 2013.

9. People's Law Office, *Report on the Failure*.

10. G. Flint Taylor, "The Chicago Police Torture Scandal: A Legal and Political History," *CUNY Law Review* 17 (2015), 329; People's Law Office, "Press Release: City Council Makes History in Passing Reparations Legislation for Burge Torture Survivors," May 6, 2015, https://peopleslawoffice.com/city-council-makes-history-in-passing-reparations-legislation-for-burge-torture-survivors/.

11. See Alexander, *New Jim Crow*; Beckett, *Making Crime Pay*; Enns, *Incarceration Nation*; Forman, *Locking Up Our Own*; Fortner, *Black Silent Majority*; Frydl, *Drug Wars in America*; Garland, *Mass Imprisonment*; Gilmore, *Golden Gulag*; Gottschalk, *Caught*; Gottschalk, *Prison and the Gallows*; Hernandez, *City of Inmates*; Hinton, *From the War on Poverty to the War on Crime*; Kohler-Hausmann, *Getting Tough*; Mauer, *Race to Incarcerate*; Murakawa, *First Civil Right*; Perkinson, *Texas Tough*; Pfaff, *Locked In*; Wacquant, *Prisons of Poverty*; Vesla Weaver,

"Frontlash: Race and the Development of Punitive Crime Policy," *Studies in American Political Development* 21 (Fall 2007): 230–265; Western, *Punishment and Inequality in America.*

12. Heather Ann Thompson and Donna Murch, "Rethinking Urban America through the Lens of the Carceral State," *Journal of Urban History* 41, no. 5 (September 2015): 751–755.

13. Quote from Margulies, *What Changed When Everything Changed*, 91.

14. Hinton, *From the War on Poverty to the War on Crime*, 11–18.

15. Gottschalk, *Caught*, 4–7.

16. Heather Ann Thompson and Donna Murch, "Rethinking Urban America through the Lens of the Carceral State," *Journal of Urban History* 41, no. 5 (September 2015): 751–755. Not only does Balto identify "Chicago's punitive turn" in an earlier post–World War II period; his chronology reinforces the argument that changes in state and federal policy after 1965 did not trigger a sea change in local policing, which had always been repressive and inequitable. Balto, *Occupied Territory*, 124–125, 152–153.

17. Gonzalez Van Cleve, *Crook County*, 8. For more on racial discourse in the post–civil rights era, see Bonilla-Silva, *Racism without Racists*, 1–8, 53–56; Kruse, *White Flight*, 42–77.

18. Jason Meisner, "Burge Detective to Face Accuser Who's Seeking to Clear His Name," *Chicago Tribune*, September 17, 2015; Kitchen, *My Midnight Years*, 229.

19. "Jon Burge et al., Case Nos. 1856, 1857, & 1858," March 2, 1992, 2414, CPB.

20. Gonzalez Van Cleve, *Crook County*, 60.

21. See, for example, Commission to Investigate Allegations of Police Corruption and the Anti-Corruption Procedures of the Police Department, *Commission Report*, 1–9. Otherwise known as the Mollen Commission Report.

22. Balko, *Rise of the Warrior Cops*, xvi, 35, 42, 51–80; Hinton, *From the War on Poverty to the War on Crime*, 2–18; Gest, *Crime & Politics*, 17–62; Parenti, *Lockdown America*, 4–5, 14–18, 21–23, 119–120.

23. Fogelson, *Big City Police*, 15–16, 34, 54–58, 61, 89–90, 94; Monkkonen, *Police in Urban America*, 37–39; Lindberg, *To Serve and Collect*, xi, xv–xvi, xviii.

24. Fogelson, *Big City Police*, 219–223, quote from 221.

25. Hervey A. Juris, "The Implications of Police Unionism," *Law & Society Review* 6, no. 2 (November 1971): 231–246; Katherine J. Bies, "Let the Sunshine In: Illuminating the Powerful Role Police Unions Play in Shielding Officer Misconduct," *Stanford Law & Policy Review* 28, no. 1 (May 2017): 109–149; Fogelson, *Big City Police*, 207.

26. Simone Weichselbaum, Beth Schwartzapfel, and Tom Meagher, "When Warriors Put on the Badge," Marshall Project, https://www.themarshallproject.org/2017/03/30/when-warriors-put-on-the-badge.

27. Julilly Kohler-Hausmann, "Militarizing the Police: Officer Jon Burge, Torture, and War in the 'Urban Jungle,'" in Hartnett, *Challenging the Prison-Industrial Complex*, 43–77. Detectives Peter Dignan and John Byrne both served in the U.S. military before joining the CPD. See Taylor, *Torture Machine*, 213, 276.

28. Hal Dardick and John Byrne, "Mayor: Approval of Burge Victims Fund a Step toward 'Removing a Stain,'" *Chicago Tribune*, May 6, 2015.

29. Steve Mills, "Burge Reparations Deal a Product of Long Negotiations," *Chicago Tribune*, May 6, 2015.

30. Fran Spielman, "Disgraced Chicago Cop Jon Burge Breaks Silence, Condemns $5.5 Million Reparations Fund," *Chicago Sun-Times*, April 17, 2015; "Exclusive: Jon Burge Responds to Torture Reparations," *Crooked City* (blog), April 16, 2015, http://martin-preib-b7is.squarespace.com/rainbo2hotmailcom/2015/4/16/conviction-project-exclusive-jon-burge-responds-to-torture-reparations.

31. Torture Inquiry and Relief Commission, "Claim of Jackie Wilson," TIRC No. 2011.021-W, May 21, 2015, https://www2.illinois.gov/sites/tirc/Pages/default.aspx.

32. Erin Fahey (remarks offered at the Illinois Torture Inquiry and Relief Commission regular meeting, James R. Thompson Center, Chicago), author in attendance, May 20, 2015.

33. Gonzalez Van Cleve, *Crook County*, 11.

34. Gonzalez Van Cleve, *Crook County*, 5.

35. Gonzalez Van Cleve, *Crook County*, 5. Emphasis in original.

36. Balto, *Occupied Territory*, 11, 5, 256.

37. Paul Butler, "One Hundred Years of Race and Crime," *Journal of Criminal Law and Criminology (1973–)* 100, no. 3 (Summer 2010), 1055–1056.

38. Describing police officers as inhabiting "a world shrouded with mystery and power," former Minneapolis police chief Anthony V. Bouza added, "[Cops] reveal what they must, when they must, and slip and slide or simply stonewall the public and the press the rest of the time." Bouza, *Police Mystique*, 1, 65.

39. Michael Goldston and Francine Sanders, *Office of Professional Standards Special Project* (Chicago Police Department, 1990), 6, People's Law Office, https://peopleslawoffice.com/wp-content/uploads/2012/02/Goldston-Report-with-11.2.90-Coversheet.pdf.

40. "Status of Ratification Interactive Dashboard," UN Office of the High Commissioner for Human Rights, http://indicators.ohchr.org.

41. UN Office of the High Commissioner for Human Rights, Convention against Torture and other Cruel, Inhuman or Degrading Treatment or Punishment, Adopted and Opened for Signature, Ratification and Accession by General Assembly Resolution 39/46 of 10 December 1984 Entry into Force 26 June 1987, in Accordance with Article 27 (1), http://www.ohchr.org/EN/ProfessionalInterest/Pages/CAT.aspx.

42. Many of the interrogation techniques and strategies employed by Burge and his men appeared in standard police textbooks of the period. See Inbau and Reid, *Criminal Interrogations and Confessions*.

43. David Simon referred to detective work as "a genuinely deceitful art," one that is, "from a moral standpoint, contemptible" yet "nonetheless essential." Simon, *Homicide*, 208.

44. Taylor, *Torture Machine*, 308; "Ex-Jailer Fined in Torture Case," *Washington Post*, January 17, 1970; "Former Police Chief, 2 Others Charged in Texas 'Torture,'" *Baltimore Afro-American*, February 3, 1979; "Ex-Officer Testifies about Torture," *Dallas Morning News*, June 7, 1979; Michael Coakley, "New York Shaken by Charges of Stun-Gun Torture by Police," *Chicago Tribune*, April 28, 1985; Terry Pristin, "Term Cut for Ex-Police Officer Involved in Stun-Gun Torture," *Los Angeles Times*, April 29, 1988.

45. See, e.g., *People v. Banks*, 192 Ill. App. 3d 986 (1st Dist. 1989); *People v. Bates*, 267 Ill. App. 3d 503 (1st Dist. 1994); *People v. Hobley*, 182 Ill. 2d 404, 231 Ill. Dec. 321, 696 N.E.2d 313 (1998).

46. Fran Spielman, "Rahm OKs $5.5M for Torture 'Reparations,'" *Chicago Sun-Times*, April 15, 2015.

47. Chicago Torture Justice Memorials, *Reparations Now, Reparations Won*; Steve Mills, "Burge Reparations Deal a Product of Long Negotiations," *Chicago Tribune*, May 6, 2015.

48. Flint Taylor, "How Activists Won Reparations for Survivors of Chicago Police Department Torture," *In These Times*, June 26, 2015.

49. Mike Royko, "Celling the Idea of More Jail Cells: Some Arresting Ideas," *Chicago Sun-Times*, February 17, 1982.

Chapter One

1. Wendell Rudacille, phone interview with author, February 14, 2013.

2. For brief descriptions of the old Area 2 headquarters at 91st and Cottage Grove, see "Jon Burge et al., Case Nos. 1856, 1857, & 1858," February and March, 1992, 112, 1149, 1186, 2023, CPB.

3. Peterson, *Report on Chicago Crime*, 5–7.

4. "District 5 (Kensington)," in Stokes, *Demographic Studies of the Chicago Police Areas and Districts*, 5, HWLC.

5. John Conroy, "Mill Town," *Chicago*, November 1976, 165.

6. Fremon, *Chicago Politics Ward by Ward*, 75.

7. Bensman and Lynch, *Rusted Dreams*, 127–129.

8. Green, *Selling the Race*, chap. 5.

9. Fremon, *Chicago Politics Ward by Ward*, 75.

10. Seligman, *Block by Block*, 35. Seligman reveals that contemporary sociologists borrowed the term *succession* from ecologists.

11. Seligman, *Block by Block*, 4–5. While Seligman writes specifically of Chicago's West Side, her analysis applies to racial transition on Chicago's West and South Sides generally.

12. This brief industrial history of South Side Chicago has been culled from the following works: John Conroy, "Mill Town," *Chicago* 25, no. 11, November 1976, 164–182; "District 4 (South Chicago)," in Stokes, *Demographic Studies of the Chicago Police Areas and Districts*, 1–29, HWLC; Bensman and Lynch, *Rusted Dreams*, 11–22; Cronon, *Nature's Metropolis*; Chicago Fact Book Consortium, *Chicago Metropolitan Area, 1990*.

13. Bensman and Lynch, *Rusted Dreams*, 7.

14. Sugrue, *Origins of the Urban Crisis*, 6. Sugrue recovered a history of postwar industrial crises stretching back to the 1940s and 1950s, when "automated production and relocated plants" threatened working-class security.

15. Caroline Hanley, "A Spatial Perspective on Rising Inequality in the United States," *International Journal of* Sociology 40, no. 4 (Winter 2010–11): 6–30; Jefferson Cowie and Nick Salvatore, "The Long Exception: Rethinking the Place of the New Deal in American History," *International Labor and Working-Class History*, no. 74 (Fall 2008): 3–32.

16. Paul Duffy, "Pushing Our Costs Up," *Chicago Tribune*, November 16, 1959.

17. Stein, *Pivotal Decade*, xi.

18. Dominic A. Pacyga, "Union Stock Yard," *Encyclopedia of Chicago*, http://www.encyclopedia.chicagohistory.org/pages/2218.html.

19. John C. Hudson, "Railroads," and Mark R. Wilson, "Railroad Supply Industry," *Encyclopedia of Chicago*, http://www.encyclopedia.chicagohistory.org/pages/2218.html.

20. Bensman and Lynch, *Rusted Dreams*, 1–3.

21. Todd Dietterle and Elke Lockette, "CA46-South Chicago," in Chicago Fact Book Consortium, *Chicago Metropolitan Area, 1990*, 146.

22. Chicago Fact Book Consortium, *Chicago Metropolitan Area, Based on the 1970 and 1980 Censuses*, 136.

23. Lieberson, *Piece of the Pie*.

24. Grossman, *Land of Hope*.

25. Seligman, *Block by Block*, 3–6.

26. Police recruits interviewing Southeast Side residents for a sociology training course in the early 1980s noticed that local whites and Latinos commonly referred to black newcomers as "invaders." "District 4 (South Chicago)," in Stokes, *Demographic Studies of the Chicago Police Areas and Districts*, 1, HWLC.

27. M.W.H. and Patt Quinn, "CA52-East Side," in Chicago Fact Book Consortium, *Chicago Metropolitan Area, 1990*, 159.

28. "District 4 (South Chicago)," in Stokes, *Demographic Studies of the Chicago Police Areas and Districts*, 1–20, HWLC; The quote concerning the isolation of Hegewisch comes from Fremon, *Chicago Politics Ward by Ward*, 76.

29. For mention of the neighborhood of Burge's childhood home as Jeffery Manor, see David Heinzmann, "Scandal Muddied Bright Future," *Chicago Tribune*, July 20, 2006. While Burge grew up at 9612 S. Luella Ave. in Merrionette Manor, not Jeffery Manor next door, the entire area later came to be called Jeffery Manor in local parlance. See Hauser and Kitagawa, *Local Community Fact Book for Chicago, 1950*, 210.

30. "District 4 (South Chicago)," in Stokes, *Demographic Studies of the Chicago Police Areas and Districts*, 31, HWLC. In 1950, Jeffery Manor was in census tract 702 and was 0 percent black. In 1980, Jeffery Manor's census tract number changed to 5103 and had become 96 percent black. In 1990, tract 5103 was 99 percent black. See the sections on the South Deering community area in the following: Hauser and Kitagawa, *Local Community Fact Book, 1950*, 211; Chicago Fact Book Consortium, *Chicago Metropolitan Area, Based on the 1970 and 1980 Censuses*, 135; Chicago Fact Book Consortium, *Chicago Metropolitan Area, 1990*, 158.

31. "District 4 (South Chicago)," in Stokes, *Demographic Studies of the Chicago Police Areas and Districts*, 15, HWLC.

32. Diamond, *Mean Streets*, 49.

33. Peter T. Alter, "Mexicans and Serbs in Southeast Chicago: Racial Group Formation during the Twentieth Century," *Journal of the Illinois State Historical Society* 94, no. 4 (Winter 2001–2002): 410.

34. "South Deering Passes Resolution Not to Sell to Anyone without a South Deering Background," *South Deering Bulletin* 1, no. 16 (August 5, 1955), 1.

35. "South Deering Passes Resolution Not to Sell to Anyone without a South Deering Background," *South Deering Bulletin* 1, no. 16 (August 5, 1955), 1.

36. Diamond, *Chicago on the Make*, 16–17, 24–25, 166–167; Adler, *First in Violence, Deepest in Dirt*, 1–3.

37. Muhammad, *Condemnation of Blackness*; Agyepong, *Criminalization of Black Children*, 3, 6; Balto, *Occupied Territory*, 42–45.

38. Roth, *American Homicide*, 441.

39. "District 4 (South Chicago)," in Stokes, *Demographic Studies of the Chicago Police Areas and Districts*, 30–31, HWLC.

40. Paul Delaney, "Chicago Latest to Feel Impact of Urban Crisis," *New York Times*, June 6, 1976.

41. Kenneth A. Stahl, "Mobility and Community in Urban Policy: An Essay on 'Great American City' by Robert J. Sampson," *Urban Lawyer* 46, no. 3 (Summer 2014): 650.

42. See, e.g., Hirsch, *Making the Second Ghetto*, 78.

43. This family tree of Jon Burge was gleaned from a variety of sources accessed through the website Ancestry Library Edition (http://www.ancestrylibrary.com), including census information from the years 1910, 1920, 1930, and 1940. In addition, a website containing the genealogy of the Van Hees family includes material on many persons related to Jon Burge. See the website Van Hees Family History, at http://vanhees.us/index.php.

44. "South Side Woman Slates Talk on Men," *Chicago Tribune*, December 29, 1960.

45. "Front Views and Profiles," *Chicago Tribune*, August 29, 1960.

46. Conroy, *Unspeakable Acts, Ordinary People*, 61; Burge, *This Business of Dressing for Business*.

47. For the address of Burge's childhood home, see John Conroy, "Tools of Torture," *Chicago Reader*, February 3, 2005.

48. "Merrionette Project Nears Halfway Mark," *Chicago Tribune*, August 15, 1948.

49. "First Homes in Project about Ready," *Chicago Tribune*, February 8, 1948.

50. Local practice can be inferred by looking at census records. There were zero African Americans listed as living in South Deering in both the 1930 and 1940 censuses. In 1950, census takers counted a mere fifteen black residents in the neighborhood. Hauser and Kitagawa, *Local Community Fact Book for Chicago, 1950*.

51. Cooley, "Moving Up, Moving Out," 225.

52. *Shelley v. Kraemer*, 334 U.S. 1 (1948).

53. Confidential Memorandum: To: File, From: J. Cassels, Subject: Merrionette Manor, January 7, 1953, AFSC, folder 86-14; Will Cooley, "Moving Up, Moving Out: Race and Social Mobility in Chicago, 1914–1972" (PhD diss., University of Illinois, 2008), 227.

54. Confidential Memorandum: To: File, From: J. Cassels, Subject: Merrionette Manor, January 7, 1953, AFSC, folder 86-14.

55. Confidential Memorandum: To: File, From: Jim Cassels, Subject: Merrionette Manor, October 15, 1953, AFSC, folder 86-14.

56. Confidential Memorandum: To: File, From: J. Cassels, Subject: Merrionette Manor, February 24, 1953; Confidential Memorandum: To: File, From: Yvonne Priest, Subject: Meeting with Members of the Merrionette Manor Improvement Association, July 30, 1953, AFSC, folder 86-14.

57. Confidential Memorandum: To: File, From: Yvonne Priest, Subject: Meeting with Members of the Merrionette Manor Improvement Association, July 30, 1953, AFSC, folder 86-14.

58. Memo: To: Jane Reinheimer, From: Yvonne Priest, August 19, 1953, AFSC, folder 86-14.

59. Memo: To: Jane Reinheimer, From: Yvonne Priest, August 19, 1953, AFSC, folder 86-14; Housing Opportunities Program, American Friends Service Committee, "Summary of Chicago Housing Opportunities Program after 21 Months," January 25, 1954, AFSC, folder 86-16.

60. Kruse, *White Flight*, chap. 2.

61. Hunt, *Blueprint for Disaster*, 57.

62. Hauser and Kitagawa, *Local Community Fact Book for Chicago, 1950*, 222–223.

63. Mary Jane Eaton, "A Community Center Groupworker in a Changing Neighborhood," *Merrill-Palmer Quarterly* 4, no. 2 (Winter 1958): 101.

64. For Lyman Trumbull's role in drafting the Thirteenth Amendment, see Roske, *His Own Counsel*, 106.

65. In 1953, there were twenty low-rent public housing developments in the city, housing about ten thousand tenants. Along with Trumbull Park Homes, the other all-white projects were Julia C. Lathrop Homes, Lawndale Gardens, and Bridgeport Homes. See Chicago Commission on Human Relations, "The Trumbull Park Homes Disturbances, Documentary Report Number I: August 1953–March 1954," 1, CHM.

66. Housing Opportunities Program, American Friends Service Committee, "Trumbull Park—A Progress Report-April, 1959; Public Housing—A Concern," 10–11, CHM.

67. Chicago Commission on Human Relations, "The Trumbull Park Homes Disturbances, Documentary Report Number I: August 1953–March 1954," 1, CHM.

68. Hunt, *Blueprint for Disaster*, 55.

69. "George A. Fuller Co.," *Wall Street Journal*, July 11, 1936; "PWA Housing to Pass to Local Authorities," *New York Times*, November 20, 1937; "2,000 Families Leave Marks on U.S. Houses,"

Chicago Tribune, June 6, 1938; quotes from Laura McEnaney, "Nightmares on Elm Street: Demobilizing in Chicago, 1945–1953," *Journal of American History* 92, no. 4 (March 2006): 1265.

70. "Negroes Charge Jim Crowism in Federal Housing," *Chicago Tribune*, June 28, 1939.

71. Lee McGraw and James Walker, "CA51-South Deering," in Chicago Fact Book Consortium, *Chicago Metropolitan Area, 1990*, 157.

72. McCoyer, "Darkness of a Different Color," 368.

73. Chicago Commission on Human Relations, "The Trumbull Park Homes Disturbances, Documentary Report Number I: August 1953–March 1954," 2, CHM; James Daniels, "Egg, Tomato Shower," *Chicago Defender*, August 30, 1952.

74. Louis Dinnocenzo, "South Deering Will Not Falter," *White Sentinel* 5, no. 3 (March 1955), 1, CHM.

75. Chicago Commission on Human Relations, "The Trumbull Park Homes Disturbances, A Chronological Report: August 4, 1953 to June 30, 1955," 59, CHM. For the standard account of the Trumbull Park housing riots, see Hirsch, *Making the Second Ghetto*.

76. Quote from "Editorial—That Truth Might Live," *South Deering Bulletin* 1, no. 3 (May 7, 1955), 1, CHM. For claims of national and international attention garnered by the Trumbull Park disturbances, see Carl Hirsch, *Terror at Trumbull* (New York: New Century Publishers, October 1955), 7, CHM. Arnold Hirsch reveals that Trumbull Park was the only one of several contemporaneous housing riots to be "covered by television" and "given national publicity." Hirsch, *Making the Second Ghetto*, 72.

77. Green, *Selling the Race*, 183–184.

78. Chicago Commission on Human Relations, "The Trumbull Park Homes Disturbances, Documentary Report Number I: August 1953–March 1954," 1–5, CHM.

79. Louis Dinnocenzo, "South Deering Will Not Falter," *White Sentinel* 5, no. 3 (March 1955) 1, CHM.

80. For the respective numbers from the 1950 census, broken down by community area, see Hauser and Kitagawa, *Local Community Fact Book, 1950*.

81. Seligman, *Block by Block*, 28.

82. "District 4 (South Chicago)," in Stokes, *Demographic Studies of the Chicago Police Areas and Districts*, 25, HWLC.

83. Sellers, *Chicago's Southeast Side*, 63.

84. Louis Dinnocenzo, "Editorial—The South Deering Improvement Ass'n," *South Deering Bulletin* 1, no. 5 (May 21, 1955), 1; Louis Dinnocenzo, "Voice of the People: Tenants are Thankful," *Chicago Tribune*, July 19, 1938.

85. Masthead of the *South Deering Bulletin* 1, no. 13 (July 15, 1955).

86. Housing Opportunities Program, American Friends Service Committee, "Trumbull Park—A Progress Report-April, 1959; Public Housing—A Concern," 2, CHM.

87. Seligman, *Block by Block*, 166.

88. For use of the euphemism "unwanted tenants," see *South Deering Bulletin* 1, no. 5 (May 21, 1955), CHM.

89. Hirsch, *Making the Second Ghetto*, 69–71.

90. Hirsch, *Making the Second Ghetto*, 74.

91. Carl Hirsch, *Terror at Trumbull* (New York: New Century, October 1955), 4, CHM.

92. Balto, *Occupied Territory*, 100–101.

93. Chicago Commission on Human Relations, "The Trumbull Park Homes Disturbances, Documentary Report Number I: August 1953–March 1954," 1–6, CHM. The name "Black Maria" comes from Green, *Selling the Race*, 184.

94. Peter T. Alter, "Mexicans and Serbs in Southeast Chicago: Racial Group Formation during the Twentieth Century," *Journal of the Illinois State Historical Society* 94, no. 4 (Winter 2001–2002): 410.

95. *South Deering Bulletin* 1, no. 15 (July 29, 1955), 4.

96. *South Deering Bulletin* 1, no. 15 (July 29, 1955), 4.

97. Louis P. Dinnocenzo, "South Deering Will Not Falter," *White Sentinel* 5, no. 3 (March 1955), 1, CHM.

98. *South Deering Bulletin* 1, no. 13, July 15, 1955, 2.

99. Robert J. Havighurst, "A Report to the Board of Education of the City of Chicago: A Design for a Survey of Public Education in Chicago," November 21, 1963, CHAIII, folder 1-5; Seligman, *Block by Block*, 119–150.

100. Louise Malis, "Report of the School Education Committee on Vacant Classrooms in the Chicago Public Schools," February 24, 1958, CHAIII, folder 1-1.

101. For the construction of new high schools in Chicago from the 1930s through the early 1960s, see Benjamin C. Willis, "High School Facilities, Yesterday, Today, Tomorrow: Progress Report," May 8, 1963, CHAIII, folder 1-3. For the holding of classes in public housing units, see Hunt, *Blueprint for Disaster*, 162–163.

102. Chicago Board of Education, "Report of Fiscal Policies Committee," June 25, 1958, CHAIII, folder 1-1.

103. Anderson and Pickering, *Confronting the Color Line*, 73–85.

104. Benjamin C. Willis, "Statement to the Board of Education," July 10, 1963, 10, CHAIII, folder 1-3; Benjamin C. Willis, "Statement re Solution re Webb Case, to the Board of Education of the City of Chicago," August 28, 1963, CHAIII, folder 1-4.

105. The most well-known study came from an independent researcher named Faith Rich, whose work was published in the NAACP's *Crisis*. See Seligman, *Block by Block*, 131–132. The Board of Education completed its own belated student count by race in October 1963. See Benjamin C. Willis, "Head Count: Report to the Board of Education of the City of Chicago," October 22, 1963, CHAIII, folder 1-4.

106. Seligman, *Block by Block*, 121.

107. Benjamin C. Willis, "Statement to the Board of Education," July 10, 1963, CHAIII, folder 1-3; "Regular Elementary Schools Analysis Based on Average Class Size per 1-8 Grade Classroom," September 27, 1963, CHAIII, folder 1-4.

108. Benjamin C. Willis, "Head Count: Report to the Board of Education of the City of Chicago," October 22, 1963, CHAIII, folder 1-4.

109. "What about Mixed Schools," *South Deering Bulletin* 4, no. 16 (October 30, 1958), 1, CHM.

110. Seligman, *Block by Block*, 133–138; Anderson and Pickering, *Confronting the Color Line*, 116–120.

111. Benjamin C. Willis, "Revised Policy on Establishment of Sub-Districts (Attendance Areas) and Student Permits and Transfers," CHAIII, folder 1-4.

112. Seligman, *Block by Block*, 135–136.

113. "Plan to Cluster Three South Side Schools," *Chicago Tribune*, January 27, 1965.

114. Lawrence Knutson, "Bowen Built Up Chicago's South Side," *Chicago Tribune*, March 18, 1965.

115. Seligman, *Block by Block*, 137.

116. Rodney Gibson, "Bowen Cluster Jeopardized: Nowinson Cites School Crowding," *Chicago Tribune*, May 8, 1966.

117. "Cluster's Last Stand Fought Again," *Chicago Tribune*, July 3, 1966.

118. Betty Washington, "Southeast Side Racial Change Brings Friction: Trouble Brewing at Bowen High School; Bias Charged," *Chicago Defender*, May 7, 1968.

119. Chicago Vocational High School lies in the Community Area of Avalon Park, a neighborhood that went from 0 percent black in 1960 to 83 percent black in 1970. See Annie Ruth Leslie, "CA 45—Avalon Park," in Chicago Fact Book Consortium, *Chicago Metropolitan Area, 1990*, 145.

120. Thomas Moffett, "Temporary Measure: S.E.C.O. Favors 3rd Bowen Branch," *Chicago Tribune*, July 18, 1965.

121. "Group Hit School Transfer Plan," *Chicago Tribune*, April 2, 1967.

122. Quote is from Ann Plunkett, "May Add Washington to Cluster Plan," *Chicago Tribune*, March 5, 1967. See also Casey Banas, "Cluster Plan Failure: Redmond," *Chicago Tribune*, March 9, 1967; "Cluster Plan's Removal Expected," *Chicago Defender*, March 22, 1967.

123. "An Editorial: The First Step," *Daily Calumet*, January 2, 1968.

124. "The People Speak: Miles of Letters Protest Bussing," *Daily Calumet*, January 9, 1968.

125. "The People Speak: No More 'Jungle,'" *Daily Calumet*, January 3, 1968.

126. "The People Speak: WAC Views AWOL to Protest Bussing," *Daily Calumet*, January 13, 1968.

127. Noble Desalvi and Joseph Sevick, "Call Bussing Hearings; Vote February 28," *Daily Calumet*, January 11, 1968.

128. Danns, *Something Better for Our Children*, 67–69.

129. Casey Banas, "A Pendulum Swings, and Redmond Falls," *Chicago Tribune*, June 4, 1975.

130. "Desegregation Option: City Schools Eye Forced Busing," *Chicago Tribune*, December 30, 1972; Robert McClory, "Bradwell Parents Threaten Boycott," *Chicago Defender*, February 23, 1974.

131. Todd-Breland, *Political Education*, 6.

132. Danns, *Something Better for Our Children*, 3.

133. John Conroy, "Tools of Torture," *Chicago Reader*, February 3, 2005.

134. For Luella's name change to Robert H. Lawrence School, see Ron Grossman, "A Return Flight Long Overdue," *Chicago Tribune*, July 7, 2008. Lawrence was the first African American selected to take part in the U.S. space program; he died during a training flight on December 8, 1967, before participating in actual space flight. He had graduated from Englewood High School on Chicago's South Side in 1952. See "Dream Ends as Astronaut Dies in Crash," *Chicago Tribune*, December 9, 1967.

135. "Gang Shoots Two in Bowen Lunchroom," *Chicago Tribune*, February 6, 1968.

136. "Metropolitan Briefs: 69 Bowen High Pupils Arrested," *Chicago Tribune*, December 14, 1974.

137. Juanita Bratcher, "Precious Life: When Will Violence End?" *Chicago Defender*, February 25, 1982; John C. White and Philip Wattley, "Teen Held in Fatal Stabbing at Bowen," *Chicago Tribune*, February 24, 1982.

138. Appy, *Working-Class War*, 27. Appy reveals that approximately 80 percent of American soldiers fighting in the Vietnam War came from working-class backgrounds (6). Out of a generation of 27 million, only 2.5 million men served in Vietnam, representing some 10 percent of the male population coming of age in time to serve between 1964 and 1973 (18). Appy also shows that American soldiers in Vietnam were exceptionally young, with an average age of 19 for draftees and volunteers (27).

139. For a firsthand account of Burge's military career, see his 1992 testimony before the Chicago Police Board, "Jon Burge, Case Nos. 1856, 1857, & 1858," March 2, 1992, 2392–2395, CPB.

140. Appy, *Working-Class War*, 59.

141. Appy, *Working-Class War*, chap. 2.

142. John Conroy, "Tools of Torture," *Chicago Reader*, February 3, 2005.

143. Jon Burge, "Voice of the People: Cadet Medals," *Chicago Tribune*, May 15, 1963; "Honors Given High School's R.O.T.C. Cadets," *Chicago Tribune*, January 24, 1963; "Honor R.O.T.C. Cadets at Bowen High," *Chicago Tribune*, May 26, 1963; "Cadets at 2 Schools Get R.O.T.C. Medals," *Chicago Tribune*, May 23, 1965.

144. John Conroy, "Tools of Torture," *Chicago Reader*, February 3, 2005.

145. John Conroy, "Tools of Torture," *Chicago Reader*, February 3, 2005.

146. Branch, *At Canaan's Edge*, 520.

147. John Conroy, "Tools of Torture," *Chicago Reader*, February 3, 2005.

148. John Conroy, "Tools of Torture," *Chicago Reader*, February 3, 2005; "Jon Burge et al., Case Nos. 1856, 1857, & 1858," Chicago Police Board Transcripts, March 2, 1992, 2394; "Neighbors in Uniform," *Chicago Tribune*, October 19, 1967.

149. Hunt, *9th Infantry Division in Vietnam*, 3.

150. "Old Reliables Return Home from War," *Old Reliable* 3, no. 31 (August 6, 1969), 1.

151. Lair, *Armed with Abundance*, 73, 214–215.

152. John Conroy, "Tools of Torture," *Chicago Reader*, February 3, 2005.

153. Frank Reysen, "Building Boom Hits Dong Tam," *Octofoil* 1, no. 4 (October–December 1968), 15; Eric B. Johns, "Division Aids Civilians: A Center of Understanding," *Octofoil* 1, no. 4 (October–December 1968), 8.

154. Ted Tindall, "America's Second Mobile Riverine Force," *Octofoil* 1, no. 1 (January–March 1968), 2.

155. Ewell and Hunt, *Sharpening the Combat Edge*, 188.

156. Appy, *Working-Class War*, 187; for more on the body count, see 156.

157. "U.S. Positions Hit, 16 Killed in 3 Dawn Attacks by Cong," *Boston Globe*, March 9, 1967. Throughout 1968 and 1969, Dong Tam frequently made headlines as the site of mortar and rocket attacks. See, e.g., "Foe Renews Viet Shelling: Allied Bases and Cities Are Attacked Again," *Baltimore Sun*, February 25, 1969; "U.S. Base in Delta Hit Hard by Enemy Shells," *Los Angeles Times*, March 26, 1969.

158. John Conroy, "Tools of Torture," *Chicago Reader*, February 3, 2005.

159. Wendell Rudacille, phone interview with the author, February 14, 2013.

160. "Jon Burge et al., Case Nos. 1856, 1857, & 1858," March 2, 1992, 2395, CPB. Downplaying his injury, Jon Burge told journalist John Conroy in 1989 that he received the Purple Heart for a minor shrapnel wound that laid him up for only "about 15 minutes." John Conroy, "House of Screams," *Chicago Reader*, January 25, 1990.

161. "2 Killed, 46 Injured by Red Rocket as Marines View Film," *Los Angeles Times*, April 21, 1969.

162. This description of the duties of military police at Dong Tam comes from David H. Furse, "Their Beat Is the Delta," *Octofoil* 1, no. 4 (October–December 1968), 37. Further information was gleaned from a telephone interview with former Ninth MP Steve Gustat, February 13, 2013.

163. David H. Furse, "Their Beat Is the Delta," *Octofoil* 1, no. 4 (October–December 1968), 37.

164. Wendell Rudacille, e-mail message to author, February 20, 2013.

165. Charlie Ochs, phone interview with author, February 17, 2013. A member of the Army's Public Information Office in Vietnam, Ochs spent two to three weeks with the Ninth MPs in 1968.

166. David H. Furse, "Their Beat Is the Delta," *Octofoil* 1, no. 4 (October–December 1968), 37.

167. Wendell Rudacille, who worked with Burge as an MP for approximately six months in 1969, recalled Burge frequently telling others of his ultimate goal of becoming a CPD detective. Rudacille, phone interview with author, February 14, 2013.

168. "Jon Burge et al., Case Nos. 1856, 1857, & 1858," March 2, 1992, 2394, CPB.

169. John Conroy, "Tools of Torture," *Chicago Reader*, February 3, 2005.

170. Wendell Rudacille, phone interview with author, February 14, 2013.

171. Wendell Rudacille, e-mail message to author, February 20, 2013.

172. Wendell Rudacille, phone interview with author, February 14, 2013.

173. Wendell Rudacille, e-mail message to author, February 14, 2013.

174. Wendell Rudacille, phone interview with author, February 14, 2013.

175. Most accounts of the Chicago police torture cases that mention Vietnam suggest that Burge learned his technique during the war and brought it back to Chicago. John Conroy's first article on Burge from January 1990 is the origin of this narrative, which has remained a stock feature of the Burge story in several articles by Conroy and lawyer Flint Taylor in the decades since. See John Conroy, "House of Screams," *Chicago Reader*, January 25, 1990; John Conroy, "Tools of Torture," *Chicago Reader*, February 3, 2005. Academic accounts of the Burge cases that mention Vietnam also draw heavily from John Conroy. See Rejali, *Torture and Democracy*, 582–583; Julilly Kohler-Hausmann, "Militarizing the Police: Officer Jon Burge, Torture, and War in the 'Urban Jungle,'" in Hartnett, *Challenging the Prison-Industrial Complex*, 43–77.

176. There is a large body of literature on Vietnam-era atrocities. This chapter relies primarily on McCoy, *Torture and Impunity*; Nelson, *War behind Me*; Turse, *Kill Anything That Moves*; Anderson, *Facing My Lai*.

177. For UN condemnation of torture, see McCoy, *Torture and Impunity*, 3.

178. McCoy, *Torture and Impunity*. For the story of American-funded academic research into psychological torture methods, see especially 62–84. McCoy argues that "sensory disorientation and self-inflicted pain" have been hallmarks of American torture since at least the early 1960s (103).

179. American interrogators distinguished between their civilized methods and the barbarities of the South Vietnamese, who were known to torture prisoners during interrogations. See Schell, *Real War*, 112–113.

180. McCoy, *Torture and Impunity*. For more on Operation Phoenix, see 88–99. Congressional hearings revealed that CIA-approved electric shock torture in Vietnam involved applying shocks to both female and male genitals (98). McCoy puts the number of deaths stemming from the Phoenix program around forty-one thousand (7), whereas the CIA concedes only around half that number (88).

181. McCoy, *Torture and Impunity*, 6. By 1984, the CIA itself came to define psychological interrogation methods as "torture" in its own service manuals while continuing the practice in the field (28–29).

182. Rejali, *Torture and Democracy*, 123.

183. Rejali, *Torture and Democracy*, 146.

184. For the use of electric shock as torture in 1950s and 1960s Algeria, see Rejali, *Torture and Democracy*, 161–165. For a Viet Minh recollection of such torture in the 1950s under Ngo Dinh Diem, see Young, *Vietnam Wars*, 61. For remnants of the "old French methods" found in South Vietnam upon U.S. arrival, see McCoy, *Torture and Impunity*, 89.

185. This comes from the testimony of Peter N. Martinsen, who served with the 541st Military Intelligence Detachment from September 1966 to June 1967 and later with the 172nd Mili-

tary Intelligence Detachment. Nelson, *War behind Me*, 50–51. For more examples of field telephone torture, see the rest of Nelson's chapter 2, particularly 49–51, 56, 62–66, and 70.

186. Nelson, *War behind Me*, 51.

187. John Conroy, "Tools of Torture," *Chicago Reader*, February 3, 2005.

188. John Conroy, "Tools of Torture," *Chicago Reader*, February 3, 2005. The first quote is from former lieutenant David Rudoi; the second veteran was former sergeant D. J. Lewis, both interviewed by Conroy.

189. Steve Gustat, phone interview with author, February 13, 2013.

190. This was the general attitude projected by former Ninth MP John Patterson. Phone interview with author, February 13, 2013.

191. John Conroy, "Tools of Torture," *Chicago Reader*, February 3, 2005.

192. Ian Wright, "GIs Doubtful on Chances of Early Trip Home," *The Guardian*, June 16, 1969. One ex-soldier who petitioned for Ewell's removal on humanitarian grounds claimed his former commander had "made his reputation in Vietnam on the body count." See "3 Ex-Officers Attack Viet Body Count," *Washington Post*, April 16, 1971. For more on the Ninth Infantry high command's obsession with statistical analysis and quantifiable measurements, see Hunt, *9th Infantry Division in Vietnam*.

193. For the division's own celebratory history, see Frank Reysen, "Fifty Reliable Years," *Octofoil* 1, no. 3 (July–September 1968), 18.

194. Steve Gustat, phone interview with author, February 13, 2013.

195. Ian Wright, "GIs Doubtful on Chances of Early Trip Home," *The Guardian*, June 16, 1969; "Old Reliables Return Home from War," *Old Reliable* 3, no. 31 (August 6, 1969), 1.

196. "S. Viets Take Over Camp; It Deteriorates," *Chicago Tribune*, October 13, 1969.

197. The CPD's Joseph Martin, who conducted an interview with the new recruit in 1969 or 1970, described Burge as "neat, polite, honest, well built, and a pleasure to deal with." Speaking with John Conroy decades later, Martin conceded: "It may appear I went overboard for this young man." John Conroy, "Tools of Torture," *Chicago Reader*, February 3, 2005.

198. "Jon Burge et al., Case Nos. 1856, 1857, & 1858," March 2, 1992, 2395, CPB.

199. See, e.g., Peterson, *Report on Chicago Crime*, 133–135.

200. Block, *Lethal Violence in Chicago*.

201. Some index crimes dropped from year to year, but the overall picture was of dramatic climb. Chicago Crime Commission, *Annual Report 1970*, 3–4.

202. Peterson, *Report on Chicago Crime for 1968*, 3.

203. Cohen and Taylor, *American Pharaoh*, 455.

204. Farber, *Chicago '68*, chap. 7.

205. Kusch, *Battleground Chicago*, 116–126.

206. Burke and O'Gorman, *End of Watch*, 486.

207. In the early 1970s, there was a surplus of applicants wishing to join the CPD, thanks in part to the large numbers of "returning veterans" who often outscored nonveterans in the civil service written exam used to weed out weaker candidates. Gilmore Spencer and Robert Nichols, "A Study of Chicago Police Recruits: Validation of Selection Procedures," *Police Chief*, June 1971, 3–6.

208. Lindberg, *To Serve and Collect*, 310.

209. Farber, *Chicago '68*, 125.

210. Although Daley was not up for reelection, he sought to unseat Republican state's attorney Benjamin Adamowski, who figured as a Daley challenger in the 1963 mayoral election. Cohen and Taylor, *American Pharaoh*, 251.

211. Lindberg, *To Serve and Collect*, 296–309.

212. When he retired as chief of the Berkeley Police Department in 1932, Vollmer was heralded as the "father of modern police administration." Parker, *Berkeley Story*; Parker, *Crime Fighter*; Alder, *Lie Detectors*.

213. Bopp, *"O.W."*

214. Lindberg, *To Serve and Collect*, 309.

215. Maverick Fifth Ward alderman Leon Despres doubted that Wilson could remain independent of City Hall. See Radio Broadcast Transcript, WMAQ, March 3, 1960, in LMD, folder 69-6. The rank and file also resented having an outsider as their new boss and wondered whether he would endanger their livelihood or bring undesired changes to the department. See Lindberg, *To Serve and Collect*, 309–310. Others feared the reorganization of the detective division would hamper tried-and-true crime-fighting strategies. See George Bliss, "New City Detective System to Begin Today," *Chicago Tribune*, April 30, 1961.

216. For Wilson's opposition to racial discrimination, see Kenneth M. Dooley, "Orlando W. Wilson and His Impact on the Chicago Police Department: 25 Years after His Superintendency" (MS thesis, Chicago State University, May 1994), 46, CHM.

217. Chicago Police Department, *Chicago Police*.

218. Lindberg claims the CPD had a "reputation for unchecked brutality for much of its history." Lindberg, *To Serve and Collect*, xi.

219. Illinois Association for Criminal Justice, *Illinois Crime Survey*, 357.

220. National Commission on Law Observance and Enforcement, *Report on Lawlessness in Law Enforcement*, 19.

221. Abusing prisoners is referred to as "work" in "Report of Committee on Lawless Enforcement of Law: Made to the Section of Criminal Law and Criminology of the American Bar Association at a Meeting of the Section at Chicago, Illinois, August 19th, 1930," *American Journal of Police Science* 1, no. 6 (November–December 1930): 579. Lindberg also describes the "sweat" process. See Lindberg, *To Serve and Collect*, 33–34. The list of methods comes from *Report on Lawlessness in Law Enforcement*, 126.

222. Balto, *Occupied Territory*, 47

223. National Commission on Law Observance and Enforcement, *Report on Lawlessness in Law Enforcement*, 125.

224. For more on the relationship between crime and policing in this period, see Jeffrey S. Adler, "Less Crime, More Punishment: Violence, Race, and Criminal Justice in Early Twentieth-Century America," *Journal of American History* 102, no. 1 (June 2015): 34–46.

225. Hopkins, *Our Lawless Police*, chap. 21. Hopkins devotes an entire chapter to lamenting the consequences of bringing a war mentality to policing.

226. Illinois Association for Criminal Justice, *Illinois Crime Survey*, 285.

227. National Commission on Law Observance and Enforcement, *Report on Lawlessness in Law Enforcement*, 130.

228. National Commission on Law Observance and Enforcement, *Report on Lawlessness in Law Enforcement*, 125. My emphasis.

229. J. A. Larson, "Present Police and Legal Methods for the Determination of the Innocence and Guilt of the Suspect," *Journal of the American Institute of Criminal Law and Criminology* 16, no. 2 (August 1925): 227.

230. The most important of these cases was *Brown v. Mississippi* (1936), in which the U.S. Supreme Court vacated the convictions of three African Americans whose confessions were coerced. See Harold G. Christensen, "Constitutional Law: Due Process of Law: Admissibility of Confessions under the Fourteenth Amendment," *Michigan Law Review* 50, no. 4 (February 1952): 567–568.

231. Noting that "most legal experts agree that the violent third degree is now relatively rare," Marilynn Johnson concluded that, "in retrospect, the 1930s campaign against the third degree was largely successful." Johnson, *Street Justice*, 148.

232. Johnson, *Street Justice*, 316.

233. Johnson, *Street Justice*, 142.

234. Faith in administrators' ability to curtail the third degree was fostered by Ernest Hopkins, whose 1931 exposé of police abuse included praise for progressive police chiefs in Boston, Cincinnati, and Philadelphia who, he claimed, had rapidly eliminated the third degree. Hopkins, *Our Lawless Police*, 229–235.

235. Chevigny, *Police Power*, xix.

236. Richard A. Leo, "From Coercion to Deception: The Changing Nature of Police Interrogation in America," *Crime, Law and Social Change* 18, nos. 1–2 (September 1992): 35–59.

237. American Civil Liberties Union, Illinois Division, *Secret Detention by the Chicago Police*, 10–12.

238. Balto, *Occupied Territory*, 149–151.

239. Peterson, *Report on Chicago Crime for 1961*, 5.

240. John Hagedorn, Bart Kmiecik, Dick Simpson, Thomas J. Gradel, Melissa Mouritsen Zmuda, and David Sterrett, *Crime, Corruption and Cover-ups in the Chicago Police Department*, Anti-Corruption Report No. 7 (Chicago: University of Illinois at Chicago, 2013), 16–20.

241. Lindberg, *To Serve and Collect*, 314.

242. Balto, *Occupied Territory*, 156. Emphasis in original.

243. Afro-American Patrolmen's League Position Paper, "Police Public Relations Programs (A Concerted Effort)," Chicago Urban League Records, series III, box 176, folder 176-1914, Special Collections, University of Illinois at Chicago.

244. Bopp, *"O.W.,"* 135–136.

245. In 1970, Burnside was 96 percent white. In 1980, the neighborhood was 89 percent black. See Chicago Fact Book Consortium, *Chicago Metropolitan Area, Based on the 1970 and 1980 Censuses*, 126.

246. In 1980, the black population of Burnside was 89 percent, 72 percent of the residents were younger than 21, and 19 percent were unemployed. See Will Hogan, "CA47-Burnside," in Chicago Fact Book Consortium, *Chicago Metropolitan Area, 1990*, 148.

247. Ron Grossman, "Children of 'White Flight' Revisit Their Old Neighborhood," *Chicago Tribune*, July 3, 2008.

Chapter Two

1. Goldstein, *Policing a Free Society*, 4–6, 307; The chapter title is drawn from a quote by CPD Superintendent Richard Brzeczek in Roger Simon, "City's Top Cop Speaks Out," *Chicago Sun-Times*, February 26, 1982.

2. Andy Meisler, "Ship to Shore With: Joseph Wambaugh; Still a Bit Paranoid among the Palms," *New York Times*, June 13, 1996. My emphasis.

3. An advertisement celebrating his seventy-fifth birthday touted Wambaugh as such. See *Publisher's Weekly* 259, no. 9 (February 27, 2012), 3.

4. Andy Meisler, "Ship to Shore With: Joseph Wambaugh; Still a Bit Paranoid among the Palms," *New York Times*, June 13, 1996. My emphasis.

5. "*The New Centurions* by Joseph Wambaugh," review by A. C. Germann, *Journal of Criminal Law, Criminology, and Police Science* 63, no. 1 (March 1972): 149.

6. Wambaugh, *Choirboys*.

7. Bill Brashler, "Cops, Thieves, Justice, and Murder in an Onion Field," *Chicago Tribune*, September 2, 1973.

8. "The Blue Light: District/Unit News," *Chicago Police Star*, June 1976, 9.

9. Roger Simon, "City's Top Cop Speaks Out," *Chicago Sun-Times*, February 26, 1982.

10. Burge made investigator in the quickest time possible, as the department required officers serve two years before becoming eligible for the necessary exam. Paul M. Whisenand, Robert E. Hoffman, and Lloyd Sealy, *The Chicago Police Department: An Evaluation of Personnel Practices* (Washington, DC: Law Enforcement Assistance Administration, Department of Justice, 1972), 5.16, AAPL, folder 58/425.

11. "Practical Instructions in Police Work and Detective Science," *Chicago Police Journal*, May–June 1960, 9; Paul M. Whisenand, Robert E. Hoffman, and Lloyd Sealy, *The Chicago Police Department: An Evaluation of Personnel Practices* (Washington, DC: Law Enforcement Assistance Administration, Department of Justice, 1972), 5.2–5.4, AAPL, folder 58/425.

12. See Jon Burge's description of exempt ranks, "Jon Burge et al., Case Nos. 1856, 1857, & 1858," March 2, 1992, 2401, CPB. In 1972 there were approximately 73 persons holding exempt ranks in the CPD, 9 of whom (12 percent) were African American. See Paul M. Whisenand, Robert E. Hoffman, and Lloyd Sealy, *The Chicago Police Department: An Evaluation of Personnel Practices* (Washington, DC: Law Enforcement Assistance Administration, Department of Justice, 1972), 5.1, 5.8, AAPL, folder 58/422.

13. Samuel W. Nolan, "Job Insecurity Goes with the Territory," *Chicago Tribune*, January 28, 1980.

14. "Jon Burge et al., Case Nos. 1856, 1857, & 1858," March 2, 1992, 2396, CPB.

15. Paul M. Whisenand, Robert E. Hoffman, and Lloyd Sealy, *The Chicago Police Department: An Evaluation of Personnel Practices* (Washington, DC: Law Enforcement Assistance Administration, Department of Justice, 1972), 5.4, AAPL, folder 58/425.

16. Area 2 headquarters at 9039 S. Cottage Grove Ave. was built in 1917. See Levering, Cavan, and Zemans, *Chicago Police Lockups*, 34. In 1975 there were 236 detectives at Area 2, including 36 in the Robbery unit. Of these, 34 were white and 2 were black. See Douglas Longhini, "More Crime, Fewer Solutions," *Chicago Reporter* 6, no. 2 (February 1977), 5.

17. *Allocations of Resources in the Chicago Police Department* (Chicago: National Institute of Law Enforcement and Criminal Justice, 1972), app. A, 188, HWLC. The Homicide, Sex, and Aggravated Assault Section would later be renamed the Violent Crimes Section during a reorganization that took effect at the beginning of 1981. See Philip Wattley, "Police to Send High-Ranking Detectives to Work the Streets," *Chicago Tribune*, November 9, 1980.

18. "New Detective Setup Bared; Force Doubled," *Chicago Tribune*, February 23, 1961.

19. During some of the period covered here, the division was called the Criminal Investigation Division and detectives were known as "investigators." I have used *Detective Division* and the title *detective* for stylistic consistency.

20. After reorganization in 1975, Area 2's jurisdiction shifted slightly to include Districts 3, 4, 5, and 22 (Morgan Park). See Chicago Police Department, *Statistical Summary, 1975*, HWLC.

21. For dedication of the new building at 727 E. 111th St., see "Gold & Sneed Inc.," *Chicago Tribune*, February 4, 1983.

22. For the total number of CPD detectives in 1972, see *Allocations of Resources in the Chicago Police Department*, app. A, 188, HWLC.

23. Of the 125 female officers in the CPD in 1972, zero held the rank of investigator. See Federal Bureau of Investigation, *Crime in America: 1972*. The department promoted its first female detective, Cindy Pontoriero, in 1973. See Lynette Miller, "City's 1st Gal Detective Gives Just the

Facts," *Chicago Tribune*, June 21, 1973. In 1972, a patrolman's annual salary was $13,680, and a detective's annual salary was $14,676. See Chicago Police Department, *Statistical Summary 1972*, HWLC.

24. Citing the often mythologized "detective instinct," one CPD official conceded in 1960 that "many men are better qualified by nature for the work than others." See "Practical Instructions in Police Work and Detective Science," *Chicago Police Journal*, November–December 1961, 7. One Chicago policeman referred to the process of developing such intelligence as "getting your street degree." See Fletcher, *What Cops Know*, 5.

25. In the early 1970s, every detective was evaluated on a monthly basis. Those who consistently ranked among the bottom 10 percent of their unit were transferred out of the division. According to a Justice Department study of the CPD, "Normally, an inferior producer is transferred after six months to one year in the Division." Paul M. Whisenand, Robert E. Hoffman, and Lloyd Sealy, *The Chicago Police Department: An Evaluation of Personnel Practices* (Washington, DC: Law Enforcement Assistance Administration, Department of Justice, 1972), 5.16, AAPL, folder 58/425.

26. Douglas Longhini, "More Crime, Fewer Solutions," *Chicago Reporter* 6, no. 2 (February 1977): 5.

27. "Minutes of Staff Meeting of 18 March 1960," 3, reel 1, OWWP.

28. For reference to "white shirts," see Francine Sanders, "Questions I Never Asked," *Chicago Reader*, September 19, 2013, 16.

29. In 1975, Area 2 homicide detectives told a reporter it was "almost impossible to solve so many murders with their present small staff." See Axe Man, "The Hot Skillet: Last Rites Held for Teacher Shot Five Times," *Chicago Metro News*, January 4, 1975, 4.

30. Federal Bureau of Investigation, *Crime in America: 1965–1974*.

31. Federal Bureau of Investigation, *Crime in America: 1960–2010*. The number of officers employed by the CPD rose from 10,026 in 1960 to 13,266 in 1974 (counting male and female officers), remaining between 11,800 and 13,700 for the rest of the 1970s, 1980s, 1990s, and 2000s despite changes in total numbers of reported index crimes.

32. In 1975, the CPD employed 1,228 detectives. Douglas Longhini, "More Crime, Fewer Solutions," *Chicago Reporter* 6, no. 2 (February 1977): 5.

33. Chicago Police Department, *Murder Analysis*, 1965–2000, HWLC; Frank Main, "Murder 'Clearance' Rate in Chicago Hit New Low in 2017," *Chicago Sun-Times*, February 9, 2018.

34. "Minutes of Staff Meeting of 15 March 1963," 6, reel 1, OWWP.

35. Zimring reveals that national homicide rates "more than doubled" in the decade after 1965, while "every street crime of significance to public fear had increased by similar magnitudes." Zimring, *Great Crime Decline*, 29.

36. Federal Bureau of Investigation, *Crime in America: 1965–1974*.

37. Zimring, *Great American Crime Decline*, 6.

38. Harris, *Fear of Crime*, 7.

39. "Minutes of Staff Meeting of 15 March 1963," 6, reel 1, OWWP.

40. Douglas Longhini, "Deploying Our Blue Knights," *Chicago Reporter* 6, no. 2 (February 1977): 1. My emphasis.

41. A 1974 Chicago Crime Commission report concluded that the police, prosecutors, and courts were all falling behind their growing caseloads during a period of rapid crime escalation. See Jack Fuller, "Crime Report Finds Justice System Lags," *Chicago Tribune*, April 8, 1974.

42. Balto, *Occupied Territory*, 176.

43. According to Sherman and Langworthy, "Criminologists have long viewed homicide as the least difficult type of crime to measure." Lawrence W. Sherman and Robert H. Lang-

worthy, "Measuring Homicide by Police Officers," *Journal of Criminal Law & Criminology* 70, no. 4 (Winter 1979): 546; Monkkonen, *Police in Urban America*, 22–23.

44. Wilson, *Truly Disadvantaged*, 22.

45. Balto, *Occupied Territory*, 175–176. Emphasis in original.

46. Pihos, "Policing, Race, and Politics," 234.

47. For the annual murders at Area 2, see Chicago Police Department, *Murder Analysis*, 1965–2000, HWLC.

48. "Excerpt of Transcript of Proceedings—Michael McDermott Testimony before the Honorable Joan Humphrey Lefkow, and a Jury," *United States v. Burge*, No. 08 CR 846 (N.D. Ill. June 14, 2010), 37.

49. Thomas Leroy, "Teacher Takes Own Life: Husband Tried to Stop Her," *Chicago Defender*, April 14, 1973; "Body Unidentified Two Weeks," *Chicago Defender*, July 22, 1975. At least 79 civilians were killed by the CPD during 1969 and 1970 alone, ranking Chicago above comparable cities in the number of civilians killed through deadly force. See Chicago Law Enforcement Study Group, "Press Release," March 28, 1972, AAPL, folder 58/422.

50. For a sample of Area 2 cases culled from local newspapers in the 1970s, see Harold Remy and James Strong, "Held 2 Hours: 3 Hostages Free; Seize Holdup Trio," *Chicago Tribune*, August 20, 1970; Leroy Thomas, "Police Arrest 3 Gunmen," *Chicago Defender*, August 20, 1970; Sheryl M. Butler, "Record 12 Deaths in Violent Weekend," *Chicago Defender*, November 23, 1970; "Elijah Muhammad Denies His Followers Had Any Part in Baton Rouge Shootout," *New Pittsburgh Courier*, January 22, 1972; "Cops Probing 4 Deaths," *Chicago Defender*, February 26, 1973; "Link Dope to Execution," *Chicago Defender*, February 27, 1973; "Charge 2 in Cop Killing: Victim's Last Rites Set Today," *Chicago Defender*, April 2, 1973; Joseph Longmeyer, "Find Loop Bank Aide's Nude Body," *Chicago Defender*, April 13, 1974; Joseph Longmeyer, "Murder Suspect Gives Up," *Chicago Defender*, November 4, 1974.

51. "Minutes of Staff Meeting of 25 March 1960," 1, reel 1, OWWP.

52. "Department Commendations," *Chicago Police Star* 12, no. 12 (December 1971): 18.

53. "Department Commendations," *Chicago Police Star* 16, no. 6 (September–October 1975): 17.

54. "Jon Burge et al., Case Nos. 1856, 1857, & 1858," March 2, 1992, 2402–2403, CPB.

55. In arguing *Miranda v. Arizona*, a state lawyer referred to the confession as "the most important piece of evidence in every case that they bring before a court." See Stuart, *Miranda*, 61.

56. Lassiter and Meissner, eds., *Police Interrogations and False Confessions*, 3.

57. Cray, *Enemy in the Streets*, 98.

58. Cray, *Enemy in the Streets*, 98.

59. Richard A. Leo, "Miranda's Revenge: Police Interrogation as a Confidence Game," *Law & Society Review* 30, no. 2 (1996): 259–288. According to Leo, "Most criminal suspects routinely waive their constitutional rights," and the new rules "had only a marginal effect on the ability of the police to successfully elicit admissions and confessions from criminal suspects" (260). For a contested view that *Miranda* both hampered law enforcement and lowered conviction rates, see Paul G. Cassell and Richard Fowles, "Handcuffing the Cops? A Thirty-Year Perspective on *Miranda's* Harmful Effects on Law Enforcement," *Stanford Law Review* 50 (1998): 1055–1145.

60. Campbell, Sahid, and Stang, *Law and Order Reconsidered*, 469–471.

61. Louis Michael Seidman, "Brown and Miranda," *California Law Review* 80, no. 3 (May 1992): 752.

62. Stuntz, *Collapse of American Criminal Justice*, 235. Several of the police torture cases demonstrate the proclivity of judges to rule in favor of police over defendants in suppression hearings. See Illinois Torture Inquiry and Relief Commission, "Case Disposition: Claim of

Shawn Whirl," TIRC Claim No. 2011.051-W, June 13, 2012, https://www2.illinois.gov/sites/tirc/Pages/TIRCDecision.aspx.

63. Leo offers several explanations for how performance of the *Miranda* ritual led suspects to waive their rights and provide incriminating statements. Richard A. Leo, "Questioning the Relevance of Miranda in the Twenty-First Century," *Michigan Law Review* 99, no. 5 (March 2001): 1012–1015.

64. Chicago Police Department, General Order No. 82-3, "Interrogations: Field and Custodial," March 19, 1982, CAR, folder 20-340.

65. Richard Rogers, Lisa L. Hazelwood, Kenneth W. Sewell, Kimberly S. Harrison, and Daniel W. Shuman, "The Language of *Miranda* Warnings in American Jurisdictions: A Replication and Vocabulary Analysis," *Law and Human Behavior* 32, no. 2 (April 2008): 135.

66. Michael Wald, "Interrogations in New Haven: The Impact of *Miranda*," *Yale Law Journal* 76, no. 8 (July 1967): 1572–1578.

67. For a discussion of how waiver forms facilitate confessions in counterintuitive ways, see Simon, *Homicide*, 211.

68. In their classic interrogation manual, Inbau and Reid recommend officers make intentional errors on each page of a statement and have the suspect sign or initial each correction, thus ensuring the defendant's cooperation appears clear throughout. Inbau and Reid, *Criminal Interrogations and Confessions*, 132.

69. Shadeed Mu'Min's signature appeared on a written confession that included a recitation of the *Miranda* warnings. Mu'Min did not deny signing the waiver form and claimed he actually interrupted the ASA who was reading it aloud to him by saying, "Just let me sign and get this over with." See "Jon Burge et al., Case Nos. 1856, 1857, & 1858," February 20, 1992, 1094, CPB. Melvin Jones recalled officers reading the *Miranda* warnings following several different arrests but dismissed their importance, as he claimed he already knew his rights. "Jon Burge et al., Case Nos. 1856, 1857, & 1858," February 19, 1992, 873–886, CPB.

70. The case was *Dickerson v. United States*, 530 U.S. 428 (2000). Yale Kamisar, "*Miranda* Thirty-Five Years Later: A Close Look at the Majority and Dissenting Opinions in *Dickerson*," *Arizona State Law Journal* 33 (Summer 2001): 396.

71. Gonzalez Van Cleve, *Crook County*, 87–88.

72. Fredric Soll and Patricia Leeds, "Last Family on the Block: Hemophiliac Beaten by Invaders," *Chicago Tribune*, July 28, 1972; "Hunt Two in Heist," *Chicago Defender*, July 29, 1972.

73. "Clear Black Youth in Mistaken-Identity Charge," *Southeast Independent Bulletin* 1, no. 4 (August 11, 1972): 7. The other white family on the block was that of Clarence Carey, the father of Bernard Carey, Republican candidate for Cook County state's attorney. See Clarence Page, "Black Neighbors Offer Aid to Beaten White Boy," *Chicago Tribune*, July 30, 1972.

74. For the use of such language, see the exchange between former first deputy state's attorney William Kunkle and former assistant state's attorney Ficaro in "Jon Burge et al., Case Nos. 1856, 1857, & 1858," March 6, 1992, 2955–2958, CPB.

75. "Start Fund for 'Bleeder': Beating Spurs Fight on Crime," *Chicago Tribune*, August 2, 1972.

76. "Raps 'Punks,' Finds Glass Shattered," *Chicago Tribune*, August 4, 1972.

77. Philip Wattley, "Wilbur Wood Pitches In: Joey's Birthday Is a Hit," *Chicago Tribune*, August 23, 1972.

78. "Attack Victim Recovering," *Chicago Tribune*, August 18, 1972.

79. "Editorial," *Southeast Independent Bulletin* 1, no. 4 (August 11, 1972): 4.

80. Joe Morang, "Suspect, 12, Is Held in Beating of 'Bleeder,' 11," *Chicago Tribune*, July 31, 1972.

81. "Clear Black Youth in Mistaken-Identity Charge," *Southeast Independent Bulletin* 1, no. 4 (August 11, 1972): 7.

82. "Summary of Evidence of *Monell* Policy and Practice of Torture and Cover-Up, and of Defendants' Martin's, Shines', Needham's, and Hillard's Involvement," 106–107, PLOTF, available at https://genius.com/University-of-chicago-chicago-police-torture-summary-of-evidence-annotated.

83. Jane Fritsch, "6 Crimes in 6 Months: 'Royal Family' Gang Reactivated," *Chicago Tribune*, October 7, 1979.

84. William R. Mooney to John Killackey, "Alleged Robbery Gang Composed of Ex-Convicts," August 16, 1972, memo from *People v. Hooper*, exhibit 101, "Law Enforcement Documents on Roger Collins and the 'Royal Family,'" located in the case files of *People v. Collins*, No. 81-1204, box CI/3B-39A-19-096, CCCA.

85. Edmund J. Rooney, "S. Side Cop Lauded in Breakup of Gang," *Chicago Daily News*, August 24–25, 1974.

86. Joseph Burke to SAC Chicago, September 20, 1973, *People v. Hooper*, exhibit 101, "Law Enforcement Documents on Roger Collins and the 'Royal Family,'" *People v. Collins*, No. 81-1204, box CI/3B-39A-19-096, CCCA.

87. FBI Memo, "Roger Collins, aka: The Royal Family," [c. 1974], *People v. Hooper*, exhibit 101, "Law Enforcement Documents on Roger Collins and the 'Royal Family,'" *People v. Collins*, No. 81-1204, box CI/3B-39A-19-096, CCCA.

88. SAC New York to SAC Chicago, "Re: Roger Collins; The Royal Family," October 31, 1974, *People v. Hooper*, exhibit 101, "Law Enforcement Documents on Roger Collins and the 'Royal Family,'" *People v. Collins*, No. 81-1204, box CI/3B-39A-19-096, CCCA.

89. "Transcript of Record Appeal," *People v. Collins*, No. 81-1204, 1293, box CI/3B-39A-19-094, CCCA.

90. "Exhibit 2: Deposition of Michael Goggin," in *Bracy v. Gramley*, October 1, 1998, 31, located in the case files of *People v. Collins*, No. 81-1204, box CI/3B-39A-19-095, CCCA. William Bracey's last name is occasionally misspelled *Bracy* in the court documents.

91. "Suspect in Evanston Slayings Held," *Chicago Tribune*, June 18, 1972.

92. Joe Morang, "Suspect in Killing Found Slain," *Chicago Tribune*, June 20, 1972.

93. Jerry Crimmins and Philip Wattley, "Drug Store Victim Had Told of Fear," *Chicago Tribune*, November 2, 1972.

94. "Transcript of Record Appeal," *People v. Collins*, No. 81-1204, 1574–1580, box CI/3B-39A-19-094, CCCA.

95. Steven Pratt, "4 Cars in Fiery Crash: 5 Hurt in High Speed Chase on Lake Shore," *Chicago Tribune*, June 15, 1972.

96. John O'Brien and Thomas Powers, "2 Are Found Slain in Trunk of Auto," *Chicago Tribune*, November 1, 1972.

97. Bonita Brodt, "'Royal Family' Are Kings of Killing," *Chicago Tribune*, September 6, 1981.

98. Circuit Court of Cook County, Adult Probation Department, "Investigation," December 21, 1973, *People v. Holmes*, 73 CR-003442, CCCA.

99. John Conroy, "Believing Satan," *Burge Trial* (blog), WBEZ 91.5, May 27, 2010, http://www.wbez.org/blog/burge-trial-believing-satan.

100. Chicago Police Department, "Criminal History of Holmes, Anthony," September 1, 1964, revised April 6, 1971, *People v. Holmes*, 73 CR-003442, CCCA.

101. Memo: William R. Mooney to John Killackey, August 16, 1972, *People v. Hooper*, exhibit 101, "Law Enforcement Documents on Roger Collins and the 'Royal Family,'" located in the case files of *People v. Collins*, 81-CR-1204, box CI/3B-39A-19-096, CCCA.

102. Kate Taylor, "'Can't Nothing Take That Pain Away': Chicago Police Torture and the Historical Construction of the Black Body" (senior honors thesis, Brown University, 2010), 139, PLOTF.

103. Tony Griggs, "2d Victim Lives, Bar Shooting Fatal," *Chicago Defender*, December 22, 1971.

104. "Killer Gets 50 Years in Tavern Slaying," *Chicago Tribune*, December 29, 1972.

105. *People v. Coburn*, 20 Ill. App. 3d 60 (1974), 313 N.E.2d 270, April 19, 1974.

106. "Memorandum in Opposition to Motion to Bar Testimony Concerning Other Alleged Victims of Police Misconduct," Chicago Police Board hearing in the case of Jon Burge et al., Nos. 1856, 1857, and 1858, 9, CPB.

107. *People v. Holmes*, 38 Ill. App. 3d 122 (1976), 347 N.E.2d 407.

108. Holmes told Luella Woods and another acquaintance who visited him at Area 2 as well as assistant public defender Lawrence Suffredin. Mike Robinson, "Official Testifies Client Was Tortured by Police," *Final Call*, June 7, 2010, http://www.finalcall.com/artman/publish/National_News_2/article_7031.shtml.

109. "Memorandum in Opposition to Motion to Bar Testimony Concerning Other Alleged Victims of Police Misconduct," Chicago Police Board hearing in the case of Jon Burge et al., Nos. 1856, 1857, and 1858, 9, CPB; Chicago Torture Justice Memorials, "Torture Victim Anthony Holmes," Vimeo, http://vimeo.com/38695585.

110. John Conroy, "Believing Satan," *Burge Trial* (blog), WBEZ 91.5, May 27, 2010, http://www.wbez.org/blog/burge-trial-believing-satan.

111. *People v. Holmes*, 73 C 3441 and 73 C 3442, "Motion for a New Trial," filed January 28, 1974, CCCA.

112. "A Resolution on Police Torture in Chicago," October 1990, CAR, folder 30-503.

113. *People v. Hooper*, 81-C-001204(3), exhibit 80, "Sworn Statement of Lawrence Poree," April 19, 2004, 19, located in the case files of *Illinois v. Collins*, 81-CR-1204, box CI/3B-39A-19-096, CCCA.

114. "Memorandum in Opposition to Motion to Bar Testimony Concerning Other Alleged Victims of Police Misconduct," Chicago Police Board hearing in the case of Jon Burge et al., Nos. 1856, 1857, and 1858, 13, CPB.

115. *People v. Hooper*, 81-C-001204(3), exhibit 80, "Sworn Statement of Lawrence Poree," April 19, 2004, 25–26, *People v. Collins*, 81-CR-1204, box CI/3B-39A-19-096, CCCA.

116. "Personnel Order No. 75-78," April 18, 1975, government exhibit 2, *United States v. Burge*, 08 CR 846 (N.D. Ill.).

117. George Bliss, "Cops Break Up Killer Gang," *Chicago Tribune*, August 24, 1974.

118. Jane Fritsch, "6 Crimes in 6 Months: 'Royal Family' Gang Reactivated," *Chicago Tribune*, October 7, 1979.

119. *People v. Sanford*, 116 Ill. App. 3d 834 (1983), 452 N.E.2d 710, filed July 29, 1983.

120. "Memorandum in Opposition to Motion to Bar Testimony Concerning Other Alleged Victims of Police Misconduct," Chicago Police Board hearing in the case of Jon Burge et al., Nos. 1856, 1857, and 1858, 13, CPB.

121. "Summary of Evidence of *Monell* Policy and Practice of Torture and Cover-Up, and of Defendants' Martin's, Shines', Needham's, and Hillard's Involvement," 104, PLOTF, available at https://genius.com/University-of-chicago-chicago-police-torture-summary-of-evidence-annotated.

122. "Transcript of Record Appeal," *People v. Collins*, No. 81-1204, 1574–1580, 1420–1422, box CI/3B-39A-19-094, CCCA.

123. Exhibit 35: *State of Arizona v. Hooper*: Request for Voluntariness Hearing/Motion to Suppress (July 29, 1982), 1–2, *People v. Collins*, 81-CR-1204, box CI/3B-39A-19-095, CCCA.

124. Exhibit 56: Deposition of Morris Nellum, July 23, 1992, 17–18, *People v. Collins*, 81-CR-1204, box CI/3B-39A-19-095, CCCA.

125. Chicago Crime Commission, *Gang Crimes Coordinating Council Conference*, July 6, 1983, app. G, HWLC.

126. "Jon Burge et al., Case Nos. 1856, 1857, & 1858," March 2, 1992, 2396–2397, CPB; Taylor, *Torture Machine*, 116.

127. See the cases of George Powell and Melvin Jones, "Memorandum in Opposition to Motion to Bar Testimony Concerning Other Alleged Victims of Police Misconduct," Chicago Police Board hearing in the case of Jon Burge et al., Nos. 1856, 1857, and 1858, 8–9, CPB.

128. Inbau and Reid, *Criminal Interrogations and Confessions*, 24.

129. "4 Charged in Robbery of S. Side Store," *Chicago Sun-Times*, September 30, 1979.

130. Sworn Statement of Tony Thompson, *Patterson v. Burge*, No. 03 C 4433, March 5, 2005, 12, 20, PLOTF.

131. Exhibit 36: *People v. Hooper*, Report of Proceedings for August 21, 1981, 937–938 (trial testimony of Murray Hooper), *People v. Collins*, No. 81-1204, 396, box CI/3B-39A-19-095, CCCA.

132. "Transcript of Record Appeal," *People v. Collins*, No. 81-1204, 396, box CI/3B-39A-19-094, CCCA.

133. Richard M. Daley mayoral campaign flier, 1983, broadsides, folder "People, Government Officials, Municipal Officials, Mayors, ILL-CHGO, Daley, Richard M," CHM.

134. Inbau and Reid, *Criminal Interrogations and Confessions*, 24.

135. "Cops Charged with Beating of Prisoner," *Chicago Tribune*, March 20, 1963.

136. "2 Cops Freed in Prisoner Beating Case," *Chicago Tribune*, April 18, 1963.

137. "State Cancels Action Against Accused Cops," *Chicago Tribune*, May 2, 1963.

138. By 1968, Murphy was involved in the Internal Investigations Division's investigation of a Ku Klux Klan ring within the department. See Donald Mosby, "KKK Planned Mayor Daley's Assassination," *Chicago Tribune*, March 2, 1968.

139. "One Charge Is a Demotion: Conlisk Promotes 12 to Captain, Transfers 15 Others," *Chicago Tribune*, February 1, 1973.

140. William Parker to Flynt Taylor [*sic*], December 13, 1991, 4, PLOTF.

141. "Sworn Statement of William Parker, Sr.," *Patterson v. Burge*, No. 03 C 4433, October 4, 2004, 4–17, quotes from 6 and 14, PLOTF. The month and year of the incident Parker describes comes from "Defendant's Memorandum of Law in Support of Request for a Hearing and Motion to Dismiss for Pre-Indictment Delay," *United States v. Burge*, No. 08 CR 846, filed May 26, 2009, 5.

142. Gonzalez Van Cleve, *Crook County*, 4.

143. "Rochford Announces New Assignments for Top Policemen," *Chicago Tribune*, April 17, 1974.

144. Robert Enstad and Charles Mount, "Daley Office Got Cop Spy Files, Log Shows," *Chicago Tribune*, March 25, 1975. For more on the Red Squad, see "The Alliance/Citizens Alert Civil Suit and Complete Text of the Cook County Grand Jury Report on Police Spying in Chicago," 1975, HWLC.

145. "Personnel Order No. 75-78," April 18, 1975, government exhibit 2, *United States v. Burge*, 08 CR 846 (N.D. Ill.).

146. "Jon Burge et al., Case Nos. 1856, 1857, & 1858," March 2, 1992, 2397, CPB.

147. Multiple sources refer to Burge and his men as the "midnight crew." See People's Law Office, *Report on the Failure*, 5.

148. The People's Law Office's list of Burge victims reveals a dearth of allegations between 1974 and 1977. See "118 Documented Burge Area 2 and 3 Torture Victims 1972–1991," People's Law Office, http://peopleslawoffice.com/wp-content/uploads/2014/01/1.6.14.-Documented-TortureSurvivorsunderBurge.pdf.

149. Philip Wattley and Jay Branegan, "Four More Charged in Slaying of 9-Year-Old Lisa," *Chicago Tribune*, November 19, 1976; "Teens Get 200 Years for Killing 9-Year-Old," *Chicago Tribune*, May 28, 1977.

150. Lee Strobel, "Witness in Lisa Slaying Recants; State's Case Ruined," *Chicago Tribune*, December 17, 1976.

151. Lee Strobel, "Lisa Witness Is Moving to Escape 'Tragedy,'" *Chicago Tribune*, June 19, 1976.

152. *Evans v. City of Chicago*, No. 06-3401, 2008 U.S. App. Lexis 1246 (7th Cir.).

153. People's Law Office, *Report on the Failure*, 32.

154. For Burge's own account of his career, see "Jon Burge et al., Case Nos. 1856, 1857, & 1858," March 2, 1992, 2395–2402, CPB.

155. Both arresting officers—Virgil Jones and Aaron Gibson—would be convicted of unrelated corruption and theft charges, respectively. When Jones (who had also become a member of Chicago's City Council) was sentenced years later, Clements wrote him from prison: "Now you know what it feels like." See Frank Main, "Did He Do It?" *Chicago Sun-Times*, June 9, 2009.

156. McWeeny described the routine while referencing a different case but admitted its use was common. See "Jon Burge et al., Case Nos. 1856, 1857, & 1858," February 28, 1992, 2241–2243, CPB.

157. Steve Bogira, "A Convict's Odyssey," *Chicago Reader*, May 5, 2011.

158. Ted Pearson, "Mark Clements Fact Sheet," Chicago Alliance against Racist and Political Repression, http://naarpr.org/mark-clements/.

159. Steve Bogira, "A Convict's Odyssey," *Chicago Reader*, May 5, 2011. Emphasis in original.

160. Ted Pearson, "Mark Clements Fact Sheet," Chicago Alliance against Racist and Political Repression, http://naarpr.org/mark-clements/.

161. William Currie, "City Report: Life Sentence in Fatal Arson," *Chicago Tribune*, September 22, 1982. For more on Clements and the role of ASA Daniel Locallo during the 1982 trial, see Bogira, *Courtroom 302*, 198–199.

162. Michael Volpe, "A Culture of Torture: Mark Clements, Jon Burge, and the Chicago Police Department," *Gaper's Block*, July 1, 2010, http://gapersblock.com/mechanics/2010/07/01/a-culture-of-torture/.

163. Rummana Hussain and Frank Main, "Guilty Plea Buys His Freedom," *Chicago Sun-Times*, August 19, 2009.

164. For abuse allegations against John McCann, see Torture Inquiry and Relief Commission, "Case Disposition: Claim of Gerald Reed," filed June 18, 2012, exhibit G, 8; Daniel McWeeny was involved in some of the most notorious of the torture cases, including all four men pardoned from death row by Governor George Ryan in 2003—Leroy Orange, Stanley Howard, Aaron Patterson, and Madison Hobley. See "118 Documented Burge Area 2 and 3 Torture Victims 1972–1991," People's Law Office, http://peopleslawoffice.com/wp-content/uploads/2014/01/1.6.14.-Documented-TortureSurvivorsunderBurge.pdf.

165. For Daniel McWeeny's own account of his career, see "Jon Burge et al., Case Nos. 1856, 1857, & 1858," February 28, 1992, 2209–2210, CPB. For the reorganization of the Detective Divi-

sion and the merging of the Homicide, Sex, and Robbery Units into the Violent Crime section, see Philip Wattley, "Police to Send High-Ranking Detectives to Work the Streets," *Chicago Tribune*, November 9, 1980.

166. Gonzalez Van Cleve, *Crook County*, 145, 150.

167. National Commission on Law Observance and Enforcement, *Report on Lawlessness in Law Enforcement*, 126. The commission found that the beatings performed by prosecutors often proved "more severe and exceptional" than those of the police.

168. For a review of the Court's decisions on criminal procedure from the 1930s through the early 1960s, see Yale Kamisar, "What Is an 'Involuntary' Confession?" in *Police Interrogation and Confessions*, 1–25.

169. Paul D. Newey, *An Introduction to the Office of the State's Attorney of Cook County Illinois* (Chicago: Gunthorp-Warren, 1960), 9, HWLC.

170. According to State's Attorney Bernard Carey, felony indictments nearly doubled from 3,514 in 1972 to 6,857 in 1974. Alan Merridew, "Half of Felony Complaints are Discharged: Survey," *Chicago Tribune*, October 23, 1975.

171. *People v. Hooper*, exhibit 92, "Transcript of Hearing before Special Committee on Prosecutorial Misconduct, Testimony of Gregg Owen" (March 8, 1999), 129, *People v. Collins*, No. 81-1204, box CI/3B-39A-19-096, CCCA.

172. Joe Ellis, "Legal Aid Defends Self," *Chicago Defender*, January 16, 1973; Donald M. McIntyre and Raymond T. Nimmer, *Survey and Evaluation of Illinois State's Attorneys Association Comprehensive Project: Second Year Illinois Law Enforcement Commission Grant*, 1972, 6, CUL, folder 174-1897.

173. Jacoby, *Report on the State's Attorneys Office*, 12.

174. In 1980, Ed Hanrahan published an editorial in the *Chicago Tribune* complaining that Carey stole credit for his idea. Edward V. Hanrahan, "Felony Review," *Chicago Tribune*, October 27, 1980.

175. "Jon Burge et al., Case Nos. 1856, 1857, & 1858," March 6, 1992, 2877, CPB.

176. Jack Fuller, "Crime Report Finds Justice System Lags," *Chicago Tribune*, April 8, 1974.

177. "Jon Burge et al., Case Nos. 1856, 1857, & 1858," March 6, 1992, 2901, CPB.

178. Michael Cahill, phone interview with author, March 20, 2013.

179. Michael Cahill, phone interview with author, March 20, 2013.

180. Jacoby, *Report on the State's Attorneys Office*, 9.

181. Tuohy and Warden, *Greylord*, 59.

182. Michael Cahill, phone interview with author, March 20, 2013.

183. Gonzalez Van Cleve, *Crook County*, 141, 143, 146. Emphasis in original.

184. Donald M. McIntyre and Raymond T. Nimmer, *Survey and Evaluation of Illinois State's Attorneys Association Comprehensive Project: Second Year Illinois Law Enforcement Commission Grant*, 1972, 13–14, CUL, folder 174-1897.

185. For comparison of clearance rates, see Chicago Police Department, *Murder Analysis*, 1965–2000, HWLC.

186. Gonzalez Van Cleve, *Crook County*, 145.

187. Bogira, *Courtroom 302*, 157–158.

188. Bonita Brodt, "Student Who 'Had It All' Charged in Rape Slaying," *Chicago Tribune*, May 18, 1981.

189. Bonita Brodt, "Officer Casts Doubt on Murder Charge," *Chicago Tribune*, April 9, 1982.

190. Rob Warden, "George Jones Gets Even," *Chicago Lawyer* 10, no. 4 (April 1987): 1.

191. My account of the street files case draws from *Palmer v. City of Chicago*, 755 F.2d 560

(7th Cir. 1985). See also John Conroy, "The Good Cop," *Chicago Reader*, January 4, 2007; Bogira, *Courtroom 302*, 151–170.

192. Nat Hentoff, "The Wrong Man," *Washington Post*, April 24, 1987.

193. Jean-Pierre Benoît and Juan Dubra, "Why Do Good Cops Defend Bad Cops?" *International Economic Review* 45, no. 3 (August 2004): 787.

194. Jerome H. Skolnick and James J. Fyfe, *Above the Law: Police and the Excessive Use of Force* (New York: Free Press, 1993), 108–112. Skolnick and Fyfe argue that fears of physical retribution for breaking the code are exaggerated.

195. Armstrong, *They Wished They Were Honest*, viii, 13; Sanja Kutnjak Ivkovic, "To Serve and Collect: Measuring Police Corruption," *Journal of Criminal Law and Criminology* 93, nos. 2–3 (Winter–Spring 2003): 604.

196. Beigel and Beigel, *Beneath the Badge*, xi.

197. Taylor, *Torture Machine*, 53.

198. John Conroy, "The Good Cop," *Chicago Reader*, January 4, 2007.

199. Anonymous Area 2 Detective to Flint Taylor, March 15, 1989, PLOTF.

200. "Sworn Statement of Ms. Doris Byrd," *Patterson v. Burge*, No. 03 C 4433, November 9, 2004, 6–7, PLOTF.

201. Bogira, *Courtroom 302*, 168.

202. John Conroy, "The Good Cop," *Chicago Reader*, January 4, 2007.

203. Elliot Riebman, "How and Why a Code of Silence between State's Attorneys and Police Officers Resulted in Unprosecuted Torture," *DePaul Journal for Social Justice* 9, no. 2 (Summer 2016): 1–30.

204. G. Flint Taylor, "A Long and Winding Road: The Struggle for Justice in the Chicago Police Torture Cases," *Loyola Public Interest Law Reporter* 17, no. 3 (Summer 2012): 182–183.

205. William Parker to Flint Taylor, December 13, 1991; "Sworn Statement of Mr. William A. Parker," *Patterson v. Burge*, No. 03 C 4433, October 4, 2004, exhibit "Parker 1, 10404 CF," PLOTF.

206. People's Law Office, *Report on the Failure*, 21.

207. Detective Frank Laverty claimed that the slur *nigger* was in common use at Area 2. People's Law Office, *Report on the Failure*, 26.

208. "Deposition of Peter F. Dignan," *Wiggins v. Burge*, No. 93 C 0199, August 8, 1996, 59–61, PLOTF.

209. Anonymous Area 2 Detective to Flint Taylor, March 15, 1989. PLOTF.

210. "Affidavit of Kenneth Caddick," *Kitchen v. Burge*, No. 10 C 4093, January 28, 2013, PLOTF.

211. "Videotaped Sworn Statement of Eileen Pryweller," *Hobley v. Burge*, March 11, 2004, PLOTF.

212. "Sworn Statement of Mr. Walter Young," *Patterson v. Burge*, No. 03 C 4433, November 2, 2004, 27, PLOTF.

213. Mort Smith to Flint Taylor, January 25, 2005, PLOTF. Smith recounted an interview with retired African American detective Barry Mastin, who said, "Black officers were not allowed to be present during interrogations by the few white detectives."

214. "Sworn Statement of Ms. Doris Byrd," *Patterson v. Burge*, No. 03 C 4433, November 9, 2004, 28, PLOTF.

215. "Sworn Statement of Mr. Sammy Lacey," *Patterson v. Burge*, No. 03 C 4433, October 12, 2004, 5, PLOTF.

216. "Sworn Statement of Ms. Doris Byrd," *Patterson v. Burge*, No. 03 C 4433, November 9,

2004, 4, PLOTF. Although this occurred while Dignan and Byrd worked at Area 1, Dignan later worked under Burge at both Areas 2 and 3 and became a frequent focus of brutality and torture accusations.

217. "Sworn Statement of Mr. Walter Young," *Patterson v. Burge*, No. 03 C 4433, November 2, 2004, 15–21, PLOTF. Doris Byrd referred to such dead-end cases as "known-but-flowns" or "ghost offenders." "Sworn Statement of Ms. Doris Byrd," *Patterson v. Burge*, No. 03 C 4433, November 9, 2004, 8, PLOTF.

218. "Sworn Statement of Mr. Walter Young," *Patterson v. Burge*, No. 03 C 4433, November 2, 2004, 18–22, PLOTF.

219. Walter Young claimed that in the early 1980s, Commander Deas "answered to Burge . . . Burge didn't answer to Deas." "Sworn Statement of Mr. Walter Young," *Patterson v. Burge*, No. 03 C 4433, November 2, 2004, 22, PLOTF.

220. "Sworn Statement of Ms. Doris Byrd," *Patterson v. Burge*, No. 03 C 4433, November 9, 2004, 12, PLOTF.

221. "Memorandum and Opinion Order," *Tillman v. Burge*, No. 10 C 4551, filed July 20, 2011, 3, PLOTF.

222. Hines and Patton were linked to the coerced confession of Michael Tillman in 1986. See "Memorandum, To: Special Prosecutors Edward Egan and Robert D. Boyle, From: Ronald F. Neville," February 28, 2005, 22, PLOTF. Hines is also linked to the 1986 abuse of Stephen Bell and Clarence Trotter.

223. "Order," *People v. Burchette*, No. 84 C 6487, 2017 Ill. App. 143236-U, No. 1-14-3236, June 29, 2017.

224. Account of Anthony Williams, tortured February 12, 1982, "Memorandum Opinion and Order," *People v. Wilson*, 82 C 001211-02, 88 CR 07771-01, June 14, 2018, 68.

225. For more on anti-brutality activists' disappointment with increased black representation, see Moore, *Black Rage in New Orleans*, 3, 9, 14, 163, 219.

226. Tera Agyepong, "The Chicago Police Department and the African American Community," *Journal of African American History* 98, no. 2 (Spring 2013): 267.

227. "Bridges of Memory: Deas, Milton (Commander)," TMB, folder 14-7.

228. Gonzalez Van Cleve, *Crook County*, 57.

229. Taylor, *Torture Machine*, 55.

230. Toussaint Losier, "Prison House of Nations: Police Violence and Mass Incarceration in the Long Course of Black Insurgency in Illinois, 1953–1987" (PhD diss., University of Chicago, 2014), 273.

231. Laurence Ralph, "The Extralegal Force Embedded in the Law," in Fassin, *Writing the World of Policing*, 261.

232. Kitchen, *My Midnight Years*, 9.

233. "Affidavit of Melvin Duncan," *Patterson v. Burge*, No. 03 C 4433, May 20, 2004, 1–2, PLOTF.

234. "Sworn Statement of Mr. Walter Young," *Patterson v. Burge*, No. 03 C 4433, November 2, 2004, 6–9, PLOTF.

235. "Sworn Statement of Mr. Sammy W. Lacey," *Patterson v. Burge*, No. 03 C 4433, November 2, 2004, 16, PLOTF.

236. People's Law Office, *Report on the Failure*, 25.

237. Taylor, *Torture Machine*, 107.

238. People's Law Office, *Report on the Failure*, 29.

239. People's Law Office, *Report on the Failure*, 29.

240. "Jon Burge et al., Case Nos. 1856, 1857, & 1858," February 19, 1992, 823–847, CPB.

241. "Amended Motion to Suppress," *People v. Jones*, 82 1 1605, respondent officers' exhibit 121, "Jon Burge, Case Nos. 1856, 1857, & 1858," CPB.

Chapter Three

1. The chapter title is drawn from attorney Daniel Reidy referring to the mind-set of Chicago police officers on February 14, 1982. "Jon Burge et al., Case Nos. 1856, 1857, & 1858," March 19, 1992, 3386–3387, CPB.

2. "Criminal History of Andrew Wilson," respondent officers' exhibit 144, "Jon Burge et al., Case Nos. 1856, 1857, & 1858," CPB.

3. This biography of Wilson draws heavily from Conroy, *Unspeakable Acts, Ordinary People*, 62–65.

4. Conroy, *Unspeakable Acts, Ordinary People*, 63.

5. "Jon Burge, Case Nos. 1856, 1857, & 1858," March 16, 1992, 3147, CPB. This quote comes attorney William Kunkle's summary of a July 15, 1988, document prepared by prison psychologist Dennis Becraft, who reported on Wilson's psychological condition for a presentencing hearing.

6. This according to attorney Daniel Reidy, "Jon Burge, Case Nos. 1856, 1857, & 1858," March 16, 1992, 3151, CPB.

7. "Criminal History of Andrew Wilson," respondent officers' exhibit 144, "Jon Burge et al., Case Nos. 1856, 1857, & 1858," CPB. These quotes come from attorney Daniel Reidy's refutation of oppositional testimony.

8. Conroy, *Unspeakable Acts, Ordinary People*, 62–64.

9. Conroy, *Unspeakable Acts, Ordinary People*, 64.

10. "Criminal History of Andrew Wilson," respondent officers' exhibit 144, "Jon Burge et al., Case Nos. 1856, 1857, & 1858," CPB.

11. For Wilson's criminal record as reported in the press, see Art Petacque and Michael Briggs, "Wilsons Are Linked to More Crimes," *Chicago Sun-Times*, February 16, 1982. For a timeline of Burge's career as he remembered it, see "Jon Burge, Case Nos. 1856, 1857, & 1858," March 2, 1992, 2392–2404, CPB.

12. Cook County Adult Probation Department, "Pre-Sentence Investigation: Andrew Wilson," March 15, 1983, respondent officers' exhibit 154, "Jon Burge, Case Nos. 1856, 1857, & 1858," CPB.

13. "Jon Burge, Case Nos. 1856, 1857, & 1858," March 16, 1992, 3158, CPB.

14. Joye Brown, "Wilson Jury Hears Crime Tally," *Chicago Tribune*, February 8, 1983.

15. "Jon Burge, Case Nos. 1856, 1857, & 1858," February 26, 1992, 2029, CPB.

16. "Jon Burge, Case Nos. 1856, 1857, & 1858," March 5, 1992, 2785, CPB.

17. For Wilson heading first to Joliet, see Conroy, "House of Screams." For Joliet's reputation for ill repair, see Illinois Prison Inquiry Commission, *Prison System in Illinois*, 227. In 1972, a U.S. congressman who toured Joliet remarked that the prison had a "medieval atmosphere about it." See Williams Gaines, "Close Joliet Prison, Congressmen Urge," *Chicago Tribune*, January 29, 1972.

18. "Joliet Correctional Center, Program Considerations," March 13, 1978, respondent officers' exhibit 154, "Jon Burge, Case Nos. 1856, 1857, & 1858," CPB.

19. John Conroy, "House of Screams," *Chicago Reader*, January 25, 1990.

20. Adult Clinical Services, Menard Unit, "Supplemental Program Considerations," August 18, 1981, respondent officers' exhibit 154, "Jon Burge, Case Nos. 1856, 1857, & 1858," CPB.

21. Conroy, *Unspeakable Acts, Ordinary People*, 64–65.

22. Adult Clinical Services, Menard Unit, "Supplemental Program Considerations," August 18, 1981, respondent officers' exhibit 154, "Jon Burge, Case Nos. 1856, 1857, & 1858," CPB.

23. In 1984, the CPD's Gang Crimes Unit commander Ed Pleines asserted, "It is not possible to be in a prison in Illinois without belonging to a gang." IDOC officials conceded, arguing that most prisoners arrived with prior gang affiliation. See William Recktenwald and Nathaniel Sheppard Jr., "Spread of Gangs Defies Police Efforts," *Chicago Tribune*, January 11, 1984.

24. Charles Mount, "Gangs Tested Us at Joliet and They Lost, Sielaff Says," *Chicago Tribune*, April 24, 1975.

25. Charles Mount, "Gangs Tested Us at Joliet and They Lost, Sielaff Says," *Chicago Tribune*, April 24, 1975.

26. "The Latest Riot at Joliet," *Chicago Tribune*, April 25, 1975.

27. "Klan Recruitment Reported; Menard: Center of White Racism," *Chicago Tribune*, September 9, 1974.

28. "Klan Recruitment Reported; Menard: Center of White Racism," *Chicago Tribune*, September 9, 1974.

29. Kim Norman, "Blame Lax Execs for Racist Cons," *Chicago Defender*, September 9, 1974, 11.

30. Testimony of Melvin Jones, in "Jon Burge et al., Case Nos. 1856, 1857, & 1858," February 19, 1992, 888, CPB. Attorney William Kunkle provided the last portion of this quote in a question he asked Jones during cross-examination.

31. Noting that Wilson was "uncooperative" and "an unreliable story teller," a prison counselor reported, "He denies gang membership." "Joliet Correctional Center, Program Considerations," March 13, 1978, respondent officers' exhibit 154, "Jon Burge, Case Nos. 1856, 1857, & 1858," CPB.

32. Attorney William Kunkle referred to Willie Washington as "some kind of shirttail relative or at least a family friend of the Wilson family." See "Jon Burge, Case Nos. 1856, 1857, & 1858," February 24, 1992, 1562, CPB. For Washington letting Wilson stay in exchange for work, see Conroy, *Unspeakable Acts, Ordinary People*, 65. For Willie's being the site of a recent homicide, see Art Petacque and Phillip J. O'Connor, "Warrants Name 2 in Killing of Cops," *Chicago Sun-Times*, February 14, 1982.

33. Conroy, *Unspeakable Acts, Ordinary People*, 65. While Conroy writes, "[Wilson] saw his daughters almost every day," prison documents claim he had no children of his own. See "Joliet Correctional Center, Program Considerations," March 13, 1978, respondent officers' exhibit 154, "Jon Burge, Case Nos. 1856, 1857, & 1858," CPB.

34. *People v. Hope*, 658 N.E.2d 391 (1995), 168 Ill. 2d 1, 212 Ill. Dec. 909.

35. For Hope as "Ace," see "Jon Burge, Case Nos. 1856, 1857, & 1858," March 5, 1992, 2811, CPB. For the Wilson aliases, see Art Petacque and Phillip J. O'Connor, "Warrants Name 2 in Killing of Cops," *Chicago Sun-Times*, February 14, 1982.

36. See "Jon Burge, Case Nos. 1856, 1857, & 1858," February 11, 1992, 368–371, CPB.

37. For the Wilson brothers' reputation, see John O'Brien and Philip Wattley, "Motive Hinted in Two Cop Slayings," *Chicago Tribune*, February 16, 1982; Art Petacque and Michael Briggs, "Wilsons Are Linked to More Crimes," *Chicago Sun-Times*, February 16, 1982. For the three men's link to the Disciples, see Art Petacque and Phillip J. O'Connor, "Warrants Name 2 in Killing of Cops," *Chicago Sun-Times*, February 14, 1982.

38. Conroy, *Unspeakable Acts, Ordinary People*, 65. Conroy mentions four armed robberies but lists only three—the December 3, 1981, robbery at the World Camera store; a later robbery of a clothing outlet; and the February 4, 1982, burglary of Laveda Downs. Wilson was later linked to

a January 11, 1982, McDonald's holdup. See "Memorandum Opinion and Order," *United States v. Burge*, Case No. 08 CR 846, 17 n. 13. Both Wilson brothers were also involved in a home invasion on the morning of February 9, 1982, and allegedly linked to another robbery at a gas station in Alsip, Illinois, two days later. See John O'Brien and Philip Wattley, "Motive Hinted in Two Cop Slayings," *Chicago Tribune*, February 16, 1982. The gas station robbery is mentioned only in February 1982 newspaper articles and nowhere else, suggesting their link to this crime was part of a flurry of media speculation following the manhunt for the Wilson brothers.

39. "Supplemental Report on World Camera Robbery," December 1981, department's exhibit 30, "Jon Burge, Case Nos. 1856, 1857, & 1858," CPB.

40. Art Petacque and Michael Briggs, "Wilsons Are Linked to More Crimes," *Chicago Sun-Times*, February 16, 1982; Joye Brown, "Wilson Jury Hears Crime Tally," *Chicago Tribune*, February 8, 1983.

41. "Jon Burge, Case Nos. 1856, 1857, & 1858," March 5, 1992, 2780–2809, CPB.

42. "Jon Burge, Case Nos. 1856, 1857, & 1858," February 26, 1992, 2031, CPB.

43. Phillip J. O'Connor and Rosalind Rossi, "Earlier Bail for Wilsons Defended," *Chicago Sun-Times*, February 17, 1982.

44. "Supplemental Violation Report," February 17, 1982, respondent officers' exhibit 154, "Jon Burge, Case Nos. 1856, 1857, & 1858," CPB.

45. "Jon Burge, Case Nos. 1856, 1857, & 1858," March 2, 1992, 2523, 2532–2533, CPB.

46. Phillip J. O'Connor and Rosalind Rossi, "Earlier Bail for Wilsons Defended," *Chicago Sun-Times*, February 17, 1982.

47. *People v. Hope*, 116 Ill. 2d 265 (1986), 508 N.E.2d 202. Lawyers dispute Hope's involvement in this robbery. See "Law School Team Says Wrong Man Convicted," *Chicago Tribune*, January 26, 2000.

48. During the 2010 criminal trial of Jon Burge, the government stipulated that Andrew Wilson long concealed his involvement in the January 1982 McDonald's robbery, leading to the wrongful conviction of a man named Alton Logan. Witnesses identified Logan instead of Wilson; Logan was charged, convicted, and sentenced for the shooting of the security guards alongside Edgar Hope. It was later proved that Wilson, not Logan, was the second shooter. After Wilson's arrest in February 1982, Hope told his lawyers that Wilson, not Logan, was his accomplice. Hope's lawyers told Wilson's lawyers, Dale Coventry and Jamie Kunz, but they felt bound by lawyer-client privilege to keep the information secret. They instead sealed a notarized affidavit in a metal box. Following Wilson's death in 2007, Coventry and Kunz went public with the information that exonerated Alton Logan after more than 25 years. The State's Attorney's Office considered retrying Logan before releasing him. See "Memorandum Opinion and Order," *United States v. Burge*, Case No. 08 CR 846, 17 n. 13. See also "Alton Logan," Center for Wrongful Convictions, http://www.law.northwestern.edu/legalclinic/wrongfulconvictions/exonerations/il/alton-logan.html.

49. My composite account of the McDonald's robbery comes from "1 Killed, 2 Shot in 2 Restaurant Hold-Ups," *Chicago Defender*, January 13, 1982; Jim Casey, "Cop Killing Suspect Tied to Guard Death," *Chicago Sun-Times*, February 9, 1982; Art Petacque and Michael Briggs, "Wilsons Are Linked to More Crimes," *Chicago Sun-Times*, February 16, 1982; "Dramatic Testimony in Cop Killer Hearing," *Chicago Tribune*, October 28, 1982; Marianne Taylor, "2 Convicted in Murder of a Guard," *Chicago Tribune*, February 17, 1983; Marianne Taylor, "Cop-Killer Gets 2d Death Sentence for Murder of Guard in Restaurant," *Chicago Tribune*, February 19, 1983. According to the *Defender* article, the guard at the second McDonald's survived his wounds.

50. Further details of the McDonald's robbery culled from *People v. Hope*, 116 Ill. 2d 265 (1986), 508 N.E.2d 202.

51. Closing statement by Daniel Reidy, "Jon Burge, Case Nos. 1856, 1857, & 1858," March 19, 1992, 3386, CPB.

52. Burke and O'Gorman, *End of Watch: Chicago Police Killed in the Line of Duty, 1853–2006*, 516.

53. Lynn Emmerman and Barbara Brotman, "CTA Rider Charged in Cop Killing," *Chicago Tribune*, February 7, 1982.

54. "Suspect Drunk at Time Cop Shot, Defense Says," *Chicago Tribune*, October 21, 1982; Manuel Galvan, "Court Hears How 'Hustler' Ended Cop's Dream," *Chicago Tribune*, October 25, 1982.

55. *People v. Hope*, 168 Ill. 2d 1 (1995), 212 Ill. Dec. 909, 658 N.E.2d 391.

56. This account of the CTA shoot-out drawn from *People v. Hope*, 168 Ill. 2d 1 (1995), 212 Ill. Dec. 909, 658 N.E.2d 391; Lynn Emmerman and Barbara Brotman, "CTA Rider Charged in Cop Killing," *Chicago Tribune*, February 7, 1982; Manuel Galvan, "Court Hears How 'Hustler' Ended Cop's Dream," *Chicago Tribune*, October 25, 1982; Manuel Galvan, "Suspect in Slaying of Cop Takes Stand in Own Defense," *Chicago Tribune*, October 26, 1982; Marianne Taylor, "Guns Common Element in 4 Police Deaths," *Chicago Tribune*, February 27, 1983; Maurice Possley, "13 Years Haven't Erased the Hurt," *Chicago Tribune*, May 19, 1995.

57. On February 9, Jesse Jackson told an audience: "The very atmosphere we live in breeds violence. We need a new standard of behavior on public transportation. For those who have to take public transportation, they should not be terrorized by uncivilized conduct. Every act of defiance is not a blow for freedom: sometimes it's just bad manners." See Chinta Strausberg, "End 'War Zone'—Jesse Jackson," *Chicago Defender*, February 11, 1982.

58. Art Petacque and Phillip J. O'Connor, "Warrants Name 2 in Killing of Cops," *Chicago Sun-Times*, February 14, 1982.

59. "Jon Burge, Case Nos. 1856, 1857, & 1858," February 11, 1992, 368–371, CPB.

60. "Statement of Derrick Martin," February 14, 1982, respondent officers' exhibit 35, "Jon Burge et al., Case Nos. 1856, 1857, & 1858," 6, CPB; John O'Brien and Philip Wattley, "Motive Hinted in Two Cop Slayings," *Chicago Tribune*, February 16, 1982.

61. "Statement of Donald White," February 13, 1982, respondent officers' exhibit 50, "Jon Burge et al., Case Nos. 1856, 1857, & 1858," 1, CPB; Art Petacque and Phillip J. O'Connor, "Warrants Name 2 in Killing of Cops," *Chicago Sun-Times*, February 14, 1982.

62. "Jon Burge et al., Case Nos. 1856, 1857, & 1858," February 21, 1992, 1210, CPB.

63. "Jon Burge et al., Case Nos. 1856, 1857, & 1858," February 25, 1992, 1860, CPB.

64. "Policeman Slain; 2nd Shot: S. Side Manhunt on for 2 Suspects," *Chicago Sun-Times*, February 10, 1982.

65. William Fahey's biography gleaned from Henry Wood and Andy Knott, "Cop Slain, Partner Critical; Big Manhunt for 2 Gunmen," *Chicago Tribune*, February 10, 1982; "Policeman Slain; 2nd Shot: S. Side Manhunt on for 2 Suspects," *Chicago Sun-Times*, February 10, 1982; Michael Cordts, "Neighbors Know 2 Cops Who Always Lent a Hand," *Chicago Sun-Times*, February 10, 1982; Michael Cordts, "Cop Mourns His 'Best Friend Ever,'" *Chicago Sun-Times*, February 12, 1982; Marianne Taylor, "Police Slaying Tragedy Knits Victims' Families," *Chicago Tribune*, February 13, 1983. Fahey's Calumet High School and Burge's Bowen High School were fewer than seven miles apart.

66. Richard O'Brien's biography gleaned from Henry Wood and Andy Knott, "Cop Slain, Partner Critical; Big Manhunt for 2 Gunmen," *Chicago Tribune*, February 10, 1982; Michael Cordts, "Neighbors Know 2 Cops Who Always Lent a Hand," *Chicago Sun-Times*, February 10, 1982; Michael Cordts, "Cop Mourns His 'Best Friend Ever,'" *Chicago Sun-Times*, February 12, 1982; Marianne Taylor, "Struggle Erupted, Gun Flashed and 2 Cops Died, Witness Says," *Chicago*

Tribune, January 25, 1983; Robert Blau, "Cop Killer's Sentence Disappoints Survivors," *Chicago Tribune*, June 29, 1988.

67. Henry Wood and Andy Knott, "Cop Slain, Partner Critical; Big Manhunt for 2 Gunmen," *Chicago Tribune*, February 10, 1982. For the October 1981 organization of the Bureau of Gang Crime Suppression, see Wilfredo Cruz, "Arrests Jump Sharply, Minority Leaders Charge Police with 'Disorderly Conduct,'" *Chicago Reporter* 11, no. 10 (October 1982): 1.

68. Michael Cordts, "Cop Mourns His 'Best Friend Ever,'" *Chicago Sun-Times*, February 12, 1982.

69. Jim Casey, "Police Check on 'Hundreds' of Cars," *Chicago Sun-Times*, February 13, 1982; Roger Simon, "City's Top Cop Speaks Out," *Chicago Sun-Times*, February 26, 1982.

70. Andrew Wilson maintained that the gun accidentally went off during the struggle, striking Fahey in the head. According to Burge's attorney William Kunkle, however, Sims's testimony and medical evidence contradicted Wilson. Sims testified that he saw Wilson deliberately place the gun to Fahey's head. In addition, Fahey's autopsy revealed a "contact wound" suggesting an "intentional killing." See "Jon Burge, Case Nos. 1856, 1857, & 1858," March 20, 1992, 3718, CPB.

71. This account culled from Conroy, *Unspeakable Acts, Ordinary People*, 21–22. See also the testimony of Detective Patrick O'Hara, reciting the signed confession of Andrew Wilson from February 14, 1982, in "Jon Burge, Case Nos. 1856, 1857, & 1858," February 25, 1992, 1860–1864, CPB; Marianne Taylor, "Struggle Erupted, Gun Flashed and 2 Cops Died, Witness Says," *Chicago Tribune*, January 25, 1983; Matt O'Connor, "Court Told How 2 Officers Died," *Chicago Tribune*, June 9, 1988.

72. "Jon Burge, Case Nos. 1856, 1857, & 1858," February 24, 1992, 1554–1555, CPB.

73. This according to Jon Burge, whose detectives interviewed Coulter and Hardin that day. "Jon Burge et al., Case Nos. 1856, 1857, & 1858," March 2, 1992, 2426, CPB.

74. Marianne Taylor, "Smile Sticks in Memory of Police Slaying Witness," *Chicago Tribune*, January 26, 1983; Conroy, *Unspeakable Acts, Ordinary People*, 22.

75. Henry Wood and Andy Knott, "Cop Slain, Partner Critical; Big Manhunt for 2 Gunmen," *Chicago Tribune*, February 10, 1982.

76. Jim Casey, "Manhunt Pushed in Killing of Cops," *Chicago Sun-Times*, February 11, 1982.

77. Henry Wood and Andy Knott, "Cop Slain, Partner Critical; Big Manhunt for 2 Gunmen," *Chicago Tribune*, February 10, 1982.

78. For the gun-control debate that winter, see David Axelrod and Robert Davis, "Byrne Pushes Strict Gun Law," *Chicago Tribune*, January 15, 1982; Robert Davis, "Byrne Scolds Council on Gun Law," *Chicago Tribune*, January 28, 1982; For descriptions of Kelley and Streeter, see Ben Joravsky, "City Council Records Show Byrne Support," *Chicago Reporter* 11, no. 12 (December 1982): 1.

79. Barbara Brotman, "Byrne to Ask State for New Crime Bill," *Chicago Tribune*, February 11, 1982.

80. Henry Wood and Andy Knott, "Cop Slain, Partner Critical; Big Manhunt for 2 Gunmen," *Chicago Tribune*, February 10, 1982.

81. Chinta Strausberg, "Gun Control Battle Continues," *Chicago Defender*, February 10, 1982.

82. Russ Meek, "The Razor's Edge: The Aim of Gun Control Is Annihilation," *Chicago Defender*, February 10, 1982.

83. Jane Byrne and Paul McGrath, "How I Got Started," *Chicago*, April 1979; Granger and Granger, *Fighting Jane*, 143; Fitzgerald, *Brass*, 192.

84. Green and Holli, *Mayors*, 168–178.

85. Not only did Daley's critics lampoon him for taking three tries to pass the Illinois Bar

Exam, they also claimed he saw the position simply as a stepping stone to the Mayor's Office. See Eric Zorn, "Daley's Oversight of Prosecutors Didn't Do Justice to the Job," *Chicago Tribune*, November 16, 1999.

86. Roger Simon, "A Hard Look at the Mayor's Crime Package," *Chicago Sun-Times*, February 13, 1982.

87. Rick Greenberg, "Chicago's Deadly '70s: Murder Victims: Most Black, Latinos Now Surpassing Whites," *Chicago Reporter* 10, no. 1 (January 1981), 1.

88. Walter Nugent, "Demography," *Encyclopedia of Chicago*, http://www.encyclopedia.chicagohistory.org/pages/962.html.

89. "Chicago Homicide Rates per 100,000 Residents, 1870–2000," *Encyclopedia of Chicago*, http://www.encyclopedia.chicagohistory.org/pages/2156.html.

90. African American murder rates hit 56 and 49 per 100,000 in 1970 and 1980, respectively, while white victimization rates were only 6 and 8 per 100,000 in the same years. Estimated Latino homicide rates were 23 per 100,000 in 1970 and 36 per 100,000 in 1980. Block, *Lethal Violence in Chicago*, 21.

91. For national media coverage of Byrne's public housing stunt, see "The U.S. Press on Jane Byrne," *Chicago Tribune*, March 29, 1981.

92. "Crime and Public Safety Debate, Byrne's Record," 1983, AAPL, box 238, folder "Attacks on Jane Byrne, 1979."

93. In July 1979 Byrne named Nolan head of the new Office of Public Safety, which coordinated the police, fire, health, and sanitation departments in times of emergency. His $50,000 salary was second only to the mayor's $80,000. Robert Davis and David Axelrod, "Big Shakeup at City Hall: Degnan Is Out, Nolan in New Job," *Chicago Tribune*, July 31, 1979. Political commentator Lu Palmer called the so-called promotion a blatant attempt to get rid of Nolan by kicking him "upstairs" and out of the superintendents' office for good. See Lu Palmer, "Lu's Views: Blacks Can See through Sam Nolan's Demotion," *Chicago Metro News*, August 4, 1979; Storer Rowley and Robert Davis, "Brzeczek Appointed as Top Cop," *Chicago Tribune*, January 12, 1980.

94. David Axelrod, "Brzeczek Nearly Quit over Gang Unit," *Chicago Tribune*, July 22, 1983; Andy Knott, "Byrne Orders Crackdown on Vandals," *Chicago Tribune*, February 4, 1982; Roger Simon, "Byrne CTA Plan: Isn't It a Crime?" *Chicago Sun-Times*, February 9, 1982; Harry Golden Jr., "'Hangouts' along CTA Raided," *Chicago Sun-Times*, February 10, 1982; "Security Plan for Seniors Put into Effect by Police," *Chicago Defender City Edition*, March 1982.

95. See Joye Brown, "200 Neighbors Demand Better Police Protection," *Chicago Tribune*, March 12, 1981; Wilfredo Cruz, "Arrests Jump Sharply, Minority Leaders Charge Police with 'Disorderly Conduct,'" *Chicago Reporter* 11, no. 10 (October 1982): 1.

96. "Minutes of the Citizens Alert Board of Directors, March 5, 1981," CAR, box 4, folder 4-56.

97. David Axelrod, "Brzeczek Nearly Quit over Gang Unit," *Chicago Tribune*, July 22, 1983.

98. For attorneys' claim that McCarthy was Byrne's representative during the manhunt for the Wilson brothers, see "Plaintiff's First Amended Complaint," *Cannon v. Burge*, No. 05 C 02192 (N.D. Ill. September 11, 2011), 7. For Richard Brzeczek's claim he had little authority over McCarthy because of the latter's personal relationship with Byrne, see Manuel Galvan and Anne Keegan, "Controversial Police Gang Unit Head Quits," *Chicago Tribune*, July 19, 1983. For community activists' belief that "McCarthy reports NOT to Brzeczek but to the Mayor," see Coalition against Police Abuse and Misconduct Meetings Minutes, November 29, 1982, CAR, folder 25-431.

99. Byrne, *My Chicago*, 160–161. Byrne incorrectly places the shooting deaths of three officers in less than a week's time in 1981, not February 1982.

100. Henry Wood and Andy Knott, "Cop Slain, Partner Critical; Big Manhunt for 2 Gunmen," *Chicago Tribune*, February 10, 1982.

101. "Plaintiff's First Amended Complaint," *Cannon v. Burge*, No. 05 C 02192 (N.D. Ill. September 2011), 7–8; "Jon Burge, Case Nos. 1856, 1857, & 1858," February 26, 1992, 1948–1949, CPB.

102. This according to black detectives who testified about their knowledge of torture at Area 2. See "Sworn Statement of Doris M. Byrd," *Patterson v. Burge*, No. 03 C 4433 (N.D. Ill November 9, 2004); "Sworn Statement of Sammy W. Lacey," *Patterson v. Burge*, No. 03 C 4433 (N.D. Ill. October 12, 2004).

103. In related litigation, civil rights attorneys argue that public officials "knew or should have known of this reign of terror led by Burge." See "Plaintiff's First Amended Complaint," *Cannon v. Burge*, No. 05 C 02192 (N.D. Ill. September 2011), 7–10.

104. "Jon Burge, Case Nos. 1856, 1857, & 1858," March 2, 1992, 2421, CPB

105. "Jon Burge, Case Nos. 1856, 1857, & 1858," March 2, 1992, 2415–2418, 2437, CPB.

106. "Jon Burge, Case Nos. 1856, 1857, & 1858," March 2, 1992, 2512, CPB.

107. "Jon Burge, Case Nos. 1856, 1857, & 1858," February 24, 1992, 1561, CPB.

108. For their home address, see Marianne Taylor, "Jury Selection Begins in Police-Murder Trial," *Chicago Tribune*, January 11, 1983.

109. "Jon Burge, Case Nos. 1856, 1857, & 1858," February 24, 1992, 1562, CPB.

110. "Jon Burge, Case Nos. 1856, 1857, & 1858," February 11, 1992, 487, CPB.

111. John O'Brien and Bonita Brodt, "Cops Check Brothers' Ties to City, Suburb Shootings," *Chicago Tribune*, February 17, 1982.

112. These quotes are from Andrew Wilson's public defender Dale Coventry, lamenting the way the press condemned his client before trial. See Jimmie Treadwell, "Defense Attorney Charges 'Pattern to Police Tactics,'" *Chicago Defender*, February 23, 1982.

113. "Jon Burge et al., Case Nos. 1856, 1857, & 1858," March 2, 1992, 2422–2424, CPB.

114. Art Petacque and Rosalind Rossi, "Lost Glasses Linked to Cop Killings," *Chicago Sun-Times*, February 19, 1982.

115. "Jon Burge et al., Case Nos. 1856, 1857, & 1858," March 2, 1992, 2428–2435, CPB.

116. "Police Sweep City in Search for Killers' Car," *Chicago Sun-Times*, February 12, 1982; The search spread to surrounding communities, see Jim Casey, "Police Check on 'Hundreds' of Cars," *Chicago Sun-Times*, February 13, 1982.

117. "Jon Burge et al., Case Nos. 1856, 1857, & 1858," March 2, 1992, 2436, CPB.

118. "Police Sweep City in Search for Killers' Car," *Chicago Sun-Times*, February 12, 1982.

119. Jim Casey, "Manhunt Pushed in Killing of Cops," *Chicago Sun-Times*, February 11, 1982.

120. Quote from Russ Meek, "Chicago on Trial—a Look at Conditions," *Chicago Defender*, February 22, 1982.

121. "Sworn Statement of Ms. Doris M. Byrd," *Patterson v. Burge*, No. 03 C 4433 (N.D. Ill. November 9, 2004), 28.

122. Attorney Ronald Samuels of the Cook County Bar Association reported that "people were being beat up, doors were being bust into, people were being held without . . . warrants issuing for their arrest," and "virtually hundreds of people were being arrested and harassed that had no relation or should not have any relation to that alleged killing because of the nature of the description of the persons that they were looking for." "Memorandum Opinion and Order," *People v. Wilson*, 82 C 001211-02, 88 CR 07771-01, June 14, 2018, 59.

123. For a lengthy, yet partial, list of abuse complaints stemming from the events of February 9–14, 1982, see Chinta Strausberg, "Brutality Complaints Continue to Mount," *Chicago Defender*, February 23, 1982.

124. Michael Goldston and Francine Sanders, *Office of Professional Standards Special Project*

(Chicago Police Department, 1990), 20–22, People's Law Office, https://peopleslawoffice.com/wp-content/uploads/2012/02/Goldston-Report-with-11.2.90-Coversheet.pdf.

125. "Memorandum in Opposition to Motion to Bar Testimony Concerning Other Alleged Victims of Police Misconduct," Chicago Police Board hearing in the case of Jon Burge et al., Nos. 1856, 1857, and 1858, 10–11, CPB.

126. This according to Doris Miller, Michael Goldston and Francine Sanders, *Office of Professional Standards Special Project* (Chicago Police Department, 1990), 94, People's Law Office, https://peopleslawoffice.com/wp-content/uploads/2012/02/Goldston-Report-with-11.2.90-Coversheet.pdf.

127. Art Petacque, "How a Tip to Byrne Assisted Police in Manhunt," *Chicago Sun-Times*, February 15, 1982.

128. "Jon Burge et al., Case Nos. 1856, 1857, & 1858," March 2, 1992, 2439–2443, CPB.

129. "Jon Burge et al., Case Nos. 1856, 1857, & 1858," February 25, 1992, 1696–1703, CPB.

130. Taylor, *Torture Machine*, 69.

131. "Jon Burge et al., Case Nos. 1856, 1857, & 1858," February 10, 1992, 251–252, CPB.

132. While there has been some dispute over the exact time, most contemporary media accounts place the arrest around 4:50 a.m. See Michelle Stevens, "'Who Would Think He Was Under Our Noses?'" *Chicago Sun-Times*, February 15, 1982.

133. Taylor, *Torture Machine*, 69.

134. "Jon Burge et al., Case Nos. 1856, 1857, & 1858," February 10, 1992, 68–70, CPB.

135. John Conroy, "Tools of Torture," *Chicago Reader*, February 3, 2005.

136. "Exhibit 1, Stipulation," *United States v. Burge*, No. 08 CR 846, filed May 10, 2010, 5–11.

137. Taylor, *Torture Machine*, 69.

138. "Memorandum Opinion and Order," *People v. Wilson*, 82 C 001211-02, 88 CR 07771-01, June 14, 2018, 75.

139. "Jon Burge et al., Case Nos. 1856, 1857, & 1858," February 25, 1992, 1707–1712, CPB.

140. Private Investigator Mort Smith to Flint Taylor, describing a September 2004 interview with African American former Area 2 detective Barry Mastin, PLOTF.

141. "Jon Burge et al., Case Nos. 1856, 1857, & 1858," February 10, 1992, 73–84, CPB.

142. "Jon Burge et al., Case Nos. 1856, 1857, & 1858," February 10, 1992, 78–90, CPB

143. "Jon Burge et al., Case Nos. 1856, 1857, & 1858," February 10, 1992, 90–104, CPB.

144. "Jon Burge et al., Case Nos. 1856, 1857, & 1858," February 10, 1992, 104–109, CPB.

145. "Jon Burge et al., Case Nos. 1856, 1857, & 1858," February 10, 1992, 111–121, CPB.

146. "Jon Burge et al., Case Nos. 1856, 1857, & 1858," February 10, 1992, 121–127, CPB.

147. "Jon Burge et al., Case Nos. 1856, 1857, & 1858," February 10, 1992, 127–134, CPB.

148. "Jon Burge et al., Case Nos. 1856, 1857, & 1858," February 10, 1992, 134, CPB.

149. "Testimony of Andrew Wilson," respondent officers' exhibit 112, "Jon Burge et al., Case Nos. 1856, 1857, & 1858, 1146," CPB. This is testimony from a November 1982 motion to suppress hearing in Wilson's first criminal trial for the murder of Officers Fahey and O'Brien.

150. "Jon Burge et al., Case Nos. 1856, 1857, & 1858," February 10, 1992, 134–146, CPB.

151. "Jon Burge et al., Case Nos. 1856, 1857, & 1858," February 25, 1992, 1882–1888, CPB.

152. "Memorandum and Opinion Order," *People v. Wilson* 82 C 001211-02, 88 CR 07771-01, June 14, 2018, 8–9.

153. "Jon Burge et al., Case Nos. 1856, 1857, & 1858," February 10, 1992, 146–150, CPB.

154. "Jon Burge et al., Case Nos. 1856, 1857, & 1858," February 21, 1992, 1188–1192, CPB.

155. "Jon Burge et al., Case Nos. 1856, 1857, & 1858," February 10, 1992, 174–175, CPB.

156. "Jon Burge et al., Case Nos. 1856, 1857, & 1858," March 2, 1992, 2489–2490, CPB.

157. For the suggestions that Mulvaney was a friend to a slain officer, see "Jon Burge et al.,

Case Nos. 1856, 1857, & 1858," February 24, 1992, 1603, CPB; Mulvaney committed suicide a year and a half later, on August 5, 1983. See "In Memoriam," *Chicago Police Star* 22, no. 3 (July–August 1983): 2.

158. "Jon Burge et al., Case Nos. 1856, 1857, & 1858," February 10, 1992, 175–177, CPB.

159. "Jon Burge et al., Case Nos. 1856, 1857, & 1858," February 10, 1992, 180–189, CPB.

160. "Transcript of Proceedings before the Honorable Joan Humphrey Lefkow," *United States v. Burge*, No. 08 CR 846, filed July 1, 2011, 124–125.

161. Quote from Irv Kupcinet, "Kup's Column," *Chicago Sun-Times*, February 15, 1982. A letter to the editor published in the *Sun-Times* on February 15, 1982, stressed the "laxity" of judges for allowing criminals like the Wilson brothers to escape for lesser crimes.

162. Chinta Strausberg, "End 'War Zone'—Jesse Jackson," *Chicago Defender*, February 11, 1982.

163. Chinta Strausberg, "Police Tactics 'Shock' Community," *Chicago Defender*, February 16, 1982.

164. In addition to Andrew and Jackie Wilson, at least a dozen others accused Area 2 detectives of abuse between February 9 and 14, 1982, including one the few documented female victims stemming from the Burge cases, Doris Miller. The others include Dwight Anthony, Roy Brown, Walter Johnson, Paul Mike, Larry Milan, Alphonso Pinex, Donnell Traylor, Donald White, Lamont White, Walter White, and Anthony Williams. "Memorandum Opinion and Order," *People v. Wilson*, 82 C 001211-02, 88 CR 07771-01, June 14, 2018, 60–74.

165. "Plaintiff's First Amended Complaint," *Cannon v. Burge*, No. 05 C 02192 (N.D. Ill. Sept. 2011), 7–8.

166. Chinta Strausberg, "Sleeping Family Startled by Police Search," *Chicago Defender*, February 11, 1982.

167. Chinta Strausberg, "Sleeping Family Startled by Police Search," *Chicago Defender*, February 11, 1982.

168. "Nab Brothers as Suspects in Police Shootings," *Chicago Defender*, February 15, 1982.

169. Natasha Folling, "Blacks Not Shocked by Policemen Murders," *Chicago Metro-News*, February 13, 1982, 1.

170. Russ Meek, "Chicago on Trial—a Look at Conditions," *Chicago Defender*, February 22, 1982; Russ Meek, "The Razor's Edge: The Betrayal of Our People," *Chicago Defender*, March 25, 1982.

171. Toni Anthony, "Mark Soto Brothers Deaths at MLK Center," *Chicago Defender*, November 4, 1970.

172. For more on this case, see Haas, *Assassination of Fred Hampton*.

173. Vernon Jarrett, "A Familiar Tale to Chicago Blacks," *Chicago Tribune*, June 5, 1977.

174. Citizens Alert memo, "God Knows This Isn't Right," n.d. (ca. September 1977), CAR, box 2, folder 2-20.

175. Bonita Brodt, "Why I Found 2 Cops Guilty: Judge," *Chicago Tribune*, December 24, 1981.

176. "Table of Contents 6—No Title," *Chicago Tribune*, February 23, 1982.

177. Jimmie Treadwell, "Unemployed Man Fires on Cops, Is Arrested," *Chicago Defender*, February 25, 1982.

178. "Interracial Squabble Ends in Terror," *Chicago Metro News*, March 6, 1982, 1.

179. "Wilson Brothers Appear in Court," *Chicago Sun-Times*, February 17, 1982.

180. Jimmie Treadwell, "Defense Attorney Charges 'Pattern to Police Tactics,'" *Chicago Defender*, February 23, 1982.

181. Roger Simon, "Cop Brutality: It's Here in Black and White," *Chicago Sun-Times*, February 23, 1982.

182. Roger Simon, "Cop Brutality: It's Here in Black and White," *Chicago Sun-Times*, February 23, 1982.

183. Mike Royko, "Celling the Idea of More Jail Cells: Some Arresting Ideas," *Chicago Sun-Times*, February 17, 1982.

184. Axe Man, "The Hot Skillet: Cop Killings Present Dilemma for Black Community," *Chicago Metro News*, February 20, 1982, 4.

185. Toussaint Losier, "Prison House of Nations: Police Violence and Mass Incarceration in the Long Course of Black Insurgency in Illinois, 1953–1987" (PhD diss., University of Chicago, 2014), 248–249.

186. "Professional Standards," *Chicago Defender*, March 16, 1982.

187. Alan P. Henry, "Was It Police Brutality or Reasonable Force?" *Chicago Sun-Times*, February 21, 1982; Chinta Strausberg, "Police, Bar Groups Ask 'Manhunt' Probe," *Chicago Defender*, February 18, 1982.

188. Chinta Strausberg, "Brzeczek Pressed to Act on Cop Brutality," *Chicago Defender*, February 22, 1982.

189. "At Police Brutality Hearing . . ." *Chicago Defender*, March 12, 1982; "Announce Hearing on Police Brutality," *Chicago Defender*, March 18, 1982.

190. Citizens Alert Press Release, "Police Superintendent Calls Brutality Complaints 'Frivolous' and 'Garbage,'" June 7, 1982, CAR, folder 3-52.

191. Citizens Alert Press Release, "Mayor Says No . . . Changes!" July 19, 1982, CAR, folder 3-52.

192. "Transcript of Proceedings before the Honorable Joan Humphrey Lefkow," *United States v. Burge*, No. 08 CR 846, filed July 1, 2011, 128, People's Law Office, http://peopleslawoffice.com/wp-content/uploads/2012/02/1.20.11.Testimony-of-Adam-Green-in-US-v.-Burge.pdf.

193. Attorney Daniel Reidy argued, "There is a series of mistakes made by the police that make this case possible," including the marks left on Wilson. "Jon Burge et al., Case Nos. 1856, 1857, & 1858," March 19, 1992, 3403, CPB.

194. Mary D. Powers to U.S. Attorney Fred Forman, September 10, 1990, CAR, folder 6-75.

195. John Conroy, "House of Screams," *Chicago Reader*, January 25, 1990.

196. Chicago Police Board, "Findings and Decisions," "Jon Burge et al., Case Nos. 1856, 1857, & 1993," CPB.

197. Matthew Walberg and William Lee, "Burge Found Guilty," *Chicago Tribune*, June 28, 2010.

198. Dr. John M. Raba to Richard J. Brzeczek, February 17, 1982, People's Law Office, http://peopleslawoffice.com/wp-content/uploads/2012/02/Brceczek-Let-to-Daley-in-Police-Torture.pdf.

199. Egan and Boyle, *Report of the Special State's Attorney*, 76–77.

200. Richard Brzeczek to Richard M. Daley, February 25, 1982, People's Law Office, http://peopleslawoffice.com/wp-content/uploads/2012/02/Brceczek-Let-to-Daley-in-Police-Torture.pdf.

201. "Sworn Statement of Richard M. Daley," June 12, 2006, *In Re: Internal Investigation by Special Prosecutor Appointed by Judge Biebel*, 18–19, People's Law Office, http://peopleslawoffice.com/wp-content/uploads/2012/02/6.12.06.-Daley-Statement.pdf.

202. Egan and Boyle, *Report of the Special State's Attorney*, 73.

203. *People v. Wilson*, 116 Ill. 2d 29 (1987), 606 N.E.2d 571.

204. For Byrne's denials, see Egan and Boyle, *Report of the Special State's Attorney*, 85–86.

205. Egan and Boyle, *Report of the Special State's Attorney*, 78, 85.

206. Egan and Boyle, *Report of the Special State's Attorney*, 77–79.

207. For McCarthy's denial, see Egan and Boyle, *Report of the Special State's Attorney*, 79. For McCarthy's reputation, see Joye Brown, "200 Neighbors Demand Better Police Protection," *Chicago Tribune*, March 12, 1981; Wilfredo Cruz, "Arrests Jump Sharply, Minority Leaders Charge Police with 'Disorderly Conduct,'" *Chicago Reporter* 11, no. 10 (October 1982): 1. For claims that McCarthy acted as Byrne's representative during the manhunt for the Wilson brothers, see "Plaintiff's First Amended Complaint," *Cannon v. Burge*, No. 05 C 02192 (N.D. Ill. September 2011), 7. For evidence that McCarthy and Brzeczek's strained relationship, see Manuel Galvan and Anne Keegan, "Controversial Police Gang Unit Head Quits," *Chicago Tribune*, July 19, 1983.

208. Testimony of Jon Burge, "Jon Burge et al., Case Nos. 1856, 1857, & 1858," March 2, 1992, 2513–2514, CPB.

209. Anonymous to Flint Taylor, postmarked February 2, 1989, People's Law Office, http://peopleslawoffice.com/wp-content/uploads/2012/02/February-2-1989-letter-regarding-chicago-police-torture.pdf.

210. Jimmie Treadwell, "Defense Attorney Charges 'Pattern to Police Tactics,'" *Chicago Defender*, February 23, 1982; "Testimony of Andrew Wilson," November 1982, respondent officers' exhibit 112, "Jon Burge et al., Case Nos. 1856, 1857, & 1858," CPB.

211. "Sworn Statement of Doris M. Byrd," *Patterson v. Burge*, No. 03 C 4433 (N.D. Ill. November 9, 2004), 28–29.

212. "Honors: Daley Hails 11 in Crime War," *Chicago Tribune*, May 20, 1983.

213. People's Law Office, *Report on the Failure*, 32.

Chapter Four

1. Leonard M. Richardson to James B. Conlisk, December 29, 1969, AAPL, folder 1-15.

2. The chapter title is drawn from "Action for Survival, Outline for Speakers Bureau," 1970, CUL, folder series III 171-1868.

3. Chicago Urban League, "Position Paper for Action for Survival: Crime in the Black Community Must Go!!" July 6, 1970, CUL, folder series III 170-1857.

4. The Latino torture survivor was named Pedro Sepulveda. See Taylor, *Torture Machine*, 452.

5. Robert Blau, "Cop Tortured Prisoners, Group Says," *Chicago Tribune*, August 18, 1989.

6. Sugrue, *Origins of the Urban Crisis*, 7.

7. Harrington, *Other America*.

8. Hubert H. Humphrey, "Lawyers and America's Urban Crisis," *American Bar Association Journal* 53, no. 10 (October 1967): 897–900.

9. Clark, *Crime in America*.

10. In 1973, Chicago's frustrated Model Cities administrator Erwin France claimed the Nixon administration "denied the existence of an urban crisis." Erwin A. France, "A Report to the Full Committee," November 9, 1973, CUL, folder series III 174-1900; Ernest Holsendolph, "Urban Crisis of the 1960s Is Over, Ford Aides Say," *New York Times*, March 23, 1975.

11. Ken O. Hartnett, "The Urban Crisis That Isn't but Is," *Boston Globe*, March 8, 1973, 20.

12. "The New Urban Crisis," *Wall Street Journal*, June 23, 1975.

13. Daniel Patrick Moynihan, "Is There Really an Urban Crisis?" *Challenge* 15, no. 2 (November–December 1966), 20–22, 49–50, 21.

14. Banfield, *Unheavenly City*, 21–22.

15. Richard A. Cloward and Frances Fox Piven, "The Urban Crisis and the Consolidation of National Power," *Proceedings of the Academy of Political Science* 29, no. 1 (1968): 159–168.

16. Cook County Urban Crisis Committee fliers, "Cities/Urban Crisis Forum," May, 1977, and "The Urban Crisis in the Middle-Sized Cities," November, 1977, LWVIL, folder 69-578.

17. The exception being African American policy makers, particularly newly elected mayors and federal executive branch appointees. See Paul Delaney, "The Black Mayors: Confronting the Urban Crisis," *Chicago Tribune*, November 10, 1974; Larry Van Dyne, "Weaver Calls Nixon's Housing Plan 'Nonsense,'" *Boston Globe*, November 12, 1968.

18. Daniel Patrick Moynihan, "Is There Really an Urban Crisis?" *Challenge* 15, no. 2 (November–December 1966): 21.

19. Banfield, *Unheavenly City*, 4.

20. Keyserling, *Progress or Poverty*.

21. Chicago Commission on Race Relations, *The Negro in Chicago*; Drake and Cayton, *Black Metropolis*.

22. Clark, *Dark Ghetto*, chap. 3, 27–41 47–50; Wilson, *Truly Disadvantaged*.

23. Hinton, *From the War on Poverty to the War on Crime*, 8.

24. Renault Robinson to Peter Fitzpatrick, Chairman of the Chicago Human Relations Committee, 1972, RJD, box SIss1B113, folder 113-10.

25. Fortner, *Black Silent Majority*; Forman, *Locking Up Our Own*.

26. Richard Block, *Violent Crime*, 43.

27. Chicago's black population was approximately 33 percent in 1970 and 40 percent in 1980. See Chicago Fact Book Consortium, *Chicago Metropolitan Area, Based on the 1970 and 1980 Censuses*.

28. Block, *Lethal Violence in Chicago*, iii, 21.

29. Rick Greenberg, "Chicago's Deadly '70s: Murder Victims: Most Black, Latinos Now Surpassing Whites," *Chicago Reporter* 10, no. 1 (January 1981): 1.

30. Law Enforcement Assistance Administration, "News Release," April 30, 1976, AAPL, folder 66-6; Block and Block, *Patterns of Change in Chicago Homicide*, 14, 27.

31. Block, *Violent Crime*, 44.

32. "Statement by Mr. James W. Compton, Executive Director, Chicago Urban League, on the Use and Control of Handguns before the Subcommittee on Crime of the U.S. House of Representatives' Committee on the Judiciary, Tuesday, April 15, 1975," CUL, folder series III 179-1938.

33. Rick Greenberg, "Out of Control? Pistols Pour through Sieve of Unenforceable Handgun Laws," *Chicago Reporter* 10, no. 2 (February 1981): 1.

34. *McDonald v. City of Chicago*, 561 U.S. 3025 (2010).

35. Vernon E. Jordan Jr., "A Question of Commitment: The Black Urban Crisis and the Carter Administration," *Black Scholar* 9, no. 2 (October 1977): 4–5.

36. Cipes, *Crime War*, xii.

37. Navasky and Paster, *Law Enforcement*, 3.

38. Hinton, *From the War on Poverty to the War on Crime*, 2.

39. Ron Dorfman, "Daley's Bluff," *Chicago*, April 1976, 123, CUL, folder series III 180-1942.

40. Joseph C. Goulden, "Tooling Up for Repression: The Cops Hit the Jackpot," *The Nation*, November 23, 1970, 521.

41. Hinton, *From the War on Poverty to the War on Crime*, 337.

42. Clark, *Crime in America*, 28, 107; Hinton, *From the War on Poverty to the War on Crime*, 9.

43. The Burge scandal first appeared in print in the middle of two 1989 trials stemming from a civil suit filed by torture survivor Andrew Wilson. "At Large: U.S. Should Probe Tor-

ture, Says Judge," *Chicago Lawyer* 12, no. 4 (April 18, 1989): 5. Extensive coverage in the *Chicago Reader* followed in January 1990. John Conroy, "House of Screams," *Chicago Reader*, January 25, 1990.

44. Balto, *Occupied Territory*, 9. See also Diamond, *Chicago on the Make*, 183–185.

45. Felker-Kantor, *Policing Los Angeles*, 19–20, 26–42.

46. "Metcalfe Maps War on Crime," *Chicago Defender*, November 7, 1974.

47. Dhoruba Moore, "Strategies of Repression against the Black Movement," *Black Scholar* 12, no. 3 (May–June 1981): 10–16. Quotation from Toni Anthony, "Black Probe Sparked U.S. Inquiry: Salons," *Chicago Defender*, December 23, 1969.

48. "Chicago Judge Slaps Back," *Jet* 28, no. 1 (April 15, 1965): 8–9.

49. "Leighton Court Decision Draws Heated Protests from Officials," *Chicago Defender*, March 8, 1965; "House Eyes 'Stop and Frisk' Law: Police Power of Search Would Be Expanded," *Chicago Tribune*, April 26, 1965; George Tagge, "Open Housing Voted: Senate Passes 'Stop and Frisk' Legislation," *Chicago Tribune*, April 28, 1965.

50. "Gov. Kerner Vetoes Stop and Frisk Bill," *Chicago Tribune*, August 18, 1965; "Stop and Frisk Law Again Asked by GOP," *Chicago Tribune*, December 6, 1966.

51. George Tagge, "Assembly Passes Stop-and-Frisk Bill: 60 Millions Needed in Financial Crisis," *Chicago Tribune*, July 25, 1969.

52. Audrey Weaver, "Cops 'Stop and Frisk' Has Black Area Fuming," *Chicago Daily Defender*, October 19, 1968; Robert Davis, "Negro Cops Form Association; Oppose Stop and Frisk Law," *Chicago Tribune*, July 13, 1968.

53. Kenwood-Oakland Community Organization Memo, August 14 and August 18, 1969, CUL, folder series III 171-1858.

54. "Memo, To: Mayor Richard J. Daley, Re: Police," April 27, 1972, RJD, box SIss1B113, folder 113-10.

55. John Dineen, "Keep Stop and Frisk," *Chicago Tribune*, April 22, 1973.

56. *Terry v. Ohio*, 312 U.S. 1 (1968); *Schneckloth v. Bustamonte*, 412 U.S. 218 (1973); "'Stop and Frisk' OK'd," *Chicago Defender*, June 13, 1972.

57. Balto, *Occupied Territory*, 160–162.

58. Chicago Urban League, "Chicago Lawn–West Englewood: A Community in Transition," August 6, 1976, 8, CUL, folder series III 180-1944.

59. Moore, *Black Rage in New Orleans*, 4, 77, 169.

60. Seale, *Seize the Time*, 66–69.

61. Newton and Blake, *Revolutionary Suicide*, 127.

62. Murch, *Living for the City*, 67, 133–134. For a Panther leader's identification with a criminal element and rejection of white-dominated laws and norms, see Cleaver, *Soul on Ice*, particular his essay "On Becoming," 21–36.

63. Bloom and Martin, *Black against Empire*, 119–124, 199–246.

64. Williams, *From the Ballot to the Bullet*, 61–66.

65. Bloom and Martin, *Black against Empire*, 226.

66. Clark and Wilkins, *Search and Destroy*, 26.

67. Williams, *From the Bullet to the Ballot*, 192–194.

68. Jon Rice, "The World of the Illinois Panthers," in Theoharis and Woodard, *Freedom North*, 55–56.

69. Foner, *Black Panthers Speak*, 219–255.

70. Williams, *From the Bullet to the Ballot*, 127–131; Sonnie and Tracy, *Hillbilly Nationalists*, 1–5, 66–101; Fernandez, *Brown in the Windy City*, 190.

71. Jon F. Rice, "Black Radicalism on Chicago's West Side: A History of the Illinois Black

Panther Party" (PhD diss., Northern Illinois University, 1998), 103–105, 121, 129–132, 136–139, 146–147.

72. Chicago Committee on National Priorities and Alliance to End Repression, "Repression 1970," AER, folder 1.1.

73. Bloom and Martin, *Black against Empire*, 230–239.

74. Haas, *Assassination of Fred Hampton*, 72–82, 255–256, 297–298.

75. U.S. District Court, Northern District of Illinois, Eastern Division, *Report of the January 1970 Grand Jury*; Clark and Wilkins, *Search and Destroy*.

76. Sonnie and Tracy, *Hillbilly Nationalists*, 87.

77. See, e.g., Roy Wilkins to Audrey Reid, November 26, 1968; Audrey Reid to Black Panthers, October 23, 1968, Papers of the NAACP, Part 28: Special Subject Files, 1966–1970, Series A, in ProQuest History Vault, folder 009056-003-0715.

78. Bloom and Martin, *Black against Empire*, 242.

79. Haas, *Assassination of Fred Hampton*, 98.

80. Bloom and Martin, *Black against Empire*, 239–246.

81. "Fact Sheet on Action for Survival," CUL, folder series III 172-1872; "Position Paper for Action for Survival: Crime in the Black Community Must Go!!" July 6, 1970, CUL, folder series III 170-1857.

82. "Position Paper for Action for Survival: Crime in the Black Community Must Go!!" July 6, 1970, CUL, folder series III 170-1857.

83. "Action for Survival, Outline for Speakers Bureau," n.d. (ca. 1970), CUL, folder series III 171-1868.

84. Press Release, Action for Survival, December 23, 1970, CUL, folder series III 172-1872.

85. Diamond, *Mean Streets*, 4, 13–14; Fernandez, *Brown in the Windy City*, 180–181.

86. Diamond, *Mean Streets*, 262; Chicago Crime Commission, *The Gang Book: A Detailed Overview of Street Gangs in the Chicago Metropolitan Area* (Chicago: Chicago Crime Commission, 2012), CHM.

87. Will Cooley, "'Stones Run It': Taking Back Control of Organized Crime in Chicago, 1940–1975," *Journal of Urban History* 37, no. 6 (November 2011): 911–932, 911.

88. "Brief History of the Young Lords Organization," January 1972, CAR, folder 30-515; Fernandez, *Brown in the Windy City*, 180–205.

89. Diamond, *Chicago on the Make*, 185–200; Balto, *Occupied Territory*, 176–179.

90. Will Cooley, "'Stones Run It': Taking Back Control of Organized Crime in Chicago, 1940–1975," *Journal of Urban History* 37, no. 6 (November 2011): 912, 919–923.

91. Arnold Rosenzweig, "Police Set Up New Intelligence Unit to Battle Street Gangs," *Chicago Daily Defender*, March 22, 1967.

92. Clark and Wilkins, *Search and Destroy*, 19–20; John M. Hagedorn, "Race Not Space: A Revisionist History of Gangs in Chicago," *Journal of African American History* 91, no. 2 (Spring 2006): 194–208, 202–203.

93. Ruth Wells, "Law Enforcement in the Minority Community," October 1974, CAR, folder 2-19.

94. Citizens Alert Memo, "Policy Matters," n.d. (ca. mid-1980s, probably 1984), CAR, folder 2-23.

95. Ruth Wells, "Law Enforcement in the Minority Community," October 1974, CAR, folder 2-19.

96. Donald Mosby, "Mayor at Odds with Gang Unit," *Chicago Defender*, May 22, 1969; "Teen Gang Crackdown Criticized," *Chicago Defender*, June 9, 1969.

97. "Petition," n.d. (ca. 1969), RJD, box SIss1B80, folder 80-6.

98. "'Que viva el pueblo,' A Biographical History of Jose Cha-Cha Jimenez, General Secretary of the Young Lords Organization," 1973, CAR, folder 30-515; Fernandez, *Brown in the Windy City*, 187–188.

99. Ruth Wells, "Law Enforcement in the Minority Community," October 1974, CAR, folder 2-19.

100. "Women Activists Escalate War on Crime," *Chicago Defender*, April 3, 1974; flier, "Coalition of Concerned Women in the War on Crime," 1974, CCUA, folder 45-801; Ethel Payne, "Cartoonist Depicts Horrors of Black-on-Black Crime," *Chicago Defender*, March 9, 1974.

101. Timothy Stewart-Winter, "Queer Law and Order: Sex, Criminality, and Policing in the Late Twentieth-Century United States," *Journal of American History* 102, no. 1 (June 2015): 62.

102. Jim Bradford to Edward Hanrahan, December 19, 1969, LMD, folder 95-6; Timothy Stewart-Winter, "Raids, Rights, and Rainbow Coalitions: Sexuality and Race in Chicago Politics, 1950–2000" (PhD diss., University of Chicago, 2009), 183–187, 186.

103. Citizens Alert, "Six Months Report, October 1, 1974 to March 31, 1975," CAR, folder 15-263; Alliance to End Repression, Meeting Minutes, January 13, 1970, AER, folder 3.29.

104. "Migrant Group Plans a Protest against Police," *Chicago Sun-Times*, August 11, 1966; Sonnie and Tracy, *Hillbilly Nationalists*; Roger Guy, "Hank Williams Lives in Uptown: Appalachians and the Struggle against Displacement in Chicago," *Journal of Appalachian Studies* 18, no. 1–2 (Spring–Fall 2012): 131–148.

105. Chicago Urban League Memo, May 20, 1980, CUL, folder series III 181-1953.

106. Charles M. Unkovic, foreword to Bopp, *Police Rebellion*, vii; "Embattled Police Taking the Offensive," *Washington Post*, December 15, 1968.

107. William J. Bopp, "The Police Rebellion," in Bopp, *Police Rebellion*, 6.

108. Charles M. Unkovic, foreword to Bopp, *Police Rebellion*, viii; "President's Message," *F.O.P. Newsletter* 1, no. 1 (July–August, 1981), 1, CHM; James Strong and Robert Davis, "Byrne Hails 'Landmark' Police Pact, No-Strike Pledge," *Chicago Tribune*, June 26, 1981; Citizens Alert Flier, "Stop Police Brutality: Support Necessary Amendments to the Mayor's Bill on OPS Reform," 2007, CAR, folder 15-256.

109. Tera Agyepong, "In the Belly of the Beast: Black Policemen Combat Police Brutality in Chicago, 1968–1983," *Journal of African American History* 98, no. 2 (Spring 2013): 253–276.

110. Pihos, "Policing, Race, and Politics," 67.

111. Ron Dorfman, "Daley's Bluff," *Chicago*, April 1976, 123, CUL, folder series III 180-1942; Pihos, "Policing, Race, and Politics," 277.

112. "National Black Police Convention, Louisville, Kentucky, October 5–10, 1976," CUL, folder series III 180-1942.

113. For example, in May 1971 independent aldermen Leon Despres (Fifth Ward), Anna Langford (Sixteenth Ward), and William Cousins (Eighth Ward) sponsored a City Council resolution calling for an independent investigation after a white police officer shot and wounded a black plainclothes officer in his unit. Leon Despres to AAPL, May 5, 1971, AAPL, folder 7-12. See other resolutions for police reform proposed by Despres in the early 1970s, in LMD, folder 22-2.

114. Leon Despres to Vernon Jarrett, February 17, 1976, LMD, folder 129-7.

115. Grimshaw, *Bitter Fruit*, 137.

116. "Conlisk Pressed on Dr. Odom," *Chicago Defender*, March 21, 1972; "S. Side Dentist Fights for Life," *Chicago Defender*, April 24, 1972; "The Misuse of Police Authority in Chicago: A Report and Recommendations Based on Hearings before the Blue Ribbon Panel Convened by the Honorable Ralph H. Metcalfe, Representative, First Congressional District of Illinois, on June 26, July 17, July 24, and July 31, 1972," July 1973, AAPL, folder 69-2.

117. Faith Christmas, "No Deals on Cop Issue, Metcalfe: Unity Victory Key," *Chicago Defender*, May 8, 1972; "Press Release," April 24, 1972, AAPL, folder 69-2.

118. Many groups claimed credit for the OPS, including the CCPR, the Afro-American Patrolmen's League, Citizens Alert, CPD Superintendent James Rochford, and the editorial board of the *Chicago Tribune*. All deserve some credit—or blame, as it were—for the controversial OPS. This account comes from "History of the Afro American Patrolman's League," TMB, folder 68-12.

119. "Report and Recommendations of Black State Legislators of Illinois on Law Enforcement—Crime in the Black Communities of Chicago," May 13, 1970, CUL, folder series III 172-1874.

120. Chicago Law Enforcement Study Group, Minutes of Meeting, May 10, 1972, CUL, folder series III 175-1907.

121. Citizen's Alert Fundraising Proposal, 1979, CAR, folder 2-16.

122. The founding members of the board of directors were Fred E. Glick, Norman E. Lapping, Jay A. Miller, Jack Korshak, and Stephen E. Whitehead. Citizens Alert, Articles of Certification, CAR, folder 1-1.

123. Mary Powers, Benefit Speech, 1982, CAR, folder 1-7.

124. Louise Kiernan, "Fighting Brutality for 25 Years," *Chicago Tribune*, May 11, 1992, CAR, folder 1-7.

125. Citizens Alert, Articles of Certification, Section 5, CAR, folder 1-1.

126. Charles Hounmenou, *Justice Advocates: Citizens Alert and Police Accountability* (Chicago: Jane Addams Center for Social Policy and Research, 2012), 6–8, CAR, folder 1-8B.

127. Press Release, *First Church News*, "Form Liberties Coalition to Fight 'Police State,' 2/17/1970," AER, folder 3.29.

128. AER press release, September 10, 1970, AER, folder 1.1.

129. AER newsletter, February 1971, AER, folder 7.12.

130. The Police Task Force was folded into the tax-exempt Citizens Alert Inc. in 1970; the Bail Task Force incorporated as the Cook County Special Bail Project; and the Prisons Task Force became the Illinois Prisons and Jail Project. Alliance to End Repression, "Statement of Purpose," n.d. (ca. 1970), AER, folder 3.29. For the jury task force, see "Alliance to End Repression—Jury Task Force," n.d. (ca. 1971), AER, folder 8.22.

131. Mary D. Powers, "From Protest to Program," *New World Outlook*, June 1972, 16–19, AER, folder 3.28.

132. AER, March 1976 Progress Report, AER, folder 7.47.

133. The Alliance to End Repression and the ACLU each filed separate suits against the CPD. A federal judge barred the city from continuing to gather intelligence on civilians not suspected of any illegal wrongdoing. William B. Crawford Jr., "City Report: Political Spying by Police Barred," *Chicago Tribune*, April 2, 1982. For more on the suit, see "The Alliance/Citizens Alert Civil Suit and Complete Text of the Cook County Grand Jury Report on Police Spying in Chicago," 1975, MRL.

134. Robert McClory, "Cop Watch," *Chicago Reader*, July 16, 1992.

135. "Crime and the Justice System, Draft Statement for Submission to the Council of the Alliance to End Repression," n.d. (ca. 1975), AER, folder 8.2.

136. Ruth Wells, "Accountability Sessions (article for Citizens Alert newsletter)," n.d. (ca. 1975), CAR, folder 19-330; Law Enforcement Study Group, "Chicago Police Board, Draft," August 21, 1973, CUL, folder series III 175-1906; Evaluation/Policy Research Associates, "Project Descriptions and Effectiveness Plan—Community Awareness Projects," n.d. (ca. 1978), 64, CAR, folder 4-64.

137. Citizens Alert, "History: The First 36 Years of the Struggle," n.d. (ca. 2003), CAR, folder 1-7.

138. Citizens Alert, Undated Partial Report, c. 1986, CAR, folder 2-23.

139. "Board Approves Medical Examiner's Office," *Bridge* 1, no. 2 (August 1976): 1, CAR, folder 15-252; Citizens Alert, "History: The First 36 Years of the Struggle," n.d. (ca. 2003), CAR, folder 1-7.

140. Evaluation/Policy Research Associates, "Project Descriptions and Effectiveness Plan—Community Awareness Projects," n.d. (ca. 1978), 70, CAR, folder 4-64.

141. "Minutes of Strategy Committee of Cairo Task Force, Office of the Alliance to End Repression," October 9, 1972, CAR, folder 19-314; Ruth Wells, Director of Citizens Alert Project of the AER, "Law Enforcement in the Minority Community," October 1974, 3, CAR, folder 2-19. With periodic fluctuations, Citizens Alert received on average one or two police complaint calls per day through the 1970s and 1980s. "Citizens Alert Board Meeting," January 6, March 4, and September 9, 1986, CAR, folder 4-57.

142. Louise Kiernan, "Fighting Brutality for 25 Years," *Chicago Tribune* May 11, 1992, CAR, folder 1-7.

143. Hounmenou, *Justice Advocates*, 22, CAR, folder 1-8B; Gladys Lewis, interview with author, April 13, 2014.

144. Citizens Alert Press Release, "Justice Delayed . . ." May 19, 2006, CAR, folder 15-256.

145. Maureen O'Donnell, "Mary D. Powers, Dead at 93, Called for Police Accountability," *Chicago Sun-Times*, June 27, 2016.

146. Mary D. Powers, "Resumé," n.d. [ca. 1996], CAR, folder 2-18.

147. Carol Marin, "Mary Powers Wins a Fight for Justice," *Chicago Sun-Times*, July 18, 2010, CAR, folder 1-12.

148. Mary Powers to AER, June 9, 1970, AER, folder 1.1; Taylor, *Torture Machine*, 118.

149. Taylor, *Torture Machine*, 118.

150. Robert McClory, "Cop Watch," *Chicago Reader*, July 16, 1992.

151. "Cabrini-Green Group Acts on Police Problems," *Citizens Alert Special Report*. November 1984, 5, CAR, folder 1-7.

152. Citizens Alert Memo, January 5, 1984, CAR, folder 3-42. See more on the Cabrini-Green Committee in CAR, folder 30-516.

153. "The Ethnic Minority Local Church: In the Midst of Social and Economic Issues," *e/sa forum* 71 (May 1981), CAR, folder 30-517. The security guard was later acquitted.

154. Susan Swanson, "Families of Deadly Force Victims Unite," *Citizens Alert Special Report*, November 1984, 1, CAR, folder 1-7.

155. Hounmenou, *Justice Advocates*, 22, CAR, folder 1-8B.

156. Mary D. Powers to Daniel K. Webb, November 3, 1981, CAR, folder 32-559.

157. "Affidavit of Mary D. Powers," May 21, 1991, CAR, folder 2-24.

158. "118 Documented Burge Area 2 and 3 Torture Victims 1972–1991," People's Law Office, http://peopleslawoffice.com/wp-content/uploads/2014/01/1.6.14.-Documented-TortureSurvivorsunderBurge.pdf.

159. Thirteen of the torture survivors who wound up on death row include Frank Bounds, Madison Hobley, Stanley Howard, Grayland Johnson, Leonard Kidd, Derrick King, Ronald Kitchen, Jerry Mahaffey, Reginald Mahaffey, Andrew Maxwell, Leroy Orange, Aaron Patterson, and Victor Safforld. Of these, seven were later released: Hobley, Howard, Kitchen, Maxwell, Orange, Patterson, and Safforld.

160. Dusty Rhodes, "Tougher Than Guantanamo," *Illinois Times*, June 18, 2009.

161. Dusty Rhodes, "Tougher Than Guantanamo," *Illinois Times*, June 18, 2009.

162. "118 Documented Burge Area 2 and 3 Torture Victims 1972–1991," People's Law Office, http://peopleslawoffice.com/wp-content/uploads/2014/01/1.6.14.-Documented-TortureSurvivorsunderBurge.pdf.

163. Taylor, *Torture Machine*, 79–80; "Jon Burge et al., Case Nos. 1856, 1857, & 1858," February 19, 1992, 972–1023, CPB.

164. Despite similarities with the Andrew Wilson case and without interviewing a single officer, the OPS found Johnson's allegations "not sustained." Egan and Boyle, *Report of the Special State's Attorney*, 87, 113–114.

165. Dusty Rhodes, "Tougher Than Guantanamo," *Illinois Times*, June 18, 2009.

166. Egan and Boyle, *Report of the Special State's Attorney*, 12–13.

167. *People v. Wrice*, 2012 IL 111860, February 2, 2012, 5–7.

168. "Deposition of Rodney Benson," *Cannon v. Burge*, 05 C 2192, October 6, 2008, 18–19, 97, PLOTF.

169. "Deposition of Rodney Benson," *Cannon v. Burge*, 05 C 2192, October 6, 2008, 18–23, PLOTF.

170. *People v. Wrice*, 2012 IL 111860, February 2, 2012, 6–7.

171. "Memorandum Opinion and Order," *Wrice v. Burge*, No. 14 C 5934, November 29, 2016, 2.

172. *People v. Wrice*, No. 1-08-0525, 940 N.E.2d 102 (Ill. 2010).

173. "Memorandum Opinion and Order," *Wrice v. Burge*, No. 14 C 5934, November 29, 2016, 4.

174. *People v. Wrice*, 2012 IL 111860, February 2, 2012, quotes from 3 and 9.

175. "Deposition of Rodney Benson," *Cannon v. Burge*, 05 C 2192, October 6, 2008, 36–62, 128–129, PLOTF.

176. "Memorandum Opinion and Order," *Wrice v. Burge*, No. 14 C 5934, November 29, 2016, 3.

177. *People v. Wrice*, No. 1-08-0525, 940 N.E.2d 102 (2010); "100 Years in Rape, Burning," *Chicago Tribune*, June 15, 1983.

178. *People v. Wrice*, 962 N.E.2d 934, 936 (Ill. 2012).

179. *Wrice v. Burge*, No. 14 C 5934 (N.D. Ill. November 29, 2016).

180. "Memorandum Opinion and Order," *Wrice v. Burge*, No. 14 C 5934 (N.D. Ill September 25, 2015), 4–6.

181. "Deposition of Rodney Benson," *Cannon v. Burge*, 05 C 2192, October 6, 2008, 56–146, PLOTF.

182. "Deposition of Rodney Benson," *Cannon v. Burge*, 05 C 2192, October 6, 2008, 56–146, PLOTF.

183. "Defendant Burge's Supplement to Motion to Dismiss for Pre-Indictment Delay and Notice of Intent to Offer Former Testimony of Charles Grunhard," *United States v. Burge*, No. 08 CR 846, filed April 23, 2010, 2–4. For Banks's gang affiliation, see Karen Hawkins, "Gregory Banks, Former Gang Member, Claims Jon Burge Suffocated, Beat Him," *Huffington Post*, June 10, 2010.

184. "Sworn Statement of Ms. Doris Byrd," *Patterson v. Burge*, No. 03 C 4433, November 9, 2004, 21–23, PLOTF.

185. "Summary of Evidence of *Monell* Policy and Practice of Torture and Cover-Up, and of Defendants' Martin's, Shines', Needham's, and Hillard's Involvement," 37–39, PLOTF, available at https://genius.com/University-of-chicago-chicago-police-torture-summary-of-evidence-annotated.

186. Karen Hawkins, "Gregory Banks, Former Gang Member, Claims Jon Burge Suffocated, Beat Him," *Huffington Post*, June 10, 2010.

187. "Meet the Death Row Ten: A Burge Torture Victim Speaks Out," *New Abolitionist*, no. 20, July 2001, https://nodeathpenalty.org/new_abolitionist/archive/.

188. *People v. Bates*, 578 N.E.2d 240 (1991), 218 Ill. App. 3d 288 161 Ill. Dec. 113.

189. "Defendant Burge's Supplement to Motion to Dismiss for Pre-Indictment Delay and Notice of Intent to Offer Former Testimony of Charles Grunhard," *United States v. Burge*, filed April 23, 2010, 2–4.

190. "Summary of Evidence of *Monell* Policy and Practice of Torture and Cover-Up, and of Defendants' Martin's, Shines', Needham's, and Hillard's Involvement," 37–39, PLOTF, available at https://genius.com/University-of-chicago-chicago-police-torture-summary-of-evidence-annotated.

191. *People v. Banks*, 192 Ill. App. 3d 986 (1989) 549 N.E.2d 766.

192. *People v. Banks*, 218 Ill. App. 3d 288 161 Ill. Dec. 113, 578 N.E.2d 240 (1991).

193. *People v. Banks*, 192 Ill. App. 3d 986 (1989), 549 N.E.2d 766.

194. *People v. Banks*. 267 Ill. App. 3d 503, 204 Ill. Dec. 873, 642 N.E.2d 774 (1994); "Summary of Documented City and County Expenditures in Burge Torture Scandal," People's Law Office, https://peopleslawoffice.com/wp-content/uploads/2018/09/8.20..18..SUMMARY-OF-DOCUMENTED-CITY-COUNTY-AND-STATE-EXPENDITURES-IN-BURGE-TORTURE-SCANDAL-3.pdf.

195. *People v. Cannon*, No. 84-1584, 150 Ill. App. 3d 1009 (December 11 1986), 502 N.E.2d 345.

196. "Plaintiff's First Amended Complaint," *Cannon v. Burge*, No. 05-C-2192, February 13, 2007, 15.

197. Andy Knott, "Paroled Murderer Gets Life in Prison," *Chicago Tribune*, June 21, 1984; "Gets 100–200 Years for Killing Merchant," *Chicago Tribune*, December 2, 1971; "Jury Asks Death Penalty for Slayer," *Chicago Tribune*, August 4, 1971; Taylor, *Torture Machine*, 234.

198. *People v. Cannon*, No. 84-1584, 150 Ill. App. 3d 1009 (December 11 1986), 502 N.E.2d 345.

199. *Cannon v. Burge*, No. 05 C 2192, February 2, 2006; "Brief of the Plaintiff-Appellant, Darrell Cannon," *Cannon v. Burge*, No. 12-1529, No. 05 CV 2192, August 8, 2012, 5–6.

200. "Summary of Evidence of *Monell* Policy and Practice of Torture and Cover-Up, and of Defendants' Martin's, Shines', Needham's, and Hillard's Involvement," 33, PLOTF, available at https://genius.com/University-of-chicago-chicago-police-torture-summary-of-evidence-annotated.

201. "Plaintiff's First Amended Complaint," *Cannon v. Burge*, No. 05-C-2192, February 13, 2007, 16–17.

202. "Darrell Cannon, Anthony Holmes and Flint Taylor on Torture," YouTube video, People's Law Office, http://peopleslawoffice.com/issues-and-cases/chicago-police-torture/.

203. *Cannon v. Burge*, No. 05 C 2192, February 2, 2006; John Conroy, "Poison in the System," *Chicago Reader*, June 24, 1999.

204. John Conroy, "Poison in the System," *Chicago Reader*, June 24, 1999.

205. Matt O'Connor, "Judge Maloney Found Guilty in Corruption Case," *Chicago Tribune*, April 17, 1993.

206. John Conroy, "Poison in the System," *Chicago Reader*, June 24, 1999.

207. *People v. Cannon*, 150 Ill. App. 3d 1009 (1986), 502 N.E.2d 345.

208. Bob Goldsborough, "John Mannion, Chicago Cop Who Became Prosecutor and Judge, Dies at 77," *Chicago Tribune*, November 20, 2014.

209. *People v. Cannon*, 293 Ill. App. 3d 634 (1997).

210. "Memorandum Opinion and Order," *Cannon v. Illinois Prisoner Review Board*, No. 04 CH 16620, November 22, 2006, 1–6.

211. Frank Main, "Alleged Burge Victim Who Settled for Just $3,000 Seeks More," *Chicago Sun-Times*, February 18, 2012; "Brief of the Plaintiff-Appellant, Darrell Cannon," *Cannon v. Burge*, No. 12-1529, No. 05 CV 2192, August 8, 2012, 8–9.

212. G. Flint Taylor, "Federal Appeals Court Rejects Torture Survivor's Case," *In These Times*, June 26, 2014.

213. Natalie Moore, "Victims of Chicago Police Torture Paid Reparations Decade Later," *NPR*, January 6, 2016.

214. John Conroy, "Town without Pity," *Chicago Reader*, January 11, 1996.

215. John Conroy, "This Is a Magic Can," *Chicago Reader*, May 25, 2000.

216. The Campaign to Prosecute Police Torture, "The Death Row Ten + 1 in 2002: Will They Finally Obtain Justice?" n.d. (ca. 2002), CAR, folder 19-331.

217. See the cases of Jerry and Reginald Mahaffey, "People's Response in Opposition to Petition for Executive Clemency," *People v. Jerry Mahaffey*, Docket No. / Inmate No. N-12780, October 2002; "People's Response in Opposition to Petition for Executive Clemency," *People v. Mahaffey*, Docket No. / Inmate No. A92127.

218. "Statement by Panelist Mary D. Powers, Marygrove College 7/31/04," CAR, folder 1-13.

Chapter Five

1. Citizens Alert Buffet Supper Invitation, "Third World Torture: Chicago Style," June 27, 1990, CAR, folder 7-103.

2. Chicago Police Board, "Findings and Decision," Case Nos. 91-1856, 91-1857, and 91-1858, 1, CPB; "Federal Indictment," *United States v. Burge*, 08 CR 846 (N.D. Ill. 2009).

3. Chicago Torture Justice Memorials, *Reparations Now, Reparations Won*; In 1989, Citizens Alert described their anti-torture coalition as having "Central American and Asian representation as well as groups working with immigrants and refugees." Citizens Alert, "Overview—1989," CAR, folder 3-43.

4. For Wilson's height and weight in the late 1970s, see "Joliet Correctional Center, Program Considerations," March 13, 1978, respondent officers' exhibit 154, "Jon Burge et al., Case Nos. 1856, 1857, & 1858," CPB.

5. "Jon Burge et al., Case Nos. 1856, 1857, & 1858," February 10, 1992, 38–39, 183–188, CPB.

6. Marianne Taylor, "Wilsons Found Guilty in Slaying of 2 Cops," *Chicago Tribune*, February 5, 1983.

7. *People v. Wilson*, 116 Ill. 2d 29, 40 (1987), 106 Ill. Dec. 771, 506 N.E.2d 571.

8. Jessica Seigel and Matt O'Connor, "Man Is Found Guilty 2d Time in Cop Killings," *Chicago Tribune*, June 21, 1988; Matt O'Connor, "Andrew Wilson Gets Life Sentence in Killing of Cops," *Chicago Tribune*, July 13, 1988.

9. "Summons in Civil Action," *Wilson v. City of Chicago*, 86 C 2360, April 22, 1986, "Jon Burge et al., Case Nos. 1856, 1857, & 1858," respondent officers' exhibit no. 43, CPB.

10. John L. Stainthorp and G. Flint Taylor, "Litigating Police Torture in Chicago," *Civil Rights Litigation and Attorney Fees Annual Handbook* 13 (1998): 1–34.

11. G. Flint Taylor, interview with author, May 15, 2018.

12. G. Flint Taylor, interview with author, May 15, 2018.

13. Flint Taylor, "To Catch a Torturer: One Attorney's 28-Year Pursuit of Racist Chicago Police Commander Jon Burge," *In These Times*, March 30, 2015.

14. Haas, *Assassination of Fred Hampton*, 36–37.

15. Haas, *Assassination of Fred Hampton*, 6–7, 13, 21, 25, 33.

16. "People's Law Office 20 Years: Working with People and Their Movements for Justice and Liberation," November 18, 1989, 4, Freedom Archives, https://search.freedomarchives.org/search.php?&keyword[]=Marilyn+Buck&title=People%27s+Law+Office-20+Years.

17. Haas, *Assassination of Fred Hampton*, 49.

18. Haas, *Assassination of Fred Hampton*, 37–38.

19. Haas, *Assassination of Fred Hampton*, 49–50.

20. "People's Law Office 20 Years: Working with People and Their Movements for Justice and Liberation," November 18, 1989, 4–5, Freedom Archives, https://search.freedomarchives.org/search.php?&keyword[]=Marilyn+Buck&title=People%27s+Law+Office-20+Years.

21. Haas, *Assassination of Fred Hampton*, 45–46; Fernandez, *Brown in the Windy City*, 187–190.

22. Fernandez, *Brown in the Windy City*, 180–192; "McCormick Take-Over," *Y.L.O.* 1, no. 2 (May 1969): 4, Oberlin College & Conservatory, http://www.oberlinlibstaff.com/omeka_projects/items/show/34.

23. G. Flint Taylor, interview with author, May 15, 2018.

24. "People's Law Office 20 Years: Working with People and Their Movements for Justice and Liberation," November 18, 1989, 4–5, Freedom Archives, https://search.freedomarchives.org/search.php?&keyword[]=Marilyn+Buck&title=People%27s+Law+Office-20+Years.

25. "History of the People's Law Office," People's Law Office, http://peopleslawoffice.com/wp-content/uploads/2012/02/HISTORYOFTHEPEOPLESLAWOFFICE.pdf.

26. "People's Law Office 20 Years: Working with People and Their Movements for Justice and Liberation," November 18, 1989, 4–5, Freedom Archives, https://search.freedomarchives.org/search.php?&keyword[]=Marilyn+Buck&title=People%27s+Law+Office-20+Years.

27. G. Flint Taylor, interview with author, May 15, 2018.

28. Haas, *Assassination of Fred Hampton*, 45–46.

29. G. Flint Taylor, interview with author, May 15, 2018.

30. James, *People's Lawyers*, 137, xxi; Haas, *Assassination of Fred Hampton*, 54.

31. Haas, *Assassination of Fred Hampton*, 54.

32. Haas, *Assassination of Fred Hampton*, 55.

33. Haas, *Assassination of Fred Hampton*, 56.

34. James, *People's Lawyers*, 130.

35. G. Flint Taylor, interview with author, May 15, 2018.

36. Haas, *Assassination of Fred Hampton*, 56.

37. James, *People's Lawyers*, 135.

38. James, *People's Lawyers*, 135.

39. G. Flint Taylor, interview with author, May 15, 2018.

40. Ted Kleine, "Still Fighting the Power," *Chicago Reader*, November 12, 1999, 10, CAR, folder 56-998; Robert McClory, "Why Don't Jeff Haas and Flint Taylor Just Give Up?" *Chicago Reader* August 4, 1978, 1, CAR, folder 30-505.

41. "People's Law Office 20 Years: Working with People and Their Movements for Justice and Liberation," November 18, 1989, Freedom Archives, https://search.freedomarchives.org/search.php?&keyword[]=Marilyn+Buck&title=People%27s+Law+Office-20+Years, quote

from page 21; "History of the People's Law Office," People's Law Office, http://peopleslawoffice.com/wp-content/uploads/2012/02/HISTORYOFTHEPEOPLESLAWOFFICE.pdf.

42. Michael J. McNamara, "Judicial Discretion and the 1976 Civil Rights Attorney's Fees Awards Act: What Special Circumstances Render an Award Unjust?" *Fordham Law Review* 51 (1982): 320–324, 320.

43. G. Flint Taylor, interview with author, May 15, 2018.

44. John Conroy, "The Shocking Truth," *Chicago Reader*, January 9, 1997.

45. Sheldon H. Nahmod, "The Mounting Attack on Section 1983 and the 14th Amendment," *American Bar Association Journal* 67, no. 12 (December 1981): 1586.

46. "First Amended Complaint," *Wilson v. City of Chicago*, 86 C 2360, October 19, 1987, "Jon Burge et al., Case Nos. 1856, 1857, & 1858," respondent officers' exhibit 117, CPB.

47. Jane Fritsch, "Gacy Sentenced to Death," *Chicago Tribune*, March 14, 1980.

48. Bonita Brodt, "Gacy Prosecutor Heads for Law Firm," *Chicago Tribune*, March 15, 1985; Joye Brown, "Wilson Jury Hears Crime Tally," *Chicago Tribune*, February 8, 1983; Matt O'Connor, "Andrew Wilson Gets Life Sentence in Killing of Cops," *Chicago Tribune*, July 13, 1988.

49. John Conroy, "House of Screams," *Chicago Reader*, January 25, 1990.

50. Egan and Boyle, *Report of the Special State's Attorney*, 136.

51. Jacquelyn Heard, "2 Officers Cleared of Torturing Suspect," *Chicago Tribune*, March 31, 1989.

52. Jacquelyn Heard, "2 Officers Cleared of Torturing Suspect," *Chicago Tribune*, March 31, 1989.

53. Anonymous to Flint Taylor, February 2, 1989, PLOTF.

54. "Corrected and Verified Supplemental Filing in Conformance with Direction of District Court," *Wilson v. City of Chicago*, No. 86 C 2360, Judge Brian Barnett Duff, June 12, 1990, CAOF, folder "Marcus Wiggins."

55. Anonymous to Flint Taylor, March 6, 1989, PLOTF.

56. G. Flint Taylor, "A Long and Winding Road: The Struggle for Justice in the Chicago Police Torture Cases," *Loyola Public Interest Law Reporter* 17, no. 3 (Summer 2012): 182–183.

57. "Corrected and Verified Supplemental Filing in Conformance with Direction of District Court," *Wilson v. City of Chicago*, No. 86 C 2360, Judge Brian Barnett Duff, June 12, 1990, CAOF, folder "Marcus Wiggins."

58. Anonymous to Flint Taylor, March 15, 1989, PLOTF.

59. Anonymous to Flint Taylor, June 19, 1989, PLOTF.

60. Anonymous to Flint Taylor, March 15, 1989, PLOTF.

61. Anonymous to Flint Taylor, March 6, 1989, PLOTF.

62. Anonymous to Flint Taylor, June 19, 1989, PLOTF.

63. *Wilson v. Burge*, 710 F. Supp. 1168 (N.D. Ill., May 4, 1989).

64. Taylor, *Torture Machine*, 65–134, quote from 76.

65. Taylor, *Torture Machine*, 87.

66. *Wilson v. Burge*, 6 F.3d 1233 (7th Cir. 1993), ¶ 7.

67. Egan and Boyle, *Report of the Special State's Attorney*, 137–138.

68. "Jon Burge et al., Case Nos. 1856, 1857, & 1858," 518–526, 1121–1122, 3499–3501, CPB.

69. *Wilson v. Burge*, 6 F.3d 1233 (7th Cir. 1993).

70. David Lombardero, "Do Special Verdicts Improve the Structure of Jury Decision-Making?" *Jurimetrics* 36, no. 3 (Spring 1996): 276.

71. Robert Dudnik, "Special Verdicts: Rule 49 of the federal Rules of Civil Procedure," *Yale Law Journal* 74, no. 3 (January 1965): 483–523.

72. *Wilson v. City of Chicago*, 6 F.3d 1233 (7th Cir. 1993).

73. *Wilson v. City of Chicago*, 120 F.3d 681 (7th Cir. 1997).

74. The title of this chapter section is drawn from "Jon Burge et al., Case Nos. 1856, 1857, & 1858," March 20, 1992, 3837–3838, CPB.

75. John Gorman, "'Torture' Charged in Rights Suit," *Chicago Tribune*, February 16, 1989.

76. Rob Warden, "Tough Prosecutor Daley Can Be Suspiciously Soft," *Crain's Chicago Business*, February 20, 1989.

77. Mary Ann Williams, "Torture in Chicago," *Chicago Lawyer* 12, no. 3 (March 1989): 1.

78. "At Large: U.S. Should Probe Torture, Says Judge," *Chicago Lawyer* 12, no. 4 (April 18, 1989): 5.

79. Rudolph Unger, "Lawyer Says Killer Was Beaten by Cops," *Chicago Tribune*, March 30, 1989; Adrienne Drell, "Convicted Cop Killer Says He Was Tortured," *Chicago Sun-Times*, February 18, 1989.

80. League of Women Voters of Illinois, Illinois Juvenile Court Watching Project, *Out of the Shadows: A Citizens' View of the Juvenile Court in Illinois*, November 1981, LWVIL, folder 36-316.

81. "Affidavit of Mary Powers," October 1996, CAR, folder 2-24.

82. Citizens Alert Memo, January 5, 1984, CAR, folder 3-42.

83. Committee to End Police Abuse and Torture Flier, "Chicago Police Torturer Gets Promoted," n.d. (ca. summer 1989), CAOF, emphasis in original.

84. Mary Powers, "CA Expects to See Improvements as Fogel Takes Charge of OPS," *Citizens Alert Special Report*, November 1984, 2, CAR, folder 1-7.

85. Keith W. Griffiths, "OPS Summary Report," July 29, 1985, "Brzeczek Exhibit No. 4," Special Prosecutor's Report, 109–111; Mary Powers to David Fogel, July 26, 1989, CAR, folder 20-340.

86. Mary Powers to David Fogel, July 26, 1989, CAR, folder 20-340.

87. Citizens Alert, "Minutes of the Board Meeting," August 1, 1989, CAR, folder 4-57.

88. Citizens Alert Newsletter, July 31, 1989, CAR, folder 6-73.

89. Citizens Alert, annual newsletter, June 21, 1994, CAR, folder 3-45.

90. Press statement, November 7, 1991, CAR, folder, 15-257.

91. Law Enforcement Study Group, "Chicago Police Board, Draft," August 21, 1973, CUL, folder series III 175-1906.

92. Robert McClory, "Cop Watch," *Chicago Reader*, July 16, 1992.

93. Robert Blau, "Cop Tortured Prisoners, Group Says," *Chicago Tribune*, August 18, 1989; "Demonstration," *Chicago Defender*, August 18, 1989, CAOF, folder B24 "Burge-Clippings, 1989."

94. Chicago Police Board Meeting Minutes, August 17, 1989, CPB.

95. Chicago Police Board Meeting Minutes, August 17, 1989, CPB.

96. Chicago Police Board Meeting Minutes, September 14, 1989, CPB.

97. Chicago Police Board Meeting Minutes, November 30, 1989, CPB.

98. Chicago Police Board Meeting Minutes, December 14, 1989, CPB.

99. Robert Blau, "Mayor Chooses New Police Boss: Martin Is a Surprise Choice," *Chicago Tribune*, November 1, 1987.

100. Philip Wattley, "Top Cop's Warning," *Chicago Tribune*, November 3, 1987.

101. "Plaintiff's First Amended Complaint," *Cannon v. Burge*, No. 05-C-2192 (N.D. Ill. February 13, 2007), 18.

102. Robert Davis, "Panel OKs 2 Byrne Police Board Nominees," *Chicago Tribune*, July 17, 1979.

103. Robert McClory, "Cop Watch," *Chicago Reader*, July 16, 1992.

104. James Strong, "Daley Picks 6 in Police Board Shakeup," *Chicago Tribune*, October 24, 1989; Citizens Alert, "Overview—1989," CAR, folder 3-43.

105. The Chicago Coalition to End Police Torture & Brutality, "No More Torture By the Chicago Police!" n.d. (ca. 1990), CAR, folder 1-11; "Citizens Alert Board Meeting, Aug. 7, 1990," CAR, folder 4-58; "Resolution Seeking to Expose and Discipline Police Commander Jon Burge for Acts of Torture and Brutality," Chicago City Council, July 31, 1990, CAOF.

106. Citizens Alert press release, February 7, 1990, CAR, folder 15-256.

107. Mary Powers to Clarence Page of the *Chicago Tribune*, April 6, 1990, CAR, folder 6-75; *The End of the Nightstick: Confronting Police Brutality in Chicago*, directed by Peter Kuttner, Cyndi Moran, and Eric Scholl (First Run Icarus Films, 1994), VHS.

108. Citizens Alert Newsletter, January 28, 1991, CAR, folder 5-69.

109. "Citizens Alert Board Meeting, July 7, 1990," CAR, folder 4-59; Citizens Alert Grant Application to the AFSC, September 12, 1989, CAR, folder 3-47.

110. "Minutes of the February 20, 1991 Board Meeting," CAR, folder 4-58.

111. "Citizens Alert Board Meeting, March 13, 1991," CAR, folder 4-58.

112. Mary Powers to "Friends and Colleagues," September 14, 1990, CAR, folder 6-75.

113. Citizens Alert Speech, n.d. (ca. February–April 1990), CAR, folder 1-7.

114. Taylor, *Torture Machine*, 84.

115. McCoy, *Torture and Impunity*.

116. Citizens Alert Grant Application to the AFSC (September 12, 1989), CAR, folder 3-47; Citizens Alert, "Overview—1989," CAR, folder, 3-43; Taylor, *Torture Machine*, 150–151.

117. Matt O'Connor, "Cops Cleared in Racial Beating Case," *Chicago Tribune*, April 3, 1991.

118. Dirk Johnson, "Blacks March to Protest Bias Incident in Chicago," *New York Times*, October 22, 1989, CAOF, folder: "Sub 21: Bridgeport March 1989"; Chinta Strausberg, "Daley, Martin to Fight Police Abuse," *Chicago Defender*, September 30, 1989; Fran Spielman and Ray Hanania, "Brutality Charges Prompt Daley to Realign Police Bd," *Chicago Sun-Times*, October 12, 1989; City of Chicago Committee on Police, Fire and Municipal Institutions, "Public Hearings on Police Brutality," October 11, 1989, 392–393, in author's possession.

119. *People v. Banks*, 218 Ill. App. 3d 288 (1991), 161 Ill. Dec. 113, 578 N.E.2d 240.

120. Don Terry, "Justice for John Conroy," *Columbia Journalism Review*, July–August 2010, https://archives.cjr.org/feature/justice_for_john_conroy_1.php.

121. John Conroy, "House of Screams," *Chicago Reader*, January 25, 1990.

122. Chicago Police Board Meeting Minutes, February 8, 1990, CPB.

123. Chinta Strausberg, "'Torture' Hearings Set,'" *Chicago Defender*, December 20, 1990.

124. Citizens Alert Flier, December 20, 1990, CAR, folder 3-47.

125. "Citizens Alert Board Meeting, Jan. 22, 1991," CAR, folder 4-58, quote from Citizens Alert Memo to Crossroads Fund, May 29, 2007, CAR, folder 15-156.

126. Amnesty International USA, "Allegations of Police Torture in Chicago, Illinois," December 1990.

127. Taylor, *Torture Machine*, 113.

128. Taylor, *Torture Machine*, 113.

129. Michael Goldston and Francine Sanders, *Office of Professional Standards Special Project* (Chicago Police Department, 1990), 1, People's Law Office, https://peopleslawoffice.com/wp-content/uploads/2012/02/Goldston-Report-with-11.2.90-Coversheet.pdf.

130. Michael Goldston and Francine Sanders, *Office of Professional Standards Special Project* (Chicago Police Department, 1990), 1, People's Law Office, https://peopleslawoffice.com/wp-content/uploads/2012/02/Goldston-Report-with-11.2.90-Coversheet.pdf.

131. "Affidavit of Mary Powers," October 1996, CAR, folder 2-24; Gayle Shines to LeRoy Martin, April 30, 1991, PLOTF.

132. Gayle Shines to LeRoy Martin, April 30, 1991, PLOTF.

133. Independent Commission on the Los Angeles Police Department, *Report of the Independent Commission*, 3–12.

134. Press release, "New National Coalition on Police Accountability," n.d. (ca. 1991), CAR, folder 30-501.

135. Citizens Alert Press Release, "Chicago Marks National Police Accountability Week," February 29, 1992, CAR, folder 15-257.

136. National Interreligious Task Force on Criminal Justice, "Press Release," May 4, 1992, CAR, folder 30-500.

137. Taylor, *Torture Machine*, 216–217.

138. "Citizens Alert Complaint Form, Marcus Wiggins," October 1, 1991, CAOF, folder "Wiggins, Marcus."

139. Hubert Williams to LeRoy Martin, October 17, 1991, PLOTF.

140. OSP Memorandum, "Gregory Banks and David Bates Allegations," May 16, 2003, Egan Report Appendices, section D, 65.

141. Egan and Boyle, *Report of the Special State's Attorney*, 277.

142. Chicago Police Board, "Findings and Decision," Case Nos. 91-1856, 91-1857, and 91-1858, 1, CPB.

143. "Coalition to End Police Torture and Brutality Minutes, January 15, 1992," CAR, folder 4-58.

144. Chicago Law Enforcement Study Group, "Chicago Police Board, Draft." August 21, 1973, CUL, folder series III 175-1906; In 1989, critics claimed that since 1982 the CPB reduced punishments recommended by the superintendent in two-thirds of their cases. See Fran Spielman and Ray Hanania, "Brutality Charges Prompt Daley to Realign Police Bd," *Chicago Sun-Times*, October 12, 1989.

145. FOP Confidential Memo, "Burge/O'Hara/Yucaitis Fund (B.O.Y.)," January 16, 1992, CAOF.

146. Colin McMahon and Christine Hawes, "Suit Alleges Cop Torture of Youth," *Chicago Tribune*, January 14, 1993.

147. FOP Confidential Memo, "Burge/O'Hara/Yucaitis Fund (B.O.Y.)," January 16, 1992, CAOF.

148. Burge-O'Hara-Yucaitis Family Fund Committee newsletter, n.d. (ca. February 1992), CAOF.

149. Taylor, *Torture Machine*, 161.

150. Task Force to Confront Police Violence Flier, "Burge Tortures Men; State's Attorneys and Police Department Throw a Party," February 25, 1992, CAOF.

151. Michael Sneed, "Sneed," *Chicago Sun-Times*, February 21, 1992, CAR, folder 20-342.

152. *Jon Burge et al.*, Case Nos. 1856, 1857, & 1858, November 25, 1991, December 1991, and January 7, 1992, CPB.

153. Eric Harrison, "Chicago Police Used Torture, Report Alleges," *Los Angeles Times*, February 8, 1992.

154. Coalition to End Police Torture and Brutality Press Release, "The Truth Is Out!" February 7, 1992, CAR, folder 25-434.

155. "Citizens Alert Board of Directors Meeting, February 4, 1992," CAR, folder 4-59.

156. "Citizens Alert Board of Directors Meeting, February 4, 1992," CAR, folder 4-59.

157. Michael Goldston and Francine Sanders, *Office of Professional Standards Special Project*

(Chicago Police Department, 1990), 62–63, People's Law Office, https://peopleslawoffice.com/wp-content/uploads/2012/02/Goldston-Report-with-11.2.90-Coversheet.pdf.

158. Michael Goldston and Francine Sanders, *Office of Professional Standards Special Project* (Chicago Police Department, 1990), 6, People's Law Office, https://peopleslawoffice.com/wp-content/uploads/2012/02/Goldston-Report-with-11.2.90-Coversheet.pdf.

159. "Abuse by Chicago Police Is Found," *Boston Globe*, February 8, 1992; "Chicago Police Dealt in Torture, Report Says," *St. Louis Post-Dispatch*, February 8, 1992; "Chicago Police Tortured Suspects," *St. Petersburg Times*, February 8, 1992; "Police Abuse Detailed," *Washington Post*, February 8, 1992.

160. Charles Nicodemus, "Report Cites 12 Years of S. Side Cop Brutality," *Chicago Sun-Times*, February 8, 1992.

161. Coalition to End Police Torture and Brutality Press Release, "The Truth Is Out!" February 7, 1992, CAR, folder 25-434.

162. Pope and John hosted a few sessions in their offices at 311 S. Wacker. "Jon Burge et al., Case Nos. 1856, 1857, & 1858, March 7, 1992, 2965," CPB.

163. "Jon Burge et al., Case Nos. 1856, 1857, & 1858," February 10–March 20, 1992, CPB.

164. Bill Nolan, "Police Persecution," *FOP Newsletter*, January 1992, 2, CHM.

165. Josh Karp, "Something He Mostly Liked," Super Lawyers, http://www.superlawyers.com/illinois/article/Something-He-Mostly-Liked/c53daba9-d1aa-4203-ab6f-7a4418af711f.html; Tuohy and Warden, *Greylord*.

166. Taylor, *Torture Machine*, 224.

167. "Jon Burge et al., Case Nos. 1856, 1857, & 1858," February 10, 1992, 56–63, CPB.

168. G. Flint Taylor, interview with author, May 15, 2018; Joey Mogul, interview with the author, May 15, 2018.

169. "Jon Burge et al., Case Nos. 1856, 1857, & 1858," March 2, 1992, 2378–2627, CPB.

170. See the department's summary and rebuttal of Kunkle's defense strategy, "Jon Burge et al., Case Nos. 1856, 1857, & 1858," March 20, 1992, 3744–3775, CPB.

171. "Jon Burge et al., Case Nos. 1856, 1857, & 1858," February 24, 1992, 1461–1466, CPB.

172. "Jon Burge et al., Case Nos. 1856, 1857, & 1858," March 19, 1992, 3526, CPB.

173. "Jon Burge et al., Case Nos. 1856, 1857, & 1858," March 20, 1992, 3837–3838, CPB.

174. Chicago Police Board, "Findings and Decision," Case Nos. 91-1856, 91-1857, and 91-1858, 3, CPB.

175. Melvin L. Oliver, James H. Johnson Jr., and Walter C. Farrell Jr., "Anatomy of a Rebellion: A Political-Economic Analysis," in Gooding-Williams, *Reading Rodney King*, 118–119; Felker-Kantor, *Policing Los Angeles*, 227–231.

176. Michael J. Rosenfeld, "Celebration, Politics, Selective Looting and Riots: A Micro Level Study of the Bulls Riot of 1992 in Chicago," *Social Problems* 44, no. 4 (November 1997): 483–502.

177. Citizens Alert Press Release, April 30, 1992, "Simi Valley Verdicts—A Wake Up Call," CAR, folder 3-47.

178. Flier, "Community Protest against Police Torture," July 9, 1992, CAR, folder, 20-342.

179. Taylor, *Torture Machine*, 187.

180. "Legislative Information System Complete Bill Status," CAR, folder 19-303; Taylor, *Torture Machine*, 188.

181. Neil Steinberg, "Groups Oppose Limit on Time to Accuse Cops," *Chicago Sun-Times*, August 21, 1992, CAR, folder 19-302.

182. Anne Zacharias-Walsh, "Amendatory Veto Softens Dudycz Bill on Police Force," *Niles Spectator*, September 24, 1992, CAR, folder 19-302.

183. "Citizens Alert Board Meeting, August 4, 1992," CAR, folder 4-59; "Sen. Dudycz Sponsors Resolution to Study Police Training on Use of Force," *The Leader*, July 5, 1992, CAR, folder 19-302.

184. "Commentary: Complaint Deadline Is Bad Idea," *Chicago Sun-Times*, August 24, 1992, CAR, folder 19-302; "Citizens Alert Board Meeting, September 1, 1992," CAR, folder 4-59.

185. Jim Edgar to "The Honorable Members of the Senate, 87th General Assembly," September 3, 1992, CAR, folder 19-303.

186. Chicago Police Board, "Findings and Decision," Case Nos. 91-1856, 91-1857, and 91-1858, 35-39, CPB.

187. "Citing Race Angle in a Float, Parade Bars a Police Entry," *New York Times*, March 10, 1993.

188. Frank Main, "Burge Works for Ex-Cop's Security Firm," *Chicago Sun-Times*, July 20, 2006; Taylor, *Torture Machine*, 270.

189. "Press Conference Statement by Coordinator Mary D. Powers, July 19, 1999," CAR, folder 15-255.

190. John Conroy, *Unspeakable Acts, Ordinary People*, 62; Mary D. Powers to Sam Lederman, December 16, 1991, CAR, folder 5-69.

Chapter Six

1. Andrea Lyon, interview with the author, May 2, 2014.

2. *People v. Banks*, 192 Ill. App. 3d 986 (1st Dist. 1989).

3. *People v. Bates*, 267 Ill. App. 3d 503 (1st Dist. 1994).

4. Banks received $92,000 in 1992 and Bates received $66,000 in 1996. "Table 14, Summary of Documented City and County Expenditures in Burge Torture Scandal," PLOTF.

5. John L. Stainthorp and G. Flint Taylor, "Litigating Police Torture in Chicago," *Civil Rights Litigation and Attorney Fees Annual Handbook* 13 (1998): 1–28.

6. *Wilson v. City of Chicago*, 900 F. Supp. 1015 (N.D. Ill. 1995).

7. John Conroy, "The Shocking Truth," *Chicago Reader*, January 9, 1997; Taylor, *Torture Machine*, 210.

8. *United States* ex rel. *Maxwell v. Gilmore*, 37 F. Supp. 2d 1078 (N.D. Ill. 1999).

9. See *People v. Wilson*, 116 Ill. 2d 29 (1987), 506 N.E.2d 571; *People v. Banks*, 192 Ill. App. 3d 986 (1989), 549 N.E.2d 766; *People v. Bates*, 642 N.E.2d 774 (1994), 267 Ill. App. 3d 503, 204 Ill. Dec. 873; *People v. Cannon*, 293 Ill. App. 3d 634 (1997), 688 N.E.2d 693, 1997 Ill. App. LEXIS 790, 227 Ill. Dec. 1000; *People v. Hobley*, 182 Ill. 2d 404 (1998), 231 Ill. Dec. 321, 696 N.E.2d 313. *People v. Patterson*, 192 Ill. 2d 93 (2000), 249 Ill. Dec. 12, 735 N.E.2d 616.

10. ICADP Meeting Minutes, December 19, 2000, ICADP, folder 1-6.

11. "Pontiac Condemned Unit," List of Prisoners, April 21, 1999, ICADP, folder 1-5.

12. Joan Parkin, "Justice for the Death Row Ten," *New Abolitionist*, no. 5, November 1998, https://nodeathpenalty.org/new_abolitionist/archive/.

13. Campaign to Prosecute Police Torture, "The Death Row Ten + 1 in 2002: Will They Finally Obtain Justice?" n.d. (ca. 2002), CAR, folder 19-331.

14. Jones, *Coalition Building in the Anti-Death Penalty Movement*, 77.

15. Andrew S. Baer, "Let Them Get Their Voices Out: The Death Row 10, Radical Abolitionists, and the Anti-Death Penalty Movement in Illinois, 1996–2011," *Journal for the Study of Radicalism* 11, no. 2 (Fall 2017): 129–160.

16. Joan Parkin, "Justice for the Death Row Ten," *New Abolitionist*, no. 5, November 1998, https://nodeathpenalty.org/new_abolitionist/archive/.

17. Don Terry, "'Live from Death Row,'" *Chicago Tribune*, November 2, 2003.

18. "Jon Burge Was Fired for Torture: But Some of His Victims Are Still On Death Row Despite Evidence of Innocence" (Aaron Patterson Defense Committee, 1995), ICADP, folder 1-1.

19. John Conroy, "Pure Torture," *Chicago Reader*, December 2, 1999.

20. *People v. Patterson*, 154 Ill. 2d 414 (1992), 182 Ill. Dec. 592, 610 N.E.2d 16.

21. *People v. Patterson*, 192 Ill. 2d 93 (2000), 249 Ill. Dec. 12, 735 N.E.2d 616.

22. *People v. Patterson*, 154 Ill. 2d 414 (1992), 182 Ill. Dec. 592, 610 N.E.2d 16. Text taken from photographs of the etchings, People's Law Office, http://peopleslawoffice.com/issues-and-cases/chicago-police-torture/.

23. *People v. Patterson*, 154 Ill. 2d 414 (1992), 182 Ill. Dec. 592, 610 N.E.2d 16.

24. John L. Stainthorp and G. Flint Taylor, "Litigating Police Torture in Chicago," *Civil Rights Litigation and Attorney Fees Annual Handbook* 13 (1998): 1–28.

25. ICADP, "Board Meeting, Tuesday, August 19, 6 p.m." (1997), ICADP, folder 1-4; Mary D. Powers to Rebecca Epstein, Department of Justice, May 5, 1999, CAR, folder 7-93; "Illinois Coalition against the Death Penalty Board Nominees," July 14, 2002, CAR, folder 26-450.

26. Aaron Patterson Defense Committee Flier, "Jon Burge Was Fired for Torture but Police Torturers under His Command Remain on the Force," June 1, 1996, ICADP, folder 1-1.

27. Alan Maass, "The Road to Victory," *Socialist Worker*, no. 438, January 31, 2003.

28. *People v. Howard*, 147 Ill. 2d 103 (1991), 167 Ill. Dec. 914, 588 N.E.2d 1044 (1991).

29. Egan and Boyle, *Report of the Special State's Attorney*, 227.

30. Cecilie Ditlev-Simonsen, "Sentenced to Death, Man Laughs," *Chicago Tribune*, May 1, 1987.

31. John Conroy, "Town without Pity," *Reader*, January 11, 1996; Steve Mills and Ken Armstrong, "A Tortured Path to Death Row," *Chicago Tribune*, November 17, 1999.

32. *People v. Howard*, No. 84 C 01313401, March 30, 2007.

33. *People v. Howard*, 147 Ill. 2d 103 (1991), 167 Ill. Dec. 914, 588 N.E.2d 1044.

34. Joan Parkin, "Meet the Death Row Ten: Stanley Howard," *New Abolitionist*, no. 14, February 2000, https://nodeathpenalty.org/new_abolitionist/archive/.

35. Stanley Howard to Andrew Baer, March 20, 2015, in author's possession.

36. Alan Maass, "The Road to Victory," *Socialist Worker*, no. 438, January 31, 2003.

37. Joan Parkin, "Justice for the Death Row Ten," *New Abolitionist* 2, no. 5, November 1998, https://nodeathpenalty.org/new_abolitionist/archive/.

38. Hylton White, "Pressure Grows for Death Row Ten," *New Abolitionist* 3, no. 3, September 1999, https://nodeathpenalty.org/new_abolitionist/archive/.

39. Joan Parkin, "Meet the Death Row Ten: Stanley Howard," *New Abolitionist*, no. 14, February 2000, https://nodeathpenalty.org/new_abolitionist/archive/.

40. *People v. Patterson*, 154 Ill. 2d 414 (1992), 182 Ill. Dec. 592, 610 N.E.2d 16.

41. *People v. Patterson*, 154 Ill. 2d 414 (1992), 182 Ill. Dec. 592, 610 N.E.2d 16; "Memorandum and Opinion Order," *Patterson v. Burge*, No. 03 C 4433, September 27, 2010, 6.

42. Noreen McNulty, "Innocent on Death Row: An Interview with Aaron Patterson," *New Abolitionist*, no. 2, February 1998, https://nodeathpenalty.org/new_abolitionist/archive/; Steve Mills, "Death Row Inmate Claims He Was Forced to Confess," *Chicago Tribune*, October 4, 1998; Steve Mills, "Devine Hears Appeal for Death Row Inmate," *Chicago Tribune*, April 27, 1999.

43. *People v. Patterson*, 154 Ill. 2d 414 (1992), 182 Ill. Dec. 592, 610 N.E.2d 16.

44. Donald Hubert to Edward Egan and Robert Boyle, July 6, 2004, in "Special Prosecutor's Report," 246.

45. E-mail printout, Bill Ryan to ICADP Board Members, October 16, 2001 09:10:31, ICADP, folder 1-9.

46. Don Terry, "Coercion, Chicago Style—Third-World-Quality Torture," in Warden and Drizin, *True Stories of False Confessions*, 387.

47. Adrienne Drell, "Petitioners Want Inmate Spared," *Chicago Sun-Times*, December 11, 1998.

48. Martha Brant, "Last Chance Class," *Newsweek*, May 31, 1999.

49. Steve Mills and Ken Armstrong, "A Tortured Path to Death Row," *Chicago Tribune*, November 17, 1999.

50. John Conroy, "Pure Torture," *Chicago Reader*, December 2, 1999.

51. John Conroy, "Pure Torture," *Chicago Reader*, December 2, 1999.

52. Robert Feder, "Tracking: Ryan on 'Oprah,'" *Chicago Sun-Times*, January 15, 2003.

53. "Madison Hobley Deposition Taken March 19, 2004," in Egan and Boyle, *Report of the Special State's Attorney*, 205–209.

54. *People v. Hobley*, 182 Ill. 2d 404 (1998), 231 Ill. Dec. 321, 696 N.E.2d 313.

55. Philip Wattley and Jack Houston, "Husband Charged in Fire Fatal to 7," *Chicago Tribune*, January 7, 1987.

56. "Seven Killed in Chicago Arson; Husband Held," *Los Angeles Times*, January 7, 1987; Roxanne Brown and Linnet Myers, "Shock Still Burns amid the Ashes," *Chicago Tribune*, January 8, 1987.

57. CPD Department of Personnel, "Employment Work History: Burge, Jon," government exhibit 6b, *United States v. Burge*, No. 08 CR 846; Testimony of Fred Rice, "Jon Burge, Case Nos. 1856, 1857, & 1858," February 28, 1992, 2158–2162, CPB.

58. Barbara Brotman, "The Verdict," *Chicago Tribune*, December 30, 1990.

59. People's Law Office, *Report on the Failure*, 32.

60. Lytle, *Execution's Doorstep*, 147.

61. Donald Hubert to Edward Egan and Robert Boyle, July 6, 2004, 5, PLOTF.

62. *People v. Hobley*, 159 Ill. 2d 272 (1994), 202 Ill. Dec. 256, 637 N.E.2d 992.

63. John Conroy, "This Is a Magic Can," *Chicago Reader*, May 25, 2000.

64. Barbara Brotman, "The Verdict," *Chicago Tribune*, December 30, 1990.

65. Lytle, *Execution's Doorstep*, 161–164.

66. Cheryl Lavin, "Angel of Death Row," *Chicago Tribune*, February 13, 1995.

67. Lyon, *Angel of Death Row*, xvii, 257.

68. Andrea Lyon and Kurt Feuer, "Petition for Executive Clemency for Madison Hobley," 2002.

69. *People v. Hobley*, 182 Ill. 2d 404 (1998), 231 Ill. Dec. 321, 696 N.E.2d 313.

70. Andrea Lyon and Kurt Feuer, "Brief on Appeal," *People v. Hobley*, No. 87-CR-2356; Steve Mills, "Retrial Denied in Fire Deaths," *Chicago Tribune*, July 9, 2002.

71. Judge Diane Wood's concurring opinion, in *Hinton v. Uchtman*, 395 F.3d 810 (7th Cir. 2005).

72. Andrew S. Baer, "Let Them Get Their Voices Out: The Death Row 10, Radical Abolitionists, and the Anti-Death Penalty Movement in Illinois, 1996–2011," *Journal for the Study of Radicalism* 11, no. 2 (Fall 2017): 129–160.

73. "People's Response in Opposition to Petition for Executive Clemency," *People v. Orange*, October 2002, 2–5; "Memorandum and Opinion Order," *Orange v. Burge*, No. 04 C 0168 (N.D. Ill. September 29, 2008).

74. Andy Knott, "Death Penalty Eases a Father's Outrage," *Chicago Tribune*, May 30, 1985; Linnet Myers, "Another Brother Guilty in 4 Killings," *Chicago Tribune*, August 6, 1985.

75. For a synopsis of Orange's case, see Bogira, *Courtroom 302*, 171–173, 80–81, 231–235, 85–87.

76. *People v. Orange*, 121 Ill. 2d 364 (1988), 521 N.E.2d 69.

77. Egan and Boyle, *Report of the Special State's Attorney*, 169–182.

78. *People v. Kidd*, 178 Ill. 2d 92 (1997), 227 Ill. Dec. 463, 687 N.E.2d 945.

79. Chicago Police Department, "Supplementary Report," August 21, 1983. *People v. Mahaffey*, 83CR-9326, box B2014-R2-02586, CCCA.

80. *People v. Mahaffey*, 128 Ill. 2d 388 (1989), 539 N.E.2d 1172, nos. 61821 and 61822.

81. *Mahaffey v. Schomig*, No. 01-4271 (7th Cir. 2002); Bonita Brodt and Philip Wattley, "Murders Stun Neighbors, Who Didn't Lock Doors," *Chicago Tribune*, August 30, 1983; Philip Wattley and Bob Wiedrich, "Cops Cite Motives in Double Murder," *Chicago Tribune*, August 31, 1983; Andy Knott, "Brothers' Statements Describe Rogers Park Killings," *Chicago Tribune*, February 2, 1985.

82. Bonita Brodt and Philip Wattley, "Murders Stun Neighbors, Who Didn't Lock Doors," *Chicago Tribune*, August 30, 1983.

83. *Mahaffey v. Schomig*, No. 01-4271 (7th Cir. 2002); Bonita Brodt and Philip Wattley, "Murders Stun Neighbors, Who Didn't Lock Doors," *Chicago Tribune*, August 30, 1983; Philip Wattley and Bob Wiedrich, "Cops Cite Motives in Double Murder," *Chicago Tribune*, August 31, 1983; Andy Knott, "Brothers' Statements Describe Rogers Park Killings," *Chicago Tribune*, February 2, 1985; Bonita Brodt, "Life after Death: Rick Pueschel Sets an Example for Other Victims of Random Violence," *Chicago Tribune*, May 12, 1985.

84. Matt O'Connor, "Survivors Cherish Memories of Slain Couple," *Chicago Tribune*, April 25, 1991.

85. Anne Keegan, "No Place Is Safe, Neighbors Discover," *Chicago Tribune*, November 24, 1983.

86. "Victims of Double Murder Mourned at Mass," *Chicago Tribune*, September 2, 1983.

87. "Victims of Double Murder Mourned at Mass," *Chicago Tribune*, September 2, 1983.

88. Bonita Brodt, "Life after Death: Rick Pueschel Sets an Example for Other Victims of Random Violence," *Chicago Tribune*, May 12, 1985.

89. Don Pierson, "Payton Gives TD Ball to Slain Couple's Son," *Chicago Tribune*, September 12, 1983.

90. Matt O'Connor, "Murder Defendant Quizzes Victims' Son," *Chicago Tribune*, April 16, 1991.

91. Chicago Police Department, "General Progress Reports," late August–early September, 1983, *People v. Mahaffey*, 83CR-9326, box B2014-R2-02586, CCCA.

92. Bonita Brodt, "Life after Death: Rick Pueschel sets and Example for Other Victims of Random Violence," *Chicago Tribune*, May 12, 1985.

93. John Byrne, pretrial testimony of February 9, 1984, 73–76. *People v. Mahaffey*, 83CR-9326, box B2014-R2-02584, CCCA.

94. Bonita Brodt, "Life after Death: Rick Pueschel sets and Example for Other Victims of Random Violence," *Chicago Tribune*, May 12, 1985.

95. *People v. Mahaffey*, 128 Ill. 2d 388 (1989), 539 N.E.2d 1172, nos. 61821 and 61822.

96. People's Law Office, *Report on the Failure*, 7.

97. *People v. Mahaffey*, 166 Ill. 2d 1 (1995), 209 Ill. Dec. 607, 651 N.E.2d 155.

98. *People v. Mahaffey*, 194 Ill. 2d 154 (2000), 252 Ill. Dec. 1, 742 N.E.2d 251.

99. *People v. Mahaffey*, 651 N.E.2d 174 (Ill. 1995).

100. *People v. Mahaffey*, 742 N.E.2d 251 (2000), 194 Ill. 2d 154, 252 Ill. Dec. 1.

101. *People v. Mahaffey*, 651 N.E.2d 174 (Ill. 1995).

102. *People v. Mahaffey*, 194 Ill. 2d 154 (2000), 252 Ill. Dec. 1, 742 N.E.2d 251.

103. Andy Knott, "Cop 'Black Box' Torture Charged," *Chicago Tribune*, February 9, 1984.

104. Chicago Police Department, "General Progress Report," September 2, 1983; *People v. Mahaffey*, 83CR-9326, box B2014-R2-02586, CCCA.

105. "People's Response in Opposition to Petition for Executive Clemency," *People v. Mahaffey*, Docket No. / Inmate No. A92127, 8.

106. Henry Locke, "Jail Escapee Grabbed, Two at Large," *Chicago Defender*, March 26, 1984.

107. Marianne Taylor and William Presecky, "Medic Charged in Jailbreak," *Chicago Tribune*, March 25, 1984.

108. Lynn Emmerman, "Cook County Jail Break Opens Some Eyes to Security Problems," *Chicago Tribune*, April 1, 1984.

109. Henry Wood and Mark Eissman, "6 Escape County Jail," *Chicago Tribune*, March 24, 1984.

110. William Recktenwald and George Papajohn, "Inmates Searched as 2 Remain Free: 4th County Jail Escapee Captured on West Side," *Chicago Tribune*, March 26, 1984.

111. John Kass and Andy Knott, "Hideout Found—But Jail Escapee Flees," *Chicago Tribune*, March 27, 1984.

112. Andy Knott, "Convicted Killer Asks for Mercy," *Chicago Tribune*, February 12, 1985.

113. Marianne Taylor and William Presecky, "Medic Charged in Jailbreak," *Chicago Tribune*, March 25, 1984.

114. Leonard Benefico to OPS Administrators, March 25, 1984, *People v. Mahaffey*, 83CR-9326, box B2014-R2-02586, CCCA.

115. St. Anthony Hospital Emergency Room Record, "Mahaffey, Reginald," March 23, 1984, *People v. Mahaffey*, 83CR-9326, box B2014-R2-02587, CCCA.

116. Leonard Benefico to OPS Administrators, March 25, 1984, *People v. Mahaffey*, 83CR-9326, box B2014-R2-02586, CCCA.

117. Leonard Benefico to OPS Administrators, March 26, 1984, *People v. Mahaffey*, 83CR-9326, box B2014-R2-02586, CCCA. Henry Wood and Mark Eissman, "6 Escape County Jail," *Chicago Tribune*, March 24, 1984.

118. Joan Parkin, "Meet the Death Row 10: Reginald Mahaffey," *New Abolitionist*, no. 25, August 2002, https://nodeathpenalty.org/new_abolitionist/archive/.

119. Andy Knott, "Brothers to Die for Killing Couple," *Chicago Tribune*, February 13, 1985.

120. *People v. Mahaffey*, 128 Ill. 2d 388 (1989), 539 N.E.2d 1172, nos. 61821 and 61822.

121. Leon Pitt, "Man Again Guilty in Rogers Pk. Slaying," *Chicago Sun-Times*, April 19, 1991.

122. Matt O'Connor, "Murder Defendant Quizzes Victims' Son," *Chicago Tribune*, April 16, 1991.

123. Andy Knott, "Brothers to Die for Killing Couple," *Chicago Tribune*, February 13, 1985.

124. *People v. Mahaffey*, 166 Ill. 2d 1 (1995), 209 Ill. Dec. 607, 651 N.E.2d 1055.

125. Leon Pitt, "Mahaffey Again Gets Death in Murder Trial," *Chicago Sun-Times*, April 24, 1991.

126. *People v. Mahaffey*, 194 Ill. 2d 154 (2000), 252 Ill. Dec. 1, 742 N.E.2d 251.

127. *People v. Mahaffey*, 128 Ill. 2d 388 (1989), nos. 61821 and 61822.

128. *People v. Mahaffey*, 194 Ill. 2d 154 (2000), 252 Ill. Dec. 1, 742 N.E.2d 251.

129. *Mahaffey v. Schomig*, 294 F.3d 907 (7th Cir. 2002).

130. Joan Parkin, "Meet the Death Row 10: Reginald Mahaffey," *New Abolitionist*, no. 25 (August 2002), https://nodeathpenalty.org/new_abolitionist/archive/.

131. The first jury included eleven whites and one Asian American. The U.S. Court of Appeals for the Seventh Circuit referred to its composition as "essentially all-white." While revers-

ing Reginald Mahaffey's conviction, it affirmed that of his brother, Jerry Mahaffey, condemned by the same "essentially all-white" jury. *Mahaffey v. Page*, 162 F.3d 481 (1998).

132. Lawrence C. Marshall, "The Innocence Revolution and the Death Penalty," *Ohio State Journal of Criminal Law* 1 (2004): 573.

133. Alice Kim, "Meet the Death Row Ten: Frank Bounds," *New Abolitionist*, no. 17, November 2000, https://nodeathpenalty.org/new_abolitionist/archive/; *People v. Bounds*, 182 Ill. 2d 1 (1998), 230 Ill. Dec. 591, 694 N.E.2d 560 (1998).

134. Campaign to Prosecute Police Torture, "The Death Row Ten + 1 in 2002: Will They Finally Obtain Justice?" n.d. (ca. 2002), CAR, folder 19-331.

135. The title of this chapter section is drawn from Governor George Ryan's speech at Northwestern University School of Law, January 11, 2003. Maurice Possley and Steve Mills, "Clemency for All: Ryan Commutes 164 Death Sentences to Life in Prison," *Chicago Tribune*, January 12, 2003.

136. "Number of Executions since 1976," Death Penalty Information Center, http://www.deathpenaltyinfo.org/executions-year.

137. "Executions in the U.S. 1608–2002: The ESPY File, Executions by State," Death Penalty Information Center, http://www.deathpenaltyinfo.org/documents/ESPYstate.pdf.

138. "Report of the Governor's Commission on Capital Punishment," April 15, 2002, 1.

139. Jodi Wilgoren, "Citing Issue of Fairness, Governor Clears Out Death Row in Illinois," *New York Times*, January 12, 2003.

140. Rob Warden, "How and Why Illinois Abolished the Death Penalty," *Law & Inequality* 30 (2012): 245, 284.

141. *Furman v. Georgia*, 408 U.S. 238 (1972).

142. *Gregg v. Georgia*, 428 U.S. 153 (1976).

143. Mary Alice Rankin to House Judiciary II Committee, May 30, 1979, ICADP, folder 10-137.

144. "ICADP Mary Alice Rankin File," ICADP, folder 8-87(A).

145. Kathryn Mozden, Coordinator of the Death Penalty Project for the ACLU IL Division to Joyce Keller, re: ICADP, December 13, 1976, ICADP, 8-87(A).

146. Rankin's family to supporters, September 10, 1990, ICADP, folder 8-87(A); Kenan Heis, "Death Penalty Opponent Mary Alice Rankin, 73," *Chicago Tribune*, September 11, 1990.

147. Charles Hoffman, "Can It Be Fixed?" n.d. (ca. Aug. 2000), ICADP, folder 1-5.

148. James Coates, "The Noose Tightens: America Could Witness a Surge in Executions," *Chicago Tribune*, August 19, 1990.

149. Tim Unsworth, "Death Row Inspiration," *National Catholic Reporter*, January 12, 2001, ICADP, folder 1-7.

150. ICADP Newsletter, June 28, 1995, ICADP, folder 1-1.

151. Linnet Myers, "4 Years on Death Row," *Chicago Tribune*, September 4, 1988.

152. Dirk Johnson, "Back to Family from Life on Death Row," *New York Times*, September 25, 1994.

153. Alex Rodriguez, "For Cruz, 'Nightmare Is Over,'" *Chicago Sun-Times*, November 5, 1995; Maureen O'Donnell, "Charges Dropped vs. 3rd Nicarico Suspect," *Chicago Sun-Times*, December 8, 1995.

154. Don Terry, "After 18 Years in Prison, 3 Are Cleared of Murders," *New York Times*, July 3, 1996; Daniel Sinker and Jeff Guntzel, "Finding Life on Death Row," *Punk Planet*, n.d. (ca. 2001); Robert Goodrich, "Suspect Innocent in Death of Child," *St. Louis Post-Dispatch*, December 13, 1996.

155. John Carpenter and Alex Rodriguez, "After 17 Yrs., Porter Freed from Death Row," *Chicago Sun-Times*, February 5, 1999; Adrienne Drell and Dave McKinney, "Another Death Row Acquittal—11th to Be Freed by State High Court," *Chicago Sun-Times*, February 20, 1999.

156. Between 1987 and 2011, there were twenty total exonerations from Illinois's death row, more than any other state. Not all of these cases were connected to Jon Burge. Death Penalty Information Canter, "Illinois," http://www.deathpenaltyinfo.org/illinois-1.

157. ICADP, "Eleven Innocent Men Spent over 100 Years on Illinois' Death Row: Fact Sheet," April 20, 1999, ICADP, folder 1-5.

158. ICADP, "Why We Need a Death Penalty Moratorium in Illinois," April 20, 1999, ICADP, folder 1-5.

159. Illinois Department of Corrections Form Letter to Exonerees, ICADP, folder 12-166.

160. Ken Armstrong and Maurice Possley, "The Verdict: Dishonor," *Chicago Tribune*, January 10, 1999.

161. Ken Armstrong and Maurice Possley, "Reversal of Fortune," *Chicago Tribune*, January 13, 1999.

162. Pam Belluck, "Officials Face Trial in Alleged Plot to Frame a Man for Murder," *New York Times*, March 9, 1999; Thomas Frisbie, "Kunkle Finally Lights Up as Power Goes Out on Trial," *Chicago Sun-Times*, May 30, 1999, 18.

163. Mark Hansen, "How a Vision Failed: Indictment Calls Prosecution a Conspiracy Against Suspect," *ABA Journal* 83, no. 2 (February 1997): 26–27.

164. Dan Rozek and Robert C. Herguth, "Verdict Not End of Line," *Chicago Sun-Times*, June 6, 1999.

165. Dan Rozek and Thomas Frisbie, "DuPage 7 Cut by Two," *Chicago Sun-Times*, May 14, 1999; Andrew Bluth, "Prosecutor and 4 Sheriff's Deputies Are Acquitted of Wrongfully Accusing a Man of Murder," *New York Times*, June 5, 1999.

166. Marianne Taylor, "Killer of 2 Sentenced to Death," *Chicago Tribune*, September 22, 1983.

167. Pam Belluck, "Class of Sleuths to Rescue on Death Row," *New York Times*, February 5, 1999.

168. Lorraine Forte, "Murder Case Witness Recants, Saying Police Coerced Him," *Chicago Sun-Times*, February 2, 1999.

169. Gary Wisby, "Taped Confession Could Help Death Row Inmate," *Chicago Sun-Times*, February 4, 1999.

170. Bryan Smith, "The Angels of Death Row," *Chicago Sun-Times*, February 5, 1999.

171. Joshua Marquis, "The Myth of Innocence," *Journal of Law and Criminology* 95, no. 2 (Winter 2005): 501–522.

172. Meg Wagner, "Illinois Judge Releases Inmate Alstory Simon, Whose Confession Freed Death Row Inmate in 1999," *Chicago Sun-Times*, October 30, 2014.

173. Mark Hansen, "More for Moratorium: ABA Conference Bolsters Momentum to Halt Executions," *ABA Journal* 86, no. 12 (December 2000): 92.

174. Adrienne Drell and Dave McKinney, "Another Death Row Acquittal—11th to Be Freed by State High Court," *Chicago Sun-Times*, February 20, 1999; "Kokoraleis Executed Despite Late Appeals," *Chicago Sun-Times*, March 17, 1999.

175. State of Illinois Supreme Court, "M.R. 15833, In re: Special Supreme Court Committee on Capital Cases, Order," March 8, 1999, ICADP, folder 1-5.

176. ICADP, "Moratorium Update Draft," April 1999, ICADP, folder 1-5.

177. "Testimony at Chicago City Council, June 24, 1999," CAR, folder 7-93.

178. See "House Bill 1054, 81st General Assembly State of Illinois, 1979 and 1980," ICADP,

folder 10-133; "House Bill 2186, 83rd General Assembly, State of Illinois, 1983 and 1984," ICADP, folder 10-137; "HB1443, 84th General Assembly, State of Illinois, 1985 and 1986," ICADP, folder 10-138.

179. Jennifer Davis, "Death Penalty Reforms Aired at Peoria Hearing," *Journal Star*, August 1, 2002, ICADP, folder 2-11; ICADP Memo/Staff Report, December 17, 2002, ICADP, folder 2-12.

180. ICADP, "Moratorium Update Draft," April 1999, ICADP, folder 1-5; Barbara J. Hayler, "Moratorium and Reform: Illinois's Efforts to Make the Death Penalty Process 'Fair, Just and Accurate,'" *Justice System Journal* 29, no. 3 (2008): 423–440.

181. ICADP "Draft of Fund-Raising Letter," n.d. (ca. Dec. 1999), ICADP, folder 1-5.

182. Ken Armstrong and Steve Mills, "Death Row Justice Derailed," *Chicago Tribune*, November 14, 1999.

183. "Report of the Governor's Commission on Capital Punishment," April 15, 2002, 1.

184. ICADP "Draft of Fund-Raising Letter," n.d. (ca. December 1999), ICADP, folder 1-5.

185. ICADP "Draft of Fund-Raising Letter," n.d. (ca. December 1999), ICADP, folder 1-5.

186. ICADP Meeting Minutes, August 15, 2000, ICADP, folder 1-5; Newsletter, "The Governor's Commission on Capital Punishment Got a Chance to Hear the Public on Tuesday, Aug 2 [*sic*]," ICADP, folder 1-5.

187. "Moratorium Project: Ideas for Information Sheets," April 20, 1999, ICADP, folder 1-5.

188. ICADP Staff Report, May 15, 2001, ICADP, folder 1-8.

189. ICADP Meeting Minutes, February 20, 2001, ICADP, folder 1-7.

190. George W. Brooks, "As I See It," *Abolition Now!* 2, no. 2 (Spring 2002): 1, ICADP, folder 2-11.

191. "Press Release: Governor Ryan's Commission on Capital Punishment Completes Comprehensive Review of Illinois System, Delivers Final Recommendations to Governor Ryan," April 15, 2002, ICADP, folder 2-10.

192. "Report of the Governor's Commission on Capital Punishment," April 15, 2002, 207.

193. "Report of the Governor's Commission on Capital Punishment," April 15, 2002, iii.

194. "Lawmakers Consider Ill. Death Penalty Changes," *Associated Press*, June 26, 2002, ICADP, 2–11.

195. ICADP Meeting Minutes, April 16, June 18, and August 20, 2002, folders 2-11 and 2-12; Taylor, *Torture Machine*, 289.

196. H. Gregory Meyer, "Death Penalty Foes Rally Near Hearings," *Chicago Tribune*, October 26, 2002, ICADP, folder 2-12.

197. "Jim Ryan's Suit over Death Appeals Tossed," *Chicago Sun-Times*, October 11, 2002.

198. John Patterson, "Clemency Hearings Open Old Wounds, New Opportunities," *Daily Herald*, October 15, 2002; News clipping, "Illinois Puts Death Penalty on Trial," BBC News, October 15, 2002, 18:45 GMT, ICADP, folder 2-12.

199. Jodi Wilgoren, "Illinois Moves to Center of Death Penalty Debate: Board to Hear 142 Requests for Clemency," *New York Times*, October 14, 2002.

200. Steve Mills, "Life-or-Death Debate Rages at Hearings," *Chicago Tribune*, October 16, 2002.

201. Mark Brown, "State's Death Penalty Hearings Miss the Point," *Chicago Sun-Times*, October 16, 2002, ICADP, folder 2-12; Eric Zorn, "Hearings Look More Like Forum on Death Penalty," *Chicago Tribune*, October 16, 2002.

202. News clipping, "Illinois Puts Death Penalty on Trial," BBC News, October 15, 2002, 18:45 GMT, ICADP, folder 2-12.

203. Jodi Wilgoren, "Illinois Moves to Center of Death Penalty Debate: Board to Hear 142 Requests for Clemency," *New York Times*, October 14, 2002.

204. Steve Mills and Christi Parsons, "Tears Send a Message; Hearings' Emotional Impact Surprises Death Penalty Foes," *Chicago Tribune*, October 27, 2002.

205. "People's Response in Opposition to Petition for Executive Clemency," *People v. Howard*, Docket No. / Inmate No. N-71620, October 2002, 11–20, 22, 39.

206. "People's Response in Opposition to Petition for Executive Clemency," *People v. Kidd*, Docket No. / Inmate No. N-23646, October 2002, 1.

207. "People's Response in Opposition to Petition for Executive Clemency," *People vs. Reginald Mahaffey*, Docket No. / Inmate No. A92127, 15.

208. John Patterson, "Clemency Hearings Open Old Wounds, New Opportunities," *Daily Herald*, October 15, 2002, ICADP, folder 2-12; John Keilman, "Murder Victims' Families Feel Twice Betrayed by Ryan," *Chicago Tribune*, January 12, 2003, 17.

209. Eric Zorn, "Halting Hearings Is Decent Thing for Ryan to Do," *Chicago Tribune*, October 18, 2002; John Kass, "Clemency Panels' Horrors Add to Shame of Ryan," *Chicago Tribune*, October 20, 2002; John Gorman, "The Public Winced in the Face of Their Pain," *Chicago Tribune*, November 29, 2002; "Halt the Anguish, Gov. Ryan," *Chicago Tribune*, October 20, 2002; Dan O'Connell, "Eye for an Eye," *Chicago Tribune*, October 25, 2002.

210. Marlene Martin, "Winning in Illinois," *New Abolitionist*, no. 27, January 2003, https://nodeathpenalty.org/new_abolitionist/archive/.

211. Eric Zorn, "Prosecutors Are Directors in Theater of Pain," *Chicago Tribune*, October 24, 2002.

212. ICADP Staff Report, October 15, 2002, ICADP, folder 2-12.

213. ICADP, "Upcoming Events around Illinois," October 2002, ICADP, folder 2-12; H. Gregory Meyer, "Death Penalty Foes Rally Near Hearings," *Chicago Tribune*, October 26, 2002, ICADP, folder 2-12.

214. Campaign to End the Death Penalty, flier, "Commute All Death Sentences!" October 16, 2002, ICADP, folder 2-12.

215. Eric Zorn, "Prosecutors Are Directors in Theater of Pain," *Chicago Tribune*, October 24, 2002.

216. G. Flint Taylor, interview with author, May 15, 2018.

217. G. Flint Taylor, interview with author, May 15, 2018.

218. "Memorandum and Opinion Order," May 9, 1997, *Wiggins v. Burge*, 173 F.R.D. 226 (N.D. Ill. 1997), CAOF, folder "Wiggins, Marcus."

219. G. Flint Taylor, interview with author, May 15, 2018.

220. Merriner, *Man Who Emptied Death Row*; "Why the Governor Changed," *Chicago Sun-Times*, January 12, 2003; Dennis Byrne, "To Kill a 'Legacy,'" *Chicago Tribune*, October 21, 2002.

221. Andrea Lyon, interview with the author, May 2, 2014.

222. Carlos Sadovi, "Governor Vows He Won't Be Intimidated," *Chicago Sun-Times*, October 30, 2002.

223. John Chase, "Victims' Families Make a Final Plea," *Chicago Tribune*, December 12, 2002.

224. Christi Parsons, "Families Wonder If Ryan Listened," *Chicago Tribune*, December 7, 2002.

225. ICADP Meeting Minutes, November 19, 2002. ICADP, folder 2-12.

226. Eric Slater, "Illinois' Exonerated to Urge Clemency for All on Death Row," *Los Angeles Times*, December 15, 2002; ICADP Memo/Staff Report, December 17, 2002, ICADP, folder 2-12.

227. Shia Kapos, "Inmates' Families Beseech Ryan," *Chicago Tribune*, January 4, 2003, 1.14.

228. Craig Findley, "Ryan's Death Penalty Decision Will Be Painful," *Chicago Tribune*, January 8, 2003.

229. "What Ryan Said Friday," *Chicago Sun-Times*, January 11, 2003.

230. Different reports cite different numbers. There were 160 persons on death row before Ryan acted. He pardoned four outright; 153 received life in prison without the possibility of parole. Three received reduced sentences of 40 years. Ryan also commuted the sentences of several men off death row on appeal. "Death Row Inmates Receive Life," *Chicago Tribune*, January 12, 2003.

231. Mary C. Galligan, "George Ryan: Republicans' Leader in the House," *Illinois Issues* 3, no. 4 (April 1977): 8.

232. "In Ryan's Words: 'I Must Act,'" *New York Times*, January 11, 2003.

233. Richard Willing, "Ill. Hearings Could Spare 167 on Death Row," *USA Today*, October 14, 2002, ICADP, folder 2-12.

234. "Ryan Draws Applause, Jeers," *Chicago Sun-Times*, January 12, 2003; John Keilman, "Murder Victims' Families Feel Twice Betrayed by Ryan," *Chicago Tribune*, January 12, 2003.

235. "Families of the Dead," *Chicago Sun-Times*, January 12, 2003.

236. Lucio Guerrero, "Prosecutors, Survivors Rip Ryan," *Chicago Sun-Times*, January 13, 2003.

237. "Newly Exonerated Death Row Inmates Speak Out," *New Abolitionist*, no. 27, January 2003, https://nodeathpenalty.org/new_abolitionist/archive/.

238. Stanley Howard, "Keeping It Real," *New Abolitionist*, no. 27, January 2003, https://nodeathpenalty.org/new_abolitionist/archive/.

239. Marlene Martin, "Illinois Death Row Emptied: Victory!" *New Abolitionist*, no. 27, January 2003, https://nodeathpenalty.org/new_abolitionist/archive/.

240. Alice Kim, "The Road to Abolition," *New Abolitionist*, no. 27, January 2003, https://nodeathpenalty.org/new_abolitionist/archive/.

241. "Messages of Solidarity from around the World," *New Abolitionist*, no. 27, January 2003, https://nodeathpenalty.org/new_abolitionist/archive/.

242. Duncan Campbell, "Death Row Clemency Splits US," *The Guardian*, January 13, 2003, 14; Rick Pearson, "Ryan Indicted: U.S. Charges Former Governor with Pattern of Corruption," *Chicago Tribune*, December 18, 2003.

243. Monica Davey and Gretchen Ruethling, "Former Illinois Governor Is Convicted in Graft Case," *New York Times*, April 18, 2006.

244. Michael Sneed, Natasha Korecki, Stefano Esposito, and Jon Seidel, "Ryan Presented with Ashes of Late Wife upon Return to Kankakee," *Chicago Sun-Times*, January 31, 2013.

245. The title of this chapter section is drawn from Citizens Alert Newsletter, July 15, 2010, CAR, folder 21-359.

246. G. Flint Taylor, "A Long and Winding Road: The Struggle for Justice in the Chicago Police Torture Cases," *Loyola Public Interest Law Reporter* 17, no. 3 (Summer 2012): 178–203.

247. Mary Powers to Superintendent Terry Hillard, CPB President Demetrius Carney, OPS Director Callie Baird, August 2, 1999, CAR, folder 20-334.

248. Needham to Benefico, August 31, 1998, in Egan and Boyle, *Report of the Special State's Attorney*, 154.

249. Quote from Citizens Alert Press Release, August 2, 1999, CAR, folder 15-257; G. Flint Taylor to Mary Howell, April 12, 2013, PLOTF.

250. Citizens Alert Press Release, "Dick Devine Opposes Community Efforts to Seek Justice for Police Torture Victims," n.d. (ca. 2002), CAR, folder 25-434.

251. In re *Appointment of Special Prosecutor, No. 2001 Misc. 4*, Petition for Appointment of a Special Prosecutor (April 5, 2001), PLOTF.

252. Citizens Alert Newsletter, May 29, 2001, CAR, folder 6-76.

253. Citizens Alert Newsletter, December 10, 2001, CAR, folder 6-76.

254. Carol Marin, "Let's Go Right Back to the Beginning: Code of Silence Got Us Where We Are on Death Penalty," *Chicago Tribune*, January 15, 2003, CAR, folder 1-7.

255. Locke E. Bowman and Randolph N. Stone, "Cop Brutality Probe Must Be Thorough, Fair; Public Confidence in Our Justice System Is at Stake," *Chicago Sun-Times*, May 16, 2002; Egan and Boyle, *Report of the Special State's Attorney*, 155.

256. "Citizens Alert Narrative," 2002, CAR, folder 1-14.

257. Charles Mount, "Carey, Egan Return to Judicial Posts," *Chicago Tribune*, May 4, 1988.

258. Michael Coakley, "Dems Tap Judge Egan for State's Attorney Slot," *Chicago Tribune*, December 2, 1975.

259. Abdon M. Pallasch and Frank Main, "Did Leaders of Burge Inquiry Favor City Hall? Emails Show Top Daley Lawyer Pleased with Their Selection," *Chicago Sun-Times*, July 31, 2006.

260. "State Cancels Action against Accused Cops," *Chicago Tribune*, May 2, 1963.

261. William Parker Sr. to Flynt [*sic*] Taylor, December 13, 1991, 4, PLOTF.

262. Taylor, *Torture Machine*, 285.

263. Taylor, *Torture Machine*, 357–358.

264. Steve Mills and Janan Hanna, "Lawyers Plan to Widen Probe of Ex-Cop's Alleged Torture," *Chicago Tribune*, June 22, 2002, CAR, folder 21-357.

265. "Release Set for Report on Alleged Torture," *Chicago Tribune*, July 16, 2006; Fran Spielman, "'We Want That Report': Black Caucus Urges Release of Probe into Police Torture," *Chicago Sun-Times*, May 6, 2006; Abdon M. Pallasch, "Report on Cop Torture Probe Delayed," *Chicago Sun-Times*, June 3, 2006.

266. Gerald Frazier Sr., President of Citizens Alert, to Honorable Ed Smith, May 11, 2006, CAR, folder 6-72; Monica Davey, "Judge Rules Report on Police in Chicago Should be Released," *New York Times*, May 20, 2006.

267. Abdon M. Pallasch, "Burge Torture-Probe Report Released Today" *Chicago Sun-Times*, July 19, 2006.

268. Citizens Alert Press Release, "Justice Delayed . . ." May 19, 2006, CAR, folder 15, 256; Egan and Boyle, *Report of the Special State's Attorney*, 227.

269. Julien Ball, "The $7 Million Whitewash," *New Abolitionist*, no. 40, September, 2006, https://nodeathpenalty.org/new_abolitionist/archive/; Julien Ball, "A $7 Million Whitewash," *International Socialist Review*, no. 49, September–October 2006, https://isreview.org/issues/49/torture.shtml; Memo, Citizens Alert to "friends" at Crossroads Fund, May 29, 2007, CAR, folder, 15-156.

270. Citizens Alert Newsletter, April 11, 2007, CAR, folder 21-359.

271. People's Law Office, *Report on the Failure*, 2–3.

272. E-mail, Gerald Frazier to Citizens Alert, July 13, 2007, CAR, folder 7-90; Dick Simpson, "Ideas: New Campaign vs. Torture," *Chicago Sun-Times*, July 6, 2007, CAR, folder 21-359.

273. Egan and Boyle, *Report of the Special State's Attorney*, 16–17.

274. Mema Ayi, "No Indictments to Follow Release of Burge Report," *Chicago Defender*, July 20, 2006.

275. Taylor, *Torture Machine*, 242.

276. Lynn Sweet, "Rush's Group Asks Reno for Brutality Probe," *Chicago Sun-Times*, July 27, 1999.

277. McCoy, *Torture and Impunity*.

278. "Abuse of Iraqi POWs by GIs Probed," CBS, 60 Minutes II (April 28, 2004), http://www.cbsnews.com/stories/2004/04/27/6011/main614063.shtml.

279. Diane Marie Amann, "Abu Ghraib," *University of Pennsylvania Law Review* 153, no. 6 (June 2005), 2085–2141.

280. Citizens Alert Flier, "Abu Ghraib or Chicago?" 2005, CAR, folder 2-17.

281. Annie Sweeney, "Global Agency Asked to Probe Police Torture," *Chicago Sun-Times*, August 30, 2005.

282. MacArthur Justice Center Press Release, "Alleged Torture by Chicago Police Draws Call for International Investigation," August 29, 2005, CAR, folder 21-357.

283. "Citizens Alert, Working for Humane Law Enforcement: Police Torture in Chicago," CAOF.

284. Steve Ivey, "Human-Rights Group Asked to Aid Burge Probe," *Chicago Tribune*, October 15, 2005, 1.9.

285. Howard Saffold to Commissioners of the IACHR, February 23, 2006; Barbara Frey to Commissioners of the IACHR, March 20, 2006, PLOTF.

286. G. Flint Taylor, "A Long and Winding Road: The Struggle for Justice in the Chicago Police Torture Cases," *Loyola Public Interest Law Reporter* 17, no. 3 (Summer 2012): 178–203.

287. UN Committee against Torture, *Consideration of Reports Submitted by States Parties Under Article 19 of the Convention, Conclusions and Recommendations of the Committee against Torture*, May 19, 2006, 7.

288. People's Law Office, *Torture in Chicago*, 24–26, PLOTF.

289. Joey Mogul, interview with the author, May 15, 2018.

290. Joey Mogul, "The Chicago Police Torture Cases: 1972–2011," in author's possession.

291. Brian Watson and Jessica Young, "Lots of Unanswered Questions Remain Regarding Area 2 Police Abuse Claims," *Chicago Defender*, May 4, 2005; Liliana Segura, "Chicago's Dark Legacy of Police Torture," *The Nation*, July 19, 2012.

292. See TIRC databases of abuse allegations, Illinois Torture Inquiry and Relief Commission, "In re: Claim of George Ellis Anderson," TIRC Claim No. 2011.016-A, June 13, 2012, exhibits D, E, F, and G; Illinois Torture Inquiry and Relief Commission, "In re: Claim of Shawn Whirl," TIRC Claim No. 2011.051-W, June 13, 2012, exhibit D, https://www2.illinois.gov/sites/tirc/Pages/default.aspx. See the case of Dan Young Jr., in Bogira, *Courtroom 302*, 199–204, 343; Fran Spielman, "City to Pay $1.25 Million in Burge Case," *Chicago Sun-Times*, October 4, 2011. See also the case of the Englewood Four, "Complaint," *Saunders v. City of Chicago*, Case 1:12-CV-09158, Document No. 1, filed November 15, 2012.

293. Maurice Possley, Steve Mills, and Ken Armstrong, "Veteran Detective's Murder Cases Unravel," *Chicago Tribune*, December 17, 2001.

294. Walker, *Sense and Nonsense about Crime*, 44; On the courtroom work group, see Eisenstein and Jacob, *Felony Justice*; Thomas W. Church Jr., "Examining Legal Culture," *American Bar Foundation Research Journal* 10, no. 3 (Summer 1985): 449–518.

295. For more on the courtroom work group in the criminal courts of Cook County, see Gonzalez Van Cleve, *Crook County*, 17–49.

296. E. Kenneth Wright Jr., "The Cook County Courts and Its Chief Judge," *Chicago Bar Association Record* 24 (January 2010): 24.

297. "Memorandum in Support of Petition to Reassign Petitioners' Cases to Judges outside the Circuit Court of Cook County," *In re Appointment of Special Prosecutor*, No. 2001 Misc. 4, July 24, 2002, 4.

298. Bob Goldsborough, "John Mannion, Chicago Cop Who Became Prosecutor and Judge, Dies at 77," *Chicago Tribune*, November 20, 2014; Steve Mills and Ken Armstrong, "A Tortured Path to Death Row," *Chicago Tribune*, November 17, 1999.

299. John Conroy, "Blind Justices?" *Chicago Reader*, November 30, 2006.

300. Gonzalez Van Cleve, *Crook County*, 46.

301. Gonzalez Van Cleve, *Crook County*, 14.

302. Mary D. Powers to U.S. Attorney Fred Forman, September 10, 1990, CAR, folder 6-75; Mary D. Powers to Scott Lassar, U.S. Attorney for Northern District of Illinois, October 22, 1997, CAR, folder, 7-94; Amnesty International, USA, "Allegations of Police Torture in Chicago, Illinois," AMR 51/42/90, December 1990.

303. Mary Powers to William N. Lovell, Stated Clerk, Chicago Presbytery, August 31, 1990, CAR, folder 6-75.

304. Bob Kemper, "Fitzgerald: Conservative and Proud," *Chicago Tribune*, February 24, 1998; "Good Morning, Mr. Fitzgerald," *Chicago Tribune*, September 4, 2001.

305. Mark Guarino, "Patrick Fitzgerald, Nemesis of Rod Blagojevich, Steps Down," *Christian Science Monitor*, May 24, 2012.

306. Annie Sweeney, "Top Prosecutor Hits Decade," *Chicago Tribune*, September 1, 2011.

307. Joey Mogul, interview with the author, May 15, 2018.

308. Carol Marin and Frank Main, "The Truth about Torture—Feds Subpoena Up to 10 Chicago Cops to Find Out," *Chicago Sun-Times*, June 11, 2008.

309. Egan and Boyle, *Report of the Special State's Attorney*, 6–9, 18.

310. People's Law Office, *Report on the Failure*.

311. *Hobley v. Burge*, Case No. 03 C 3678 (N.D. Ill. June 2, 2004).

312. "Federal Indictment," *United States v. Burge*, 08 CR 846 (N.D. Ill. 2009).

313. Natasha Korecki, Frank Main, and Carol Marin, "Feds: It's Just the Beginning," *Chicago Sun-Times*, October 22, 2008.

314. Steve Mills and Jeff Coen, "Feds Catch Up with Burge," *Chicago Tribune*, October 22, 2008.

315. "Defendant's Supplement to Motion to Vacate Trial Date," *United States v. Burge*, 08 CR 846 (N.D. Ill. 2009); Rummana Hussain, "'You Don't Expect to Get Electrocuted'—Man Testifies on First Day of Burge Trial," *Chicago Sun-Times*, May 27, 2010.

316. "Government's List of Potential Witnesses," *United States v. Burge*, 08 CR 846 (N.D. Ill. 2009).

317. "Defendant's Motion for Reconsideration of Ruling Denying Motion *In Limine* to Admit Prior Testimony," *United States v. Burge*, 08 CR 846 (N.D. Ill. 2009).

318. "Excerpt of Transcript of Proceedings," *United States v. Burge*, No. 08 CR 846, June 21, 2010, 28–325.

319. "Transcript of Proceedings," *United States v. Burge*, No. 08 CR 846, June 24, 2010, 3371–3489.

320. Rummana Hussain, "'A Long, Long Time Coming—Burge Found Guilty of Lying about Torture, Faces 45 Years in Prison," *Chicago Sun-Times*, June 29, 2010.

321. Natasha Korecki, "Burge Wants a Light Sentence Based on His Service in Korea, Vietnam," *Chicago Sun-Times*, January 11, 2011; "Transcript of Proceedings—Sentencing—Judge's Ruling before the Honorable Joan Humphrey Lefkow," January 21, 2011, *United States v. Burge*, No. 08 CR 846.

322. Anthony Holmes, "Violent Victim Impact Statement," *United States v. Burge*, No. 08 CR 846, PLOTF.

323. Natasha Korecki and Art Golab, "'It Should Never Happen Again,'—U.S. Attorney Fitzgerald," *Chicago Sun-Times*, January 22, 2011.

324. "Transcript of Proceedings—Sentencing—Judge's Ruling before the Honorable Joan Humphrey Lefkow," January 21, 2011, *United States v. Burge*, No. 08 CR 846.

325. "Newly Exonerated Death Row Inmates Speak Out," *New Abolitionist*, no. 27, January 2003, https://nodeathpenalty.org/new_abolitionist/archive/.

326. Rummana Hussain, "Two Freed: 'It Took 20 Years,'" *Chicago Sun-Times*, July 8, 2009.

327. Ashahed M. Muhammad, "After 20 Years in Jail, Burge Accuser Walks Free," *Final Call*, September 28, 2010, http://www.finalcall.com/artman/publish/National_News_2/article_7301.shtml.

328. Frank Main and Rummana Hussain, "1986 Murder Confession Was Coerced in Beating, Judge Says," *Chicago Sun-Times*, March 17, 2011.

329. Rummana Hussain, "Going Home after Three Decades," *Chicago Tribune*, December 12, 2013.

330. John O'Connor, "Bill to Abolish Illinois Death Penalty Heading to Governor," *Chicago Defender*, January 12, 2011.

331. Steve Mills, "Illinois Bans Death Penalty," *Chicago Tribune*, March 10, 2011.

332. "Statement from Governor Pat Quinn on Senate Bill 3539," March 9, 2011, Chicago Press Release Services, http://chicagopressrelease.com/news/statement-from-governor-pat-quinn-on-senate-bill-3539http://www3.illinois.gov/PressReleases/ShowPressRelease.cfm?SubjectID=2&RecNum=9265.

333. "Death Penalty Repeal—A Victory for Justice," *Chicago Sun-Times*, March 10, 2011.

334. Eric Zorn, "A Toast, of Sorts, to the Warriors," *Chicago Tribune*, March 10, 2011.

335. Natasha Korecki, "Burge Headed to Same Prison as Madoff," *Chicago Sun-Times*, March 14, 2011.

Epilogue

1. Flint Taylor, "How Activists Won Reparations for the Survivors of Chicago Police Department Torture," *In These Times*, June 26, 2015.

2. Kim D. Chanbonpin, "Truth Stories: Credibility Determinations at the Illinois Torture Inquiry and Relief Commission," *Loyola University Chicago Law Journal* 45 (2014): 1103–1104.

3. Illinois Torture Inquiry and Relief Commission Act, http://www.illinois.gov/tirc/Pages/RulesForms.aspx.

4. "Order," *People v. Plummer*, Class Certification Proceeding Nos. 91CR21451, 84C10108, March 12, 2014.

5. "Order," *People v. Plummer*, Class Certification Proceeding Nos. 91CR21451, 84C10108, March 12, 2014.

6. Chicago Torture Justice Memorials, *Reparations Now, Reparations Won*, 23–35.

7. Alice Kim, interview with author, January 25, 2016.

8. For a brief history of the Black Lives Matter movement, see Jelani Cobb, "The Matter of Black Lives," *New Yorker*, March 14, 2016, https://www.newyorker.com/magazine/2016/03/14/where-is-black-lives-matter-headed.

9. Andrew S. Baer, "#RahmRepNow: Social Media and the Campaign to Win Reparations for Chicago Police Torture Survivors, 2013–2015," in Melgaco and Monaghan, *Protests in the Information Age*, 40–55.

10. Justin Glawe, "Lawyers Went to Rahm Emanuel, Then Quashed the Laquan McDon-

ald Video," *Daily Beast*, January 6, 2016, https://www.thedailybeast.com/lawyers-went-to-rahm-emanuel-then-quashed-the-laquan-mcdonald-video.

11. Jamie Kalven, "Sixteen Shots," *Slate*, February 10, 2015, https://slate.com/news-and-politics/2015/02/laquan-mcdonald-shooting-a-recently-obtained-autopsy-report-on-the-dead-teen-complicates-the-chicago-police-departments-story.html.

12. Chicago Torture Justice Memorials, *Reparations Now, Reparations Won*, 49.

13. Flint Taylor, "How Activists Won Reparations for the Survivors of Chicago Police Department Torture," *In These Times*, June 26, 2015, http://inthesetimes.com/article/18118/jon-burge-torture-reparations.

14. Steve Mills, "Burge Reparations Deal a Product of Long Negotiations," *Chicago Tribune*, May 6, 2015.

15. Taylor, *Torture Machine*, 461.

16. Chicago City Council Ordinance, "Reparations for Burge Torture Victims," May 6, 2015, Record No. SO2015-2687, https://www.chicago.gov/content/dam/city/depts/dol/supp_info/Burge-Reparations-Information-Center/ORDINANCE.pdf.

17. Andrew S. Baer, "#RahmRepNow: Social Media and the Campaign to Win Reparations for Chicago Police Torture Survivors, 2013–2015," in Melgaco and Monaghan, *Protests in the Information Age*, 40–55.

18. G. Flint Taylor, "The Chicago Police Torture Scandal: A Legal and Political History," *CUNY Law Review* 17 (2015): 368.

19. Citizens Alert Newsletter, July 15, 2010, CAR, folder 21-359.

20. Michael Goldston and Francine Sanders, *Office of Professional Standards Special Project* (Chicago Police Department, 1990), People's Law Office, https://peopleslawoffice.com/wp-content/uploads/2012/02/Goldston-Report-with-11.2.90-Coversheet.pdf.

21. G. Flint Taylor, "Richard M. Daley: A Central Figure in the Chicago Police Torture Scandal," *Huffington Post*, August 2, 2012.

22. See, for example, controversy over the CPD's facilities at Homan Square. Zach Stafford, "#Gitmo2Chicago: Protests Target Police 'Black Site,'" *The Guardian*, February 28, 2015.

23. Taylor, *Torture Machine*, 240; Anthony Holmes, "Violent Victim Impact Statement," *United States v. Burge*, No. 08 CR 846, in author's possession.

24. Jeremy Gorner, "Former Chicago Police Cmdr. Jon Burge Released from Home Confinement," *Chicago Tribune*, February 13, 2015.

25. "Exclusive: Jon Burge Responds to Torture Reparations," *Crooked City* (blog), April 16, 2015, http://www.martinpreib.org/rainbo2hotmailcom/2015/4/16/conviction-project-exclusive-jon-burge-responds-to-torture-reparations.

26. G. Flint Taylor, interview with author, May 15, 2018.

27. Megan Crepeau, Christy Gutowski, Jason Meisner, and Stacy St. Clair, "Van Dyke Taken into Custody after Jury Convicts Him of 2nd-Degree Murder, Aggravated Battery for Each of Sixteen Shots," *Chicago Tribune*, October 5, 2018.

28. Joey Mogul, interview with author, May 15, 2018.

Bibliography

Adler, Jeffrey S. *First in Violence, Deepest in Dirt: Homicide in Chicago, 1875–1920*. Cambridge, MA: Harvard University Press, 2006.

Agee, Christopher Lowen. *The Streets of San Francisco: Policing and the Creation of a Cosmopolitan Liberal Politics, 1950–1972*. vChicago: University of Chicago Press, 2014.

Agyepong, Tera. *The Criminalization of Black Children: Race, Gender, and Delinquency in Chicago's Juvenile Justice System, 1899–1945*. Chapel Hill: University of North Carolina Press, 2018.

Alder, Ken. *The Lie Detectors: The History of an American Obsession*. New York: Free Press, 2007.

Alexander, Michelle. *The New Jim Crow: Mass Incarceration in the Age of Colorblindness*. New York: New Press, 2010.

American Civil Liberties Union, Illinois Division. *Secret Detention by the Chicago Police: A Report of the American Civil Liberties Union, Illinois Division*. Glencoe, IL: Free Press, 1959.

Anderson, Alan B., and George W. Pickering. *Confronting the Color Line: The Broken Promise of the Civil Rights Movement in Chicago*. Athens: University of Georgia Press, 1986.

Anderson, David L., ed. *Facing My Lai: Moving beyond the Massacre*. Lawrence: University Press of Kansas, 1998.

Appy, Christian G. *Working-Class War: American Combat Soldiers and Vietnam*. Chapel Hill: University of North Carolina Press, 1993.

Armstrong, Michael F. *They Wished They Were Honest: The Knapp Commission and New York City Police Corruption*. New York: Columbia University Press, 2012.

Balko, Radley. *Rise of the Warrior Cop: The Militarization of America's Police Forces*. New York: Public Affairs, 2014.

Balto, Simon. *Occupied Territory: Policing Black Chicago from Red Summer to Black Power*. Chapel Hill: University of North Carolina Press, 2019.

Banfield, Edward C. *The Unheavenly City: The Nature and Future of Urban Crisis*. New York: Little, Brown & Co., 1970.

Baum, Dan. *Smoke and Mirrors: The War on Drugs and the Politics of Failure*. Boston: Little, Brown & Co., 1996.

Beckett, Katherine. *Making Crime Pay: Law and Order in Contemporary American Politics*. New York: Oxford University Press, 1997.

Beigel, Herbert, and Allan Beigel. *Beneath the Badge: A Story of Police Corruption*. New York: Harper & Row, 1977.

Bensman, David, and Roberta Lynch. *Rusted Dreams: Hard Times in a Steel Community*. New York: McGraw-Hill, 1987.

Biondi, Martha. *To Stand and Fight: The Struggle for Civil Rights in Postwar New York City*. Cambridge, MA: Harvard University Press, 2003.

Block, Carolyn Rebecca. *Lethal Violence in Chicago over Seventeen Years: Homicides Known to the Police, 1965–1981*. Chicago: Illinois Criminal Justice Information Authority, 1985.

Block, Carolyn Rebecca, and Richard L. Block. *Patterns of Change in Chicago Homicide: The Twenties, the Sixties, and the Seventies*. 3rd ed. Chicago: Criminal Justice Information Systems, 1981.

Block, Richard. *Violent Crime*. New York: Lexington Books, 1977.

Bloom, Joshua, and Waldo E. Martin Jr. *Black against Empire: The History and Politics of the Black Panther Party*. Berkeley: University of California Press, 2013.

Bogira, Steve. *Courtroom 302: A Year behind the Scenes in an American Criminal Courthouse*. New York: Vintage Books, 2005.

Bonilla-Silva, Eduardo. *Racism without Racists: Color-Blind Racism and the Persistence of Racial Inequality in the United States*. Lanham, MD: Rowman & Littlefield, 2003.

Bopp, William J. *"O.W.": O. W. Wilson and the Search for a Police Profession*. Port Washington, NY: Kennikat Press, 1977.

———, ed. *The Police Rebellion: A Quest for Blue Power*. Springfield, IL: Charles C. Thomas, 1971.

Bouza, Anthony V. *The Police Mystique: An Insider's Look at Cops, Crime, and the Criminal Justice System*. New York: Plenum, 1990.

Boyle, Kevin. *Arc of Justice: A Saga of Race, Civil Rights, and Murder in the Jazz Age*. New York: Henry Holt, 2005.

Branch, Taylor. *At Canaan's Edge: America in the King Years, 1965–68*. New York: Simon & Schuster, 2006.

Brazier, Arthur M. *Black Self-Determination: The Story of the Woodlawn Organization*. Grand Rapids, MI: Wm. B. Eerdmans, 1969.

Brown, Frank London. *Trumbull Park*. 1959. Lebanon, NH: University Press of New England, 2005.

Burge, Ethel. *This Business of Dressing for Business*. Chicago: Dartnell, 1970.

Burke, Edward M., and Thomas J. O'Gorman. *End of Watch: Chicago Police Killed in the Line of Duty, 1853–2006*. Chicago: Chicago's Books Press, 2007.

Byrne, Jane. *My Chicago*. New York: W. W. Norton & Co., 1992.

Campbell, James S., Joseph R. Sahid, and David P. Stang. *Law and Order Reconsidered: A Staff Report to the National Commission on the Causes and Prevention of Violence*. Washington, DC: U.S. Government Printing Office, 1969.

Chevigny, Paul. *Edge of the Knife: Police Violence in the Americas*. New York: New Press, 1995.

———. *Police Power: Police Abuses in New York City*. New York: Pantheon, 1969.

Chicago Crime Commission. *The Gang Book: A Detailed Overview of Street Gangs in the Chicago Metropolitan Area*. Chicago: Chicago Crime Commission, 2012.

———. *Annual Report 1970, Crime Trends—1971*. Chicago: Chicago Crime Commission, 1971.

Chicago Fact Book Consortium, ed. *Local Community Fact Book Chicago Metropolitan Area, Based on the 1970 and 1980 Censuses*. Chicago: Chicago Review Press, 1984.

———. *Local Community Fact Book: Chicago Metropolitan Area, 1990*. Chicago: Chicago Review Press, 1995.

Chicago Police Department. *The Chicago Police: A Report of Progress, 1960–1964*. Chicago: Public Information Division, Chicago Police Department, 1964.

Chicago Torture Justice Memorials. *Reparations Now, Reparations Won*. Chicago: Chicago Torture Justice Memorials, 2016.

Cipes, Robert M. *The Crime War: The Manufactured Crusade*. New York: New American Library, 1968.

Clark, Kenneth B. *Dark Ghetto: Dilemmas of Social Power*. New York: Harper Torchbooks, 1965.

Clark, Ramsey. *Crime in America: Observations on Its Nature, Causes, Prevention and Control*. New York: Pocket Books, 1970.

Clark, Ramsey, and Roy Wilkins. *Search and Destroy: A Report by the Commission of Inquiry into the Black Panthers and the Police*. New York: Metropolitan Applied Research Center, 1973.

Cleaver, Eldridge. *Soul on Ice*. New York: Delta, 1968.

Cohen, Adam, and Elizabeth Taylor. *American Pharaoh: Mayor Richard J. Daley, His Battle for Chicago and the Nation*. Boston: Little, Brown & Co., 2000.

Commission to Investigate Allegations of Police Corruption and the Anti-Corruption Procedures of the Police Department. *Commission Report*. New York: City of New York, 1994.

Conley, John A., ed. *The 1967 President's Crime Commission Report: Its Impact 25 Years Later*. Cincinnati, OH: Anderson Publishing, 1994.

Conroy, John. *Unspeakable Acts, Ordinary People*. Berkeley: University of California Press, 2000.

Cooley, Will. "Moving Up, Moving Out: Race and Social Mobility in Chicago, 1914–1972." PhD diss., University of Illinois, 2008.

Cowie, Jefferson. *Stayin' Alive: The 1970s and the Last Days of the Working Class*. New York: New Press, 2010.

Cray, Ed. *The Enemy in the Streets: Police Malpractice in America*. Garden City, NY: Anchor Books, 1972.

Cronon, William. *Nature's Metropolis: Chicago and the Great West*. New York: W. W. Norton & Co., 1992.

Cusac, Anne-Marie. *Cruel and Unusual: The Culture of Punishment in America*. New Haven, CT: Yale University Press, 2009.

Danns, Dionne. *Something Better for Our Children: Black Organization in the Chicago Public Schools, 1963–1971*. London: Routledge, 2002.

Davis, Angela J. *Arbitrary Justice: The Power of the American Prosecutor*. New York: Oxford University Press, 2007.

Diamond, Andrew J. *Chicago on the Make: Power and Inequality in a Modern City*. Berkeley: University of California Press, 2017.

———. *Mean Streets: Chicago Youths and the Everyday Struggle for Employment in the Multiracial City, 1908–1969*. Berkeley: University of California Press, 2009.

Drake, St. Clair, and Horace R. Cayton. *Black Metropolis: A Study of Negro Life in a Northern City*. 1945. Chicago: University of Chicago Press, 1993.

Egan, Edward J., and Robert D. Boyle, *Report of the Special State's Attorney: Appointed and Ordered by the Presiding Judge of the Criminal Court of Cook County in No. 20001 Misc. 4*, Circuit Court of Cook County, 2006.

Eisenstein, James, and Herbert Jacob. *Felony Justice: An Organizational Analysis of Criminal Courts*. Boston: Little, Brown & Co., 1977.

Enns, Peter K. *Incarceration Nation: How the United States Became the Most Punitive Democracy in the World*. New York: Cambridge University Press, 2016.

Ewell, Julian J., and Ira A. Hunt Jr. *Sharpening the Combat Edge: The Use of Analysis to Reinforce Military Judgment*. Washington, DC: Department of the Army, 1995.

Farber, David. *Chicago '68*. Chicago: University of Chicago Press, 1988.

Fassin, Didier. *Writing the World of Policing: The Difference Ethnography Makes*. Chicago: University of Chicago Press, 2017.

Federal Bureau of Investigation. *Crime in America*. Washington, DC: Government Printing Office, 1960–2010.

Felker-Kantor, Max. *Policing Los Angeles: Race, Resistance, and the Rise of the LAPD*. Chapel Hill: University of North Carolina Press, 2018.

Fernandez, Lilia. *Brown in the Windy City: Mexicans and Puerto Ricans in Postwar Chicago*. Chicago: University of Chicago Press, 2012.

Fitzgerald, Kathleen Whalen. *Brass: Jane Byrne and the Pursuit of Power*. Chicago: Contemporary Books, 1981.

Flamm, Michael W. *Law and Order: Street Crime, Civil Unrest, and the Crisis of Liberalism in the 1960s*. New York: Columbia University Press, 2005.

Fletcher, Connie. *What Cops Know: Cops Talk about What They Do, How They Do It, and What It Does to Them*. New York: Villard Books, 1991.

Fogelson, Robert M. *Big City Police*. Cambridge, MA: Harvard University Press, 1977.

Foner, Philip S., ed. *The Black Panthers Speak*. 1995. Cambridge, MA: Da Capo, 2002.

Forman, James, Jr. *Locking Up Our Own: Crime and Punishment in Black America*. New York: Farrar, Straus & Giroux, 2017.

Fortner, Michael Javen. *Black Silent Majority: The Rockefeller Drug Laws and the Politics of Punishment*. Cambridge, MA: Harvard University Press, 2015.

Fremon, David K. *Chicago Politics Ward by Ward*. Bloomington: Indiana University Press, 1988.

Frydl, Kathleen J. *The Drug Wars in America, 1940–1973*. New York: Cambridge University Press, 2013.

Garey, Diane. *Defending Everybody: A History of the American Civil Liberties Union*. New York: TV Books, 1998.

Garland, David, ed. *Mass Imprisonment: Social Causes and Consequences*. Thousand Oaks, CA: Sage, 2001.

Gest, Ted. *Crime & Politics: Big Government's Erratic Campaign for Law and Order*. New York: Oxford University Press, 2001.

Gilmore, Ruth Wilson. *Golden Gulag: Prisons, Surplus, Crisis, and Opposition in Globalizing California*. Berkeley: University of California Press, 2007.

Goldstein, Herman. *Policing a Free Society*. Cambridge, MA: Ballinger Publishing, 1977.

Gonzalez Van Cleve, Nicole. *Crook County: Racism and Injustice in America's Largest Criminal Court*. Stanford, CA: Stanford University Press, 2016.

Gooding-Williams, Robert, ed. *Reading Rodney King, Reading Urban Uprising*. New York: Routledge, 1993.

Gottschalk, Marie. *Caught: The Prison State and the Lockdown of American Politics*. Princeton, NJ: Princeton University Press, 2015.

———. *The Prison and the Gallows: The Politics of Mass Incarceration in America*. New York: Cambridge University Press, 2006.

Gottschalk, Petter. *Policing the Police: Knowledge Management in Law Enforcement*. New York: Nova Science Publishers, 2009.

Granger, Bill, and Lori Granger. *Fighting Jane: Mayor Jane Byrne and the Chicago Machine*. New York: Dial Press, 1980.

Green, Adam. *Selling the Race: Culture, Community, and Black Chicago, 1940–1955*. Chicago: University of Chicago Press, 2007.

Green, Paul M., and Melvin G. Holli, eds. *The Mayors: The Chicago Political Tradition*. 3rd ed. Carbondale: Southern Illinois University Press, 2005.

Grimshaw, William J. *Bitter Fruit: Black Politics and the Chicago Machine, 1931–1991*. Chicago: University of Chicago Press, 1992.

Grossman, James R. *Land of Hope: Chicago, Black Southerners, and the Great Migration*. Chicago: University of Chicago Press, 1991.

Grossman, James R., Ann Durkin Keating, and Janice L. Reiff, eds. *The Encyclopedia of Chicago*. Chicago: University of Chicago Press, 2004.

Haas, Jeffrey. *The Assassination of Fred Hampton: How the FBI and the Chicago Police Murdered a Black Panther*. Chicago: Lawrence Hill Books, 2010.

Hagedorn, John, Bart Kmiecik, Dick Simpson, Thomas J. Gradel, Melissa Mouritsen Zmuda, and David Sterrett. *Crime, Corruption and Cover-ups in the Chicago Police Department*. Anti-Corruption Report No. 7. Chicago: University of Illinois at Chicago, 2013.

Harrington, Michael. *The Other America: Poverty in the United States*. 1962. New York: Touchstone, 1993.

Harris, Richard. *The Fear of Crime*. New York: Praeger, 1969.

Hartnett, Stephen John, ed. *Challenging the Prison-Industrial Complex: Activism, Arts, and Educational Alternatives*. Urbana: University of Illinois Press, 2011.

Hauser, Philip M., and Evelyn M. Kitagawa, eds. *Local Community Fact Book for Chicago, 1950*. Chicago: University of Chicago Press, 1953.

Hawes, Joseph M., ed. *Law and Order in American History*. Port Washington, NY: Kennikat Press, 1979.

Hernandez, Kelly Lytle. *City of Inmates: Conquest, Rebellion, and the Rise of Human Caging in Los Angeles*. Chapel Hill: University of North Carolina Press, 2017.

Hinton, Elizabeth. *From the War on Poverty to the War on Crime: The Making of Mass Incarceration in America*. Cambridge, MA: Harvard University Press, 2016.

Hirsch, Arnold R. *Making the Second Ghetto: Race and Housing in Chicago, 1940–1960*. Chicago: University of Chicago Press, 1983.

Hopkins, Ernest Jerome. *Our Lawless Police: A Study of the Unlawful Enforcement of the Law*. New York: Viking, 1931.

Horne, Gerald. *Fire This Time: The Watts Uprising and the 1960s*. Charlottesville: University Press of Virginia, 1995.

Hounmenou, Charles. *Justice Advocates: Citizens Alert and Police Accountability*. Chicago: Jane Addams Center for Social Policy and Research, 2012.

Hunt, D. Bradford. *Blueprint for Disaster: The Unraveling of Chicago Public Housing*. Chicago: University of Chicago Press, 2009.

Hunt, Ira A. *The 9th Infantry Division in Vietnam: Unparalleled and Unequaled*. Lexington: University Press of Kentucky, 2010.

Illinois Association for Criminal Justice. *Illinois Crime Survey*. Chicago: Blakely Printing Co., 1929.

Illinois Prison Inquiry Commission. *The Prison System in Illinois*. Springfield: Illinois Prison Inquiry Commission, 1937.

Inbau, Fred E., and John E. Reid. *Criminal Interrogations and Confessions*. Baltimore: Williams & Wilkins Co., 1967.

Independent Commission on the Los Angeles Police Department. *Report of the Independent Commission on the Los Angeles Police Department*. Los Angeles, 1991.

Jacoby, Joan E. *Report on the State's Attorneys Office: Cook County, Illinois*. Washington, DC: National Center for Prosecution Management, November 22, 1972.

James, Marlise. *The People's Lawyers*. New York: Holt, Rinehart and Winston, 1973.

Jenkins, Philip. *Decade of Nightmares: The End of the Sixties and the Making of Eighties America*. New York: Oxford University Press, 2006.

Johnson, Marilynn. *Street Justice: A History of Police Violence in New York City*. Boston: Beacon, 2003.

Jones, Sandra J. *Coalition Building in the Anti-Death Penalty Movement: Privileged Morality, Race Realities*. Lanham, MD: Rowman & Littlefield, 2010.

Kamisar, Yale. *Police Interrogation and Confessions: Essays in Law and Policy*. Ann Arbor: University of Michigan Press, 1980.

Kennedy, Randall. *Race, Crime, and the Law*. New York: Vintage Books, 1997.

Keyserling, Leon H. *Progress or Poverty: The U.S. At the Crossroads*. Washington, DC: Conference on Economic Progress, 1964.

Kitchen, Ronald, and Thai Jones. *My Midnight Years: Surviving Jon Burge's Police Torture Ring and Death Row*. Chicago: Chicago Review Press, 2018.

Kohler-Hausmann, Julilly. *Getting Tough: Welfare and Imprisonment in 1970s America*. Princeton, NJ: Princeton University Press, 2017.

Kruse, Kevin M. *White Flight: Atlanta and the Making of Modern Conservatism*. Princeton, NJ: Princeton University Press, 2005.

Kusch, Frank. *Battleground Chicago: The Police and the 1968 Democratic National Convention*. Chicago: University of Chicago Press, 2008.

Lair, Meredith H. *Armed with Abundance: Consumers & Soldiering in the Vietnam War*. Chapel Hill: University of North Carolina Press, 2011.

Lassiter, G. Daniel, and Christian A. Meissner, eds. *Police Interrogations and False Confessions: Current Research, Practice, and Policy Recommendations*. Washington, DC: American Psychological Association, 2010.

Leo, Richard A. *Police Interrogation and American Justice*. Cambridge, MA: Harvard University Press, 2008.

Levering, Johnson, Ruth Shonle Cavan, and Eugene S. Zemans. *Chicago Police Lockups: A His-*

tory of Reform in Police Handling of Persons in Detention, 1947–1962. Chicago: John Howard Association, 1963.

Levinson, Sanford, ed. *Torture: A Collection*. New York: Oxford University Press, 2004.

Lieberson, Stanley. *A Piece of the Pie: Blacks and White Immigrants since 1880*. Berkeley: University of California Press, 1980.

Lindberg, Richard C. *To Serve and Collect: Chicago Politics and Police Corruption from the Lager Beer Riot to the Summerdale Scandal, 1855–1960*. Carbondale: Southern Illinois University Press, 1998.

Losier, Toussaint. "Prison House of Nations: Police Violence and Mass Incarceration in the Long Course of Black Insurgency in Illinois, 1953–1987." PhD diss., University of Chicago, 2014.

Lyon, Andrea D. *Angel of Death Row: My Life as a Death Penalty Lawyer*. New York: Kaplan Publishing, 2010.

Lytle, Leslie. *Execution's Doorstep: True Stories of the Innocent and near Damned*. Boston: Northeastern University Press, 2008.

Margulies, Joseph. *What Changed When Everything Changed: 9/11 and the Making of National Identity*. New Haven, CT: Yale University Press, 2013.

Mauer, Marc. *Race to Incarcerate*. New York: New Press, 2006.

McArdle, Andrea, and Tanya Erzen, eds. *Zero Tolerance: Quality of Life and the New Police Brutality in New York City*. New York: New York University Press, 2001.

McCoy, Alfred W. *Torture and Impunity: The U.S. Doctrine of Coercive Interrogation*. Madison: University of Wisconsin Press, 2012.

McCoyer, Michael. "Darkness of a Different Color: Mexicans and Racial Formation in Greater Chicago, 1916–1960." PhD diss., Northwestern University, 2007.

Melgaco, Lucas and Jeffrey Monaghan, ed. *Protests in the Information Age: Social Movements, Digital Practices and Surveillance*. London: Routledge, 2018.

Merriner, James L. *The Man Who Emptied Death Row*. Carbondale: Southern Illinois University Press, 2008.

Moore, Leonard N. *Black Rage in New Orleans: Police Brutality and African American Activism from World War II to Hurricane Katrina*. Baton Rouge: Louisiana State University Press, 2010.

Monkkonen, Eric H. *Police in Urban America, 1860–1920*. New York: Cambridge University Press, 2004.

Muhammad, Khalil Gibran. *The Condemnation of Blackness: Race, Crime, and the Making of Modern Urban America*. Cambridge, MA: Harvard University Press, 2010.

Murakawa, Naomi. *The First Civil Right: How Liberals Built Prison America*. New York: Oxford University Press, 2014.

Murch, Donna Jean. *Living for the City: Migration, Education, and the Rise of the Black Panther Party in Oakland, California*. Chapel Hill: University of North Carolina Press, 2010.

National Commission on Law Observance and Enforcement. *Report on Lawlessness in Law Enforcement*. Washington, DC: National Commission on Law Observance and Enforcement, 1931.

National Institute of Law Enforcement and Criminal Justice. *Allocations of Resources in the Chicago Police Department*. Washington, DC: National Institute of Law Enforcement and Criminal Justice, 1972.

Navasky, Victor S., and Darrell Paster. *Law Enforcement: The Federal Role: Report of the Twentieth Century Fund Task Force on the Law Enforcement Assistance Administration.* New York: McGraw-Hill, 1976.

Nelson, Deborah. *The War behind Me: Vietnam Veterans Confront the Truth about U.S. War Crimes.* New York: Basic Books, 2008.

Newton, Huey P., and J. Herman Blake. *Revolutionary Suicide.* New York: Penguin Books, 1973.

Parenti, Christian. *Lockdown America: Police and Prisons in the Age of Crisis.* New York: Verso, 2000.

Parker, Alfred E. *Crime Fighter: August Vollmer.* New York: Macmillan, 1961.

———. *The Berkeley Story.* Springfield, IL: Charles C. Thomas, 1972.

Parkin, Joan, Tonya D. McClary, and Eric Ruder. *Justice for the Death Row 10: Victims of Police Torture.* Chicago: Campaign to End the Death Penalty, 2001.

Pattillo, Mary. *Black on the Block: The Politics of Race and Class in the City.* Chicago: University of Chicago Press, 2007.

People's Law Office. *Report on the Failure of Special Prosecutors Edward J. Egan and Robert D. Boyle to Fairly Investigate Systemic Police Torture in Chicago.* Chicago: People's Law Office, April 24, 2007. https://peopleslawoffice.com/wp-content/uploads/2012/02/5.8.07.Final-Corrected-Version-of-Report.pdf.

———. *Torture in Chicago: A Supplementary Report on the On-Going Failure of Government Officials to Adequately Deal with the Scandal.* Chicago: People's Law Office, October 29, 2008. https://www.prisonlegalnews.org/media/publications/torture_in_chicago_with_appendices_2008.pdf.

Perkinson, Robert. *Texas Tough: The Rise of America's Prison Empire.* New York: Metropolitan Books, 2010.

Perry, Imani. *More Beautiful and More Terrible: The Embrace and Transcendence of Racial Inequality in the United States.* New York: New York University Press, 2011.

Peterson, Virgil W. *A Report on Chicago Crime for 1961.* Chicago: Chicago Crime Commission, 1962.

Pfaff, John. *Locked In: The True Causes of Mass Incarceration and How to Achieve Real Reform.* New York: Basic Books, 2017.

Pihos, Peter Constantine. "Policing, Race, and Politics in Chicago." PhD diss., University of Pennsylvania, 2015.

President's Commission on Law Enforcement and Administration of Justice. "The Challenge of Crime in a Free Society." Washington, DC: U.S. Printing Office, 1967.

Rejali, Darius M. *Torture and Democracy.* Princeton, NJ: Princeton University Press, 2007.

Rivlin, Gary. *Fire on the Prairie: Chicago's Harold Washington and the Politics of Race.* New York: Henry Holt & Co., 1992.

Roske, Ralph J. *His Own Counsel: The Life and Times of Lyman Trumbull.* Reno: University of Nevada Press, 1979.

Roth, Randolph. *American Homicide.* Cambridge, MA: Belknap Press of Harvard University Press, 2009.

Royko, Mike. *Boss: Richard J. Daley of Chicago.* New York: E. P. Dutton & Co., 1971.

Sale, R. T. *The Blackstone Rangers: A Reporter's Account of Time Spent with the Street Gang on Chicago's South Side.* New York: Random House, 1971.

Sampson, Robert J. *Great American City: Chicago and the Enduring Neighborhood Effect.* Chicago: University of Chicago Press, 2013.

Schell, Jonathan. *The Real War: The Classic Reporting on the Vietnam War*. Cambridge, MA: Da Capo, 1988.

Schulman, Bruce J. *The Seventies: The Great Shift in American Culture, Society, and Politics*. Cambridge, MA: Da Capo Press, 2001.

Seale, Bobby. *Seize the Time: The Story of the Black Panther Party and Huey P. Newton*. Baltimore: Black Classic Press, 1970.

Seligman, Amanda I. *Block by Block: Neighborhoods and Public Policy on Chicago's West Side*. Chicago: University of Chicago Press, 2005.

Sellers, Rod. *Chicago's Southeast Side Revisited*. Chicago: Arcadia, 2001.

Simon, David. *Homicide: A Year on the Killing Streets*. New York: Picador, 1991.

Simon, Jonathan. *Governing through Crime: How the War on Crime Transformed American Democracy and Created a Culture of Fear*. New York: Oxford University Press, 2007.

Simpson, Dick. *Rogues, Rebels, and Rubber Stamps: The Politics of the Chicago City Council from 1863 to the Present*. Boulder, CO: Westview, 2001.

Skolnick, Jerome H. *Justice without Trial: Law Enforcement in Democratic Society*. 2nd ed. New York: John Wiley & Sons, 1975.

Skolnick, Jerome H., and James J. Fyfe. *Above the Law: Police and the Excessive Use of Force*. New York: Free Press, 1993.

Sonnie, Amy, and James Tracy. *Hillbilly Nationalists, Urban Race Rebels, and Black Power*. New York: Melville House, 2011.

Stein, Judith. *Pivotal Decade: How the United States Traded Factories for Finance in the Seventies*. New Haven, CT: Yale University Press, 2010.

Stokes, Bernard H., ed. *Demographic Studies of the Chicago Police Areas and Districts: Chicago Police Department Area 2*. Chicago: Chicago Police Department, 1982.

Strickland, Arvarh E. *History of the Chicago Urban League*. Urbana: University of Illinois Press, 1966.

Stuart, Gary L. *Miranda: The Story of America's Right to Remain Silent*. Tucson: University of Arizona Press, 2004.

Stuntz, William J. *The Collapse of American Criminal Justice*. Cambridge, MA: Harvard University Press, 2011.

Sugrue, Thomas. *The Origins of the Urban Crisis: Race and Inequality in Postwar Detroit*. Princeton, NJ: Princeton University Press, 1998.

Sullivan, Patricia. *Lift Every Voice: The NAACP and the Making of the Civil Rights Movement*. New York: New Press, 2009.

Taylor, Flint. *The Torture Machine: Racism and Police Violence in Chicago*. Chicago: Haymarket Books, 2019.

Theoharis, Jeanne F., and Komozi Woodard, ed. *Freedom North: Black Freedom Struggles Outside the South, 1940–1980*. New York: Palgrave Macmillan, 2003.

Thomas, George C., III, and Richard A. Leo. *Confessions of Guilt: From Torture to* Miranda *and Beyond*. New York: Oxford University Press, 2012.

Todd-Breland, Elizabeth. *A Political Education: Black Politics and Education Reform in Chicago since the 1960s*. Chapel Hill: University of North Carolina Press, 2018.

Tuohy, James, and Rob Warden. *Greylord: Justice, Chicago Style*. New York: G. P. Putnam's Sons, 1989.

Turse, Nick. *Kill Anything That Moves: The Real American War in Vietnam*. New York: Metropolitan Books, 2013.

U.S. District Court, Northern District of Illinois, Eastern Division. *Report of the January 1970 Grand Jury*. Washington, DC: U.S. Government Printing Office, 1970.

U.S. Riot Commission. *Report of the National Advisory Commission on Civil Disorders*. New York: Bantam, 1968.

Venkatesh, Sudhir Alladi. *American Project: The Rise and Fall of a Modern Ghetto*. Cambridge, MA: Harvard University Press, 2000.

Wacquant, Loïc. *Prisons of Poverty*. Minneapolis: University of Minnesota Press, 2009.

———. *Punishing the Poor: The Neoliberal Government of Social Insecurity*. Durham, NC: Duke University Press, 2009.

Walker, Samuel. *Popular Justice: A History of American Criminal Justice*. 2nd ed. New York: Oxford University Press, 1998.

———. *Sense and Nonsense About Crime: A Policy Guide*. Pacific Grove, CA: Brooks/Cole, 1989.

Wambaugh, Joseph. *The Choirboys*. New York: Delacorte Press, 1975.

Warden, Rob, and Steven A. Drizin, eds. *True Stories of False Confessions*. Evanston, IL: Northwestern University Press, 2009.

Watson, Dwight. *Race and the Houston Police Department, 1930–1990: A Change Did Come*. College Station: Texas A&M University Press, 2005.

Western, Bruce. *Punishment and Inequality in America*. New York: Russell Sage Foundation, 2006.

Williams, Jakobi. *From the Ballot to the Bullet: The Illinois Chapter of the Black Panther Party and Racial Coalition Politics in Chicago*. Chapel Hill: University of North Carolina Press, 2013.

Wilson, William Julius. *The Truly Disadvantaged: The Inner City, the Underclass, and Public Policy*. Chicago: University of Chicago Press, 1990.

———. *When Work Disappears: The World of the New Urban Poor*. New York: Alfred A. Knopf, 1996.

Young, Marilyn B. *The Vietnam Wars, 1945–1990*. New York: Harper Perennial, 1991.

Zimring, Franklin E. *The City That Became Safe: New York's Lessons for Urban Crime and Its Control*. New York: Oxford University Press, 2012.

———. *The Great American Crime Decline*. New York: Oxford University Press, 2007.

Index

Page numbers in italics refer to illustrations.